SECRET FRANCE

CHARMING VILLAGES

&

COUNTRY TOURS

Produced by AA Publishing

W·W·NORTON

NEW YORK · LONDON

Edited by Helen Douglas-Cooper, Barbara Mellor
Contributors: Paul Atterbury, David Hancock, Keith Howell,
John Lloyd, Robin Neillands, Tony Oliver, Ian Powys, Mary Ratcliffe,
Kev Reynolds, Richard Sale, Melissa Shales, John White
Ian Ousby, Paul Sterry (features)

© The Automobile Association 1994
Reprinted 1996

Maps © The Automobile Association 1994
Touring maps extracted from the Institut Géographique National de France
(IGN) 1:25,000 Série Bleu with the permission of IGN © 1993

This edition published by W.W. Norton & Company, Inc.
500 5th Avenue, New York, New York 10110
http://www.wwnorton.com

ISBN 0-393-31942-3

The contents of this book are believed correct at the time of printing.
Nevertheless, the publishers cannot be held responsible for any errors or
omissions or for changes in the details given in this book or for the consequences
of any reliance on the information provided by the same.
Assessments of attractions and locations are based upon the author's own
experience and, therefore, descriptions given in this guide necessarily contain an
element of subjective opinion which may not reflect the publisher's opinion or
dictate a reader's experiences on another occasion. We have tried to ensure
accuracy in this book, but things do change and we would be grateful if readers
would advise us of any inaccuracies they may encounter.

Colour separation by Fotographics Ltd
Printed in Italy by G Canale & C SpA – Turin

CONTENTS

REGIONS AND DEPARTEMENTS

In this book France has been divided into 18 regions as numbered and colour-coded on the map opposite. Individual maps of these regions appear at the beginning of each section.

The map also shows the *départements* into which France is divided. Each *département* has a standard number, as shown on the map and in the key, which for postal purposes replaces its name. These numbers also form part of the registration number of French cars, thus indicating the *département* in which the car was registered. The *départements* are listed here alphabetically under the regional headings of the book.

BRITTANY (Bretagne)
Côtes-du-Nord 22
Finistère 29
Ille-et-Vilaine 35
Morbihan 56

NORMANDY
(Normandie)
Calvados 14
Eure 27
Manche 50
Orne 61
Seine-Maritime 76

THE NORTH (Nord)
Aisne 02
Ardennes 08
Aube 10
Marne 51
Marne (Haute-) 52
Nord 59
Oise 60
Pas-de-Calais 62
Somme 80

ALSACE AND LORRAINE
(Alsace et Lorraine)
Meurthe-et-Moselle 54
Meuse 55
Moselle 57
Rhin (Bas-) 67
Rhin (Haut-) 68
Vosges 88

THE LOIRE (Loire)
Cher 18 (part)
Eure-et-Loir 28
Indre 36 (part)
Indre-et-Loire 37
Loir-et-Cher 41
Loire-Atlantique 44
Loiret 45
Maine-et-Loire 49
Mayenne 53
Sarthe 72
Sèvres (Deux-) 79 (part)
Vienne 86 (part)

THE ILE DE FRANCE AND PARIS
(Ile de France et Paris)
Essonne 91
Hauts-de-Seine 92
Paris 75
Seine-et-Marne 77
Yvelines 78
Seine-St-Denis 93
Val-de-Marne 94
Val-d'Oise 95

BURGUNDY
(Bourgogne)
Côte-d'Or 21
Nièvre 58
Saône-et-Loire 71
Yonne 89

FRANCHE-COMTE
(Franche-Comté)
Belfort (Territoire-de-) 90
Doubs 25
Jura 39
Saône (Haute-) 70

THE ATLANTIC COAST
(Côte Atlantique)
Charente 16
Charente-Maritime 17
Gironde 33
Landes 40
Sèvres (Deux-) 79 (part)
Vendée 85
Vienne 86 (part)

BERRY AND LIMOUSIN
(Berry et Limousin)
Cher 18 (part)
Creuse 23
Indre 36 (part)
Vienne (Haute-) 87

AUVERGNE
(Auvergne)
Allier 03
Cantal 15
Loire (Haute-) 43
Puy-de-Dôme 63

THE RHONE VALLEY
(Vallée du Rhône)
Ain 01 (part)
Ardèche 07 (part)
Drôme 26 (part)
Isère 38 (part)
Loire 42
Rhône 69

THE ALPS (Alpes)
Ain 01 (part)
Alpes (Hautes-) 05
Drôme 26 (part)
Isère 38 (part)
Savoie 73
Savoie (Haut-) 74

PERIGORD AND QUERCY
(Périgord et Quercy)
Aveyron 12 (part)
Corrèze 19
Dordogne 24
Lot 46
Lot-et-Garonne 47
Tarn-et-Garonne 82

LANGUEDOC
(Languedoc)
Ardèche 07 (part)
Aveyron 12 (part)
Gard 30 (part)
Hérault 34
Lozère 48
Tarn 81

THE PYRENEES
(Pyrénées)
Ariège 09
Aude 11
Garonne (Haute-) 31
Gers 32
Pyrénées-Atlantiques 64
Pyrénées (Hautes-) 65
Pyrénées Orientales 66

PROVENCE AND THE COTE D'AZUR
(Provence et Côte d'Azur)
Alpes-de-Haute-Provence 04
Alpes Maritimes 06
Bouches-du-Rhône 13
Drôme 26 (part)
Gard 30 (part)
Var 83
Vaucluse 84

CORSICA (Corse)

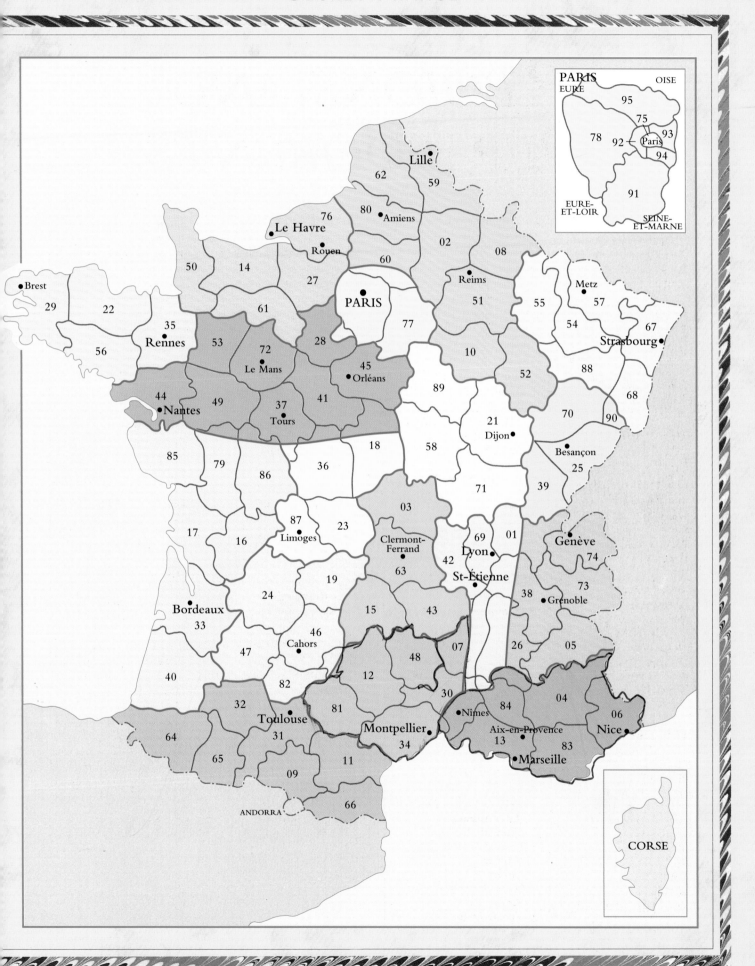

ABOUT THIS BOOK

Secret France has been divided into 18 chapters according to the regions on pages 6–7. The opening of each chapter includes a general description of the area and a more detailed map of the selected region, showing the locations which are described through that chapter and the starting points for the car tours.

International Distinguishing Signs

The following symbols are used on the individual regional maps to indicate adjacent countries.

- ⓑ Belgium
- ⓓ Germany
- ⓛ Luxembourg
- Ⓒ️ⓗ Switzerland
- ⓔ Spain
- ⓘ Italy

Regional Information

Within each region is a selection of some of the most attractive and interesting villages of France, including many of those officially designated 'most beautiful' and specially protected. The villages are of all shapes and sizes, some well known and loved by visitors of all nationalities, and many others that are less familiar and further from the beaten track, but which nevertheless offer their very own brand of rural charm or historic interest, allowing the visitor just a little nearer the secret heart of the country. Distances and directions are given from the nearest main town to help you locate each village.

Secret Places

Sometimes we have found places that are obscure or little enough known to warrant the special category of 'secret places', and these include strange châteaux, legendary valleys, unusual little churches and other odd stories which demand to be followed up. Again, distances and directions from main centres are given, and 'secret places' are picked out on the regional maps with a star.

Features

Feature panels expand points of interest both local and national, touching on all sorts of things, from the birdlife of the Alps and Breton separatism, to the sport of pelota and the French taste in bread.

Motoring Tours

Finally, there are 33 motoring tours spread throughout the book, designed to be completed in a day or spread over several, to help you explore a region in greater depth. They vary in total distance from about 100km to about 185km, but most are around 130km, and the approximate distance is given in each case. After an introduction, there are detailed instructions for driving the route, and a separate list of places of special interest. Each car tour is accompanied by a full route map, specially prepared using the detailed cartography of the famous Institut Géographique National de France (IGN), the French national mapping agency. The road maps are extracted from their major 1:250 000 Série Bleu.

Motorway (1) - Road with motorway characteristics (2) _____

Service area (1) - resting area (2) - toll-gate (3) _____

Exit number of an interchange _____

Main road with separate roadways (1) - Main roads (2) (3) _____

Secondary roads _____

National roads (1) and départment roads (2) have an official number _____

Distances in kilometres (between   or two outlined cities) _____

Other roads: regularly maintained (1), not regularly maintained (2) - Footpath _____

Railways: double track (1), single track (2), metre gauge track (3) _____

Marshalling yard (1) - Tunnel (2) - Station or stopping-place (3), open to passenger traffic (4)_____

Level crossing (1), underpass (2), overpass (3) _____

Military camp boundary (1), boundary of firing range restricted zone (2) _____

Height-tension line (225 kV and over) (1) - State Boundary (2) _____

Boundary of region (1), of département (2), of arrondissement (3) _____

Populated places: over 3 000 inhabitants (1), under 3 000 inhabitants (2) _____

over 100 000 inhabitants_____

25 000 to 100 000 inhabitants _____

5 000 to 25 000 inhabitants (1), 3 000 to 5 000 inhabitants (2)_____

under 3 000 inhabitants: commune (1), important hamlet (2) _____

Castle (1) - Religious building (2) - Shelter (3) - Isolated Landmark (4) - Ruins (5) _____

Industrial complex (1) - Fort (2) - Cave (3) - Lighthouse (4) _____

Navigable canal (1), non navigable canal (2) - Salt pans (3) - Marsh or swamp (4)_____

Aerodromes: international (1), hard surfaced runway (2), soft surfaced runway (3) _____

Area exposed at low tide: Beach (1) - Rocks (2) _____

Wood _____

Cathedral - Abbey - Church - Chapel_____

Castle - Castle open to public - Prominent building_____

View point - Curiosity _____

District of interest to tourists - Spa-Winter sports resort _____

Civil architecture (ancient house, bastide, covered market) - Rampart _____

Ancient remains - Interesting ruins - Memorial _____

Pilgrimage - Traditional festival - Museum _____

Military cemetery - Cave - Shelter - Lighthouse _____

Tourist Railway - Rack-railway - Aerial cableway, cable car or chair lift _____

Custom-houses: French, foreign _____

Start point of tour _____

Tour route _____

Direction of tour _____

Alternative route _____

Highlighted point of interest _____

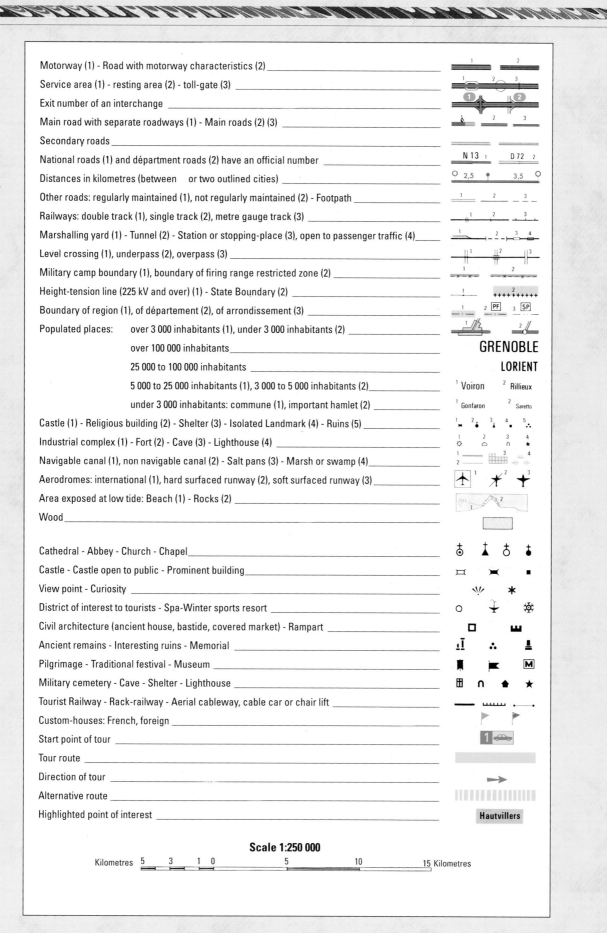

GRENOBLE

LORIENT

[1] Voiron   [2] Rillieux

[1] Gonfaron   [2] Saretto

Hautvillers

Scale 1:250 000

Kilometres 5   3   1 0   5   10   15 Kilometres

LA FRANCE TRANQUILLE

Away from the bustle of its ultra-modern cities and busy towns, the explorer in France will discover that this is a country firmly rooted to the land, with customs and traditions that are the essence of an older culture. The following chapters celebrate some of the loveliest villages of France, the most appealing quiet corners, and the charm of its varied landscapes, reflecting a style of architecture, of landscape, of living that is uniquely French. Over thirty guided car tours, to be achieved in a day or savoured slowly at leisure, can lead you through less familiar areas of the French countryside. Combining well-loved beauty spots with the hidden, secret places they don't normally tell you about, this is a very special companion to discovering France, revealing perhaps just a few of the reasons why people remain fascinated by this lovely country.

SECRET FRANCE

BRITTANY

Brittany is a province of varied and very beautiful countryside, with rich, rolling pastures and a rugged coastline, a land of farmers and fishermen that has also provided the inspiration for countless numbers of artists over the last 100 years.

Breton villages are small and composed in the main of whitewashed stone and glittering granite. Thatch is rare, for it takes a good slate or tile roof to resist the buffeting of the Atlantic winds. The centrepiece of every Breton community is the village church, a number of which are also endowed with that splendid monument to civic pride and religious fervour, the *enclos paroissial*. These are found in all parts of Brittany, with a small concentration in the north of Finistère, around St-Thégonnec.

The fishing ports tend to be smaller than the inland villages, but in some ways they are even more picturesque, consisting typically of white-painted or granite houses set around a small harbour crammed with gaily painted boats. There will be a bar or two and perhaps a quay-side restaurant. The fishermen work on their boats, the hulls braced against the harbour walls, or may be observed on the quays, mending their nets or lobster pots in the traditional way.

Although Brittany is best known for it long and beautiful coastline, the centre of the country also has its attractions. The Parc Regional d'Armorique, which stretches inland from the Pointe de Penhir, has many places that are perfect centres for walking, and any community of any size will have one or two small hotels where visitors can stay while exploring the surrounding countryside.

Lovers of the odd or the unusual will have a field day in Brittany, this most special of French provinces. Nearly every place has its own Celtic or Breton twist, prehistoric remains, isolated chapel or much-loved, hidden statue, making a visit to Brittany quite different from a visit anywhere else, and those who probe about along the coast and in the hinterland will find a host of rare and curious things to marvel at. Unlike other parts of France, Brittany did not suffer too much from the ravages of World War II. Many of the medieval and Celtic attractions are therefore still intact and still protected and cared for by the local people.

coquille de Bretagne

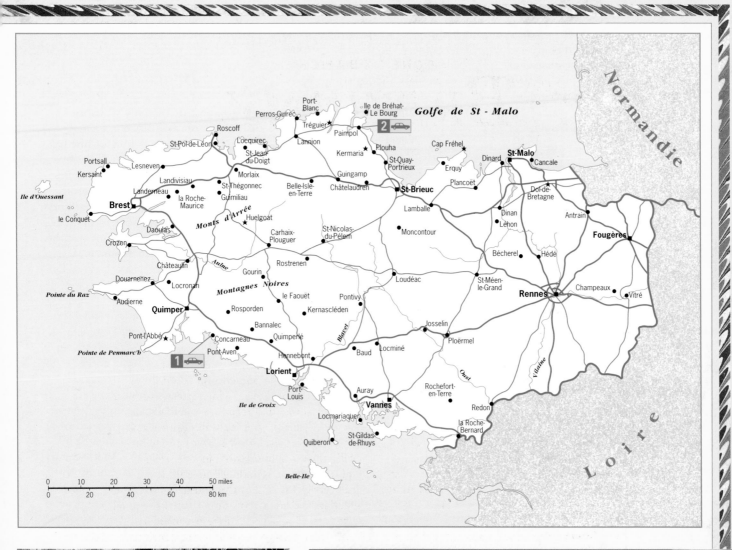

Above, girls dressed in bright, traditional Breton costumes for a Pardon procession
Right, a striking relief on an ossuary door at Lampaul-Guimilau
Far right, low tide in scenic Locquirec Bay

BAUD

A small village noted for its attractive setting and a curious relic, the Vénus de Quinipily. Just south of the N24 between Lorient and Josselin.

The central attraction of Baud is the 16th century chapel of Notre Dame-de-la-Clarté. The statue of Our Lady stands in a side chapel off the nave and is the focal point of a *pardon* on the first Sunday in July.

However, while most Breton villages will have a church and many will have a *pardon*, few others have anything as curious as the Vénus de Quinipily. This battered, life-sized statue stands above a fountain at Coët-Vin, about 1km from the village on the Hennebont road. It may be Greek or Roman, or even Egyptian, but whatever the details, it is certainly very old and of pagan rather than Christian origin. The local priests therefore detested it, and on their instructions the Vénus has often been taken from her position and hurled into the Blavet – only to be fished out again later by the local people.

BELLE-ISLE-EN-TERRE

Famous as the home of Breton wrestling, this attractive village stands at the junction of the Guic and Léguer rivers. 16km west of Guingamp.

This quaint village, hardly disturbed by the heavy traffic hurtling past on the roads to Morlaix and St-Brieuc, has a small château and a lot of old houses.

The chief attraction, however, is the Chapelle de Locmaria, 1km north

A mouthwatering display to tempt diners at Cancale

of the village, which contains a fine 16th-century rood screen. Keep an eye open for local festivals during the summer, which might feature the ancient sport of Breton wrestling, traditional singing and dancing, and Breton women in their fine lace *coiffes*.

From the village there are good excursions to the hill of the Menez-Bré, some 6km to the north-east. From the chapel of St-Hervé, which occupies the 302m summit, there are magnificent views over this part of Brittany.

BELLE-ILE

The largest of Brittany's offshore islands, with magnificent scenery and a colourful history, Belle-Ile lies forty-five minutes by ferry from the port at Quiberon. Ferries run all year and are frequent in number. Car reservations may be made in advance.

The ferry docks at Le Palais, a pretty seaport dominated by a huge 16th-century citadel. Fortified by Fouquet, Louis XIV's embezzling chancellor, it was to become his stronghold before later being fortified again by Vauban.

From this attractive port, narrow roads circle the island, north-west to the pretty port at Sauzon, south-east to Locmaria and its sandy bay, or south-west to the village of Bangor – given its name by some Welsh shepherds who came to live on the island during the British occupation of 1761–5. The island was eventually handed back to the French in exchange for the Canadian province of Nova Scotia.

BAUD

THE VENUS OF QUINIPILY

Baud lies in the south of Brittany, north-east of Lorient. The Vénus can be found in the hamlet of Coët Vin, off the road to Hennebont. Follow signs from the car park along a path to a small spring.

No-one really knows the origins of the Vénus of Quinipily, but she is very old, possibly dating back to Roman times. However, the local people have always had a great attraction to this well-worn statue, and protected it from destruction again and again down the centuries.

Because the statue dates from the pagan era, the Church has never been fond of it and whenever any of the local people displayed any signs of affection for it, the local priests would come and hurl the Vénus into the River Blavet nearby. The local people, after a discreet interval, would dredge her

BÉCHEREL

Once a fortified village, an outpost on the road leading from the coast to Rennes, Bécherel perches dramatically on a hilltop 21km south of Dinan.

The first castle to exploit this strategically positioned hill was built in the 12th century, and succeeding layers of fortifications followed. The village's most turbulent period came in the 14th century, when it came under constant siege or assault by the French or English armies, until the English ceded it in 1374.

The ravages of war and time have destroyed a large part of Bécherel's fortifications, though the eastern section of its defensive wall is well preserved. Bécherel retains a nice old-fashioned air, with 16th–18th-century granite houses lining the narrow streets around the market square. Street names such as Rue de la Filanderie recall the fact that the village derived its wealth from spinning the local flax.

From Bécherel's hilltop there are fine views north to Dinan and south to the village of Combourg with its turreted château.

CANCALE

The great oyster port of Brittany, and attractive in its own right, Cancale lies on the western side of the bay of Mont-St-Michel, 14km from St-Malo.

Every oyster-lover should visit Cancale. Although this little fishing village has many other attractions, not

least its favoured position in the bay of Mont-St-Michel, its principal attraction remains its seafood.

Oysters apart, Cancale is a pretty nest of whitewashed and pastel-painted hotels and houses running round the harbour, protected from high tides and gales by a high sea wall. In former times only fishermen lived in the houses by the harbour, while tradespeople and farmers lived in the upper town along the headland. The rooftops are over-

Oyster beds on the beach at Cancale provide a great opportunity for sellers of the freshest seafood

looked by the tower of the church of St-Méen, which at the end of an exhausting climb will reward the visitor with a tremendous view over the surrounding countryside and the great bay, away to Mont-St-Michel and the hump of Mont Dol, and down to the harbour between the quays far below.

---

out and set her up again.

The Vénus, a slightly larger than life-sized statue at over 2m high, stands above a granite basin. It was recarved in the 18th century on the

A battered tribute to the Roman Godess of Beauty, larger than life-size, and truly 'pedestalled in triumph' above an icy spring

orders of the local lord of the manor, but is now showing the effects of a rather turbulent life, and is a somewhat battered figure.

CAP FREHEL

FORT LA LATTE

The fortress at Fort la Latte lies on the headland, just east of Cap Fréhel, 35km west of St-Malo.

Fort la Latte is a fine but grim medieval château-fort built on a rock that juts out into the sea, protected by deep gullies that provided a natural defence. It has all the essential accoutrements, including two drawbridges spanning the gullies and a curtain wall. It was built by the local robber-barons,

the Goyon-Matignon families, in the 13th and early 14th centuries, and restored as a coastal fortification in the 17th century, when the glacis were put in against cannon. The Governor's quarters, the guardhouse and the cannon-ball factory that forged shot for the garrison are still intact and can be visited. From the parapet there are great views around the coastline as far as St-Malo to the east.

CHAMPEAUX

The collegiate church of the d'Espinay family is the central attraction of this charming brownstone village set in the heart of the Ille-et-Vilaine. 9km north-west of Vitré.

Champeaux is a very pretty village spread out along the slope of a long hillside. As the seat of the illustrious d'Espinay family, who were related to King François II, it played a prominent part in Breton life in the 15th and 16th centuries. Their château, which lies just south of the village, dates from this time, as does the village church. The church is still surrounded by some of the elegant houses in which 16 church canons lived until the Revolution, attached to the collegiate church of Ste-Madeleine. Light and airy, it contains impressive tombs of members of the d'Espinay family as well as some finely carved choir stalls and two notable stained-glass windows, all of 15th-century workmanship.

CHATELAUDREN

Along the green valley of the River Leff, one of the attractive minor streams of northern Brittany, lie five villages. Châtelaudren sits on a hill some 12km east of Guingamp, on the D4 road to St-Quay-Portrieux.

Though officially designated a town, present-day Châtelaudren has a population of well under 1000. Its superior status derives from its historic role as capital of the Goelo district, having been chosen by Comte Audren in the 11th century as the site for his castle, Château d'Audren. In 1773 the weir containing the artificial lake burst, and

A game of boules is taken very seriously at the little seaside resort of Erquy

in the catastrophic floods that followed, medieval Châtelaudren was virtually destroyed. Only a few traces remain among the mainly 18th-century stone houses that now make up the village.

There are two excellent churches, one dedicated to St-Magloire, the other to Notre-Dame-du-Tertre. The latter contains a remarkable collection of 132 painted panels depicting the life of Ste-Margaret. Built by St-Vincent Ferrier in 1400, it can be reached along the winding Venelle Notre-Dame.

DAOULAS

A very pretty and historic village set on the banks of the River Daoulas

at its estuary with the Brest roads, Daoulas contains one of the most attractive and least-known calvaries and *enclos paroissiaux* in Brittany, set around a medieval abbey. The city and port of Brest lie 20km to the west.

Set astride the tidal river, Daoulas grew up around two focal points: its abbey, founded in the 6th century, and early medieval fortifications on an island which has now been swallowed up by the sea. The village boasts a number of remarkably fine monuments to its long history. The abbey, occupied by Franciscan nuns, is now a lively cultural centre with interesting exhibitions.

From the 12th century to the 17th, Daoulas was a thriving centre of the weaving and porcelain trades, and this prosperity is reflected in a wealth of

DOL-DE-BRETAGNE

MONT-DOL

Dol-de-Bretagne lies inland from the coast, halfway along the Bay of Mont-St-Michel. The Mont lies just to the north of the town.

Mont-Dol is hardly a mountain. It rises just 65m above the surrounding plain, yet it can be seen for miles away. The Mont is featured under seige in the Bayeaux Tapestry, but its real fame is much older.

According to legend, the Devil and St Michael had a fight here. The Devil was thrown so violently to the ground by St Michael that he dented the rock. St Michael then gouged a hole in the rock with his sword and thrust the Devil into it, only to see the Devil reappear dancing on top of Mont-St-Michel. Furious, St Michael leapt

from Mont-Dol to Mont-St-Michel to continue the struggle, leaving the imprint of his foot behind in the granite of Mont-Dol.

Look out for the Devil's claw-marks left behind on Mont-Dol

monuments and architectural details. Perhaps the finest is the Romanesque cloister, built in the 12th century. The Romanesque church and Renaissance chapel are dedicated to Ste-Anne.

The somewhat battered calvary is one of the oldest in Brittany, dating from the middle of the 16th century – though it is some-what overshadowed by the splendid and detailed 16th-century carvings on the porch to the cemetery.

ERQUY

Once a busy fishing port, this little seaside village on the eastern side of the great bay of St-Brieuc is now one of the most attractive resorts in northern Brittany. St-Brieuc lies 30km along the coast to the south-west.

The *coquilles St Jacques*, or scallops for which the little port of Erquy is renowned are still an important source of income for local fishermen. In recent years, however, Erquy's attractive position has earned it a place as one of the finest family resorts along the magnificent north coast of Brittany.

Perhaps the best of the beaches is the Plage de Caroual, just to the south of the port with fine views out over the Baie de St-Brieuc and north to the tip of Cap d'Erquy. Erquy itself is a pretty jumble of whitewashed houses, each with its garden filled with the profusion of plants and flowers, notably fuchsias, mimosa and camellias, which flourish in this suntrap on the cliffs.

A good breezy walk along a coastal footpath leads through the fishing hamlet of Tu-es-Roc and on to the tip of the Cap d'Erquy.

LE FAOUET

This large village to the south of the Montagnes Noires stands in the beautiful undulating countryside of the Argoat, and is a good touring centre. It lies 21km north of Quimperlé.

Lying as it does on the border of northern and southern Brittany, at the meeting point of the ancient counties of Cornouaille, Broërech and Porhoët, le Faouët has been famous since time immemorial for its weekly market and annual fairs. These take place in and around the magnificent covered market hall, which is now the focus of this extensive village. Built originally in the 16th century, it is remarkable for its forest of wooden pillars and beams sup-porting a massive slate roof, with an octagonal bell-tower above.

Le Faouët's church also dates from the 16th century, but more interesting chapels are to be found in the surround-ing countryside (see Kernascléden, page 21).

Le Faouët also serves as an excellent base for exploring the lovely green hills of the Montagnes Noires which lie to the north, or the delightful wooded valley of the River Ellé.

TRADITIONAL BRETON COSTUME

Black predominates for both men and women, relieved by the men's embroidered waistcoats and the ribbons round their felt hats, and by the women's white aprons. Most distinctive of all are the women's lace *coiffes*, or caps, whose design differs from place to place. They range from the tall, cylindrical *bigouden* of Pont-l'Abbé, through the ribboned *coiffe* of Plougastel, to the skimpy cap of Huelgoat. Despite Brittany's pride in its regional heritage, such costumes play a larger role in its tourist image than they do in ordinary life. They can still be seen on market days at Quimper, however, and nearby Pont l'Abbé, and at religious festivals such as the *pardons*, or processions in honour of local saints.

TOUR 1 – 110KM

FISHERMEN AND ARTISTS IN SOUTHERN BRITTANY

Brittany is more often thought of as a country of farmers and fishermen than artists, but it is a province where artists abound, drawn to the region by the wide variety of subjects and the clear Atlantic light. This tour circles the southern centre of the province on the borders of the Morbihan and Finistère, touching the coast at well-chosen spots like Concarneau and Brigneau. This indented coastline is full of estuaries and rivers, and little yachting havens such as Pont-Aven, which is popular with yachtsmen but has also been a haven for artists for over 100 years.

Capturing the view on canvas

ROUTE DIRECTIONS

Leave the centre of Concarneau by the new bridge over the River Moros, and at the round-about pick up the **D783**, following signs for Pont-Aven and Quimperlé. Follow this for 14km into Pont-Aven.

Continue on to Riec-sur-Bélon (4.5km) and turn right onto the **D24** towards Moëlan-sur-Mer. Fork right off the **D24** on **D116** and continue down to Brigneau, returning to Moëlan-sur-Mer round the coast (11km).

From here follow the **D116** inland for 5km to the **D16**, and follow this into Quimperlé (5km). Follow 'Toutes Directions' signs from the centre and head for the **D790** to le Faouët (21km).

From le Faouët take the **D782** to Scaër (17km). Continue on the **D782**, south to Rosporden (14km). From Rosporden take the **D70** back to Concarneau.

PLACES OF INTEREST

PONT-AVEN

This pretty little town on the estuary of the River Aven is famous in painting circles as the home of the Pont Aven School founded by Paul Gauguin and his friends around 1888, and still draws a host of painters every year. Sights to see include the chapel at Trémalo, which contains the statue on which Gauguin based his Yellow Christ.

QUIMPERLÉ

Quimperlé is an interesting town full of narrow streets and old buildings dating back to the 13th and 15th centuries. The church of Ste-Croix was built in the early years of the 12th century in the style of the Church of the Holy Sepulchre in Jerusalem leading to the belief that it was designed by local knights returning from the First Crusade. The crypt and the apse are the only parts of the original building that remain, as the rest was rebuilt in 1862 when the belfry collapsed. Other sights include the Archers' House in the Rue Dom-Morice, which is now a museum dedicated to the local bowmen.

LE FAOUET
See page 17.

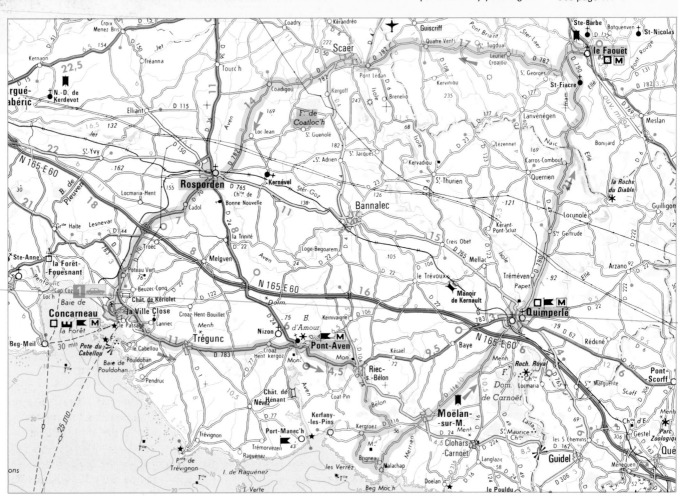

This curious place just to the south of Scaër was used by the local craftspeople to grow wood for the wooden clogs, or *sabots*, for which Scaër was famous. Constantly replanted over the years, the wood was protected in the Middle Ages by a high stone wall, which, remarkably, is still intact. Today it is a popular spot for picnics and forest walks.

ROSPORDEN

Like Pont-Aven, Rosporden – a pretty town with the River Aven flowing through it – has been a popular artists' centre since the 19th century. The original town was put to the torch during the Wars of Religion, and was not rebuilt until the early years of the 17th century. The 14th–15th century church, with its splendid bell-tower, was remodelled in the 17th century. The most popular local product is *chouchen*, a form of mead.

Off-loading a varied catch

GUIMILIAU

The village of Guimiliau, noted for its splendid *enclos paroissial*, lies 18km to the south-west of Morlaix.

This tiny village, with a population of less than 800, is a jewel which no visitor to Brittany should miss.

The church, in the Flamboyant Gothic style of the 17th century, shelters in its porch a statue of St-Miliau, the 6th-century King of Cornouaille who gave his name to the village. The rich decorations of the interior include scenes from the saint's life in the sacristy and on the altar.

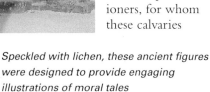

Speckled with lichen, these ancient figures were designed to provide engaging illustrations of moral tales

The overwhelming feature of Guimiliau is its large and magnificent 16th-century *enclos paroissial*, which is alive with more than 200 meticulously carved figures. On the platform a grotesque group tells the tale of Kate Gollet, who took the Devil as her lover and at his instigation stole a consecrated Host at confession. Condemned to eternal hellfire, the unhappy sinner is shown pinned down by a fork while demons tear at her flesh: a fearsome example to the local parishioners, for whom these calvaries served as pictorial representations of Bible stories and morality tales.

HEDE

Once a stronghold on the road to Rennes, this tiny village is one of a number of attractive hamlets in the green and hilly country south-east of Dinan. 22km north-east of Rennes.

Small, quaint and extremely picturesque, Hédé sits on a low hill between a lake and the winding Ille-et-Rance canal. The summit of the hill is occupied by the ruins of a fortress which affords views over the rooftops of the Romanesque church.

The Ille-et-Rance canal offers good walks along the towpath. To the north it is especially interesting, leading to the remarkable 'ladder' of 11 linked locks over 2km, by which barge traffic is able to negotiate the 26m difference in height between the valleys of the Ille and the Rance.

THE LAND FACING THE SEA

The ancients knew Brittany as Armorica, 'the land facing the sea'. When the Roman grip on Gaul weakened, the Gaulish inhabitants of Brittany were joined not by the Frankish tribes who overran the rest of France but by Britons from the other side of the Channel. These settlers helped confirm Brittany's Celtic distinctiveness, setting it apart from the rest of France and leaving it a legacy of separatism that today finds political expression in the UDB (the Union Démocratique Bretonne, or, in Breton, the Unvaniezh Demokratel Breizh) and a terrorist group, the FLB (the Front de Libération de Bretagne). Manifest in its music, dance, costume and folklore, Brittany's heritage has survived most emphatically in its language. Though today it is spoken by only about a third of the region's 2.3 million inhabitants, Breton is still written into place names that declare affinities with Cornwall and Wales. The prefixes Plou-, Lan-, Tré- and Ker-, are common examples.

ILE DE BREHAT— LE BOURG

With no cars, a climate so mild that Mediterranean plants grow freely and a wealth of wildlife – especially migrating seabirds in spring – this little rocky outcrop is a paradise for nature-lovers. Allow a full day here for a good visit. A ferry from the Pointe de l'Arcouest, near Paimpol, carries visitors on the 10-minute crossing to the island.

The Ile de Bréhat consists of two tiny islands linked by an 18th-century bridge built by the great military engineer Vauban. Each of the islands nevertheless has its own character: the northerly one more rugged and windswept; the southerly one – on which lies the village of le Bourg – softer and prettier.

Le Bourg, the island's capital, is a tiny cluster of houses around a 12th–18th century church. Bréhat was the object of vicious struggles during the Hundred Years War and again during the Wars of Religion, when many inhabitants were hanged from the sails of the old windmill to the west of the village, and the island's castle was razed to the ground.

KERMARIA

THE CHAPEL OF KERMARIA- AN-INSKUIT

This exquisite chapel lies 4km north-west of Plouha, north of St-Brieuc-Armor.

The Chapel of Kermaria-an-Iskuit (the Place of Mary, the Health Giver), was built as a baronial chapel in the 13th century, although the building was enlarged in the 15th and 18th centuries as it became a popular pilgrimage site. The 16th-century room above the porch was once used for the barons' court.

However, the great secret of Kermaria, and the reason for going there, is to see the magnificent 15th-century frescos, especially the one in the nave This shows a medieval 'Doom' or Last Judgement, which here is represented as a Dance of Death, the inevitable end of life, and starkly depicts the nobility and common-

KERNASCLEDEN

This tiny village, once a possession of the Ducs de Rohan, who for centuries ruled great swathes of Brittany from their sumptuous château at Josselin, boasts one of the finest churches in Brittany. The village lies 31km north of Lorient.

Tiny as Kernascléden is, it nevertheless possesses a magnificent church, one of the great masterpieces of Flamboyant Gothic architecture in Brittany. Completed in 1453, it has exquisite stone vaulting and tracery. The south façade has two finely sculpted stone porches, one containing statues of the apostles, and a beautiful rose window. Inside, the vaulting and upper walls of the choir are decorated with exceptional frescoes dating from the 15th century. A vividly gruesome Dance of Death mural in one of the transepts is another rare survivor.

A Grande Randonnée footpath, the GR38, leads south from Kernascléden to the Forêt de Pont-Calleck, a beauty spot on the banks of the River Scarff.

LEHON

This wonderfully picturesque little hamlet on the banks of the Rance should not be missed. It lies 2km to the south of Dinan.

The Rue de Léhon runs past the château in Dinan before leading out through the walls and steadily downhill to the banks of the Rance. There lies the golden village of Léhon, the soft stone of its 16th- and 17th-century houses and pretty bridge picked out with great hanging baskets of flowers and beds of geraniums.

A great menhir at Locmariaquer emerges from the sun-baked earth like a giant whale

The hamlet grew up on this ancient crossing place of the River Rance, around the abbey of St-Magloire. The Gothic refectory and the 12th-century abbey church still stand, but the rest of the abbey buildings are 17th-century or later. The church contains the tombs of the lords of Beaumanoir, one of the ancient noble families of the area, and some fine woodwork, as well as a curious holy water stone on which it is still the custom for the local *paysans* to sharpen their sickles in order to ensure a good harvest.

LOCMARIAQUER

In a magnificent setting on the western headland above the entrance to the Golfe du Morbihan, this pretty fishing village is so rich in megaliths, dolmens and tumuli that it has become a place of pilgrimage for anyone interested in the mysteries of the prehistoric age. It lies on the coast, 13km south of Auray and opposite Port-Navalo.

The hour when the tide is in full flood is the time to visit Locmariaquer, when the Atlantic surges into the Golfe de Morbihan, through the narrow channel between this village and Port-Navalo. That apart, the undisputed claim to fame of this village is the wealth of huge prehistoric dolmens and menhirs near by.

The Grand Menhir, now in four pieces, would have stood over 20m high when intact and erected; the Table des Marchands, 36m across, was the covering stone of a vast chamber tomb, carved with cryptic designs; and the Mané-Lud dolmen forms an underground chamber 80m long. Other dolmens are actually set among the village houses.

ality, emperors, kings, princes, lords down to peasants and humble folk, all dancing before the spectre of Death. The cross over the altar is 14th- century, as is the small statue of the Virgin suckling the infant Jesus, and the chapel is decorated with numerous other wooden statues dating from the 13th to 16th centuries.

The 'danse macabre', or dance of death, was a particularly popular choice for artists, who could portray whoever they liked (or disliked) in the line-up for the Last Judgement.

LOCQUIREC

Set on the western edge of the Baie de Lannion, this pretty little port is now a popular resort and a yachting centre. It lies 18km north-east of Morlaix.

Even among all the pretty places in which the north coast of Brittany is so rich, Locquirec is outstanding. Once a thriving fishing port, it still shelters the vestiges of the fleet along its quay. Today the livelihood of the village depends on tourism and yachting.

The village church was built in the Middle Ages by the Knights of St John, who had a commandery here. From the church, narrow alleys thread their way into the village and there is a very good, breezy walk out to the tip of the Pointe de Locquirec.

LOCRONAN

Granite-built Locronan is a beautifully preserved masterpiece of 16th- and 17th-century domestic architecture, very beautiful and not to be missed on any visit to Brittany. The village lies 10km east of Douarnerez, in Finistère.

Built of silvery granite, which simply sparkles in the clear Atlantic sunlight, Locronan grew up in the late Middle Ages as a weaving centre for the manufacture of sailcloth. A visit to this enchanting village is like a trip back in time, for there is not an electricity pylon or a television aerial to be seen,

Sturdy chimneys and high dormers adorn the roofs of Locronan, a jewel in Finistère's crown of attractive villages

and the superb Renaissance houses are well preserved and immaculately maintained. The magnificent main square contains the beautifully sculpted church of St-Ronan, the 15th-century Irish monk who gave the settlement its name. An ornate porch links it to the 16th-century Chapelle du Penity, which shelters the Saint's empty tomb.

Above the village stands the Montagne de Locronan, just 289m high, on which there is a chapel which is the focus for one of Brittany's most celebrated *pardons*.

SECRET PLACES

PONT-L'ABBE

NOTRE-DAME-DE-TRONOEN

The calvary of Notre-Dame-de-Tronoën stands beside the road, 12km west of Pont l'Abbé.

The 15th-century chapel of Notre-Dame-de-Tronoën is set among the dunes at the south end of Audierne Bay. The late 15th-century calvary beside the chapel, much eroded by wind and weather, is the oldest in Brittany. Scenes of the Judgement and the Last

MONCONTOUR

Though its redoubtable defences were partly destroyed by order of Richelieu, this pretty village remains a splendidly atmospheric reminder of the medieval and Renaissance art of fortification. It occupies a strategically positioned and much fought-over spur of land high above two deep river valleys, 24km south of St-Brieuc.

A great Chancellor of France though he may have been, Cardinal Richelieu did irreparable damage to the historic fabric of the north of France when he destroyed the old fortresses of the turbulent provincial nobility. With its 12th-century ramparts guarded by 15 towers, Moncontour must have been immensely imposing before the cardinal's canon arrived in 1626.

Happily a great deal of the old curtain wall still stands, and within the village remains a confusing jumble of narrow streets. The church contains a remarkable series of six 16th-century stained-glass windows.

PORT-BLANC

A tiny chapel set on a rock just off the shore is the unforgettable image engraved on the memory of every visitor to the pretty resort of Port-Blanc, one of the small jewels of the Côte Granit-Rose, 16km east of the larger resort of Perros-Guirec.

Now a seaside resort with a row of hotels along the shore, Port-Blanc began life as a fishing port, set among the rocks and sand dunes which now provide shade and shelter for holiday-makers. The most striking feature of this pretty village is the Chapelle Notre Dame-de-Port-Blanc, set on its rock above the esplanade and reached up a flight of steps. A calvary in the church includes a notable group of St-Yves, patron saint of lawyers, arbitrating between a rich man and a poor man. An annual *pardon* is held here on 8 September.

PORTSALL-KERSAINT

These two little ports set on either side of a tranquil bay have now merged into one, and offer an attractive combination of seaside resort and pleasant touring centre. They lie 25km north-west of le Folgoët, and 28km north of Brest.

Kersaint is an agreeable village set around a tree-filled central square, from which roads lead to the coast and directly into Portsall. This little port still retains a small harbour as a reminder of the days when fishing was its livelihood, though most of the many sailing craft that come here now anchor in the sheltered waters of the bay. From Portsall there is a good walk to a calvary at the end of the point, from where there are fine views to the ruins of Château de Tremazan to the west, and out over the Roches de Portsall, which earned notoriety in 1978 when the oil tanker *Amoco Cadiz* came to grief there and polluted the whole coast.

BRETON DELICACIES

Arguably the most common speciality is the *crêpe*, treated as a meal in itself rather than just a snack. *Galettes*, made with buckwheat flour, hold savoury fillings; white-flour *crêpes* go with dessert fillings. Freshwater fish that feature on the table may include elvers, or young eels (*civelles*), yet for many visitors, Brittany means seafood, particularly shellfish: scallops, or *coquilles St-Jacques*; cockles, grilled or stuffed; lobsters, sometimes served *à l'armoricaine*, in a rich sauce; and oysters, matured in the farms at Cancale (the *véritables Cancales*) and Morlaix. *Cotriade* is a northern equivalent of *bouillabaisse*, a fish stew which – like its Provençal cousin – should contain as many types of fish as possible. And in France even red meat can take on a tang of the sea: *agneau pré-salé* is lamb from sheep grazed on the saltmarshes of the Médoc or the Cotentin peninsula.

Supper, which face the sea, are very worn, but those on the north face showing scenes from the life of Christ between the Nativity and the Crucifixion, carved in Kersanton granite, are in better condition.

St Yves – well-loved patron saint of lawyers

MINIHY-TREGUIER
TOMB OF ST-YVES

Minihy-Tréguier lies 1km south of Tréguier, in north-west Brittany, 16km west of Paimpol.

Unlike so many of the legendary Breton saints, the popular St-Yves actually existed. He was born Yves Hélori at Minihy-Tréguier in 1253, studied law in Paris, and in the 1270s returned to Tréguier to practise. He soon built up a formidable reputation, not least because he refused to be brow-beaten by the local barons and refused to take bribes. He became known as the protector of the poor and the 'advocate of the forgotten', the 'righter of wrongs'. He died in 1303 and was canonised in 1347, becoming the patron saint of lawyers.

The churchyard at Minihy-Tréguier is the scene of the *Pardon* of St-Yves on 19 May, when devout pilgrims crawl through an arch in the 13th-century monument known as the tomb of St-Yves. His actual tomb lies in the cathedral of St-Tugdual at Tréguier, though the existing tomb is a 19th-century copy.

TOUR 2 – 135KM
THE NORTH COAST OF BRITTANY

This tour of the north coast of Brittany takes in a great variety of Breton country-side, covering a part of the province where the two very different cultures of France and Brittany collide. The first part travels through a mixture of rolling farmland and small forests, interspersed with attractive villages and small towns such as Pontrièux and Châtelaudren, and taking in the magnificent Château de Tonquédec on the way.

ROUTE DIRECTIONS

From Paimpol follow signs for Pontrieux out of town onto the **D15**, and follow this for 10km to Quemper-Guézennec, and on into Pontrieux (5km). On leaving Pontrieux pick up the **D15** again, turning right after 1km for Runan on the **D21** (4km). Continue to follow the **D21** west from Runan to Prat, and continue on the **D93** to meet the **D33** (7km), then turn left, following signs for Bégard to the **D767**. Turn north on the **D767** for 2km to Cavan. Turn right on the **D767** at the north end of the village, and follow signs for Tonquédec and the Château fort-de Tonquédec (5km). At Tonquédec turn south and follow the **D31** through Pluzunet and St-Eloi to Louargat (15km). Turn left here and follow the **N12** for Guingamp. In Guingamp follow 'Autre Directions' signs to the war memorial and pick up the road signposted to St-Quay-Portrièux, turning right after 2km on to the **D86**, signposted to Châtelaudren and Plouagat. Follow the **D86** and then the **D7** into Châtelaudren (1km).

Leave here on the **D4** for Plélo and St-Quay, following the **D4** all the way to the **D786**, a main road, and on into Binic (16km). From Binic centre return to the **D786** and follow this north, past the church of Notre Dame into St-Quay-Portrieux (4km).

From the harbour at St-Quay pick up signs to Plouha and Paimpol, which lead back to the **D786** and to Plouha (8km). From there head north along the coast back to Paimpol (17km).

PLACES OF INTEREST

CHURCHES
Many French churches lost their treasures and beauty at the Revolution, but the Bretons protected theirs and they are always warm and friendly places, full of interest. The great parish-close churches of Brittany are not as common as the tourist posters lead visitors to suppose, but the best of them lie around St Thégonnec, south of Morlaix, and further west. The churches on this tour are those of the fishing and farming communities, generally well-looked after and often of surprising beauty. The church at Lanloup near Paimpol, the ruins of Beauport Abbey, the Basilica of Notre-Dame-de-Bon-Secours in Guingamp or the 15th-century Chapel of Notre-Dame-de-Restudo are all worth visiting.

PONTRIEUX
Not to be confused with Portrieux near St-Quay on the coast, this little town at the head of the Trieux estuary is also a sailing centre. The town is attractive but the great sight hereabouts is the château of Roche-Jagu, to the north, which dates from the 15th century and is a blend of warlike castle and domestic manor.

CHATEAU DE TONQUEDEC
It is easy to miss this splendid château-fort, which overlooks the deep valley of the river Léguer, because it is half hidden in the trees. The castle was built in the 13th century, rebuilt in the 15th century, and dismantled again by Cardinal Richelieu, who was determined to destroy the fortresses of the turbulent provincial nobility. In spite of all this, a great deal of Tonquédec still remains, and it is worth visiting for the site alone.

CHATELAUDREN
See page 16.

BINIC
This charming little resort was once a fishing port,

Above left, the lonely lighthouse at St-Quay-Portrieux.
Above, mending nets

though the great pier where cod was unloaded is now used to shelter a host of visiting yachts and smaller sailing craft. Binic has a museum that recalls the great days of the Grand Banks schooners that once fished off Newfoundland.

ST-QUAY-PORTRIEUX
St-Quay is a fishing port that has turned more and more to tourism in recent years. Excellent beaches close by include the Plage Bonaparte, reached via a tunnel through the cliffs, and the smaller Plage-Palus, which looks out to St-Brieuc Bay.

The clifftop footpath, the Chemin de Ronde, is a former *sentier des douaniers*, or customs' officers path, used in the search for smugglers.

LA ROCHE-BERNARD

Once an important seaport, this large village at the top of the Vilaine estuary is one of the most attractive and interesting places to visit in the Morbihan. It lies just inside the frontiers of the modern province, 28km south-west of Redon.

It was in the 10th century that Bernard, a Norman descendant of the Vikings, built a castle on a rocky outcrop overlooking the Vilaine estuary, with a convenient cove below in which his boats could shelter.

In the 17th century la Roche Bernard was celebrated for its naval shipyards, tucked well away from the Atlantic gales, far up the tidal estuary of the Vilaine river; it is now better known as a yachting centre.

A fine suspension bridge, opened in 1960, spans the deep valley of the Vilaine here, carrying the N165 road from Vannes to Nantes. Boat trips are available from the port, up the river to Redon or down to the tidal dam which spans the river at Arzal.

LA ROCHE-MAURICE

This charming cluster of white-washed or granite stone houses, each with a flower-filled garden, has a little-known but very fine *enclos paroissial*. The village lies 4km north-east of Landerneau.

Once a strategic bastion of Finistère between the north and west coasts, la Roche-Maurice lies on the slopes of a hill topped by the remains of a 13th-century castle. There are good views over the surrounding countryside and down the valley of the Elorn.

The *enclos paroissial* is not as elaborate as those at Guimiliau or St-Thégonnec, with a cavalry consisting simply of the traditional Crucifixion, but it contains a remarkable ossuary. Built in 1639, it is among the largest in the province and bears fascinating carved panels showing the different classes in society. Above the holy water stoup is an image of Death – 'Ankou' in Breton – declaring, 'I kill you all'.

The figure of Death, a grim reminder above the holy water stoup, la Roche-Maurice

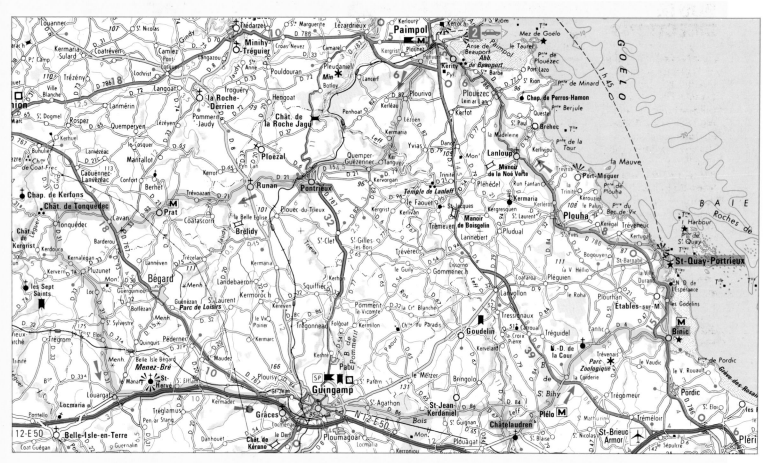

Rochefort-en-Terre

Famed for its picturesque streets and lovely squares of 16th- and 17th-century houses, wreathed in flowers throughout the summer, and treasured for its delightful atmosphere, this historic stronghold should not be missed on any visit to the Morbihan – or indeed to Brittany. It lies 20km north-west of Redon.

A pleasant seat in the sunshine at Rochefort-en-Terre

Scattered in a delightful jumble down the slopes of a promontory which earned the little settlement its strategic importance in the Middle Ages, the streets and alleyways of Rochefort-en-Terre offer an irresistible invitation to explore.

Of the original 12th-century château, destroyed in1793, only a gateway and parts of the wall survive. What the visitor now sees are the 17th-century outbuildings, restored by an American benefactor at the beginning of this century. The church, dedicated to Notre Dame-de-la-Tronchaye and built and rebuilt over the 12th to 15th centuries, has delightful carvings of oxen at the corners of its 12th-century tower and has fine 16th-century woodwork and a calvary of the same periods. A *pardon* takes place on the Sunday after 15 August each year.

St-Gildas-de-Rhuys

With its cliffs and beaches and the vestiges of its ancient abbey, this small village is the centrepiece of the Presqu'île du Rhuys. It lies 28km south of the city of Vannes.

Two clerics are responsible for the fame of St-Gildas-de-Rhuys. The first is St Gildas, who founded the abbey here in the 6th century and became the first abbot. The next illustrious clerical visitor arrived in 1125. This was the eminent scholar Abelard, who had been sent for by the Duke of Brittany in the hope that he might be able to restore order to a by now notoriously wayward community.

In 1132, however, he was obliged to flee for his life, as the monks, none too pleased with their new abbot and his unwelcome strictures, had resorted to desperate measures – including an attempt at poisoning – to oust him.

The former abbey church, altered in the 17th century, retains its magnificent 12th-century Romanesque choir. Relics of St Gildas are preserved in the sacristy, together with other fine pieces.

HUELGOAT

Roche-Tremblante

Huelgoat is the great walking centre of Brittany, a small town by a lake set in the centre of the countryside south of Morlaix. The spectacular Roche Tremblante can be reached by following a path beside the signboard, just across the main road from the lake.

The green woods and great moss-covered rocks that litter the streams and tumbled little hills around Huelgoat could almost have been created as a backdrop for some

Excellent view over the town from la Roche Cintrée, near the Promenade du Canal

ST-JEAN-DU-DOIGT

This picturesque little village owes its singular name to the unusual relic that has made it a famous centre for pilgrimage since the 15th century. The village lies inland from the coast, 18km north of Morlaix.

The finger of St John the Baptist, cut off at his execution, has been preserved in the Chapelle St-Mériadec since about 1440, although the chapel was not finished until 1513, and then only after a generous donation from the Duchesse Anne.

The result is a rather battered Flamboyant Gothic chapel – unfortunately it was badly damaged by fire earlier this century – with a treasury full of sumptuous reliquaries, including a small part of John the Baptist's index finger. Supposed to restore vision and hearing, among other afflictions, it is carried in procession around the village on the last Sunday of every June for the annual *pardon*.

The church has a small parish close, entered through a Flamboyant Gothic arch, with a Renaissance fountain. The village has a great many old and attractive houses, each with its well-kept garden.

The church at Lanmeur, 7km to the south-east, is worth visiting for its 6th-century crypt. To the south-west lies the impressive Tumulus de Barnenez, containing the most ancient of all Brittany's dolmens – it's well worth a detour.

ST-NICOLAS-DU-PELEM

This little village has been turned into a superb walking centre, perfect for enjoying the lovely countryside and historic monuments of the surrounding area. It lies in the open green county 30km south of Guingamp.

If Huelgoat has a rival as a walking centre, it undoubtedly lies in the pretty little village of St-Nicolas-du-Pélem, for the Syndicat d'Initiative has created a linked network of foot-paths all around the village, leading to lakes, crosses and menhirs, all by the most attractive routes.

Originally a settlement, strung out along the side of a hill, St-Nicolas-du-Pélem has a number of fine churches and chapels, including that of St-Nicolas which dates from around 1470.

ST-THEGONNEC

The enclos paroissial here is one of the three most celebrated in Brittany, and together with the church makes a fine ensemble of Breton Renaissance architecture. One of the great sights of Brittany, the village lies 10km south-west of Morlaix.

Unique to Brittany, parish closes consisted traditionally of a ceremonial gateway, a cemetery, a calvary and an ossuary, as well as the church.

Built under the *ancien régime* as symbols both of civic pride and an evangelical fervour in the wake of the Reformation, their construction was financed by the thriving linen industry.

A royal edict at the end of the 17th century forbidding unnecessary building work combined with the decline of the linen industry to put an end to the construction of such parish closes. The stately and well-preserved parish close here has a tall, elegant calvary of 1610, showing, among other events, St-Thégonnec harnessing his cart laden with stores to a wolf after the wolf-pack had eaten his donkey. The

The figures at St-Thegonnec were dressed by their creator in contemporary costume

ossuary, built some 60 years later, is one of the best examples of Renaissance architecture in Brittany. The church itself is 16th-century, and contains some superb woodwork. Clustered beneath its massive tower, which dwarfs the surrounding houses, the village contains another attraction in the famous little Auberge St-Thégonnec, one of the best small restaurants in this corner of Brittany.

Arthurian legend.

The *Grotte d'Artus* (Arthus's Cave), the *Ménage de la Vièrge* (Virgin's Kitchen, so-called because the rocks there are shaped like cooking pots), and the *Grotte du Diable* (Devil's Grotto, reached down a ladder), add extra mystery, to the scene, but the biggest attraction here, in every sense of the word, is the great 100-tonne rock known as the Roche Tremblante or rocking stone, which is to be found in the wood beyond the Théâtre de Verdure, the open-air amphitheatre.

Finding the rock is quite easy; actually getting it to rock is much more difficult, but legend has it that if the back is applied to the rock at a specific point, it will indeed tremble.

The rocks are found together in a beautiful area of woodland – foot-paths lead through to scenic walks beside the canal and the river.

SECRET FRANCE

NORMANDY

The five departments that go to make up the great province of Normandy – Manche, Calvados, Orne, Eure and Seine-Maritime – contain within their borders a richness and variety of landscape that is perhaps unrivalled in France. From the wild, craggy granite coastline of the northern Cotentin to the long sandy beaches and chalk cliffs of the south, from the ancient beech forests of the east to the apple orchards of Calvados, and from the meandering valleys and wooded hillsides of the Suisse Normande to the windswept plateaux of the west and the open, fertile farmland of the Pays de Caux, Normandy offers a wealth of quiet villages and unspoilt countryside for leisurely exploration.

Normandy is justly celebrated for its cuisine. Fresh fish, cream and cheese figure prominently on the menus of the many good and reasonable restaurants throughout the region – washed down, inevitably, with a finger of apple-scented Calvados.

Life in Normandy is still ordered according to the rhythm of the seasons, much as it has been for centuries. The fields of the Normandy *bocage* may have lost many of their hedges, and are now more open and more suitable for mechanised farming, but still the chequerboard landscape, a mixture of arable fields, grazing pasture and apple orchards, retains its charm.

One of the best ways to experience the diversity offered by this region is by visiting its villages. Built of local materials and designed to suit local needs, the houses, churches, barns and overall layout are as individual and varied as the landscapes in which they lie.

Driving around the province, travellers will soon sense that they have moved from the Pays d'Auge to the Pays de Bray, or up among the dovecotes and small farms of the Pays de Caux, the great chalk plateau that runs across Normandy from the Seine to the Channel coast.

Normandy lost a great many of her small, beautiful and secret places when the tide of war washed over the province in 1944. No other part of France suffered so much, or was so comprehensively destroyed, so the traveller with an eye for the amusing, the interesting or the unusual may have to work a little harder, and with an even keener eye, to catch something special. However, that said, there is still plenty to see in this attractive region.

maquereau de Normandie

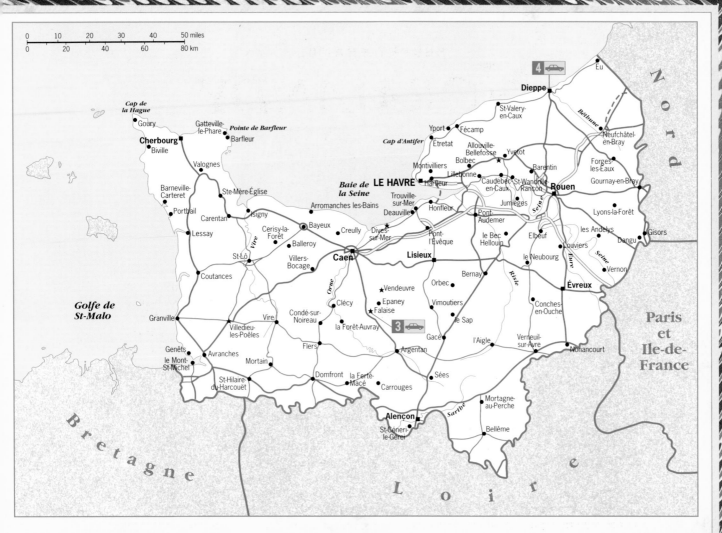

0   10   20   30   40   50 miles
0   20   40   60   80 km

Cap de la Hague
Goury
Gatteville-le-Phare
Pointe de Barfleur
Barfleur
Cherbourg
Biville
Valognes
Barneville-Carteret
Ste-Mère-Église
Portbail
Carentan
Isigny
Lessay
Cerisy-la-Forêt
Bayeux
Creully
St-Lô
Balleroy
Villers-Bocage
Coutances
Caen
Golfe de St-Malo
Granville
Vire
Condé-sur-Noireau
Clécy
Villedieu-les-Poêles
Flers
Genêts
Avranches
Mortain
le Mont-St-Michel
St-Hilaire-du-Harcouët
Domfront
la Ferté-Macé
Carrouges
Alençon
St-Céneri-le-Gérei

Eu
Dieppe
St-Valery-en-Caux
Yport
Fécamp
Béthune
Neufchâtel-en-Bray
Cap d'Antifer
Étretat
Allouville-Bellefosse
Yvetot
Forges-les-Eaux
Montivilliers
Bolbec
Baie de la Seine
LE HAVRE
Lillebonne
Barentin
Gournay-en-Bray
Harfleur
Caudebec-en-Caux
St-Wandrille-Rançon
Rouen
Trouville-sur-Mer
Jumièges
Lyons-la-Forêt
Deauville
Honfleur
Arromanches les-Bains
Pont-Audemer
Seine
les Andelys
Dives-sur-Mer
Pont-l'Évêque
le Bec Hellouin
Elbeuf
Dangu
Gisors
Lisieux
le Neubourg
Louviers
Vendeuvre
Orbec
Bernay
Risle
Vernon
Epaney
Falaise
Vimoutiers
Évreux
Orne
la Forêt-Auvray
le Sap
Conches-en-Ouche
Gacé
Argentan
l'Aigle
Verneuil-sur-Avre
Nonancourt
Sées
Eure
Mortagne-au-Perche
Sarthe
Bellême

Paris et Ile-de-France
Nord
Bretagne
Loire

[4] 🚗
[3] 🚗

Left, in Normandy they take their bread seriously – this tempting display offers thirty different sorts, or something to suit every palate
Below, low tide at Barfleur gives a fisherman a chance to maintain his vessel
Right, a pretty window box offsets the diamond panes of an old window

UN PAIN POUR CHAQUE PLAT
30 Sortes de Pains

BALLEROY

Conceived as a fitting approach and an elegant accessory to Mansart's beautifully proportioned château, this unusually harmonious 17th-century village lies 18km south-west of Bayeux.

When the great François Mansart designed the château at Balleroy – one of his finest works – for Jean de Choisy, chancellor to Duc d'Orléans, he included the village in his majestic scheme. Thus the main street forms a stately avenue leading the visitor to the château gates and on to the entrance itself.

The château, built 1626–36 and of soberly perfect proportions, has magnificent interior decorations. The parish church, also by Mansart, was originally the chapel to the château. The fine stable building now houses a museum of hot-air ballooning, and there is an annual balloon festival in June. The château park is also superb, with gardens attributed to Le Nôtre.

BARFLEUR

Once an important naval base and a busy fishing port, this picturesque village on the north coast of the Cotentin is now a popular tourist and yachting centre. It lies 27km east of Cherbourg.

Barfleur reached the height of its importance in Norman times, when it was frequented by the vessels of the Anglo-Norman kings. Local tradition has it that the boat which carried

Fishing boats idle at rest on a summer evening in Barfleur

William the Conqueror to England in 1066 not only sailed from Barfleur but was also built there. What is certain is that his grandson William, along with some 300 of the flower of the Anglo-English nobility, later perished there in the wreck of the *White Ship*. A commemorative plaque stands just off-shore, visible from the harbour.

Now, with its pretty streets and harbour and its attractive houses, Barfleur is popular with the yachting fraternity and tourists, who come to eat or stay at the village restaurants and hotels, the latter including the ever-popular Hôtel de Phare.

By the harbour is the massive 17th-century church of St Nicolas, patron saint of mariners, standing defiantly against the sea with great anchors on the outside.

LE BEC HELLOUIN

On the outskirts of this lovely village of half-timbered houses stands the great abbey which in medieval times was one of Europe's greatest centres of learning. It lies 21km south-east of Pont-Andemer.

This village on the banks of the Bec, or stream of Bec Hellouin is a rambling little place, full of cottages with trim lawns and sloping gardens, including a number of the charming black-and-white half-timbered houses that are typical of Normandy. One of these is the Auberge

BARFLEUR

BARFLEUR POINT LIGHTHOUSE

The lighthouse at Barfleur stands on the tip of the Pointe de Barfleur, 2½ km north of the village of Gatteville-le-Phare.

Few sights above the north coast of the Cotentin are as splendid as that of the Gatteville lighthouse, the *phare de Gatteville*. This is one of the tallest lighthouses in France, the lantern standing at a height of 71m. The light can be seen 56km away, and the tower is topped by a radio mast beaming

signals to ships negotiating the rocky seas as they head towards Cherbourg or Le Havre.

The lighthouse can be visited and a flight of 365 steps – one for every day of the year – leads up to the top, from where there are spectacular views along the coast to Cherbourg and Barfleur, to the west, the Isles St-Marcouf and the Baie de la Seine to the east.

The offshore waters are very dangerous. It was

here that William Atheling, the only son of the English King Henry I, was drowned in the loss of the *White Ship* in 1120, long before a lighthouse was built on its wild and rocky coast.

Guarding sea areas Portland and Wight – or Manche East, to the French

BIVILLE

This tiny windswept village has been a famous centre of pilgrimage locally since the 15th century. It lies on the west coast of the Cotentin peninsula, 20km west of Cherbourg.

Biville clings to the open heathland above the vast empty sands of the Anse de Vauville, which sweeps south here from the Nez de Jobourg.

Built of enduring silver granite, the village has a very splendid and well-preserved church, rebuilt in the 13th century to house the mortal remains of the Blessed Thomas Hélye, a saintly local missionary and priest who died in 1257.

His glass coffin is enclosed in a marble tomb, and the church is the focus of an annual midnight pilgrimage on 18/19 October each year.

CARROUGES

This large village with its château is a popular touring centre for the Suisse Normande and the Orne country. It lies on the western edge of the Forêt d'Ecouves, 21km south of Argentan.

Businesslike rather than pretty, the narrow streets of Carrouges are lined with shops serving the needs of the local farming community. The main attraction here is the château of le Veneur de Tillières, which lies just down the road from the village centre.

Now owned by the nation, this great moated brick-and-granite building belonged to the Veneur de Tillières family from its construction in the 15th century until 1936. The gatehouse is especially fine.

Most of the interior is open to visitors and contains a fine collection of tapestries and furniture, including a well-equipped kitchen. The elegant park surrounding the château now lies at the heart of these 23,000ha of protected countryside.

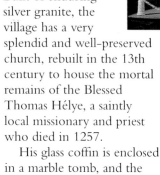

Half-timbering smothered in flowers – a restaurant at le Bec Hellouin

de l'Abbaye, popular for its good food and hospitality.

An idealistic nobleman named Herluin (hence the name Hellouin) founded this austere Benedictine community on the little River Bec in 1041. Driven out at the Revolution, the Benedictines have returned (as recently as 1946) to what remains of their abbey. The new abbey contains elements of the old buildings. The 17th-century cloister is reached up a superb staircase, and the Tour St-Nicolas contains a plaque detailing the abbey's links with England. Services are held in the abbey church on Sundays and feast days. A classic car museum lies in the adjoining park.

IVORY CARVING AT THE PORT OF DIEPPE

Even the very name Dieppe, from the Germanic 'deep', pays tribute to this deep-water harbour at the mouth of the Arques estuary. It has been a major port since at least Saxon times; by the end of the 15th century there were regular transatlantic voyages to the Americas, and by the end of the 17th century Dieppois ships were in fierce competition with the Portuguese for trade in West Africa. One result of this far-flung activity was the growth of a local craft of ivory carving which, by the end of the 17th century, already employed at least 250 people.

Today the craft is richly commemorated in the museum which occupies the former château. The carvings here cover several centuries and range from small, eveyday items, like hatpins or fans, and absurdly fanciful knick-knacks to more ambitious works, like the 18th-century copy of Girardon's group of statues, 'The Four Seasons' (the original is at Versailles). But most characteristic of all, and most fitting to the local style, are the beautiful and intricately carved model ships which recall the days of Dieppe's maritime greatness.

TOUR 3 – 140KM

THE HORSE COUNTRY AND THE CHEESE COUNTRY OF NORMANDY

This tour into the very heart of Normandy celebrates two of the best-known aspects of the province: William the Conqueror and cheese. The tour begins in the Conqueror's birthplace, the attractive town of Falaise, and then takes a great swing through the heart of the province, visiting several fine provincial towns such as Argentan, and the French National Stud at Haras du Pin. Much of the tour is made on minor roads that lead through beautiful countryside, past fields filled with cattle that provide milk for the cheese that has made Livarot and Camembert world famous.

ROUTE DIRECTIONS

Leave Falaise on the **N158**, signposted to Argentan. Carry on for Argentan (22km). From here follow signs for Dreux and l'Aigle out of town to a main roundabout, and pick up signs to Haras du Pin. Follow the **N26** through le Bourg-St-Léonard (10km) for Haras du Pin (4km). From Haras du Pin turn on to the **D26** to Exmes (5km). Continue on the **D14** to Gacé (12km). Turn left in the centre of Gacé on to the **D979** towards Vimoutiers, and after 4km turn right to Mardilly, and there turn left on the **D33**. Continue up the valley of the River Touques to Ticheville (9km). At Ticheville turn left on to the **D12**, signed for Vimoutiers, then right on to the **D979** again for Vimoutiers (7km). Leave Vimoutiers on the **D979** towards Lisieux, taking the **D16** right after 1km, towards Orbec. Head for le Bourg (8km), then turn left on the **D64** to les Moustiers-Hubert (3km). Turn left here for Bellou (3km) on the **D110**. Continue past Bellou on the **D110**, dropping down through St-Ouen-le-Houx (6km) and la Brévière. Turn right on to the **D579** for Livarot (3km).

Follow the **D4**, 'Route des Fromages', signposted for St-Pierre-sur-Dives, out of Livarot for 4km. Then fork left on to the **D250**, signposted to Montviette. Continue to crossroads and turn left on to the **D111** for 100 metres, then fork right past the church on to the **D250**, to Ecots. Cross the **D40** and continue on the **D250** to Monières, turn left on the **D511** and shortly right to Vendeuvre. At Vendeuvre take the **D271** to Pont du Jort. At the junction turn right onto the **D251**, and at the crossroads of the **D148**, turn right to Vicques and continue to Morteaux-Couliboeuf (11km) and turn right onto the **D39A**

The Marie Harel statue at Vimoutiers

for Falaise, crossing the River Dives onto the **D39**, into Falaise centre (12km).

PLACES OF INTEREST

ARGENTAN

Set below the forest of Gouffern, Argentan is a market town for the surrounding countryside and was severely damaged in the fighting of 1944. The

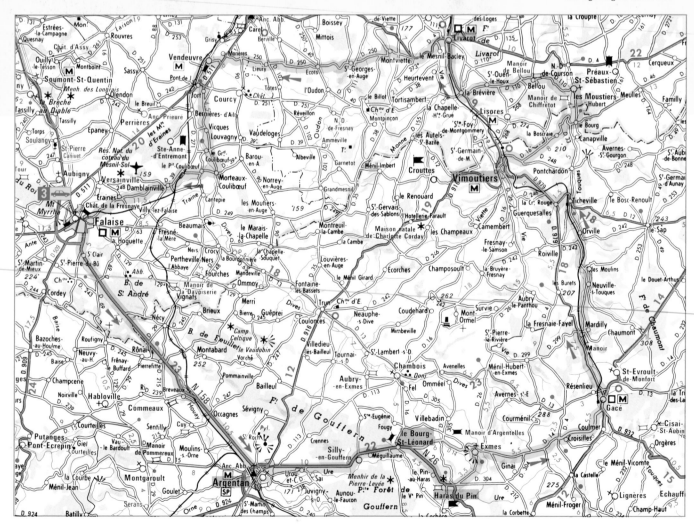

town was once a famous centre for lace-making, and examples can be inspected in the Benedictine abbey in the rue de l'Abbaye. Other interesting sights include the 15th–17th-century church of St-Germain, a riot of Flamboyant Gothic, and the château of the dukes of Alençon.

LE BOURG-ST-LEONARD

The fine 18th-century château at Bourg-St-Léonard was built by Cromot, treasurer to King Louis XV. The Classical-style château has elegant gardens open to the public, and contains a splendid collection of furniture and tapestries and fine examples of wood panelling.

HARAS DU PIN

Haras du Pin is the home of the French National Stud, which was established by Colbert in 1665 to improve the quality of cavalry mounts for the army of Louis XIV, and only the finest craftsmen were employed for its construction. Jules Hardoin-Mansart and the great Le Nôtre worked on the grounds, and the

Sturdy Percherons display at an open day, Haras du Pin

place became known as 'The Horses' Versailles'.

The buildings and stables are magnificent, and the facilities for horses second to none. This is a working stable where 80–90 stallions, representing a large number of breeds including Arabs, English Thoroughbreds, and the local breed, the Percheron, are kept at stud. Tours are available,

and the sight of the horses setting off on exercise is well worth seeing.

VIMOUTIERS

Vimoutiers owes its fortune, and a certain amount of fame, to a local milkmaid, Marie Harel, who is credited with creating the popular and famous Camembert cheese in the early years of the 19th century. The main

square contains a bronze cow to commemorate the source of it, and a statue of Marie Harel. There is also a Camembert Museum, and several hotels and restaurants where Camembert features on the menus.

LIVAROT

Livarot is another famous Norman cheese, and much of it is produced in Livarot.

Old houses and narrow streets complement a thriving cheese industry in this pleasant town. The Conservatoire des Fromages in the rue Levesque goes into cheese making in some depth. Livarot is also the starting point for the 'Route des Fromages', which visits a number of places concerned with cheese production.

CERISY-LA-FORET

The magnificent remains of one of the noblest of Normandy's Romanesque abbeys still dominate this little village, set on the edge of the forest, 22km south-west of Bayeux.

This little village, straggling up the road from the abbey, once offered a home to the servants and huntsmen of the great abbey of St-Vigor, founded by Duke Robert I of Normandy in 1032.

The abbey was closed at the Revolution and many of the buildings pulled down to provide dressed stone for new buildings nearby, or even to pave the roads. Fortunately, however, much remains, in particular the superb abbey church, which became the parish church. The nave (though

now less than half its original length) and the choir together form one of the most beautiful examples of Norman Romanesque architecture. The arches soar upwards to create a space of unusual grace and lightness, and the mellow colour of the stone is complemented by the early 15th-century choir stalls, of local workmanship. Later additions to the abbey buildings have done nothing to detract from the unusual harmony of the ensemble.

CLÉCY

A picturesque village offering a great variety of attractions, this is the principal tourist centre of la Suisse Normande and a popular base for walking excursions along

the lovely Orne valley. It lies 36km south-west of Caen.

Clécy is always busy. People come here to fish or canoe on the beautiful, meandering River Orne, to climb the Pain de Sucre (Sugarloaf), a local viewpoint and beauty spot, to follow some of the many waymarked local walks, or to hang-glide from the cliffs overlooking the deep river valley. Those with less active tastes come to stay or dine at Le Site Normand, or at the Moulin du Vey down by the river.

The pleasant, grey-stone village rises from the banks of the river by the Vey bridge, and every street leads out to the surrounding countryside. The charming 16th-century Manoir de Placy is now an hotel, but also contains a craft museum, and children will enjoy a visit to the Musée du Chemin de Fer Miniature – a miniature train museum.

D-DAY MEMORIALS

The 6 June 1944, when the Allies launched the largest seaborne invasion in military history, has left a permanent mark on the Normandy coast. Scarcely a mile between Cherbourg and Caen – the stretch divided into Utah, Omaha, Gold, Juno and Sword beaches – is without its memorial to the conflict. A Circuit du Débarquement (Landing Tour) links the main sites, which include relics of the Germans' Atlantic Wall, like the batteries at Pointe du Hoc and Port-en-Bessin; the artificial 'Mulberry' harbour built by the British at Arromanches-les-Bains; a host of small museums and plaques promoting rival claims to be the first town, village or building liberated; and military cemeteries at Colleville-St-Laurent, Bayeux, Bény-sur-Mer and Ranville.

Museums in Bayeux, the first major town to be liberated, and Caen, almost destroyed in the conflict, place D-Day in the wider context of the war.

CREULLY

This large village, on the edge of the Caen plain and overlooking the meandering valley of the Seulles, has some fine public buildings and a splendid medieval castle. It lies off the D12, 12km east of Bayeux.

Creully grew up around the imposing fortress that occupies the north end of the wide main street. Built originally in the 12th century, the château was enlarged and embellished in the 16th century, when more towers were added and the great rectangular keep was extended. Impressive vestiges of the original buildings remain and can be visited.

Like every village on this war-torn coast, Creully played its part in World War II. One of the outbuildings was used as a BBC studio immediately after the Allied landings in June 1944, and the studio is still preserved much as it was when the armies moved away in the autumn. From the terrace there is a view across the valley of the River Seulles to the château at Creullet, where General Montgomery established his headquarters in June and July 1944.

DANGU

The tranquil valley of the River Epte belies its battle-scarred history as the frontier between ancient Normandy and France. Lying well off the main tourist routes, 8km south-west of Gisors, it makes a good touring base for the region.

Dangu is a pleasant village that caters for the local farming community, with a garage and a café or two. However, the chief attraction for visitors is the 16th-century Gothic church, which con-

Watching the world go by from a peaceful corner in Dangu

tains fine 18th-century woodwork and an imposing memorial chapel to the Montmorency family, great public servants and soldiers of France during the Wars of Religion. From Dangu it is an 8km drive south to the ruins of the Château-sur-Epte, and another 4km to the Château de Baudemont.

EPANEY

This modest and quietly pretty village is a rare surviving example of the type of layout that for centuries was typical of settlements on the Falaise plain. It lies just off the D511, 8km to the north-east of Falaise.

DIVES-SUR-MER

COVERED MARKET

Dives-sur-Mer lies a little inland, 2km south-east of Cabourg, of which it is now a suburb. Dives is a smart and lively little town, full of fine sights and historical connections, but none is more fascinating than the magnificent 15th–16th century covered market, which is still in use. With its wonderful oak structure still in good condition, and intricately wrought signs indicating different types of merchandise, it is a sight well worth seeing.

Check out the local market day

The view inland from the lighthouse –
Gatteville-le-Phare, awash in a rolling sea
of little fields

The village pond – one of the few remaining in this region – lies at the heart of Epaney. In former times it provided all the water for the village's needs, and all roads led to it.

Along these roads cluster the village houses, all built of limestone and roofed with small flat tiles, and together presenting a remarkably harmonious picture. Rising above the domestic scale are the church, 15th-century in part, the tithe barn and the outbuildings and a tower belonging to the former manor house.

A short drive from Epaney will bring you to the attractive and historic town of Falaise, famous birthplace of William I of Normandy – remembered as William the Conqueror.

LA FORET-AUVRAY

With its gorges and meanders, its rocky summits and rolling hills, the Orne valley is the central feature of the lovely Suisse Normande region. This little village 15km south-west of Falaise makes a good touring base.

La Forêt-Auvray stands on a hill high above the rocky Gorges de St Aubert which funnels the River Orne on its way to Pont-d'Ouilly. It is a snug little place, full of old stone houses clustered around a small central square, where a small covered market is a popular sheltering spot for locals and walkers passing through on the GR36 long-distance footpath.

Close by on the banks of the Orne lies the fortress of la Forêt-Auvray, and 4km downstream is the great viewpoint, the Roche d'Oëtre, dominating the valley from a steep cliff high above the River Rouvre.

GATTEVILLE-LE-PHARE

The windswept and sea-lashed north coast of the Cotentin is one of the most tempestuously beautiful parts of Normandy. This village and its towering lighthouse are one of the great features of this treacherous coastline, 29km east of Cherbourg.

Set astride the narrow rocky headland of the Pointe de Barfleur, Gatteville is a little granite-built village of simple houses, centring on its church. The 12th-century Romanesque belltower rises above the village streets; the rest was rebuilt in the 18th century.

But above all this, at the end of a long causeway, towers the great lighthouse on the Pointe de Barfleur. Built in 1834 and soaring up to a height of 71m (233ft), it casts a beam that can be seen by shipping up to 56km away. From the top, reached up a flight of 365 steps, the views are superb.

FALAISE

ARLETTE'S FOUNTAIN

Falaise lies to the south of Caen, on the main road to Argentan.

Just beside the stream that runs below the walls of the great castle of Falaise, seat of the early dukes of Normandy, lies a small *lavoir* or washing place, fronted by a large, stone plaque. This is Arlette's Fountain and marks one of the few romantic legends connected with William the Conqueror.

Arlette, a tanner's daughter, was very beautiful. One evening in 1027, the duke of Normandy, Robert the Devil, was leaning on the battlements when he saw her washing linen in the stream below and was immediately smitten. Young and somewhat hot-blooded, he sent for her, making no secret of his desires. In time she bore him a son who, in 1035, replaced his father as Duke of Normandy, and was known, at least until 1066, as William the Bastard.

GENETS

Once a busy port and important staging post on the pilgrim route to Mont-St-Michel, this dignified, granite-built village is now a pleasant seaside resort. It lies 9km west of Avranches.

From Genêts there are superb views across the sand dunes and salt marshes, beyond the little bare hump of Tombelaine Island, to the magical silhouette of Mont-St-Michel. In former times parties of pilgrims would set out from here to walk across the sands to the abbey. The walk can still be done today: from the Maison de la Baie, behind the church, parties set out on a four-hour return trip from the beach at Bec d'Andaine. It must not be attempted without a guide.

Sober and dignified in its architecture, Genêts was built around a priory that no longer exists, and the port which used to be its bustling focus silted up long ago. There remains the church, however, the last stopping place for pilgrims. Built in the 12th–14th centuries, it is solid and beautifully proportioned.

From here there are good walks up the western coast of the Cotentin, and the towns of Coutances, Granville and Avranches all lie within easy reach.

GOURY

This little port and seamen's refuge is a lifeboat station of crucial importance on this wild and rocky coast. It perches on the top of Cap de la Hague, 29km west of Cherbourg.

Goury is where the road west from Cherbourg ends; beyond lie the rocks and currents of the wild Alderney

Sandy bays curve around the village of Goury on a calm day

race, the island of Alderney itself and, on a good day, the outline of the other Iles Anglo-Normands, the Channel Islands.

The village has an hotel and a café or two, as well as a small fishing harbour, but its principal and vital role is as a lifeboat station. Its long beach and rocky coves, with atmospheric views out to the offshore islands, the lighthouse and the distant Atlantic, are its chief attractions. Just to the south along the coastal footpath lie the desolate strand of Baie d'Ecalgrain and the gorse-covered cliffs of the western Cotentin, all combining to make this one of the most wildly beautiful spots on the Normandy coast.

JUMIEGES

Huddled beneath the breathtaking ruins of one of the most powerful abbeys in Christendom, this typical little Normandy village lies in the crook of a great meander of the Seine, 28km west of Rouen.

Though it has lain in ruins since the Revolution, when its beautifully carved and dressed stones were cannibalised indiscriminately, the great abbey of Jumièges still dominates the village that clusters around it.

St Philibert founded an abbey here in the 7th century. It was sacked two centuries later by the Vikings, whose Norman descendants founded the Benedictine abbey of Notre-Dame on the site. After a long and illustrious

VENDEUVRE

MINIATURE FURNITURE MUSEUM

Vendeuvre is a small village south-west of St Pierre-sur-Dives. The museum is in the château by the river.

The former orangery of this early 18th-century château is the setting for a wonderful collection of miniature furniture. It was common in the 18th

century for craftsmen to produce miniature samples to show to clients before starting on the full-sized work, and over 100 exquisite examples are on display here. Some are

very small, about 11cm, others tower to 75cm, but all are made in the same wood and with the same fine detail as their full-sized counterparts.

Look out for the miniature canopied bed, an exclusive construction for Louis XV's daughter's cat!

history it came to an ignominious end at the Revolution. The majestic proportions of the surviving fragments are an indication of the splendour and purity of the original buildings, constructed in the golden age of Norman Romanesque. Behind the west façade, flanked by two towers soaring to 43m, the roofless nave reaches skywards, and a single great arch supports one wall of a lantern tower. The 17th-century lodge now houses a Musée Lapidaire, containing among other stonework the gravestone of Charles VII's mistress, Agnès Sorel.

LESSAY

This pretty and remarkable village lies 21km north of Coutances.

Founded in 1056 by monks from le Bec-Hellouin, the magnificent abbey at Lessay survived the Revolution only to be totally destroyed in the fighting of July and August 1944. Hardly a single stone remained in place, but the local people decided – in the face of all advice – that their abbey church must be restored. For 12 years they worked, salvaging every scrap of the original fabric, quarrying new stone from the original quarry near Caen, and commissioning craftsmen who worked

with tools modelled on the medieval originals. Every detail was painstakingly repaired or replaced, and the result – completed in 1957 – is one of the loveliest Romanesque churches in all France.

South of the abbey lies the Lande de Lessay, celebrated in poetry by the 19th-century Norman Romantic writer Barbey d'Aurevilly.

DOVECOTES OF THE PAYS DE CAUX

The Pays de Caux, bounded by the Channel, the Seine and the River Bresle, forms an undulating chalk plateau topped by clay, and away from the water its countryside is thinly populated. The farms are fortified by earth and rubble walls, which enclose grassy courts large enough to protect cattle during the exposed and windy winters. But perhaps the most distinctive local feature the is the dovecotes (*colombiers*), which may be square or polygonal, though they are more often round. Their combination of white stone, dark flint and red brick produces lovely multi-coloured effects. A projecting stone string-course was to protect the birds from rats. The Château de Filières, near Gommerville and Bolbec, and the Manoir d'Ango, west of Dieppe, have fine examples to compare with the eccentric half-timbered dovecote of the château at Crèvecoeur-en-Auge.

LYONS-LA-FORET

The Forêt de Lyons was one of the great hunting forests of the Dukes of Normandy, and today it is still the finest beech forest in all France. At its heart lies this delightful timber-built village, 33km east of Rouen.

The great trees of the surrounding forest have provided the building material for the houses of the village, which include some very fine examples of 17th-century timber-framed construction. The superb 17th-century market building is also timber-framed, as is the bell-tower of the 15th-century church. Inside are substantial polychrome wooden statues of the saints carved by local woodsmen at some time during the 16th and 17th centuries.

The local Syndicate d'Initiative has waymarked many walks and rides through the immemorial oaks and beeches of the forest: one of the most notable is at la Bunodière, a beech tree which stands 42m high, amid a grove of centenarian trees.

Left, pitted by weather and adorned by lichens, an old stone head at Jumièges

MONT-ST-MICHEL

Abbey, fortress and village, this fairytale construction clinging to a needle of granite presents an image of legendary and breathtaking beauty.

A place of religious significance since the time of the Celts, Mont-St-Michel has been a place of Christian worship and pilgrimage since the 8th century when the first oratory was built.

Standing proud: the citadel of Mont-St-Michel is unmistakable, reached now across a sandy causeway scattered with summer flowers

TOUR 4 – 110KM

THE PAYS DE BRAY AND THE PAYS DE CAUX

The tour begins in the seaport of Dieppe and travels north of the Seine into the *département* of Seine Maritime, out of the lush heartlands of Normandy dotted with small fields and apple orchards, onto the high, wide plateau of the *pays de Caux*, with its stunning open expanses of plain and sky. The return to the chalk country of the province and Dieppe is made via the high cliffs that stand about the port. The northern part of Normandy is an area that many people pass through on their way to Rouen or Paris, but there is much to see and the region is well supplied with attractive towns and villages.

ROUTE DIRECTIONS

Starting from the wide seafront promenade in Dieppe, just below the castle, follow first the 'Toutes Directions' signs, then Paris-Rouen signs out of town to the first round-about (3km). Take the third exit, **N27**, marked for Eu

Moulding cheese in a traditional heart-shape, at Neufchâtel-en-Bray

and le Tréport, descending the hill towards the race-course to pick up signs for Arques-la-Bataille, sign-posted **D154E**. Follow this for 10km to Arques. Continue on the **D154** – which becomes the **D149**

for 6km – to Torcy-le-Petit and Torcy-le-Grand (10km). Keep straight ahead on the **D154** again to Bellencombre (14km), through attractive rolling countryside. Go through St-Saëns (5km) to pick up the **D38** towards la Boissière (5km). Go under the **N29** on to the **N28** for 50m, then fork left onto the **D41** to Buchy (9km). From the market square in Buchy, take the **D7**, heading towards Sommery and Neufchâtel-en-Bray. At Sommery (9km) cross the **D915** and continue on the **D7** towards St-Saire, later the **D117**. Continue on to Neufchâtel-en-Bray (12km). Carry on through the centre of Neufchâtel, past the church of Notre-Dame to the traffic lights, then turn left on the **D1314**, heading for Londinières (15km). At Londinières, continue up the main street to pick up the **D920** towards Dieppe, and continue to Envermeu

(13km). Stay on the **D920** until Neuville-lès-Dieppe, then turn left on to the **D485**, and continue into Dieppe centre and the seafront (15km).

PLACES OF INTEREST

ARQUES LA BATAILLE

Arques is a small town nestling at the foot of a long steep-sided ridge, on which lies a great château, much of it in an excellent state of preservation. The château was built and rebuilt between the 11th and 16th centuries, and endured a great many sieges. There are fine views from the ramparts.

NEUFCHATEL-EN-BRAY

Neufchâtel is the market town for the Bray area and famous in its own right as the birthplace of Neufchâtel cheese, though the Petit-Suisse cheese is also made here now. The most striking feature of the town centre in the week is the great church of Notre-Dame, which has 13th-, 15th- and 16th-century elements and takes up most of the square. The rest of the town slopes up the hill and there are many pleasant squares and streets.

LONDINIERES

This is a sprawling village in the valley of the tiny River Eaulne, a river noted

for its fish and therefore fringed with fishermen for most of its length. The church at Londinières is new, being built only in 1957, but it has some fine stained glass and a great array of saints' statues, including Sainte Suzanne.

ENVERMEU

This little village in the Eaulne valley is noted locally for the church, which is pure Gothic and unfinished. The parts that have been completed, notably the chancel, are very fine indeed and although there can be too many churches on any tour in France, this one is worth a stop.

VARENGEVILLE-SUR-MER

Eight kilometres west of Dieppe lies the seaside resort of Varengeville, once a favourite place for artists. Georges Braque is buried in the cemetery, and created stained-glass windows in the church and in the Chapel of St-Dominique on the outskirts of the village.

Other sites that are well worth seeing include the beautiful 16th-century Manoir d'Ango, once the home of the famous Dieppe seafarer, and the beach where No. 4 Commando landed in August 1942 during the Dieppe Raid.

Tiers of building have succeeded the first abbey church, Notre-Dame-sous-Terre, a 10th-century Carolingian construction that later served as part of the foundations of the Romanesque church. Destroyed by fire, it was replaced by the present monolithic structure, built against enormous odds on that 80m-tall narrow pinnacle.

Visitors now drive down the causeway and park below the defensive walls. The abbey buildings are a marvel. The dazzling Flamboyant Gothic and Romanesque architecture, the labyrinth of stairways and passages leading the visitor on, the shady corridors that open out into magnificent views of the vast sandy expanses of the bay – and all contribute to an unforgettable experience.

NONANCOURT

An ancient stronghold on the south-eastern frontier of Normandy, this historic riverside village contains many beautiful buildings and some fine domestic architecture. It lies just off the N12, 16km west of Dreux.

Nonancourt was built on the banks of the River Avre – the Norman frontier line – to defend the duchy of Normandy against the incursions of the kingdom of France. Only a few traces remain of the castle where Richard Lionheart and Phillipe Augustus of France met in 1189 to agree plans for their joint participation in the Third Crusade. Securely walled, the village kept its defences in repair (and occasional use) until the Hundred Years War ended in 1453.

Straggling picturesquely along the banks of the River Avre, it contains a number of fine half-timbered houses especially in the lower half of the village, beneath the old walls. Only the 13th-century bell-tower remains of the old church of St-Martin, destroyed in the Hundred Years War. The present building dates from the early 16th century, and has some fine stone tracery and stained-glass windows.

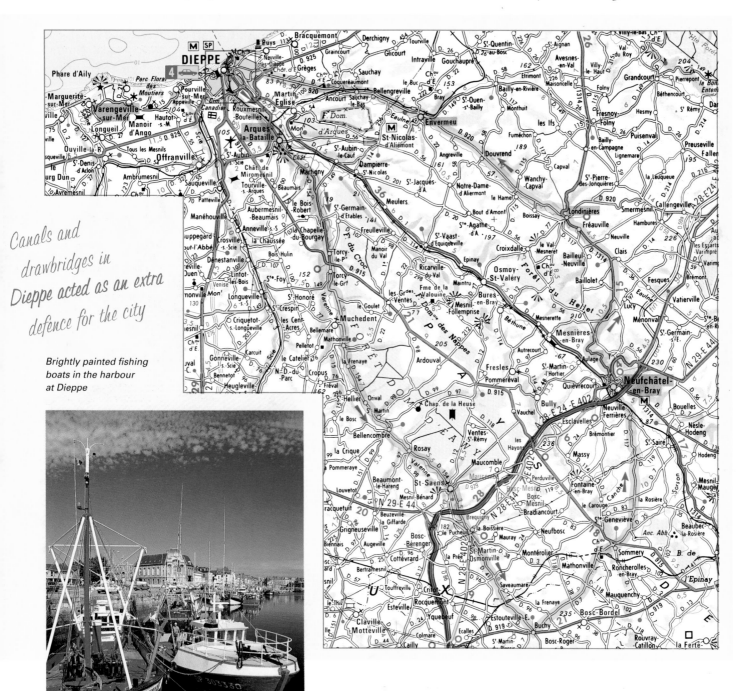

Canals and drawbridges in Dieppe acted as an extra defence for the city

Brightly painted fishing boats in the harbour at Dieppe

CALVADOS

Cows grazing in fields and apple trees growing in neat rows: these are what first strike visitors to rural Normandy. The cream is made into the cheeses and rich sauces that typify the local cuisine, while the apples are – literally – pressed into service to make an alcoholic drink for a region whose climate is unfriendly to the vine. Calvados, colloquially *calva*, is apple brandy matured in oak for up to 10 years. It is taken, like cognac, at the end of the meal, though some traditionalists still observe the custom of drinking it during pauses in the meal itself, to make the *trou normand*, or 'Norman hole'. The best Calvados, twice distilled, comes from the Pays d'Auge. Here, in the village of Coquainvilliers, the Moulin de la Foulonnerie demonstrates the various stages by which it is made. Those apples that do not end up as Calvados may be pressed for cider (*bon bère*), which sparkles gently when bottled as *cidre bouché*.

PORTBAIL

Here the gorse-covered cliffs and rocky inlets of the north-western coast of the Cotentin peninsula give way to a shimmering, atmospheric prospect of sand dunes and marram grass, threaded with tidal streams. The village lies 9km south of Barreville-Carterets.

The best way to snatch a breathtaking first view of Portbail is to approach it from the north, down the coast road from Carteret and across the cause-way. From there the village stands dream-like across the glinting waters of the bay, its church tower like a beckoning finger.

A number of Gallo-Roman remains indicate the great age of the village. The early Romanesque church was built in the 11th century on the site of an earlier abbey, but the fortified tower that stands out so clearly was not added until the 15th century. The church has been secularized, but the fittings remain and there is a fine statue of St James beside the altar, a reminder that pilgrims on the way to Santiago de Compostela once landed here.

LE SAP

The Pays d'Auge is famous for the excellence of its cuisine, based on delicious local products such as dairy cream and butter, cider and Camembert cheese. This attractive little village is a good centre for touring the region. It lies 10km east of Vimoutiers.

On the map, little le Sap resembles a star with roads converging on its main square

from all over the Pays d'Auge. This is farming country, and le Sap is a centre for the local farmers: in the main square lies a large market building with the Mairie above it. The village streets are lined with red-brick, half-timbered and slate-hung houses. The church, at the southern extremity of the village, has a 14th-century nave and fine Gothic windows. Five kilometres to the south lies the world-famous village of Camembert, at whose market in 19th century the local dairymaid Marie Harel came to sell the cheese which was to be christened 'Camembert'.

ST-CENERI-LE-GEREI

Popularly known as the prettiest village in France, this picturesque little village is clustered beneath its church in a loop of the river Sarthe, 14km south-west of Alençon.

On this spot in the early Middle Ages an Italian ascetic and hermit built a chapel; as he attracted followers so the settlement grew, taking his name. The monastery built by his followers was destroyed by the Normans, who in their turn constructed the exceptionally beautiful Romanesque church at the summit of this rocky crag.

The best view of it is perhaps from the medieval stone bridge across the Sarthe, but the church and the ochre-

VILLEDIEU-LES-POELES

BELL FOUNDRY

Villedieu-les-Poêles – 'God's town of the Pots', lies 28km east of Granville, at the foot of the Cotentin peninsula.

Villedieu is a fine and busy little town, famous for the manufacture of brass and copper pots and milk churns. The town was once a recruiting centre for the Knights of St John of Jerusalem – hence 'God's town'.

The Knights established the bell foundry in the 12th century and it has been supplying bells to churches, abbeys and cathedrals ever since. The craft continues and the foundry can still be visited. There is nothing romantic about it, for this is a working foundry with a thriving export trade.

The tour is conducted by whichever craftsman is

tiled roofs of the village are so picturesque, and have proved irresistible to many artists. A short walk leads to a charming 15th-century chapel marking the original site of St-Céneri's oratory.

ST-WANDRILLE-RANÇON

The Seine valley, running westwards to its estuary at Honfleur and le Havre, contains a number of lovely villages and great abbeys. The earliest, and one of the finest is at St-Wandrille, 34km west of Rouen.

In the 7th century the ascetic nobleman Wandregesilus founded an abbey in this lovely spot. It was put to the torch by the Vikings, in the 9th century, but the monks soon raised another monastery on the ashes. The Benedictine community flourished until the Revolution, when it was dispersed. The monks finally returned in 1931 to establish a Benedictine community at St-Wandrille once more.

During all this time, miraculously only the abbey church fell into ruin. The lovely 14th-century cloister and 12th-century refectory have survived and are still in use.

The village that grew up to serve the monastery and local farmers now caters for the many tourists who come to see the abbey. There are good walks from St-Wandrille into the Parc Régional de Brotonne, crossing the Seine on the new Pont de Brotonne.

Chalk-white cliffs at Yport

YPORT

Nestling in one of the small coves that pierce the high chalk cliffs of the Côte d'Albâtre, picturesque Yport has attracted painters for many years. It lies 8km south of Fécamp.

Founded by fishermen in 1830, this little community in its sheltered sun-trap is now more of a holiday resort than a fishing port, though a few fishing boats still lie on the strand and most of the restaurants specialise in seafood. Built of brick and flint from the shingle beach, the village gains a quaint *belle-époque* charm from the fashionable villas that sprang up on the front at the turn of the century.

---

not engaged in bell-making at the time, and includes a visit to the furnace moulds lined with the traditional mixture of clay, hair and manure, into which the molten bronze is poured. The rough-worked casts are then polished and trimmed to the required thickness, the diameter and thickness of each bell being responsible for its tone and therefore its place in the bell-peal.

Bells make an unusual export for this little town, also known for copperware.

ALLOUVILLE-BELLEFOSSE

OLDEST TREE IN FRANCE

Allouville-Bellefosse lies 2km south-west of the market town of Yvetot, some 10km north of Caudebec-en-Caux, on the Seine.

Next to the church, beside the D34, is an ancient oak tree that has stood there for the last 1,000 years, and said to be the oldest tree in France. The tree has had to be propped up, but it is so fine and large that two chapels have been hollowed out of the trunk, and can be reached by ladders.

SECRET FRANCE

THE NORTH

Despite – or perhaps because of – the fact that the North is on people's routes to somewhere as they rush southwards from the Channel ports, overlooking the special qualities of this diverse and distinct region, many parts of it have remained unspoilt and undeveloped. It is also a region that has been at the heart of many European struggles over the centuries. Famous battlefields abound, as do cemeteries and war memorials that are as architecturally distinguished as they are moving.

In the west, along the Côte d'Opale, so-called because of its smooth white waves, are many reminders of the region's turbulent past, from grim medieval fortresses to the cemeteries and memorials dedicated to the dead of two world wars. To the east of Boulogne-sur-Mer extends a landscape of rolling, fertile pastures and woodland dotted with the traditional low, stone-built farms and villages. From Boulogne-sur-Mer down to the Somme the coast is characterised by shifting dunes and pockets of pine trees, while the Somme estuary is wide and muddy, home to a variety of migratory bird life. Inland and south are long vistas of rolling farmland broken by little rivers and well-scattered with pockets of forest and woodland. It is quiet, sparsely populated country with peaceful villages and churches that provide evidence of the glorious achievements of French Gothic architecture.

In the north-east of the region lie the Pas-de-Calais and Northern Flanders, areas that have a quiet beauty. Deep forests, peaceful valleys and tranquil lakes are interspersed with dykes, canal networks, windmills and watermills. The old, flower-filled villages, consisting of houses built long and low to protect them from the strong winds coming off the North Sea, have a distinctive architecture that makes use of decorative and patterned brickwork.

In the south-east, this attractive landscape gives way to the great champagne-producing area around Reims, home to the most famous champagne houses in the world. To the south of Reims is the region of the Parc Naturel Régional de la Montagne de Reims, with its prosperous villages and splendid views of gently sloping vineyards topped by groups of trees.

coquelicots de Nord

Right, some fine examples of French architecture are to be found in this area, such as the splendid Gothic façade of the church at St-Riquier

Left and above, best-known perhaps as the scene of so many spectacular battles through the centuries, the North nevertheless offers a wealth of quiet, peaceful locations and interesting, historic towns

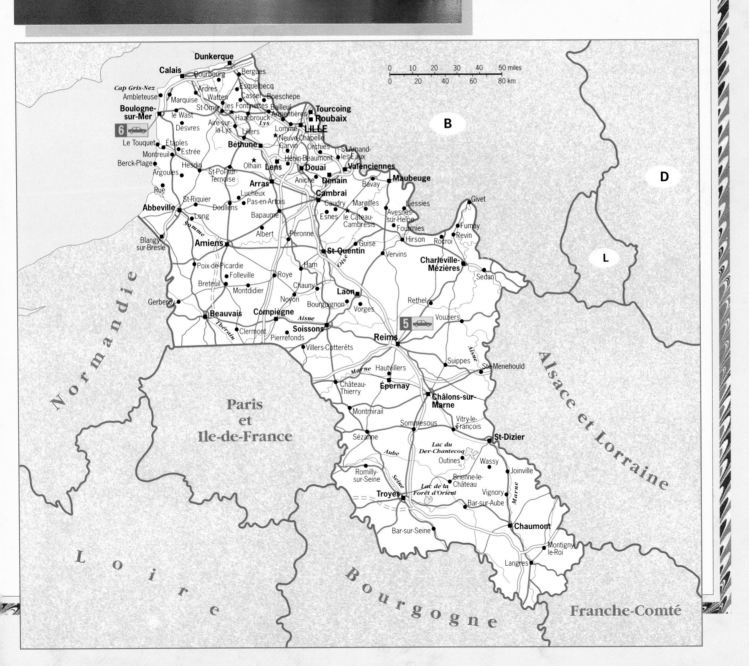

0 10 20 30 40 50 miles
0   20   40   60   80 km

Dunkerque
Calais
Bourbourg
Bergues
Cap Gris-Nez
Ardres
Esquelbecq
Cassel
Boeschepe
Ambleteuse
Marquise
Watten
Boulogne-sur-Mer
St-Omer
les Fontinettes
Bailleul
Tourcoing
le Wast
Aire-sur-la-Lys
Hazebrouck
Armentières
Roubaix
Desvres
Lillers
Lomme
LILLE
Le Touquet
Étaples
Béthune
Neuve-Chapelle
Garvin
Orchies
St-Amand-les-Eaux
Montreuil
Estrée
Olhain
Henin-Beaumont
Valenciennes
Berck-Plage
Argoules
Hesdin
St-Pol-sur-Ternoise
Lens
Aniche
Douai
Denain
Maubeuge
Rue
St-Riquier
Lucheux
Arras
Cambrai
Bavay
Abbeville
Dodlens
Pas-en-Artois
Gaudry
Margilles
Liessies
Long
Bapaume
Esnes
le Cateau-Cambrésis
Avesnes-sur-Helpe
Givet
Blangy-sur-Bresle
Albert
Péronne
Fourmies
Fumay
Amiens
Guise
Hirson
Rocroi
Revin
Poix-de-Picardie
St-Quentin
Vervins
Charleville-Mézières
Folleville
Ham
Breteuil
Roye
Chauny
Bourguignon
Sedan
Gerberoy
Montdidier
Noyon
Laon
Rethel
Beauvais
Compiègne
Vorges
Vouziers
Clermont
Soissons
Aisne
Reims
Pierrefonds
Villers-Cotterêts
Suippes
Ste-Menehould
Marne
Hautvillers
Château-Thierry
Épernay
Châlons-sur-Marne
Montmirail
Vitry-le-François
St-Dizier
Sommesous
Sézanne
Aube
Lac du Der-Chantecoq
Outines
Wassy
Joinville
Romilly-sur-Seine
Seine
Brienne-le-Château
Vignory
Troyes
Lac de la Forêt d'Orient
Bar-sur-Aube
Bar-sur-Seine
Chaumont
Montigny-le-Roi
Langres

B
D
L

Normandie
Paris et Ile-de-France
Loire
Bourgogne
Alsace et Lorraine
Franche-Comté

Somme
Thérain
Oise
Aisne
Marne

AMBLETEUSE

This tranquil village on the Côte d'Opale is especially rich in traces of this region's turbulent military past, from the Middle Ages to World War II. It lies 12km north of Boulogne.

The former importance of this little village among the dunes at the mouth of the River Slack is revealed by the great bulk of Vauban's Fort Mahon. Built in the 1680s to guard the harbour, the battered fortress still stands offshore. Today, the only craft using the silted anchorage and the beaches are the local fishing boats, but it was here that Napoleon assembled a large part of his British invasion fleet. Earlier, in 1689, James II landed here after his flight from England.

Despite its fine beaches and magnificent views to Boulogne and across the Channel to England, Ambleteuse remains surprisingly undeveloped. It is a quiet place, full of faded seaside charm, and with old shops and cafés to greet the visitor.

ARGOULES

The delightful River Authie winds its way to the sea through a landscape of water meadows and woodland, flanked by abbeys, mills and pretty villages. One of the prettiest is Argoules, 12km north of Crécy-en-Ponthieu.

With its little Gothic manor, its 16th-century church and its cluster of traditional Picardy whitewashed cottages set in flowery gardens, Argoules seems to have escaped the march of time. Yet, for centuries it has had illustrious neighbours: 2km to the

north is the famous Cistercian abbey of Valloires, a 12th-century foundation, largely rebuilt in the 18th century with flowing Rococo-style decoration by the Viennese artist Baron Pfaff von Pfaffenhoffen. It was here that the bodies of French knights killed at Crécy were brought after the battle. Today, with its soft stone buildings and gardens surrounded by woodland, Valloires is a delightful place to visit.

BOESCHEPE

The surprisingly hilly landscape between St-Omer and the Belgian border is dotted with windmills, some of them centuries old. One of the finest stands just outside the pretty Flemish village of Boeschèpe, 9km north-west of Bailleul.

A traditional Flemish village of brick and timber-framed houses, only 2km from the Belgian border, Boeschèpe is set among the undulating hills that surround the Mont des Cats, famous for its cheese and its Trappist monastery. Rising high above the village to the west are the sails of the Ondankmeulen, or Moulin de l'Ingratitude, a postmill bought and restored by the commune. The bottom part of the mill houses an exhibition on the windmills of Flanders. Near by is an old *estaminet*, a popular and typical local inn complete with tiled stoves and an old-fashioned bar. An even more authentic *estaminet* can be seen in the nearby village of Godewaersvelde, while further to the west, beyond Steenvoorde, is an exceptional group of three more windmills.

LE CATEAU-CAMBRESIS

MATISSE MUSEUM

Le Cateau-Cambresis lies east of Cambrai.

This small Flemish town has a number of features of interest, but the most unexpected is Musée Henri-Matisse. The painter was born in le Cateau in 1869, and before his death he presented the town with a collection of his works.

Hidden away in the town's back streets is another memorial to Matisse. In the local infants school, the Ecole Maternelle Matisse, is a huge stained-glass window by the artist.

The great artist trained first in Paris as a lawyer

The fine stone architecture of Bourguignon looks its best against the autumn colours

BOURGUIGNON

The rural landscape south of Laon has hardly changed since it was painted in the 17th century by the Le Nain brothers, who owned a house in Bourguignon, 8km south-west of Laon.

Set in delightful countryside – a bucolic mixture of vineyards, woods and farmland spread over rolling hills and out by small rivers – Bourguignon is a protected village, a typical cluster of attractive stone houses in the local style, reflecting the unchanging quality of French rural life. These landscapes and buildings, along with fascinating portraits of the inhabitants, are depicted with great realism in the works of the three Le Nain brothers.

From the hilltops of les Creuttes, just to the north of Bourguignon, there is a wide panorama over the Montagne de Laon, rising to 180m, and towards the distinctive skyline of Laon itself, high on its outcrop of rock. The troglodyte caves at les Creuttes, once inhabited, are now largely disused.

ESNES

The prominence of this region in the Middle Ages is reflected by the great number of châteaux and abbeys to be found around here. 12km south-east of Cambrai.

The chief feature of this farming village with its characteristic turreted houses is its magnificent fortified château. The entry is through a handsome classical gateway, framed by great 15th-century pepperpot towers, and the main buildings are ranged round a central square. Originally moated and fiercely fortified, the château has seen many changes during its long occupation by 29 generations of the same family. Today, battered and softened by time, and domesticated by the superb adjacent barns and dovecote, its old stone walls still echo the spirit of the Middle Ages. The site of Esnes has been occupied since antiquity, and two Meroringian tombs can be seen near the 17th-century church.

Six kilometres to the west are the remains of the Cistercian abbey of Vaucelles, founded in the 12th century, an impressive range of largely ruined buildings set in the quiet valley of the Escaut.

BATTLEFIELDS OF WORLD WAR I

The battlefields of the Somme – in fact, largely fought over its tributary, the Ancre – lie north-east of Amiens. Albert makes a good centre for visitors, and the view from the memorials near Pozières and Villers-Bretonneux give a good idea of the terrain so closely contested in 1916–18: Thiepval (with a memorial by Lutyens to more than 73,300 troops recorded missing), la Boiselle, Flers (where the world's first tank attack took place in 1916) and Beaumont-Hamel. Most poignant of all – unless it be the pockmarked hills ringing Verdun, where 700,000 French and Germans died in the bloodiest battle Europe has yet seen – is Vimy Ridge, north of Arras. Its trenches, dugouts and tunnels still survive and the crest of the ridge ('Hill 145'), captured by Canadians in April 1917, is crowned by a memorial to their 60,000 dead.

OLHAIN

CASTLE FARM

A picturesque 15th-century moated fortress farm, concealing a turbulent history of local and world affairs

Olhain lies north-west of Arras.

An unexpected treasure in a region of pleasant but unremarkable farmland is to be found in the moated medieval fortress and farm at Olhain. Irresistibly picturesque, it dates mostly from the early 15th century, when it was rebuilt during the Hundred Years War.

The fortress is set on two adjacent islands, and its towers and powerful stone walls appear to float on the waters of the moat.

The inner courtyard is protected by a gatehouse with drawbridge, and a watchtower containing a staircase with 100 steps. There are also a Gothic guardroom, cellars and a chapel at the fortress. Surrounded today by ducks and swans, it is a romantic and peaceful sight that belies its turbulent past.

Regularly beseiged in the wars that ravaged Artois over several centuries, it is also supposed to be haunted by a monk killed by a past lord of the manor during a drunken orgy.

Olhain can be visited on Sunday afternoons in summer, but it can easily be seen from the road at other times.

TOUR 5 – 115KM
CHAMPAGNE COUNTRY AND THE MARNE VALLEY

From the north-west to the south-east, Reims is surrounded by hills, whose steep slopes are covered in vineyards and woodland. Best known is the region to the south, the so-called Montagne de Reims. The tour takes in several well-known champagne villages, which also afford wonderful views over the vineyards and back towards the fine old city of Reims. It continues through quiet farming villages and gentle wooded landscapes, and also takes in tranquil towns beside the Marne with their quaint old riverside quays, together with splendid châteaux and ancient churches.

The enjoyable task of pruning the vines in the sunshine in anticipation of the harvest to come later in the year

towards Reims. Cross a railway, a river and a canal and then take the first left, the **D1**, to Cumières. From Cumières, follow signs north to Hautvillers. Return to Cumières and take the **D1** to Damery.

Follow the road past Venteuil to Reuil. At a roundabout by a church, bear right in the direction

of Châtillon-sur-Marne. From Châtillon, take the **D24** to Baslieux-sur-Châtillon, and continue on to Cuchery. By a war memorial bear left to la Neuville-aux-Larris, still on the **D24**, and continue to Chaumuzy.

In Chaumuzy, turn left on to the **RD386**. Follow the road through Sarcy and Poilly and after the village, turn right on to the **D227** to Bouleuse. Follow the road through Méry-Prémecy and Gueux, and back into Reims.

PLACES OF INTEREST

RILLY-LA-MONTAGNE
This prosperous champagne-producing village has a 12th–14th century church, whose delightful carved choir stalls illustrate the various stages of wine production.

VERZY
This old wine-making village is famous for the quality of its champagne. Verzy originally grew under the protection of the Benedictine abbey of St-Basle, founded in the 7th century and destroyed in the Revolution. Near the chapel of St-Basle just outside the village are the famous 'hêtres tortillards', strangely twisted beech trees – a phenomenon that has never been explained.

LOUVOIS
The lavish château of Louvois was built by Mansart and belonged to the daughters of Louis XV, although much of it was

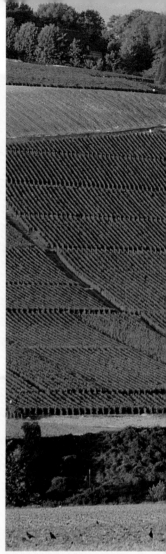

ROUTE DIRECTIONS

Leave Reims on the **RD380** Château-Thierry road. After 8km, at Pargny-les-Reims, turn left on to the **D26** towards Jouy-lès-Reims, and follow this road past Sacy, through Ecueil and Sermiers until it meets the **N51**. Here turn left, and almost immediately right (the first right), back on to the **D26**. Continue through Villers Allerand, past Rilly-la-Montagne and Chigny-les-Roses to Verzenay. Bear right, towards Verzy.

After 1km, turn right on to the **D34** to Mount Sinai. Follow this road, steeply climbing, then steeply dropping to Louvois. Leave Louvois on the **D9**. Continue to Tauxières-Mutry and Avenay-Val-d'Or, and down to Mareuil-sur-Ay. Here, bear right to Ay and then take the **D201**, into Epernay.

From the centre of Epernay take the **N51**

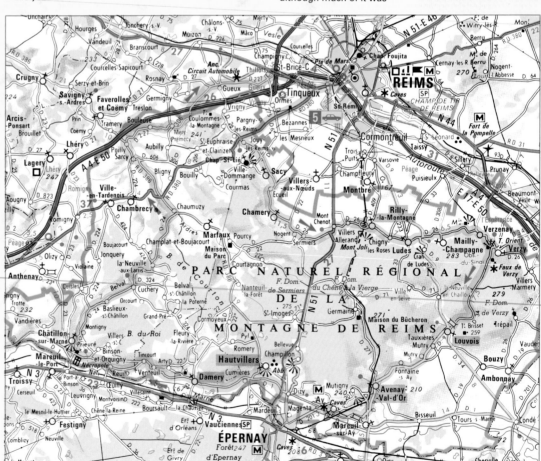

subsequently destroyed. The park was laid out by Le Nôtre. A section of the château was partly rebuilt in the 19th century. It can be seen from the gates and provides a good idea of the original building.

AVENAY-VAL-D'OR
This old village on the banks of the River Livre has a church originally built in the 13th century and rebuilt during the 16th, with a beautiful Flamboyant façade. The organ dates from the 16th century, and the church contains paintings from the former Benedictine abbey at Breuil, which was destroyed during the Revolution.

HAUTVILLERS
See page 48.

DAMERY
Grouped at the foot of a cliff on the banks of the River Marne, this peaceful town has a picturesque old quay on the riverside. The 12th–13th century church has a Gothic choir.

Left, typical patterned brickwork in the charming village of Esquelbecq

ESQUELBECQ

Distinctive Flemish decorative and patterned brickwork and a fine *hallekerke* (a combined church and market building) can both be seen at Esquelbecq, 10km south of Bergues.

With its large central square flanked by a variety of 16th to 19th-century houses, its grand *hallekerke* in patterned pink brickwork, its old-fashioned shops and its creeper-clad inn, Esquelbecq is a fine example of a Flemish village. The church, built in the 16th century, is dedicated to St-Folquin, whose statue stands above the doorway in the central nave. With its three naves, the church is a good example of the traditional *hallekerke*, with several naves of equal height and size, intended to double as a market building.

Behind the inn is a formal garden of trellised and espaliered parterres, leading the eye to the picturesque moated château, a decorative mass of brick, pepperpot towers and steep roofs set on stepped gables. Sadly, one of the château's main features, a 45m high octagonal tower, collapsed in 1984.

ESTREE

Here is rural France at its traditional best, with old farms and pretty villages set beside a gently winding river. 5km north of Montreuil.

The valley of the River Course between Desvres and Montreuil, unfolding peacefully between wooded hills, makes a delightful introduction to Estrée. The best approach is from the north, through water meadows and fields of poplars. Some of the grand farms, notable at Doudeauville, are entered across a ford, while others have added the rearing of trout and the growing of watercress to more conventional types of husbandry. Estrée, whose houses spread eastwards away from the river, is an old-fashioned village dominated by its church, set on a mound beside the road.

At Montcavrel, 2km to the north-east, is a grander church in the rural Flamboyant Gothic style. Inside are attractive primitive friezes depicting, among other tales, the life of the Virgin Mary.

FOLLEVILLE

The north of France has been famous for its stone carvings since the Middle Ages. Particularly remarkable are those to be found in the little village of Folleville, 8km north-east of Breteuil.

Today an unassuming village with superb views over the valley of the Noye, Folleville was once a place of some importance. At its centre stand the remains of a once-powerful château, an overgrown jumble of largely 15th-century work ruined since 1789. However the main treasure of the village is not here, but in the nearby church built in the early 16th century.

In that time, ownership of the village passed by marriage to Raoul de Lannoy, a famous soldier and friend of two kings, Louis XI and Louis XII. While serving as Governor of Genoa he commissioned a tomb for himself and his wife from two Milanese masters, Antonio della Porta and Pace Gaggini. Thus it was that, after his death in 1513, two lifelike recumbent effigies surrounded by a riot of Renaissance decoration but set in a Gothic sepulchre, were installed in the church at Folleville, to be consecrated in 1524.

CHAMPAGNE

Cole Porter, in *Anything Goes*, must have been one of the few people who got no kick from Champagne. Indeed, it is so universally associated with celebration and affluence that some may be surprised to find it has so precise, and small, a point of origin. The French, of course, firmly insist on this fact. Other places may produce sparkling wines but true Champagne comes only from designated vineyards on the chalk-land south of Reims. Though medieval popes and kings favoured the wine from these parts, it remained for centuries a still drink. The sparkle was added, so tradition says, by Dom Pérignon (1638–1715), cellarmaster of Hautvillers abbey. The secret of the *méthode champenoise*, as now practised, lies not just in blending red and white grapes, but in letting the wine undergo its second fermentation in the bottle. Champagne-makers are as hospitable as all French *viticulteurs*. Follow the Routes du Champagne through the Montagne de Reims, the Vallée de la Marne and the Côte des Blancs, where the best vineyards lie.

GERBEROY

A medieval fortified village with panoramic vistas over the rolling countryside to the west of Beauvais, Gerberoy is popular with visitors. It lies 13km north-east of Gournay-en-Bray.

Perched on its plateau high above the surrounding landscape, peaceful little Gerberoy has a turbulent and romantic history. Fought over for centuries because of its strategic position on the borders of Normandy and the Ile de France, it finally succumbed in the 16th century to the twin disasters of plague and fire, and slid into oblivion. Virtually abandoned during the 18th and early 19th centuries, it was rescued from total ruin when its battered charms attracted the painter Le Sidaner to come and live here. Following his lead, other artists and writers adopted Gerberoy, restoring its ruined houses with their typical dovecotes. Today it is a pretty, smart little place, full of visitors who come to enjoy its cobbled streets, its timber-framed houses, its quaint atmosphere and its 16th-century church.

Gerbreoy has been restored to medieval charm by the artists who have settled here

HAUTVILLERS

Overlooking the meandering valley of the Marne, this lively vigneron village is famous for its abbey, where the celebrated Dom Pérignon was cellarer. 6km north of Epernay.

Vines have been cultivated on the steep slopes of the Marne valley at least since Roman times, and the Benedictine abbey at Hautvillers, founded in AD660 by St-Nivard, has always taken part in this local industry. However, it was the abbey's cellarer at the start of the 18th century, Dom Pérignon, who developed the double fermentation process, which led directly to the invention of champagne. Hautvillers is still surrounded by vistas of vineyards and still has the abbey at its heart.

The abbey was already famous in the 9th century, when the monks created a new style of manuscript illumination, noted for its dynamic and lively approach to drawing, based for the first time on naturalism. The abbey's most famous production was the *Utrecht Psalter*, completed between AD820 and 830.

the Revolution, after which it was closed and steadily demolished. Near by is the 16th-century church, which contains an interesting group of statues of saints, and a Romanesque gilded cross in Byzantine style.

South of the village is the Château de la Motte, built in the 18th century as part of the abbey. This long, low building, with its sweeping expanses of slate roof is a fine example of the traditional local building styles.

LONG

The valley of the Somme is a fisherman's paradise, and the area to the south of the attractive village of Long is particularly favoured. 18km north-west of Amiens.

Approach Long from the south, across the water meadows of the Somme, for one of the village's loveliest features is its skyline. A theatrical backdrop is provided by the church with its spiky Gothic spire, and the eccentric town hall with its cupola and extravagant Renaissance-style ornamentation, a building far too grand for so small a village. The château, built in 1733, is a contrast in elegant classicism, and is open to visitors in high summer.

A few kilometres to the east along the river is the railway bridge at Hangest-sur-Somme. Here, in 1940, the tanks of Rommel's 7th armoured division crossed the Somme on the only bridge still passable, so precipitating the fall of France.

LIESSIES

From the Middle Ages the River Helpe Majeure powered the mills and forges which provided the wealth of the region's great abbeys, such as that at Liessies, 14km east of Avesnes-sur-Helpe.

Liessies is an attractive village, with many of its houses built from the rose

An expertly crafted clock in Liessies, set in the local blue stone

brick and bluish stone characteristic of the local region.

The village came into existence to serve the Benedictine abbey founded here in AD751, which became a great centre of culture and learning, famous for its library. It continued to flourish until

---

SECRET PLACES

FOLLEVILLE

THE LANNOY TOMBS

Folleville lies south of Amiens.

This small and unassuming village south of the Somme contains, in the church of St-Jacques-le-Majeur, some of the most remarkable sculpture to be found in the north of France. In the choir are the tombs of the Lannoy family, whose ruined 15th-century chateau stands near by.

The first, recumbent effigies of Raoul de Lannoy, chamberlain and advisor to Louis XI, Charles VIII and Louis XII, and his wife, Jeanne, carved in Genoa in

1507 by Antonio della Porta and Pace Gaggini, are an extravagant and delightful riot of Renaissance detail set into a Gothic frame.

Adjacent, but executed some 50 years later in a much more restrained and classical style, is the tomb of Raoul's son, François and his wife, Marie. The contrasting styles underline the dramatic changes that affected architecture and sculpture in France during the 16th century.

It was from the Baroque pulpit in this church that St-Vincent de Paul first preached in 1617.

TOUR 6 – 185KM
THE BOULONNAIS AND NORTHERN FLANDERS

The Boulonnais, a little-known region spreading east from Boulogne-sur-Mer, has a varied landscape where the valleys of the rivers Wimereux and Liane cut through vistas of cider orchards, woods and farmland. Traditional villages and stone-built farms are a particular feature of the region. Starting from Boulogne, the tour travels through the Boulonnais and into northern Flanders, a flat area of canals, windmills and brick-built villages. Circling back through the historic town of Montreuil, it returns up the sparkling modern resorts of the Channel coast.

ROUTE DIRECTIONS

Leave Boulogne-sur-Mer heading north on the **D940** coast road towards Wimereux. In the centre of Wimereux turn right on to the **D233** towards Wimille. At Wimille go under the A16 and continue on the **D233** through Souverain Moulin to Pernes-lès-Boulogne. Turn left, still on the **D233** to Conteville-les-Boulogne and Belle-et-Houllefort.

Continue past Belle on the **D233** to the junction with the **D252**, and turn left on this road to le Wast and Colembert. After Colembert, turn left on to the **N42** in the direction of St-Omer, then take the first left, the **D224**, and follow it into Ardres.

Leave Ardres on the **N43**, towards St-Omer. Pass through Nordausques, turn left on to the **D221** towards Watten. Follow this through Eperlecques, turning on to the **D222** at Ganspette. At the T-junction turn right and follow the road to Watten.

From Watten take the **D213**, later the **D928**, to St-Omer. Leave St-Omer heading south-east to Arques. Here take a right turn to les Fontinettes. Continue south-east on the **N43** to Aire-sur-la-Lys.

In Aire centre, turn right on to the **D157**, to Thérouanne, joining the **D341** just before the village. Cross the River Lys, then turn left on to the **D157**. Continue along this road, which becomes the **D126**, and further on joins the **D343**. Continue in the direction Montreuil, through Maninghem. At the roundabout where the road joins the **N1** north of Montreuil take the **N39** to Etaples.

From Etaples, take the **D940** towards Neufchâtel-Hardelot. 2km beyond Etaples is the Lutyens cemetery and memorial, on your left (parking is on the right). Continue north on the **D940** towards Boulogne. At Neufchâtel-Hardelot, bear left on to the **D119** towards Hardelot and Condette. Follow this road through le Portel and back into Boulogne.

A street lined with old shops in the old part of Boulogne

PLACES OF INTEREST

LE WAST
See page 54.

ARDRES
This ancient town, which is well worth exploring, was the headquarters of François I during the conference of the Field of the Cloth of Gold, held in 1520 between himself and Henry VIII of England. It has a 14th-century church and fine old buildings.

BLOCKHAUS D'EPERLECQUES
This 22m high concrete hill, the largest blockhouse ever built, was constructed in 1943-44 by the Germans, who planned to build V2 bombs there with which to attack London. However, in August 1943 it was disabled by British bombers, and was subsequently converted into a factory for the production of liquid oxygen.

WATTEN
See page 55.

LES FONTINETTES
The barge lift at les Fontinettes, which was in use from 1888 to 1967, replaced five locks on the Neuffossé Canal and lifted boats up and down a 13m drop. Two water-filled tanks were used to lift the barges – as one came down the lift, the other went up.

The lift has now been replaced by a large lock some 500m upriver that holds six barges and takes a mere 20 minutes to operate.

Enjoying sea air at Boulogne

MONTREUIL
Montreuil originally developed around a monastery founded in the 7th century.

The present ramparts mainly date from the 16th–17th centuries, although traces of the original 13th-century walls remain. The 17th-century Citadel is built around the ruins of an older castle. The Hospital Chapel has wonderful Flamboyant carved confessionals and pulpit, and a baroque altar. The church of St-Saulve contains notable paintings and its treasury displays relics and treasures going back to the 7th century.

Windmills are still a common sight in northern Flanders

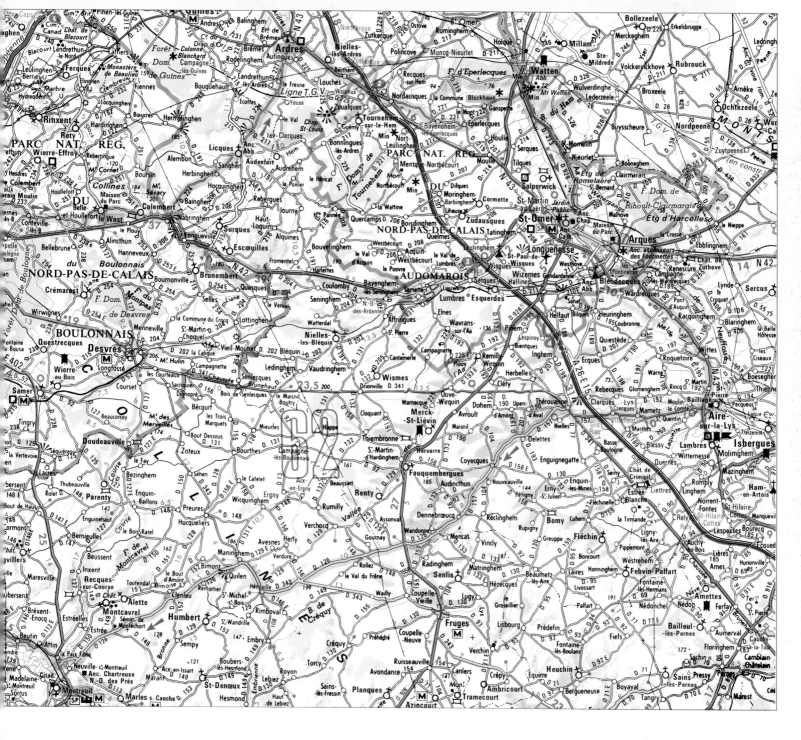

handsome trees, a bandstand and a curious little triumphal arch built in 1807. At its centre is a pleasantly simple 18th-century church, made unusual by the curious memorials on its façade. A few battered fragments remain of the Benedictine abbey where the famous local cheese was developed in the Middle Ages. A crusted cheese with a strong, distinctive flavour, Maroilles is still made locally, and can be bought in the village. Also made locally is Dauphin equally strong and with added herbs and spices. Maroilles is rinsed in beer to make *flamiche au Maroilles*, a richly flavoured cheese tart which is a local delicacy. A cheese festival is held here every year.

The pretty old village of Maroilles, which sits on the River Helpe Mineure, is famous for the distinctively flavoured cheese that is produced locally, production of which dates back to the 10th century. Maroilles cheese can be purchased in several places in the village

LUCHEUX

Set in an attractive wooded valley, Lucheux is still dominated by the ruins of its great fortress, where Joan of Arc was imprisoned by the English. It lies 7km north-east of Doullens.

Lucheux is made memorable by its distinctive blend of the historical and the domestic. Rising high above the village to the north and entered via a handsome gateway is the medieval château where Joan of Arc was held after her capture by the English. The surviving buildings span four centuries of military architecture, from the Romanesque period onwards.

Also from the 12th century is the church, notable both for its carved capitals depicting the Seven Deadly Sins in an original manner, and for the primitive ogival vaulting in the choir, one of the first appearances of the Gothic style in northern France. The old town gate and belfry further underlies the importance of Lucheux in the Middle Ages.

The village today is rather different, however, living easily with its powerful history, and its old-fashioned shops and quiet streets lined with 18th-century houses setting the scene for a pleasantly relaxed provincialism.

MAROILLES

The attractive village of Maroilles is celebrated for its cheese, the legacy of its now-ruined Benedictine abbey. It lies 12km west of Avesnes-sur-Helpe.

The pretty main street of Maroilles twists and turns its way down to the River Helpe Mineure. At its northern end is a village green, complete with

OUTINES

A typical farming village of the isolated and distinctive Der region, which takes its name from the Celtic word for oak, Outines now attracts many visitors. It lies 26km south of Vitry-le-François.

The delightful houses and barns of Outines – known as 'little Alsace' – have been beautifully restored and are fine examples of the local architectural style: low timber-framed buildings, with the silvery oak framework filled in with cob, or compacted mud and straw, painted in white or grey. The shallow roofs are covered with shingles and there are many decorative dovecotes. The houses cluster around the church, which is equally characteristic with its pointed spire covered with shingles. All these buildings reflect the strong tradition of timber-framed construction in this heavily forested area.

Part of the forest and three villages were submerged by the massive Der-Chantecoq reservoir, completed in 1974. This vast area of water is now France's largest lake, famous for watersports, sailing, fishing and birdwatching.

PAS-EN-ARTOIS

One of the most attractive features of the varied Picardy landscape are its little river valleys. Typical is the Authie, whose route to the sea can be explored from its source near Pas-en-Artois, 12km east of Doullens.

Wooded and pleasantly meandering through traditional farmland, the valley of the River Authie is one of those remote Picardy valleys which are so often overlooked by visitors in a hurry. Set in this lovely valley, Pas-en-Artois is a delightful village with all the characteristics of rural France at its most authentic. At its heart is a pretty church surrounded by a fine range of 17th- and 18th-century houses, built in brick and stone in the local styles. There are plenty of old shops and cafés and just to the east, in a wooded park that runs down to the river, is a plain little 18th-century château. A place to savour for its atmosphere and its setting, Pas-en-Artois is a village well worth visiting, away from the usual tourist routes.

PIERREFONDS

Throughout this region noted for its extraordinary architectural wealth and diversity, little can compare with the fairy-tale fantasy château outside Pierrefonds, 15km south-east of Compiègne.

Pierrefonds' setting, in a steep valley surrounded by woods is dramatic, particularly when approached from the north-west through the forest of Compiègne. At its centre is a lake, ringed by old hotels that reflect the town's former eminence as a spa, and spreading westward from the lakeside are steep old streets lined with houses that reveal Pierrefonds' medieval ancestry. However, its crowning glory is the château, with its staggering skyline of turrets, battlements and pinnacles rising high above the roofs of the town.

There has been a medieval fortress here since the 11th century, but the present building is the responsibility of Napoleon III, who in 1857 commissioned the Gothic revivalist architect Viollet-le-Duc to create a new château

at Pierrefonds. The result is a remarkable and flamboyant study in 19th-century medievalism, notable for its extraordinary diversity and extravagance of decorative detail.

ST-RIQUIER

One of the finest examples in France of the final, exuberant flowering of Gothic architecture known as the Flamboyant style is to be seen in the abbey church of the fortified village of St-Riquier, 9km east of Abbeville.

Scattered down its hillside, and best approached from the north, St-Riquier is a series of architectural delights. The

The splendid Flamboyant façade of the abbey church at St-Riquier dominates the main street of the village

first is the view down the steep main street, flanked by 18th-century houses, including the Hôtel Dieu, the former hospital of 1719. Next is the 16th-century belfry tower, followed by the main square and finally, set back to the left, the abbey. Founded by the Benedictines in 780, the present abbey dates largely from the 17th century. Towering over these elegant classical buildings in golden stone is the church, whose great façade, completely covered with sculptures and lively Flamboyant decoration, dominates not only the village but the surrounding landscape.

VIGNORY

The Canal de la Marne adds a relatively recent footnote to the ancient history of this region, reflected in the venerable buildings of Vignory, 20km north of Chaumont.

Set in a hollow in the wooded hills to the west of the River Marne and the Canal de la Marne, Vignory is dominated by its ruined château, standing high above the village to the south. The village has many attractive houses with interesting architectural details, but by far the most distinguished building is the church of St Etienne, a fine and superbly preserved early Romanesque construction from the middle of the 11th century. The exterior, with its square tower, is simply decorated with arcading, while the interior reflects the powerful primitivism of its era. The nave has three storeys, with the central storey marked by an exciting range of decorative capitals that reflect the full repertoire of the Romanesque stone-carvers, including geometric patterns, foliage and animals.

VORGES

Many of the villages of the Aisne can claim a history going back to Roman times, with many vestiges of the Carolingian and Merovingian eras. A particularly fine example is Vorges, 8km south of Laon.

Tidy and well-cared for as befits its protected status, Vorges is still predominantly a traditional farming village, unaffected by tourism. Its solid stone cottages surround the large, open central square of trees and grass, which is dominated by the grand 13th-century church.

This fine Gothic building with its tall pierced tower, its high nave and its rose window, is an unusually impressive church for a small village. Fortified during the Hundred Years War, it is now all that remains, except for the corner towers, of a formidable system of defences.

Other buildings in Vorges evoke a more domestic and pastoral past: an old pump stands outside the church, and scattered around the village are a classical wash-house, a mill and various agricultural buildings.

Catching the morning bread round in the attractive old village of Vignory, where life continues at a leisurely pace

WASSY

Remembered in history for its notorious massacre, one of the seeds of the terrible Wars of Religion, Wassy today is a tranquil riverside village. 18km south of St-Dizier.

It was on 1 March 1562 that the soldiers of Françoise de Guise massacred a group of Protestants in the little village of Wassy. The event provoked shock waves throughout the French Protestant community, and served to forment the religious turmoil that led to the Wars of Religion. Today Wassy is a quiet place with a large and decorative church that spans the Romanesque and early Gothic periods.

In the 19th century the Blaise valley was renowned for its ironworks, and the arrival of the railway brought about a great expansion of iron-making in the region. Now that the iron industry has slipped into history, Wassy has become a pleasant small town, with echoes of its former grandeur to be seen in the late 18th-century town hall, complete with astronomical clock.

LE WAST

Typical features of the Boulonnais – a little-known region of woodland, cider orchards and pastures – are its low-lying stone-built farms and old-fashioned villages. A good example is le Wast, 15km east of Boulogne-sur-Mer.

The Boulonnais spreads eastwards from Boulogne-sur-Mer, a quiet, bucolic landscape cut by the pretty Liane and Wimereux rivers, largely overlooked by motorists speeding eastwards on the nearby N42.

SECRET PLACES

FONTINETTES

BARGE LIFT

Fontinettes lies on the south-eastern side of Arques.

Hidden in the depths of Arques, famous for the manufacture of glass, is an extraordinary legacy of 19th-century engineering.

The Fontinettes canal boat lift on the Neuffossé Canal was built in 1888 to raise loaded *péniches*, or canal barges, 12m verti-cally, and thus bypass a bottleneck caused by an old flight of locks. It was designed by the English

Explore a historic feat of British engineering, hidden in the heart of Arques

Terraces of white-painted single-storey cottages with brown and blue shutters spread along the main street of le Wast. Colourful window boxes greet the visitor in the summer, while the old cafés and shops preserve, unconsciously, the leisurely atmosphere of an earlier era, echoed by the small grey stone château that faces on to the main street. The focal point of the village is the church, to the east of the main street. The last vestige of a daughter priory of Cluny, it has a famous Romanesque portal which is decorated unusually with oriental motifs, perhaps inspired by a Crusader's travels.

WATTEN

With its flat fields, dykes and brick-built villages the landscape of northern Flanders has echoes of Holland, emphasised by its network of canals. Several waterways come together at Watten. 12km north of St-Omer.

The best approach to Watten is from the south, along the road from St-Omer that runs beside the curiously named River Aa, a waterway busy with *péniches*. The little village straddles the river, a cluster of houses and shops set against a wooded hill topped by a restored windmill, its long quays often lined with barges.

Sitting at the intersection of waterways linking Calais, Dunkerque and Belgium with the mighty French canal network, Watten is a traditional canal village, unaffected as yet by the rising tide of leisure boating. From the hill above the village is a splendid panorama north towards the coast, over the Aa valley and the Flanders plain.

Traditional colourful houses in the Boulonnais village of le Wast

THE SMART SET AT LE TOUQUET

Some 30km down the coast from Boulogne, le Touquet-Paris-Plage is a fine example of a turn-of-the-century seaside resort. Attractively faded villas beautifully set among pinewoods and poplars tell a tale of luxury in days gone by, for this was a centre for high living, endless beach parties, and especially gambling. The comparatively relaxed laws of the casinos drew the British jet-setters in their thousands, and many a fortune was won and lost here. At one time, according to the legends, flights from the UK were landing here every ten minutes. Le Touquet's heyday came during the roaring '20s and 1930s, but the frivolity evaporated with the advent of World War II, and today this is a quieter town – with a lot of memories.

engineer, Edwin Clark, and based on the similar boat lift he had built in 1875 at Anderton in Cheshire, using the same principle of two great counterbalanced tanks in which the barges travelled up and down.

Clark's lift remained in use until 1967, when it in turn was replaced by one huge lock, just to the north.

Preserved now as a major industrial monument, the lift can be fully explored. There is a small but informative museum-cum-visitor-centre in one of the buildings. The massive new lock, which can take six barges and is still busy with barge traffic, is just a short walk from the lift's upper level.

NEUVE-CHAPELLE

UNUSUAL MEMORIALS

Two particularly elaborate war memorials

Neuve-Chapelle lies southwest of Lille. In a part of France famous for its cemeteries and war memorials, two at Neuve-Chapelle are particularly unusual.

First, by the crossroads, is Sir Herbert Baker's Memorial to the Missing of the India Corps, commemorating soldiers killed in World War I who have no known grave. The elegant and decorative structure, circular, and guarded by stone tigers, is a charming mixture of classical and Indian motifs.

Just down the road is more bizarre memorial cemetery, in this case to the soldiers of the Portuguese army. It is entered by an arched gateway in the Manueline, or Portuguese Gothic, style.

SECRET FRANCE

ALSACE AND LORRAINE

This region, divided by the mountain country of the Vosges that runs north to south down the middle, encompasses a variety of landscapes. Lorraine, on the western side of the Vosges, is an area of gentle farmland full of evidence of its long and varied history, from old Celtic sites and Roman remains, to reminders of Joan of Arc, who was born in the region. Alsace, to the east of the Vosges, with the Rhine running down its eastern side, consists of a narrow, flat plain squeezed between the river and the Vosges, with a succession of medieval fortified villages running down the foothills of the mountains.

Mon Village, written and illustrated in the aftermath of the Franco-Prussian War of 1870 by Jean-Jacques Waltz, curator of the Unterlinden museum in Colmar, under the pen name of Hansi, was full of regret that Alsace was no longer French, envying the storks, still free to fly into France. Hansi's village – nowhere in particular, everywhere in general – is still here today. The children no longer mockingly tie balloons to the scabbards of Prussian officers, but the medieval streets and cobbled alleyways are still to be seen, some crowded within ramparts, with timber-framed houses in all colours of plaster from pink and terracotta through orange and even in shades of green and blue.

Being a frontier region Alsace has seen more than its fair share of wars and destruction. Though welcoming, the people are fiercely proud of their identity, and this pride is reflected in the local costume, worn now mainly on high days and holidays, and in the Alsatian dialect. There are two dialects, softer Rhenish around Strasbourg and a more Germanic form further south. French was only gradually spoken here from the days of Louis XIV. Between 1870 and 1918 Alsace was incorporated into Germany, with the name Elsass, and German was taught in the schools.

One of the pleasures for the traveller in Alsace is its manageable scale; it is possible to sample the delights of the Route des Vins and to explore the picturesque mountains of the Vosges within the same day. In contrast, Lorraine, whose countryside is flatter and quieter, fed by the Meurthe, Moselle and Meuse rivers, has rolling farmland and vast areas of forest that repay leisurely exploration.

cigognes d'Alsace et Lorraine

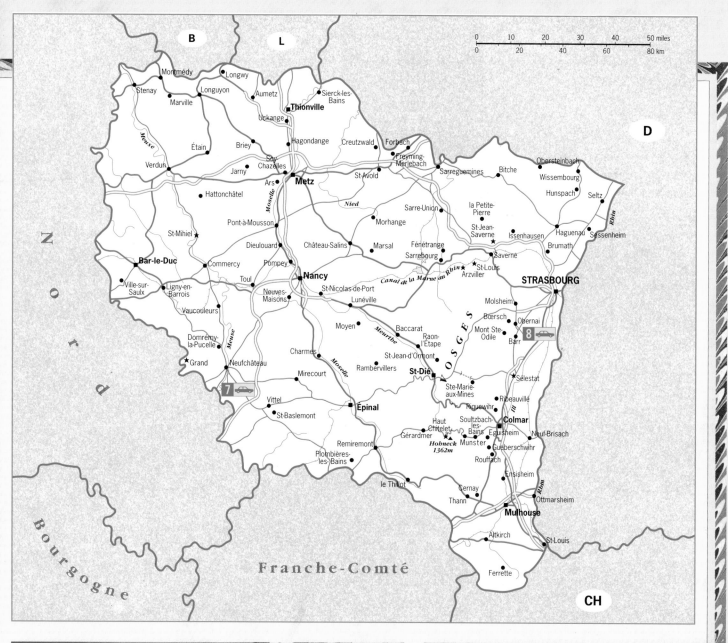

B L

0 10 20 30 40 50 miles
0 20 40 60 80 km

D

Montmédy
Longwy
Stenay
Longuyon
Marville
Aumetz
Sierck-les-Bains
Uckange
Thionville
Étain
Briey
Hagondange
Creutzwald
Forbach
Verdun
Jarny
Soy-Chazelles
St-Avold
Freyming-Merlebach
Sarreguemines
Bitche
Obersteinbach
Wissembourg
Ars
Metz
Hunspach
Seltz
Hattonchâtel
Nied
Sarre-Union
la Petite-Pierre
St-Jean-Saverne
Issenhausen
Haguenau
Sessenheim
Pont-à-Mousson
Morhange
St-Mihiel
Moselle
Château-Salins
Marsal
Fénétrange
Sarrebourg
Saverne
Brumath
Rhin
Dieulouard
Bar-le-Duc
Commercy
Pompey
Nancy
Canal de la Marne au Rhin
Arzviller
St-Louis
STRASBOURG
Ville-sur-Saulx
Ligny-en-Barrois
Toul
St-Nicolas-de-Port
Molsheim
Vaucouleurs
Neuves-Maisons
Lunéville
Boersch
Obernai
Domrémy-la-Pucelle
Moyen
Baccarat
Mont Ste-Odile
Barr
8
Meuse
Charmes
Meurthe
Raon-l'Étape
St-Jean-d'Ormont
Grand
Neufchâteau
Mirecourt
Moselle
Rambervillers
St-Dié
Sélestat
7
Vittel
Ste-Marie-aux-Mines
Ribeauvillé
St-Baslemont
Épinal
Riquewihr
Haut
Chitelet
Soultzbach-les-Bains
Colmar
Remiremont
Gérardmer
Hohneck
1362m
Munster
Eguisheim
Neuf-Brisach
Plombières-les-Bains
Gueberschwihr
Rouffach
Rhin
Ensisheim
le Thillot
Cernay
Ottmarsheim
Thann
Mulhouse
V O S G E S
Ill
Altkirch
St-Louis
Bourgogne
Ferrette
Franche-Comté
CH

Cobbled streets and timber-framed
houses are typical of the region

Decorative details
adorn many
village buildings,
and there is a
tradition of
decorating the
streets with flowers
in summer

HUGEL DEPUIS 1639

57

BOERSCH

A picturesque walled village with fine medieval fortifications and Renaissance architecture, Boersch used to be famous for its orchards and is now surrounded by vines. It lies 5km north-west of Obernai.

In the shadow of Mont Ste-Odile, Boersch is still a walled *bourg*. Elevated to the status of a town by a war-like 14th-century bishop of Strasbourg, it still has three fortified 14th-century gateways through the defensive walls which remain the only way into the cluster of houses within the ramparts. There are *caves* to be visited and *dégustations* to be made, and a pleasant half-hour stroll will take you all around this picturesque village.

In the centre is the magnificent 16th-century town hall, outside which is a fine carved stone Renaissance wellhead, now decorated with plants and flowers.

Nearby Klingenthal, 7km to the south-west, was in the 1730s the site of the royal armaments factory, where many of the swords, bayonets and pikes were produced for Louis XV's armies.

DOMREMY-LA-PUCELLE

This tiny village, forever associated with Joan of Arc, preserves the house in which she was born and a museum devoted to 'La Pucelle'. It is 21km south-west of Toul.

This small, unassuming village tucked away in the top corner of the Vosges department attracts many visitors because of its most famous daughter, Joan of Arc, described by Napoleon as a 'symbol of the unity and resistance of the French nation'.

Where the road bridge turns to cross the Meuse is the little house in which Joan was born, and the chapel in which she prayed. Both have been much restored: of the church little except the base of the tower can be said to be from Joan's time. The house was last completely restored in August 1820, but the work has left it much as it would have been when it was home to a relatively well-off farming family in the 15th century.

The downstairs rooms, including the room in which Joan was born in 1412, are open to visitors.

A small museum contains documents and maps relating to Joan's life, her mission and death, and the extraordinary revival of fervour which surrounded her memory early in this century.

Above Domrémy is the basilica of le Bois-Chenu. Consecrated in 1926, it marks one of the sites where Joan had her visions of the saints Michael, Catherine and Marguerite.

HAUT CHITELET

JARDIN D'ALTITUDE

The garden is beside the D430, 2km south of the Col de la Schlucht, 15km east of Gérardmer.

There are three high-altitude gardens in France, the ones at Lautaret in the Hautes-Alpes and at Samoëns in Savoie being the best known.

The garden at Haut Chitelet, 1,228m above sea level, consists of 10ha of woods and rocky ground.

Here, there are over 3,000 specimens of South American, Himalayan and Scandinavian high-altitude plants on display, arranged according to their place of origin.

Himalayan species of wild flowers are among the many on display

Some of the houses in Eguisheim date back to the 16th century

EGUISHEIM

One of the most ancient 'concentric' fortified villages of Alsace, Eguisheim, grouped around its 8th-century fort, has hardly changed since the 16th century. It is 5km south-west of Colmar.

'Twelve centuries of history' is the proud boast of one of the oldest settlements in Alsace. Traces of Cro-Magnon man, a wanderer from the Dordogne, have even been unearthed here. The 8th-century fort, built by Count Eberhard, nephew of Ste-Odile, still stands at the very centre of the village, which was first fortified in 1257. Narrow streets and alleyways of 16th-and 17th-century houses winding in concentric circles with the massive stone ramparts lend Eguisheim its special interest and charm.

The Grand'Rue, lined with multi-coloured half-timbered houses, leads up to a small square in front of the

castle and church, where carp swim lazily in the octagonal fountain. The red sandstone church and castle were restored in the 1890s and are presently being refurbished again. Fascinating for its architecture and its history, Eguisheim is now also an important wine-making centre.

FENETRANGE

A large fortified village with a notable château and church overlooking the Sarre, Fénétrange has preserved its medieval heart virtually intact. It lies on the edge of the forest, 15km north of Sarrebourg.

Driving along the D38 it would be easy to miss Fénétrange, perched above the River Sarre, and guarding its medieval heart within and around its old castle. Where the road makes a right-angle bend, turn up to the Porte de France. Practically every building within the ancient walls stands on foundations which date from before 1400.

The collegiate church of St-Rémi stands on the old Place de la Justice. Late Flamboyant Gothic, it was started by Jean de Fénétrange in the early 15th-century. The west door pillars carry the very distinctive latticework trademark of the master mason Hans Hammer, whose best-known work is possibly the pulpit of Strasbourg cathedral, and who here built the tall, simple nave.

On the way back to the Porte de France lies the entrance to the horseshoe-shaped castle courtyard. The watchtower guarding the riverside approach to the walls dates from 1070. In times of danger the river would be allowed to flood encircling ditches in order to protect Fénétrange and its castle.

Among its remarkably rich and varied architectures, Fénétrange boasts many interesting Renaissance houses in the town, each with its mason's marks. A particularly large and fine example with a corner oriel window rising through the first and second floors was in 1539 a hostel for ladies visiting the castle, and later was home to young candidates for the priesthood.

REGIONAL CHEESES

'How can one possibly govern a country which makes more than three hundred and seventy different cheeses?' General de Gaulle is supposed to have asked. Alsace and Lorraine have done more than their fair share to make France ungovernable in this respect. Particularly fertile for cheese-making are the high pastures of the Vosges, the mountains straddling the boundary between the provinces. Munster, on the Alsatian side, gives its name to a famous cheese with a red rind, a pungent smell and a spicy taste sometimes sharpened by the addition of caraway. Its history goes back at least to the Middle Ages, but nowadays it is usually produced by commercial dairies rather than on the farm. When young, it makes an ideal companion for Gewürztraminer, the flowery local wine. Gérardmer, on the western side of the Vosges, is known for Géromé, a cousin of Munster that can also be

flavoured with herbs. Carré de l'Est, often sold under the brand name of Recollet, is a square-shaped cheese, made in Lorraine and resembling Camembert in its white rind and soft texture.

SOUTHERN LORRAINE

Southern Lorraine is an area of gentle farmland with large, open fields of pasture and cereals, dotted with quiet towns and many ancient sites. The region is traversed by the River Meuse, which in the time of Joan of Arc formed the frontier between France and the Holy Roman Empire. Reminders of Joan are everywhere, as the route passes through her birthplace. The region is rich in Celtic and Roman remains, and la Colline Inspirée, a horseshoe-shaped ridge running from Sion to Vaudémont, is among the most dramatic. It has been a place of worship and of defence since prehistoric times. Lorraine is also famous for its spa towns, two of which are included on the tour.

ROUTE DIRECTIONS

Leave Neuchâteau, heading north on the **D164** signposted to Domrémy-la-Pucelle. At Coussey, turn left onto the **D3**, then right onto the **D53**, running parallel to the **D164**, leading to the basilica at Bois-Chenu. Continue into Domremy. Follow the road to Greux, and turn on to the **D19**. Cross the river and continue into Maxey-sur-Meuse.

Stay on the **D19** through Jubainville and Ruppes. Keep sight of the pylons to the right, for there are few other signs along this stretch of road. At the T-junction with the **N74**, turn left towards Autreville and turn right by the church on to the **D27** to Harmonville. At the war memorial turn left and continue to Saulxerotte. Over a stone bridge, take the left fork, signposted to Favières. Once into the Forêt de St Amond, turn

left at a sawmill towards the church, where 'toutes directions' signs point the way to Favières.

Turn right at the next junction on to the **D12**, signposted to Vandeléville. Do not follow signs to Sion/Vaudémont in Battigny. Continue on the **D12**, then turn almost back on your tracks in Vandeléville on to the **D51** to Thorey-Lyautey. The road passes la Colline Inspirée on the right, with the basilica at one end and the monument to Maurice Barrès at the other.

Turn onto the **D56** into Thorey-Lyautey. From here take the **D58** towards Chaouilley and just before the village turn right on to the **D53**. Turn left, still on the **D53** to Vaudémont and then follow the **D53** and then **D50e** to Sion. At the T-junction turn right and after a short while turn left on to the **D64** to Diarville. From Diarville follow the **D913**, later the **D413**, into Mirecourt.

From Mirecourt, take

the the **D66** then left on the **D17** (at Domjulien the **D68**) to Vittel. From Vittel follow the **D429** to Contrexéville, and take the **D13** through Belmont-sur-Vair across the **D166** to St-Paul. Turn on to the **D3** to Removille, and continue on through Harchéchamp to Soulosse. Turn left on to the **N74** and back into Neufchâteau.

PLACES OF INTEREST

BOIS-CHENU

The basilica of Bois-Chenu was built by Joan of Arc's great-nephew in the late 19th century, on the site where Joan heard the voices of saints Catherine, Margaret and Michael. It was dedicated in 1926.

Entry to the basilica, a place of prayer for all soldiers, living and dead, is through the crypt. Inside, it is bright with mosaics, and contains paintings done by Lionel Royer in the romantic style just before World War I, depicting well-known episodes in Joan's tragically short life and her death at the stake in Rouen.

DOMREMY-LA-PUCELLE
See page 58.

SION-VAUDEMONT

First a Celtic centre of worship for over 2,000 years, then Roman, and then Christian, this horseshoe-shaped ridge has been a pilgrimage centre for thousands of years. Today pilgrims still come to 'la Colline Inspirée', so named by Maurice Barrès. In the 18th century the present church, Notre-Dame-de-Sion, was built on the site.

At the other end of the hill is the Signal de Vaudémont, with a *table*

Below, the fertile Lorraine plain around Sion
Below right, fleur de lys decorate a doorway in Domremy-la-Pucelle

FERRETTE

Medieval capital of the Sundgau, and outpost of the Jura mountains, Ferrette has for centuries been a frontier stronghold. It lies 40km south of Mulhouse, close to the Swiss border.

From the 10th century this distinctive region was ruled by the Comtes de Ferrette. Ruins of two châteaux dominate the village in its picturesque site. When a 12th-century count began to build his castle, the market and then the village moved, and the old site

The peaceful village of Gueberschwihr hosts an arts festival each summer

became 'Vieux' Ferrette. From the higher ruins there is a good view over the village to the Vosges, the Rhine and the high Jura. The houses of the village bear witness to a prosperous past. The town hall is a stone-built 'Rhenish Renaissance' building which now houses the tourist information office.

GUEBERSCHWIHR

A peaceful wine village with some imposing buildings, Gueberschwihr is now famous for its local arts festival each August. It lies 12km south-west of Colmar.

The road climbs up the vine-covered ridge into Gueberschwihr, providing a stunning view out across what was once the flood plain of the Rhine and is now a wide swathe of cultivated fields. Narrowing as it passes older half-timbered houses, it leads into the square, with its large chestnut tree in the centre. The Mairie fronts the square and in the far corner is the church, dedicated to St-Pantaléon, a doctor in the court of Diocletian who was martyred in the 4th century. The bell-tower that dominates the village is all that remains of the original church, which was rebuilt in the 19th-century.

Since 1970 there has also been an arts festival here, held in August.

d'orientation and magnificent views south across Lorraine.

MIRECOURT
Since the early 18th-century Mirecourt has been known as the 'stringed-instrument capital' of France. It is also justly famous for its lace and embroidery. Displays of both crafts can be seen in the museum, and are usually transferred during summer to the striking 17th-century market hall.

The church of Notre Dame was started in 1303. The Chapelle de la Oultre (chapel across the river), built between the 11th and 16th centuries, serves the St-Vincent quarter of the town, St Vincent being the patron saint of wine and vineyards.

VITTEL
Vittel is the most important of the spas of the Vosges, which include Contrexéville, Bains-les-Bains and Plombières. However, one of its specialities – and this in a town best known for its water and its treatment of liver and kidney disorders – is a particularly delicious soft-centred chocolate.

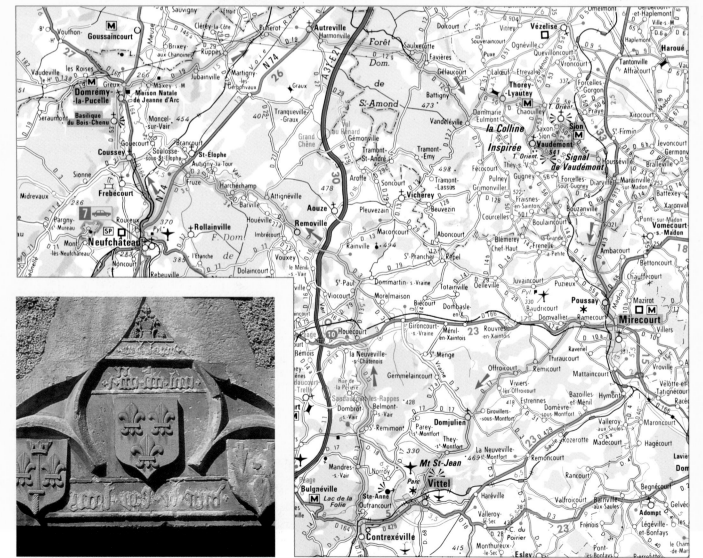

HATTONCHATEL

A historic village perched imposingly on a rocky promontory, Hattonchâtel is 36km south-east of Verdun, 17km south of the Metz-Verdun road.

It was in the 9th century that Bishop Hatton, 29th Bishop of Verdun, built himself an episcopal palace at the tip of this rocky promontory. Richelieu ordered its destruction in 1634, and it was extensively rebuilt between 1923 and 1928, by the efforts of Belle Skinner. She came from Massachussetts at the end of World War I to visit the grave of her nephew (the more romantic say her fiancé), killed in the St-Mihiel salient battle. The dead are commemorated at the Butte de Montsec, visible across the Woëvre plain and the Lac de Madine. Belle Skinner fell in love with the village and its people and did much to rebuild the lives of both.

The château was for many years the principal residence of the Bishops of Verdun. The prosperity and renown they brought to the village is reflected in some of its old houses, notably a particularly fine example with Gothic arcading. The village can be entered via what was once the guardroom of the medieval Porte Notre-Dame, a reminder that the village was fortified until the destruction of the Thirty Years War. The 14th-century collegiate church, reached through a 15th-century cloister, formed part of these defences. In a side chapel is a polychrome carved stone reredos, quaintly dated 1000-500-20-3 and still bearing traces of its original bright colours, said to be by Ligier Richier. If not by the

master's own hand it is undoubtedly the work of a supreme sculptor of the St-Mihiel school of that period.

HUNSPACH

A beautifully preserved example of a Bas Rhin village, Hunspach has become a focus for everything traditional in this remote, forested region. 11km south of Wissembourg.

One of the most picturesque of northern Alsace villages, Hunspach owes its remarkable architectural

The flower-filled streets of Hunspach, one of the best-preserved traditional villages in Alsace

harmony and integrity to the ravages of the Thirty Years War, when it was completely destroyed. Rebuilt over a relatively brief period in the late 17th and early 18th centuries, it remains today one of the finest and most complete examples of Alsatian vernacular architecture of the period. Picturesque half-timbered houses, often intricately carved, line the streets, which in summer are decked with flowers.

ST-LOUIS-ARZVILLER

INCLINED PLANE

To find the inclined plane on the Marne-Rhine canal, take the D98 south from Lutzelbourg and turn right to St-Louis.

On this section of the busy Marne-Rhine canal there used to be a stair-

An ingenious structure, clearly visible from the D98

Strict building regulations preserve the village's characteristic appearance (there are no shop windows, for example); but Hunspach is not a museum piece, rather a living centre of local tradition. The church, very plain, betrays the influence of the Swedes who settled here and established thriving Lutheran communities.

ISSENHAUSEN

A pretty village in a gentle landscape where traditional mixed farming is still practised, Issenhausen is 20km west of Haguenau.

Issenhausen is a traditional and attractive agricultural community, and its large houses are an indication that land here is not at the same premium as in prime vineyard areas.

The village consists of a long main street, lined with chestnut trees and leading up to a tiny Lutheran church. The houses are typically Alsatian, built of red sandstone on the ground floor with half-timbering above. Each has its high, wide gateway opening into a large courtyard. Some barns still remain, and others have been converted into spacious living quarters. Like so many other Alsatian villages, medieval Issenhausen was destroyed in the Thirty Years War, and its present buildings date mostly from the 18th century.

MARSAL

Rising as though on an island above the marshy valley of the Seille, Marsal used to be an important strategic point and centre of the salt trade, 30km north-east of Nancy.

From prehistoric times until the Seille valley was drained in the 19th century, salt was the main industry here. Samphire, an edible plant found normally only on saltwater marshes and seashores, grows profusely around Marsal village.

Because of Marsal's strategic position on the road from France into Alsace, it was fortified by the Dukes of Lorraine in the 17th century. On Louis XIV's orders, the great military architect Vauban then elaborated and completed them. His Porte de France makes an impressive entrance to a village of under 300 inhabitants. With three of the four original barracks blocks, this is virtually all that remains of Vauban's fortifications, which were dismantled after the Franco-Prussian war, but their former line around the village is well marked.

MARVILLE

Sited on a promontory in the attractive rolling countryside near the Belgian border and inhabited since antiquity, Marville today retains many reminders of its historic importance. It lies 12km south-east of Montmédy.

On a hill to the west of Marville there once stood a Roman villa with a temple to Mars. Early Christians came here in about AD700, destroyed the temple and on its site built a church dedicated to St-Hilaire. St-Hilaire remained the parish church until the building of St-Nicolas on the Grande-Place in the 13th and 14th centuries.

Gothic in style, St-Nicolas was enlarged in the 15th century.

For a century from 1555 Marville was occupied by the Spanish, who built splendid houses in Renaissance style. Many of these have survived. But remarkable façades, doorways, chimney breasts and staircases from the 16th and 17th centuries are to be found at every turn in Marville and the church of St-Nicolas, too, has wonderful examples of Renaissance architecture, carvings and statues and funerary monuments.

Marville contains a wealth of fine Gothic and Renaissance sculpture

St-Hilaire now houses a collection of gravestones, memorials and statues. Most remarkable, however, is its ossuary, which contains 40,000 skulls piled neatly around the walls.

---

way of 17 locks, totalling 4km in length, that took a whole day to get through. In 1969 this was replaced with an inclined plane, an ingenious system for hauling boats up or down a slope, getting rid of the need for locks altogether. The boats are carried in a 43m- long tank that sits across a concrete ramp and is hauled up or down by a system of weights and counterweights, in just 20 minutes.

ST-MIHIEL

SCULPTURES BY LIGIER RICHIER

St-Mihiel is a small town north of Commercy.

St-Mihiel was the home of the 16th-century sculptor, Ligier Richier (1500–67). Richier studied in Rome during the years 1515–20/21, then returned home and worked for the most part for the Dukes of Lorraine. Two of the churches in St-Mihiel contain fine examples of his work.

In the abbey church of St-Mihiel, constructed between the 12th and 17th centuries, in the first chapel on the right-hand side, is Richier's 'Pâmoison de la Vierge et St-Jean' (Swooning Virgin with St John), carved in 1531 in walnut as part of a larger group of figures. In another part of the church is a piece sculpted by Jean Richier, Ligier Richier's grandson, in 1608.

In the 13th–18th century church of St-Etienne is a sepulchre carved by Richier in 1554–1564. It is an impressive piece incorporating 12 larger than life-size figures, illustrating scenes from the Entombment of Christ, including Salome preparing the funeral couch, Mary Magdalen washing the feet of Christ, and Joseph of Arimathea and Nicodemus carrying his body.

Further sculpture by Ligier Richier may be seen at Hattonchâtel.

CHATEAU DE FLECKENSTEIN

Perched on its rocky outcrop, 370m high, among the northern Vosges, within a stone's throw of the present German border, the ruined castle of Fleckenstein makes a dramatic spectacle. Built in the 13th century, it was later acquired by the powerful family of Rohan-Soubise and finally destroyed in 1680, but the staircases and rooms which the original builders cut into the solid rock can still be seen. A tower gives a superb panorama of the valleys of the Sauer and the Steinbach, land fought over in the bloody disputes that have plagued the history of Alsace well into the present century.

MONT STE-ODILE

The romantic tale of Ste-Odile, a breathtaking view and a remarkable prehistoric monument continue to draw tourists and pilgrims alike to this ancient sanctuary. 5km north-west of Barr.

The Celtic inhabitants of the plain sought refuge here in time of war behind their *mur païen*, or pagan wall, built of large 'puddingstone' blocks, many of them originally held in place with oak mortise-and-tenon joints, in the 7th century BC. A walk, difficult in some places, gives access to most parts of the 10km-long wall.

It was in the 7th century AD that Ste-Odile was born, the blind, unwanted daughter of Duke Etichon of Hohenbourg. Narrowly escaping death at her father's hands, Odile was brought up by nuns, and at her baptism miraculously regained her sight. The convent that she subsequently founded here was to become the focus of some of the greatest pilgrimages in medieval Alsace, and home to some of its noblest ladies. Ste-Odile's sarcophagus in the Chapelle Ste-Odile, on the east terrace, still attracts thousands of pilgrims today. The huge lime trees in the courtyard are descendants of three planted by Odile herself, in honour of the Trinity.

Further along the rocky spur is the Chapelle des Larmes, a 12th-century foundation on the site of the convent cemetery, outside which there are still some tombs cut into the living rock. The Chapelle de la Croix, the oldest part of the convent buildings, dates from the 11th century.

MOYEN

Rising above the plain and the prettily meandering River Mortagne, Moyen and its curiously named château lie 18km south-east of Lunéville.

Moyen's square church tower with its octagonal spire stands like a beacon high above the village and the surrounding plain. The southern end of the hill is occupied by the ruins of the castle, begun by the Bishop of Metz in 1444. This substantial edifice, which originally had two concentric rings of defences, the inner one bristling with seven towers, was built by grudging conscript labour from Epinal. They bestowed on it the unforgettable name of 'Qui-qu'en-Grogne' (grumble who may) which it has kept to this day.

Most of the castle was destroyed after a siege in 1639. However, the north wing of the inner courtyard buildings has been restored, and its carved sandstone lintels and door frames carefully refurbished.

OBERSTEINBACH

A typical village of the northern Vosges, Obersteinbach seems to have slept unchanged for centuries in its little clearing in the forest. It lies on the River Steinbach, 34km north-west of Haguenau.

Obersteinbach and its near neighbour Niedersteinbach are two picturesque villages on the banks of the River Steinbach, in a pretty valley that until recently had been virtually deserted for generations. Now people are

---

SECRET PLACES

GRAND

CELTIC SANCTUARY

Grand is a small village west of Neufchâteau.

Five hundred people live in this village sitting atop what was once a healing sanctuary of the Celtic god, Grannus. The important Gallo-Roman town of Gallum once occupied the site, but was destroyed in the 5th century. The Romans built aqueducts, a basilica, and an amphi-theatre that held 20,000 people. There is a magnifi-cent and well-preserved mosaic pavement dating from the 1st century, and archaeological finds and more mosaics are on dis-play in the local museum.

Further information may be obtained from the local museum.

returning to these villages, to restore and inhabit once more their attractive houses – half-timbered above, red sandstone below – which are typical of the Vosges. Obersteinbach also has several fountains and two little churches, and in summer the whole village is decked with flowers.

Overlooking the village, perched on a great outcrop of sandstone is Château de Petit Arnsberg, and a few kilometres to the north-west is the 13th-century Château de Lutzelhardt – just two of the many medieval fortresses that dot this mountainous frontier country.

OTTMARSHEIM

Ottmarsheim is remarkable for possessing the only surviving example of Carolingian church architecture in Alsace. It is 10km east of Mulhouse, on the Grand Canal d'Alsace.

The celebrated church that constitutes industrial Ottmarsheim's claim to fame is unique in Alsace. Octagonal in shape, it is a simplified and scaled-down version of Charlemagne's 9th-century chapel at Aix-la-Chapelle. Although for many years these polygonal structures were believed to have pagan origins, the church was actually part of a Benedictine abbey founded here, on the Roman road from Basle to Strasbourg, in the 11th century. The church now stands somewhat incongruously in the middle of a village that has become a busy Rhine port.

LA PETITE-PIERRE

With its lovely walks, its well-preserved monuments and its fine domestic architecture, la Petite-Pierre makes a perfect base for exploring 'Alsace Bossue'. It is 20km north-west of Saverne.

The village owes its origins to Drogo, one of Charlemagne's illegitimate sons, who became Bishop of Metz and lord of the region, and who built his first castle on the Altenberg in about 1173. The castle is now headquarters for the Parc Naturel Régional des Vosges du Nord.

The Chapelle St Louis, built in 1684 and largely disused since 1737, is now a

One of the medival fortified gateways into the attractive old village of Riquewihr

museum of Alsatian seals: a surprising fund of information on local heraldry, history, fashions, weaponry and trades.

La Petit-Pierre is now a noted centre of gastronomy and of walking. Over 100 kilometers of walks in the surrounding forest are signposted from outside the Mairie, and there is a small wild animal reserve with a children's play park nearby.

RIQUEWIHR

Dubbed the 'pearl of the vineyards', Riquewihr is as celebrated for its delightful position and its superb architecture as for its delicious wines. It is on the Route du Vin, 11km north-west of Colmar.

The village was first fortified in 1291 and raised to the status of a town in 1320. The double rampart built round the village at this period still survives on three sides, as do two of its fortified gateways: the tall, balconied Dolder belfry, now the symbol of Riquewihr, and the Tour des Voleurs, so-called because it served as the prison (it now contains an 'authentic' torture chamber). Beautiful half-timbered and carved medieval and Renaissance houses abound in this popular village, complete with cantilevers, gables, towers and oriel windows.

There is no shortage of places to taste the local vintages, and a local speciality, *matelotte de poissons*, is a mixture of tench, pike, perch, eels and vegetables with a delicious sauce of cream and Riesling.

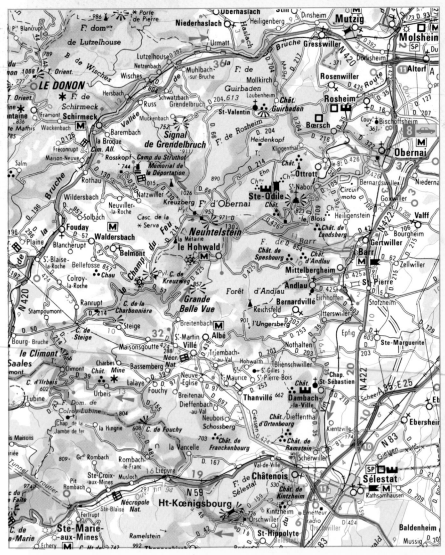

TOUR 8 - 160KM
ROUTE DU VIN

The first part of the tour travels down part of Alsace's Route du Vin, which runs along the foothills of the Vosges from Marlenheim to Thann. Neatly groomed vineyards are squeezed between the forest mountains behind them and the walls of old medieval villages. The tour starts at the picturesque old town of Obernai, and then turns west and climbs into the Vosges, winding its way over mountain tops and plunging down into deep valleys, before lastly passing one of the grimmest reminders of World War II in the whole of France.

ROUTE DIRECTIONS

Leave Obernai on the **D109**, and just beyond St-Nabor turn on to the **D33** and continue to Mont Ste-Odile.

Leave Mont St-Odile on the **D854** and continue into

Barr's excellent range of wines provide it with a just cause for celebration

Barr. Take the **D362** to Mittelberg-heim, and then turn right to Andlau. Take the Route du Vin towards Epfig, the **D603**, and at the **N422** turn back towards Itterswiller. At Itterswiller turn left on the **D35** and continue through Nothalten to Dambach-la-Ville.

Leave Dambach by the south gate and turn right on to the **D35** towards Dieffenthal. On the slopes above are the two ruined castles of Ortenbourg and Ramstein.

towards le Climont (966m). At the junction with the **D50** turn right and continue on the **D214**. At the junction with the **D57** turn right, and then join the **D425**, which leads past the Col de Kreuzweg and drops down into le Hohwald.

Take the **D426** out of Hohwald and at Welsch-bruch turn left on to the **D130** towards Neutelstein. Follow the **D130** through Neuntelstein, and continue on to the extermination

Continue on the **D35** through Scherwiller to Châtenois. From here take the road to Kintzheim, and then the **D159** to Ht-Koenigsbourg. From the castle, take the **D48** to Lièpvre, and then the **D48i** through Rombach-le-Franc and over the Col de Fouchy. Continue on towards Fouchy, and at the entrance to the village, turn left on to the **D39** signposted to Col d'Urbeis (602m). At the col, turn right on to the **D214**

Traditional timer-framed houses in Barr

camp, Natzwiller-Struthof, and into Schirmeck.

Leaving Schirmeck, take the smaller road, the **D392**, to Mutzig through Hersbach and Urmatt.

Just before Heiligenberg, turn right on to the **D704** to Mollkirch and left on to the **D216** just before Klingenthal. Follow the **D216** through Boersch and take the **D322** back into Obernai.

PLACES OF INTEREST

MONT STE-ODILE

See page 64.

BARR

Barr, on the 'Route du Vin' that runs from Marlenheim to Thann, is a charming village with winding streets between the over-hanging roofs of half-timbered houses. It produces an excellent selection of good wines.

The museum in the Folie Marco has an interesting collection of pottery and displays on local life in the area, including hauled sledges on which felled timber was once brought down special log trackways from the forest.

ANDLAU

A walk round the ramparts here is an hour well spent on a bright day. The largely 17th-century abbey church has an 11th-century crypt and a marvellous stone frieze round the exterior of the building, with naïve carvings of Adam and Eve, mermaids riding on fish, demons punishing dishonest merchants and tales from Nordic sagas. It is undoubtedly one of the loveliest Romanesque jewels of Alsace.

DAMBACH-LA-VILLE

Prettiest of the *villages fleuris* along the 'Route du Vin', Dambach still has three of its old defensive towers, two gates and part of the walls. It could be, however, that the excellence of the local wines has more than a little to do with the influx of summer visitors.

A forest road leads off the D35 up to the Chapelle St-Sébastian, which has a Baroque sculpted wooden altar screen.

CHATEAU DE KINTZHEIM

Within the ruined 15th-century château is housed a collection of many different species of birds of prey, including eagles, condors and vultures. Demonstrations of their flying and hunting skills are given during the tour.

NATZWILLER/ STRUTHOF

A truncated hollow white column commemorates the 10,000 prisoners who died here between 1941 and 1944. It was the only extermination camp built by the Nazis on French soil. Several grim build-ings remain, one now housing a museum.

Dambach-la-Ville provides many opportunities to sample the local wines

St-Baslemont

The centuries-old oak forest of Darney in the southern Vosges shelters a number of interesting villages. Notable for its château-fort is St-Baslemont, 12km south-east of Vittel.

The forest of Darney, which for centuries supplied wood to fuel the local glass industry, is now a place of ancient trees, still lakes and mysterious calm. Above the tree-tops rises the church tower of St-Baslemont, together with the two round towers of its 14th-century castle.

Medieval on the outside, with the full panoply of military defences, the château and its courtyard were trans-formed during the Renaissance period into an elegant manorhouse, with a steep, high roof and extensive outbuildings.

The 16th-century church, which is actually dedicated to St John the Baptist rather than St-Basle, contains a notable reredos.

In the Vallon de Chèvre-Roche, to the south-east of the village, are the remains of a hermitage which was presumably St-Basle's dwelling place, but the only church dedicated to him is to be found in Lignéville, just south of Vittel.

St-Jean-d'Ormont

Nestling at the end of a little valley, its church bell-tower silhouetted against the dark pine woods, this ancient settlement lies 6km north-east of St-Dié.

There has been a chapel at St-Jean d'Ormont since the 7th century, when Déodas founded a monks' cell high in the mountains. He named this spot Sanctus Johannes de Hurimonte.

The village was spared much damage in both the First and Second World Wars, though it saw its fair share of fighting during the Thirty Years War. The older part of the village, along the Ban de Sapt, has some lovely houses dating from the early 17th century. Around the church are houses built by the families who moved into the village as workers in the tannery, sawmills and a small local copper mine, back in the 1830s.

SCY-CHAZELLES

Two picturesque little vigneron villages overlooking the valley of the Moselle, just 6km west of Metz.

Scy-Chazelles consists of Scy up on its hill and Chazelles with its Romanesque fortified church dedicated to St Quentin below. Since 1809 they have formed one commune, largely inhabited by wealthy *vignerons* from Metz.

The narrow winding streets are lined with fine 18th- and 19th-century houses and punctuated with fountains, with every now and then a glimpse of the superb view over the valley of the Moselle. Each village has its ancient forti-fied church, but that of Chazelles is more remark-able. A 12th-century foundation, it is an interesting example of the defensive arrangements of the period when it was fortified, in the 14th century. In the transept crossing of the church, beneath a plain marble slab with a bronze medallion, rests the body of the 'Founder of Europe', Robert Schuman, buried here in 1963. His house, across the street, is now a museum, open in the mornings only.

SESSENHEIM

A pretty agricultural village between the Rhine and the forest of Haguenau, Sessenheim is 15km east of Haguenau.

The name of Goethe will always be closely linked with Sessenheim. In 1770 Goethe came with a fellow law student to visit the Pastor Brion at Sessenheim, fell deeply in love with the pastor's younger daughter, Frédérique. She returned his love, and for the following year the pair lived a tenderly romantic idyll that inspired some of Goethe's most lyrical poetry.

In the inn beside the Lutheran church is displayed a collection of docu-ments and portraits tracing the course of this famous romance.

At the end of this time, however, Goethe had to return to Frankfurt to

There are many tempting opportunities to try the traditional local specialities of the region

continue his studies. Frédérique was not to see Goethe again for another eight years, but the flame of love was never re-kindled.

Where once the dukes of Lorraine minted their coinage, where tanneries, mills and fishing flourished, the visitor can now conjure up some of the atmosphere on a quiet walk round this welcoming little community.

Today, half-timbered houses line the quiet streets of Sessenheim, which are all geraniums and begonias in the sum-mertime. Along the arcade outside the Mairie, is a romantic mural of the two lovers. The church key may be borrowed from here to visit the severely plain Lutheran church.

SIERCK-LES-BAINS

On its loop in the Moselle, near the frontier between France, Germany and Luxembourg, picturesque little Sierck-les-Bains has grown up at the foot of an 11th-century castle. It lies 18km north-east of Thionville.

The Tour de l'Horloge, on the Quai des Ducs de Lorraine, is part of the town defences erected in 1294, and remained the town gate until the 15th century.

It was given its clock after a siege in 1643, and served as a prison before becoming a museum and the Syndicat d'Initiative. Details of Sierck's many hidden Renaissance houses as well as the 15th-century church and 11th-century castle are available from here. The Tour des Sorcières and the Porte Nente are also vestiges of the 13th-century fortifications that once surrounded the largely medieval and Renaissance streets that tumble and twist up to the castle.

SOULTZBACH-LES-BAINS

This quiet little medieval village in the Vosges was once a celebrated spa – a prosperous past to which its imposing buildings still bear witness. It is 12km west of Colmar.

SELESTAT

BIBLIOTHEQUE HUMANISTE

Sélestat is just off the 'Route du Vin', south of Obernai.

The town's greatest glory is its library, founded in 1452 as part of the Humanist School that flourished here during the 15th and 16th centuries. It contains a precious collec-tion of manuscripts and early printed books,

This peaceful village of some 700 inhabitants, close to the confluence of the Soultzbach and Fecht rivers, was first mentioned for its salt springs in 1211.

By the 17th and 18th centuries illustrious visitors such as Archduke Leopold of Austria and even Casanova were coming here to take the waters, and fine buildings sprang up, to house the spa and lodge visitors. This thriving trade continued until the Revolution, and there is still a source of sparkling spring water here, now owned and exploited by Perrier.

The Rue des Ramparts, which follows the course of the village's medieval fortifications, leads to the centre of the village, and is lined with substantial 18th-century half-timbered houses. The parish church, heavily restored, contains three remarkable baroque altarpieces, carved by the celebrated local sculptor Jean-Baptiste Werle between 1720 and 1740.

VILLE-SUR-SAULX

A tranquil village in a shallow wooded valley, one of a number of pretty settlements along the River Saulx. 13km south-west of Bar-le-Duc.

Ville-sur-Saulx was the centre of a metal-working and paper industry in the 16th century, which accounts for the many Renaissance buildings hiding along its village streets. Here, unusually, the château is down by the riverbank and the long main street stretches along the ridge overlooking it. The houses are nearly all built in the pale yellow local stone, hewn into carefully measured blocks. The château is a square Renaissance building with four corner towers.

THE STORK OF ALSACE

Traditionally believed to bring good luck, the stork has long been the emblem of Alsace. The birds arrive in March after spending their winter in western Africa, and proceed to rebuild the same nests that they use from year to year – circular structures about a metre wide, perched on roofs, gables and chimneys. In the middle of August, when the breeding season is over and the young have been reared, they set out again for Africa, completing an annual round trip of more than 11,000km. Yet today the Alsatian stork is more likely to be found portrayed in the decorative arts of the region than alive in nature. Stork hunting in Africa and the growing scarcity of frogs, their traditional prey in Alsace, have drastically reduced the migratory population, and a recent census found only 30 pairs. You can still see inhabited nests at villages such as Sélestat, but many stand empty. In response to the crisis, Hunawihr has developed a centre for breeding non-migratory storks.

---

including the *Lectionnaire mérovingien* dating back to the 7th century, and *Le Livre des Miracles de Ste Foy* from the 12th century.

The collection also includes 2,000 books that once belonged to Beatus Rhenanus, a friend of Erasmus. A selection from the library's collection is usually on display.

ST-JEAN-SAVERNE

L'ECOLE DES SORCIERES

Near the Chapelle St-Michel just north of St-Jean-Saverne, north-west of Saverne, is a strange rock. Take the road from St-Jean to St-Michel and turn left to the chapel after 1.5km.

To the right of the chapel at the end of a promontory is a rock platform, the 'école', in the surface of which a circular depression has been hollowed out. According to legend, witches congregate on the rock at night in order to cast their evil spells. Having done this, they then move on to a cave under the chapel itself. There is a superb view from the rock across Alsace to the Black Forest in the distance.

A natural feature with a supernatural purpose?

SECRET FRANCE
THE LOIRE

Extending to the Atlantic coast in the west and to Burgundy in the east, within easy reach of the Channel ports and Paris, the Loire region is probably one of the best known and at the same time one of the least known regions in France. Away from the banks of the great river and its magnificent and justly famous châteaux are numerous areas and lesser rivers that are just as beautiful and interesting as those along the Loire itself.

The real character of the area is found in the more remote areas off the tourist route, still hidden on minor roads and often located in the less familiar parts, such as the river's south bank between Angers and Saumur, and along its tributaries the Vienne, Indre and Cher. In ancient, sleepy villages life continues as it has done for centuries, agriculture being a more important feature of local life than tourism. One of the characteristics of buildings in the region is the soft white tufa stone, used for construction and for ornamentation, and which is quarried from the hills along the southern bank of the Loire.

To the north of the Loire is the valley of the River Loir, in some ways more attractive that its namesake with a final 'e'. Delightfully uncrowded, it winds through water meadows and gentle woodland, its banks decorated with fine towns and villages and a good variety of châteaux of its own. It is an old and unchanging landscape in which the soft stone of the buildings seems an integral part. The long history of civilisation in the region is also echoed by the great variety of primitive and troglodyte dwellings, secret houses carved from the rock, that occur in many parts of the Loire region.

To the west, the region takes on a rather different character. Hauntingly beautiful salt-marshes, with their unique colouring and fascinating wildlife, give way to long stretches of sandy beaches along the Atlantic coast, dotted with smart resorts and quiet harbour towns. To the south of the Loire is the mysterious area of the Sologne, a secret and hidden region of marshes and moorland, spread with lakes and plantations of birch, pine and Spanish chestnut. It has developed distinct characteristics of its own and is a paradise for hunters and fishermen.

brochet de Loire

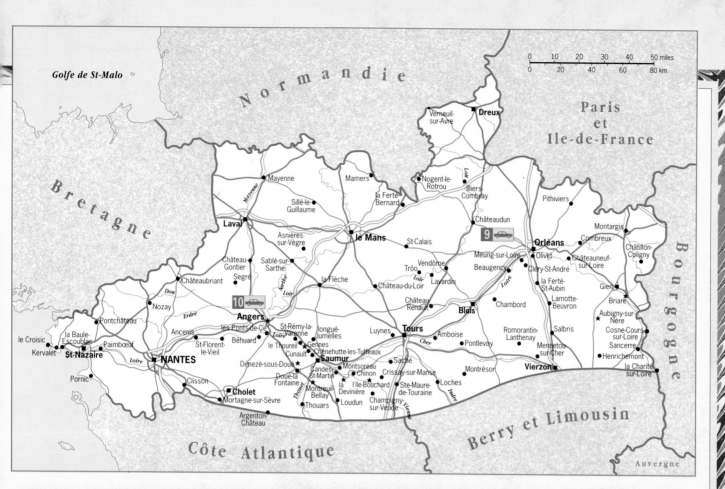

Golfe de St-Malo

N o r m a n d i e

Paris et Ile-de-France

B r e t a g n e

Bourgogne

Mayenne
Mamers
Verneuil-sur-Avre
Dreux
Nogent-le-Rotrou
Illiers-Combray
Pithiviers
Sillé-le-Guillaume
la Ferté-Bernard
Châteaudun
Montargis
Combreux
Laval
le Mans
St-Calais
Orléans
Châtillon-Coligny
Asnières-sur-Vègre
Meung-sur-Loire
Olivet
Châteauneuf-sur-Loire
Château-Gontier
Sablé-sur-Sarthe
Vendôme
Cléry-St-André
Châteaubriant
Segré
Trôo
Beaugency
la Ferté-St-Aubin
Gien
la Flèche
Château-du-Loir
Lavardin
Briare
Nozay
Château-Renault
Blois
Chambord
Lamotte-Beuvron
Aubigny-sur-Nère
Angers
les Ponts-de-Cé
Tours
Amboise
Romorantin-Lanthenay
Salbris
Cosne-Cours-sur-Loire
Ancenis
St-Rémy-la-Varenne
longué-Jumelles
Luynes
Pontlevoy
Mennetou-sur-Cher
Sancerre
Pontchâteau
St-Florent-le-Vieil
Béhuard
le Thoureil
Gennes
Saché
Vierzon
Henrichemont
la Baule-Escoublac
Paimbœuf
Denezé-sous-Doué
Chênehutte-les-Tuffeaux
Saumur
Montsoreau
Chinon
Crissay-sur-Manse
Montrésor
la Charité-sur-Loire
le Croisic
Kervalet
St-Nazaire
Doué-la-Fontaine
Candes-St-Martin
la Devinière
l'Ile-Bouchard
Ste-Maure-de-Touraine
Loches
Pornic
Clisson
Montreuil-Bellay
Loudun
Champigny-sur-Veude
Cholet
Mortagne-sur-Sèvre
Thouars
Argenton-Château

Côte Atlantique

Berry et Limousin

Auvergne

Above, while the Loire region is famous for its châteaux, some of these are less ostentatious and showy than others, while retaining a style that is distinctive

Above right, another local speciality in past centuries was cave-dwelling – this is at Denezé-sous-Doué
Right, still living close to the land

ARGENTON-CHATEAU

Nestling among the trees above the confluence of the Rivers Argenton and Ouère, this tranquil village is surrounded by historic monuments, with a wide variety of water sports also available. 17km north of Bressuire.

Of the château which gave this sleepy stone village its name, only the 15th-century guardroom and a few

A charming room with a view at Asnières-sur-Vègre

walls survive. Other reminders of the village's long history are the 14th-century Porte Gaudin, and the 13th-century church of St Gilles with its intricately carved Romanesque porch. The houses of the village, solid, granite-built and slate-hung, are a reminder of its former prosperity, founded on a flourishing textile industry.

Three kilometres to the

north are the pink granite, moated ruins of the Château d'Epaubinay, with the region's only remaining windmill nearby. Five kilometres to the east is the spectacular Pont de Grifférus, where the Argenton foams through a dramatic gorge.

ASNIERES-SUR-VEGRE

The Sarthe is a delightfully rural river, winding northwards from Angers through an attractive but little-known landscape, collecting the waters of equally pretty tributaries. One of these is the River Vègre, on which lies Asnières, 10km north-east of Sablé-sur-Sarthe.

A lovely little river following a secret route through wooded hills, the Vègre is most accessible as it makes its way through the golden stone village of Asnières. At the heart of the village is a steeply humped medieval bridge, flanked by an old mill and a fine 17th- and 18th-century turreted manor house. Stone houses with their typically steep roofs line the streets, and near the bridge is the church, built between the 11th and 13th centuries. It is celebrated for its medieval wall paintings, powerfully evoking images of hell and New Testament scenes.

They are an indication of the village's former importance, which is also underlined by the Grand Gothic building of the Cour d'Asnières, a splendid edifice with highly decorative windows built in the 13th century as a courthouse.

SECRET PLACES

ANGERS

MUSEE LURCAT

Brilliant modern tapestries displayed in a medieval hall

Housed in the splendid 12th-century hospital of St-Jean – the oldest hospital in France – on the north side of the Maine, near the Pont de la Haute Chaîne, this museum is dedicated to the work of the artist, painter and designer Jean Lurçat (1892–1966).

Inspired by the magnificent 'Apocalypse Tapestry', which narrates the Gospel of St John and hangs in the town's formidable 9th-century

château, Lurçat initiated the revival of the art of tapestry.

Adorning the walls of the great hall in this fine medieval building are a series of 10 tapestries, known collectively as 'Le Chant du Monde' (The Song of the World), and totalling 80m in length. Completed in 1966 after nine years of weaving, Lurçat's enigmatic work is full of brightly coloured symbols and allegories on

The present village developed in the 15th century, after Louis XI, saved from shipwreck by the intercession of the Virgin, ordered the building of the present church. This is a remarkable building, standing on an outcrop of rock, and with some of its walls carved from solid rock. Its timber roof is like an upturned boat, and there are unusual carved choir stalls. Close by is a small and decorative mansion of the same date, where Louis apparently stayed when visiting his church.

CANDES-ST-MARTIN

Among the many sites of religious significance along the banks of the Loire and its tributaries is Candes-St-Martin, 15km south-east of Saumur.

This old-fashioned village stands on the steep southern side of the river valley, at the confluence of the Vienne and the Loire. St-Martin, the patron saint of soldiers who cut his cloak in half to help a beggar, died here in AD397, and the grand church that dominates the village was built as a shrine to him. Dating from the 12th and 13th centuries, it was fortified some 200 years later. The entrance, through a vaulted porch, leads into a high, well-lit nave.

From the steep cobbled street beside the church a path leads upwards past old cottages, the ruins of a mill and overgrown stone quarries, to a level field high above the village, from where there is a memorable view over the Loire and the Vienne, with the wine-growing slopes of Bourgueil in the distance.

BÉHUARD

Picturesque cottages cluster round the church in the island village of Béhuard

From the pre-Christian era onwards, shrines were erected along the River Loire in order to protect boatmen. One of the most famous is at Béhuard, 15km south-west of Angers.

Béhuard stands on a rocky island in the middle of the Loire, a cluster of medieval and later cottages surrounding the 15th-century church. Established initially as a shrine to a pagan river goddess, the site was Christianized in the 5th century with a small oratory where prayers could be offered for mariners in peril.

a sombre background of black. As Lurçat was a humanist, many see the tapestry as the 'answer' to St John's prophecy in Revelations of the end of the world; others view it as a modern interpretation, while some simply find it difficult to decipher. Lurçat's informative and well-illustrated pamphlet should enrich understanding of the message in this classic piece of work.

GENNES

MEMORIAL TO THE CADETS OF SAUMUR

A moving tribute to a brave action during World War II

14km north-west of Saumur, Gennes is built at the top of a steep knoll, crowned by the 12th-century steeple and ruins of St-Eusèbe church. Tucked away at the base of the ruined south wall are the graves of several cadets from the Saumur Cavalry Academy who were killed here during World War II.

In June 1940 Colonel Michinon, the commander of the Academy, refused to withdraw to Montauban, and instead deployed his tiny force of 1,200 men and 800 cadets to hold three bridges – Montsoreau, Gennes and Saumur – along the Loire, against the advancing German army. With a limited assortment of dated weaponry, the Academy force checked the Germans' progress by blowing up tanks and destroying the mined bridges as the Germans rushed forward.

Surprised by such effective resistance, the Germans took 24 hours to reinforce and pontoon the river. The cadets only surrendered when they had run out of ammunition, and their brave stand has been compared to the Charge of the Light Brigade.

By delaying the German advance, the cadets enabled Marshall Pétain and his French forces to escape deeper into southern France.

LESSER-KNOWN LOIRE CHATEAUX

The Loire region has over 1,000 grand châteaux, yet many tourists visit only a handful of the best known, such as Blois, Amboise, Azay-le-Rideau or Chenonceaux. If you want to get away from the crowds, however, you might try the Manoir de la Possonnière near Couture-sur-Loir (don't confuse the river with the Loire itself), or le Gué-Péan, hidden away in a valley near Montrichard, or the Chanteloup pagoda, an 18th-century folly on the edge of the Forêt d'Amboise. If you are near Orléans, why not seek out the partly medieval château at Meung-sur-Loire, where the poet Villon was imprisoned – and if you are near Angers, you should certainly pay a visit to the moated, 15th-century Château du Plessis-Bourré.

CHAMPIGNY-SUR-VEUDE

The châteaux of the Loire are astounding in their number and variety, yet there used to be even more. Among those that have disappeared was the great mansion at Champigny-sur-Veude, 19km south-east of Chinon.

Early in the 16th century a mighty and splendid château was built at Champigny, in the wooded valley of the Veude. A hundred years later it was demolished on the orders of Cardinal Richelieu, who feared that it would overshadow his new château being built a few kilometres to the south, in the new town that came to be called Richelieu. At Champigny only some outbuildings survived, along with a chapel, and it is this extraordinary building that makes the village so memorable.

Champigny-sur-Veude is a pleasant place, but its focus is the Renaissance masterpiece that stands at its heart. This glorious chapel in glowing white stone perfectly expresses the spirit of the early Renaissance in France, in its blend of proportion and balance. Inside is a marvellous collection of 16th-century stained glass, and a fine 17th-century sculpture of Henri de Bourbon.

CHATILLON-COLIGNY

With its old locks and cottages, the 17th-century Canal de Briare is a gentle way to explore the country between the Loire and the Seine. A good place to start is Châtillon-Coligny, 25km south-east of Montargis.

Once a medieval walled town of some importance, Châtillon-Coligny is now a restful old village. Much of the old wall survives, along with the battered remains of a 12th-century château that was rebuilt in the 16th century and then destroyed during the Revolution. Quiet streets of 17th-and 18th-century houses hint at the village's prosperity following the arrival of the Canal de Briare, which passes just west of the centre.

In its heyday the canal carried a steady stream of barges. Hauled initially by teams of men and then by horses, they carried to Paris cargoes of wine, pottery, timber, coal and iron. Today, the canal is busy with pleasure boats, many of which stop to enjoy this pleasant old village.

CHENEHUTTE-LES-TUFFEAUX

Much of the characteristic white tufa stone of Loire buildings came from quarries cut deep into the hills that flank the river's southern shore, such as those around Chênehutte-les-Tuffeaux, 8km north-west of Saumur.

One of the most characteristic features of the village is the white tufa stone of its buildings, a material used both for building blocks and architectural ornament. In earlier centuries Chênehutte was an important centre for the stone industry, as its name indicates. The village is built against a backdrop of steep, wooded hills, which are riddled with the quarries and caverns from which the tufa stone was

BRIARE

EIFFEL'S CANAL AQUEDUCT

Briare lies south-east of Gien.

The little town of Briare is associated with the Briare–Loing Canal, a 104km-long waterway that was built to link the Loire to the Seine, thus extending the Canal Latéral to reach the Channel and the North Sea, and thus the waterways of northern Europe.

Construction began in the 17th century and took 200 years to complete.

The work included such engineering achievements as the building of 52 locks and the spectacular Pont Canal, a fine 'Art Nouveau' iron aqueduct that spans the Loire at Briare.

The aqueduct was designed by Gustave Eiffel in 1896 to enable barges to

extracted. Many of these were subsequently used as habitations, while others served as stores. Wine and mushrooms are now among the commodities that benefit from these old caves.

Typically of the villages of this region, Chênehutte has a pretty but simple Romanesque church with a decorative carved doorway, and a range of old cottages that enjoy fine views across the Loire.

COMBREUX

The route of the 17th-century Canal d'Orléans, closed in 1954, is still easily followed from Orléans to Montargis, and preserves the atmosphere of France's rural past. A typical canalside village is Combreux, 11km north-east of Châteauneuf-sur-Loire.

The Canal d'Orléans, planned and financed by Louis XIV's brother, the Duc d'Orléans, was opened to traffic in 1692. It passes just to the north of this little farming village, and the overgrown locks are now mostly the province of local fishermen. A quiet village with narrow streets and terraces of cottages around the church, Combreux has one remarkable feature. Just across the canal is an astonishing Gothic-revival château, a glorious mass of pinnacles, spires and towers, all in brick with stone detailing. Dating originally from the 16th century but largely rebuilt during the 19th, this crumbling pile presents a most romantic skyline above the trees that line the canal.

CRISSAY-SUR-MANSE

The River Manse winds its way eastwards from the Vienne through an open landscape of rolling hills and forgotten villages, the best of which is Crissay-sur-Manse, 7km north-east of l'Ile-Bouchard.

Set on the steep northern side of the Manse valley, Crissay is a remarkable village, seemingly little changed since the Middle Ages. It is a cluster of delightful buildings in soft-coloured stone, dating largely from the medieval period to the 18th century, and enriched with a wealth of decorative

Quiet roads wind through the unspoilt old village of Crissay-sur-Manse, parts of which date back to the Middle Ages

architectural details that hint at former grandeur. The reason for this is the château, built in the 15th century but now a series of picturesque ruins surrounded by extensive fortifications in the fields above the village.

Walking the village's narrow streets provides a series of delights, with each corner revealing something new to see – the old village school, the church with its pointed stone spire, and the variety of houses with their turrets and dovecotes.

---

cross the Loire, avoiding the dangerous currents. It is the largest aqueduct in the world at 660m in length and – like Eiffel's more famous tower, in Paris – quite breathtaking. Ornately decorated pillars grace each corner, and visitors can walk the length of the aqueduct using the wide balustraded pavements on either side, which afford delightful views up and down the river and across serene countryside. Attractive lamp standards make it a splendid sight, particularly at night.

Boats still use the canal aqueduct and surrounding waters, and there is a *bateau mouche*, or tourist craft, for those wishing to explore the canal further.

L'ILE-BOUCHARD

RUINS OF THE PRIORY OF ST-LEONARD

L'Ile-Bouchard lies 15km west of Ste-Maure-de-Touraine.

Lying to the south of the town is the scenic ruin of the 11th-century Romanesque priory of St-Léonard, which was built on a hillock on the left bank of the river.

All that remains of the priory today is a remarkable apse of white tufa, with ambulatory and radiating chapels; its arcades were reinforced by unusual arches during the 12th century. The well-preserved carved capitals on four pillars are of particular interest, representing scenes from the Life of Christ. Various figures and creatures relate the story from the Annunciation to the Resurrection of Christ.

TOUR 9 – 120KM
THE SOLOGNE

The Sologne region, with its great tracts of wood and heathland, and its hidden rivers and lakes, is an acquired taste. Remote and undeveloped, it is renowned for its hunting and fishing, and for its distinctive gastronomy. The Sologne villages, buried deep in this secret landscape, enjoy a character all of their own and are well worth leisurely exploration. The tour starts from the great city of Orléans and travels through this unusual and unspoilt region, taking in pleasant river villages and examples of a wide range of architectural styles.

ROUTE DIRECTIONS

From the centre of Orléans head south on the **N20** in the direction of Vierzon. Cross the Loire. After 0.5km turn right on to the **D951**, in the direction of Cléry-St-André and Blois.

Intricate carvings on a statue of Joan of Arc in Orléans

Continue to Cléry, and at the main crossroads, in the town centre, turn right on to the **D18** towards Meung-sur-Loire. Cross the Loire and continue into the centre of Meung. From the town centre take the **N152** in the direction of Beaugency. Continue to Beaugency.

Leaving town, head south. Cross the Loire, and immediately after the bridge, bear right on to the **D925** towards St-Laurent-Nouan. After 6km, at a major crossroads, turn right on to the **D951** to St-Laurent-Nouan. Continue on to St-Dyé-sur-Loire.

In the centre of St-Dyé, turn left on to the **D112A** towards Chambord. Entering the park of Chambord, turn right at the first junction, then left

at the next junction, and follow the road round Chambord, then through the park to Thoury.

In the centre of Thoury, continue straight ahead on the **D33** to Crouy-sur-Cosson. Here bear right on to the **D103** towards la Ferté-St-Cyr. Keep on this road to Ligny-le-Ribault. In Ligny turn right, then left on to the **D61** to la Ferté-St-Aubin.

In la Ferté turn left on to the **N20** in the direction of Orléans. After 10km, turn right on to the **D326** towards St-Cyr-en-Val. At a large roundabout in St-Cyr take the **D14** towards Orléans-la-Source. Follow this road, passing the Parc floral de la Source, and Source du Loiret on the right, back into the centre of Orléans.

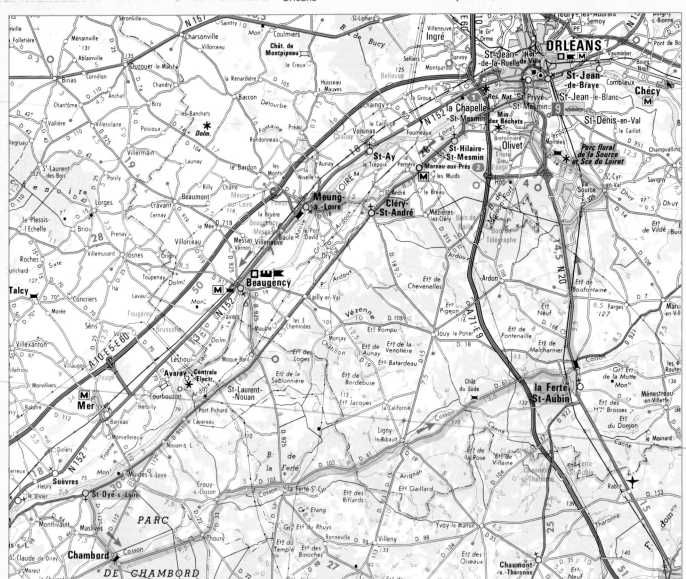

interior dates from the 19th century. The church of St-Liphard was built in the 12th and 13th centuries, and the fortified building adjacent to it is the remains of its venerable predecessor.

ST-DYE-SUR-LOIRE

On the edge of the park of the great château of Chambord, surrounded by fields of asparagus and terraces of vines, lies the old town of St-Dyé. Within its ancient encircling walls, the heart of the old town contains many fine and beautiful examples of turreted Gothic houses, together with richly decorated mansions in the Renaissance and classical styles.

Left, plants and traffic compete for space in the narrow streets of St-Dyé-sur-Loire.
Below, a welcome sight in la Ferté-St-Auban

LA FERTE-ST-AUBIN

The tall tower of the church of St-Aubin, parts of which date back to the 12th century, dominates the surrounding countryside. The low, timber-framed houses that cluster around the château, roofed with flat tiles, are among the finest examples of the traditional Sologne style of village architecture. The château, an imposing building, was constructed in the 17th century.

LA SOURCE FLORAL PARK

Covering 37 hectares, the park is a gardening enthusiast's delight, containing a wide range of types of plants and styles of planting, including parkland, woodland, formal flower gardens, a rock garden, shrubs and evergreens. It has been carefully planned so that the displays change with each month.

PLACES OF INTEREST

CLERY-ST-ANDRE

This modest but attractive village contains a jewel of a church, built in the Flamboyant style in the 15th century through the generosity of Louis XI, who loved the village. He and his queen were even-

tually buried in the church here. The statue of Louis is by the Orléans sculptor, Michel Bourdin (1622). On the other side of the nave is a tomb containing the heart of Charles VIII. The choir stalls were presented by Henri II.

MEUNG-SUR-LOIRE

From the banks of the Loire, where the old bridge

was repeatedly fought over during the Hundred Years War, this typical medieval fortified village climbs up the slope overlooking the river. The château, parts of which date back to the 13th century, was once the residence of the bishops of Orléans. Alterations were made in the 16th and 18th centuries, and much of the

CUNAULT

A wealth of Romanesque churches is to be found along the banks of the Loire and its tributaries. One of the finest stands in the centre of the little riverside village of Cunault, 13km north-west of Saumur.

Between Angers and Saumur the route along the Loire's wooded southern shore is punctuated by a series of fine churches, by far the most exciting of which is at Cunault. Built in the soft cream stone of the region, and dating from the 11th to the 13th centuries, the magnificent church was originally part of a priory. The exterior is a

powerful exercise in the Romanesque style, but even more impressive is the interior. Visitors enter through a door set high in the west front, and the vista thus revealed along the great vaulted nave with its flowing sequence of arches and pillars is unforgettable. Traces of medieval wall painting suggest that the interior was once very different.

HENRICHEMONT

Scattered throughout the remote landscape between the Loire and the Cher are isolated châteaux and villages that stand as memorials to the ambitions of once-powerful

aristocratic families. This is one such village, 28km north-east of Bourges.

Between the Loire and the Cher the landscape is remote and undeveloped, a wilderness of heath and woods broken by little rivers and hidden lakes.

Here it was, in the 17th century, that the Duc de Sully created Henrichemont as a Huguenot haven. The village he built was far from rustic however – more an exercise in sophisticated urban planning. At its centre is a large square, complete with decorative fountain, the meeting place for the eight roads that lead into the town, and all around are narrow streets laid out on a formal grid. Little has changed in this incongruous village.

KERVALET

From Nantes westwards to its estuary by St-Nazaire, the Loire seems to belong more to Brittany. Several villages preserve the traditional atmosphere of the saltmarshes and their industry, notably Kervalet, 8km west of la Baule-Escoublac.

The Atlantic coast is here characterized by resorts and smart fishing villages, but inland is the distinctive landscape of the saltmarshes, with its salt pans, sea birds and wonderful colours. Overlooking the marshes that stretch northwards towards Guérande, Kervalet has retained the particular flavour of this formerly remote and self-contained region. Around the Romanesque church are terraces of traditional stone-built cottages, largely unaltered since they were inhabited by the salt workers. Some are derelict, some have been smartly restored, and one or two are now restaurants or shops, but the essential spirit of Kervalet survives. The saltmarshes and their villages have a particular quality that is not immediately to everyone's taste, but their appeal, once appreciated, can easily become addictive.

The village of Luynes nestles below its solid medieval chateau

LAVARDIN

The course of the River Loir is marked by a series of lovely villages and small towns, and particularly exciting is that at Lavardin, 2km south-east of Montoire-sur-le-Loir.

Despite its protected status and obvious picturesque qualities, Lavardin is still primarily a working village. It is best to enter it along the wooded southern bank of the Loir, a secret approach that conceals the impact of the ruined 11th-century château until the last moment. Set on a craggy summit high above the surrounding woods, the ruins are the spectacular, battered remains of the medieval fortress of the Counts of Vendôme that defied many attackers, including Henry II and Richard the Lionheart. Below the château is the large 11th-century Romanesque church, notable for the range of its wall paintings. Below, the old stone houses of the village, dating from the 12th to the 16th centuries, spread gracefully down to the river and the old bridge.

SALT COUNTRY

The region known as La Grande Brière confronts the Atlantic coast between the mouths of the Loire and the Vilaine, which both flowed into the sea here until accumulated silt diverted them into their present courses. The result was an expanse of salt marsh dotted with granite 'islands' which became little centres of population. Until tourism created the Côte d'Amour and developed the resort of la Baule, the traditional activities of the Briérons were those suggested by the strange and uncompromising landscape: cutting peat and bog-oak; pasturing cattle and sheep to produce an *agneau pré-salé*; and shooting wildfowl, thus supplying duck for the regional speciality, *canard nantais*. The area between Guérande and Batz on the southern coastal promontory is salt-making country. Seawater is fed into canals and then into a series of progressively shallower lagoons until it reaches the *oeillet*, only a few centimetres deep. Here the salt crystallizes and can be skimmed off by the *paludiers*.

LUYNES

Despite the popularity of the Loire's major tourist sites, the discerning visitor can still find plenty of villages that are frequently overlooked. A typical example is Luynes, 19km west of Tours.

Set back from the Loire's northern bank in a gently undulating landscape covered with vineyards, Luynes is an enjoyably old-fashioned place nestling below the walls of its great château. This uncompromising 13th-century fortress is an impressive sight, particularly from the hills to the west, from where its great round towers can be seen to best advantage. Owned by the same family since the 17th century, it has

MENNETOU-SUR-CHER

East of Montrichard, though little known, the Cher is a lovely river, its banks marked by fine and decorative villages. Particularly unusual is Mennetou-sur-Cher, 16km north-west of Vierzon.

A medieval fortified village, complete with its 13th-century walls and guarded by three severe entrance gates, should be high on any visitor's list, yet few people come to Mennetou. The narrow winding streets, best explored on foot, are lined with 13th-, 15th- and 16th-century houses, all rather dilapidated, but offering a wide variety of architectural detail. Hidden in the centre is the church, originally part of the priory that once stood here.

The Cher flows to the south, and just outside the walls of Mennetou is the old Canal de Berry, part of a 261km network of narrow canals completed in the 1820s and finally closed in 1955. The old quays and a timber bridge keep alive the memory of this rural waterway and its horse-drawn barges.

MONTRESOR

The River Indrois, a short tributary of the Indre, boasts an architectural gem that would be far better known if it were on the banks of any of the great Loire rivers. It may be found 25km east of Loches.

Standing high above the wooded northern bank of the Indrois, Montrésor is set in a natural amphi-theatre. Its houses rise in irregular rows, half-hidden by trees and gardens, from the river to the château, a 16th-

In Montresor no opportunity is lost to decorate the streets with flowers

century fortress which was restored in the 19th century by a Polish count.

Elsewhere in the village are some fine 15th-century houses and a 17th-century wooden covered market. A fine 16th-century Renaissance mansion now houses the *gendarmerie*, and a number of old-fashioned shops. The delicate Gothic church has good Renaissance stained glass and woodwork, and the powerful tomb of the de Bastarnay family, original lords of the château.

never been opened to the public, and so Luynes has been spared the tourist hordes. Medieval and Renaissance houses decorate the narrow streets, and in the centre is the 15th-century wooden covered market.

In the hills to the north-east, 2km away, are the remains of a Gallo-Roman aquaduct, a striking structure whose original purpose is still hotly debated.

AUBIGNY-SUR-NERE

THE STUART CONNECTION

A little town with strong, historic Scottish links

On the D940 between Gien and Bourges. The signs along the road that read 'La Cité des Stuarts' lead to this picturesque, well preserved small town, nestling beside the River Nère.

Scottish connections with the town date back to 1423, when Charles VII gave Aubigny to John Stuart of Darnley, as a reward for his services against the English at the Battle of Baugé in 1421. Gentlemen and craftspeople from Scotland settled here as a result, establishing the glassworks and cloth mills that made the town prosperous.

The 15th- and 16-century Stuart château is now the town hall. Its entrance gateway dates from the time of Robert Stuart, and the vault displays the Stuart coat of arms.

Built by the Stuarts at the edge of the Forêt d'Ivoy, 11km south-east of the town, is the large, isolated Château de la Verrerie. In an idyllic setting beside a lake, visitors can view the graceful Renaissance gallery, the fine 15th-century chapel decorated with frescos, and various rooms containing furnishings dating from the Renaissance to the Louis XVI periods.

MONTSOREAU

Where the Loire flows from Touraine into Anjou, just below its confluence with the Vienne, there rises the romantic silhouette of the Château de Montsoreau. The village lies 11km south-east of Saumur.

Montsoreau's 15th-century château, half-fortress, half-mansion, rises sheer from the Loire's southern shore, a towering structure in creamy stone. It was home in Renaissance times to the lovely countess whose affair with the dashing Bussy d'Amboise was to inspire Alexandre Dumas to write the romantic tale of *La Dame de Montsoreau*.

The château now houses a museum devoted to the Goums, French cavalry units recruited in Morocco, and to the history of the Moroccan campaigns of Maréchal Lyautey. The village is grouped tightly on the hillside behind the château, a complex series of interwoven narrow streets that offer fine views over the Loire across a townscape of grey slate roofs and pale stone walls. To the south the hillsides are covered with vineyards and dotted with old windmills.

PONTLEVOY

Well placed on high ground between the Loire and the Cher, Pontlevoy's attractive domestic architecture is greatly enlivened by the presence of some surprisingly grand buildings. 8km north-east of Montrichard.

Pontlevoy lies at the heart of a rich agricultural region, and its houses look out over fields of fruit, vines and sunflowers. The first impression of a traditional farming village is deceptive, however, for the handsome carved details in white tufa stone that decorate

Above, intricate carvings decorate the interior of Pontlevoy abbey
Left, an old water pump

many doors and windows hint at grander things.

At its heart is a great abbey, founded in the 11th century, but what remains is largely 17th century, together with the ambitious but incomplete 15th-century church. In its heyday a famous centre of learning, the abbey was later used as a military school. Unexpected features include a massive stove covered with Delft tiles and – a recent addition – a museum of heavy lorries housed in one of the massive 19th-century buildings.

Pontlevoy was the birthplace, in 1825 of Auguste Poulain, the famous chocolate maker of Blois, who features in the museum.

DENEZE-SOUS-DOUE

TROGLODYTE CAVE, AND CAVE SCULPTURES

Dénezé-sous-Doué lies north of Doué-la-Fontaine.

The underlying rock in the immediate area of Doué-la-Fontaine is a soft, porous limestone, known as tuffeau or falum, and is riddled with quarries and caves. For centuries the underground caves have been excavated and exploited, as either underground defensive systems, or farms, barns, prisons and wine cellars. Caves hollowed out in riverside cliffs were used for housing, and continued to be inhabited as late as the 19th century.

At Dénezé-sous-Doué and at nearby la Fosse and Rochemenier there are some fine examples of this type of rural architecture. Furnished cave dwellings and old farm tools and machinery present a true picture of the life of a troglodyte.

At Dénezé-sous-Doué there is also a most extraordinary cave, its walls carved with symbols and grotesque figures depicting sexual antics. These unusual sculptures date from the 16th century and are probably the work of a secret society of stonemasons.

Deserted cave-dwellings reveal a secret past

SACHE

Many famous artists and writers have been attracted to the Loire region over the centuries, and some villages, like Saché, maintain the memory of these important visitors. 8km east of Azay-le-Rideau.

The attractive valley of the Indre winds its way eastwards from Azay, passing on its way to Montbazon a series of delightful villages. The first is Saché, built on a hillside around a large, open square, with streets running gently down to the river. To one side of the square is the small church, but far more prominent is the large, multi-coloured mobile by the American sculptor, Alexander Calder, who spent the latter part of his life here, until his death in 1976.

Saché's other famous resident was the writer Honoré de Balzac, who lived in the handsome grey stone château beside the river. Built between the 16th and 18th centuries, the château now contains a museum of Balzac memorabilia, including the room in which he wrote a number of his novels, including *Le Père Goriot*.

ST-FLORENT-LE-VIEIL

Rising above the south bank of the Loire, the peaceful village of St-Florent-le-Vieil contains a powerful reminder of its central role in a little-known civil war. 14km east of Ancenis.

It was at St-Florent that the Angevin Vendéen uprising by the White Monarchists was launched to turn back the tide of Republicanism on 12 March 1793, and it was here during the following October that the White Monarchist revolutionaries, their hopes in ruins, made what was effectively their last stand. Their leader was

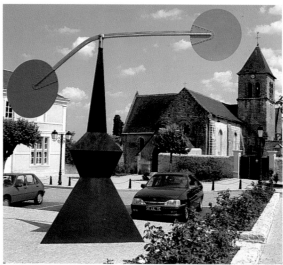

A mobile by Alexander Calder enlivens the village square in Saché

Bonchamps, and his role in bringing a sense of order to what had been a notably violent campaign is commemorated by a striking statue by the local sculptor David d'Angers. This stands in the church, above Bonchamps' tomb, and shows the dying Monarchist demanding that the lives of a group of Republican prisoners, among whom had been d'Anger's father, be spared. Powerful and moving, it is one of the best pieces of sculpture in the Loire.

The setting is also notable, in a fine early 18th-century church whose elegant classicism is out of place in its village surroundings. Set high on a rocky bluff above the river, the church is a fine sight, and from it there is a magnificent panorama over the landscape of the western Loire, and down to the village below, clustered round the bridge.

ST-REMY-LA-VARENNE

The real qualities of the Loire are to be found in such traditional, remote villages, where agriculture is much more important than visitors. 16km east of Angers.

The approach to the Loire from the south is across a rolling landscape of fruit fields, which drop suddenly down to the river, itself hidden until the last moment by thickly wooded banks. St-Rémy, on the southern bank, is a sleepy farming village devoted to an old-fashioned view of life in which tourism plays little part.

The large church dates back, in parts, to the 10th century, and its grandeur in a village setting is probably due to the famous Abbey of St-Maur, 2km to the east. Founded originally in AD542, the abbey has been steadily and continuously rebuilt, and now incorporates a Romanesque chapel, 17th-century cloisters, a splendidly formal façade, and another chapel, added in the 1950s with unusual stained glass. The old walls are covered with flowers, making it a delightfully attractive place.

LA DEVINIERE

RABELAIS MANOR

A famous satirist's delightful 15th-century country retreat

La Devinière lies 6km south-west of Chinon.

This simple old stone farmhouse is full of character, in a tranquil location overlooking the château of Coudray and the tiny hamlet of Seuilly. It was the country retreat of the Rabelais family, and the birthplace in 1494 of the monk, witty satirist and eminent physician, François Rabelais. Educated at the (now ruined) Benedictine abbey in Seuilly and at Montpellier University, Rabelais eventually became a doctor in Lyon. During this time he began writing fantasy and coarse, satirical novels that made serious comment on the changing times, as medievalism gave way to the Renaissance.

One particular tale, *Gargantua*, is set around the farmhouse and evokes Rabelais' vivid childhood memories of the valley, including the abbey and various local houses.

TOUR 10 – 145KM
ANCIENT VILLAGES OF THE GATINAIS

The abbey church of St Peter and Paul, Ferrières, with the neighbouring church of Our Lady

At the eastern end of the Loire valley, bounded by the Ile de France and Burgundy, is an area of gently undulating, quiet countryside that is much loved by hunters and fishermen, its woods being rich in game birds and its rivers abounding with fish. The area was once a royal hunting ground. Starting from Montargis, the tour proceeds through gentle countryside of rolling wheatfields, market gardens and flower-producing areas, visiting ancient villages with their beautiful old churches and ruined château, where a traditional and unique way of life continues unchanged.

ROUTE DIRECTIONS

From the centre of Montargis take the **N7** north towards Paris for 11km. At Puy-la-Laude turn right on to a minor road to Ferrières. In the centre of Ferrières turn left back on to the **N7**.

After 1km, at Fontenay-sur-Loing, turn left on to the **D32**, towards Nargis and Château-Landon. This is a dangerous turn off, so beware. Continue into Nargis, and there bear left on to the **D31** to Préfontaines. Continue on the **D31** to Corbeilles.

In Corbeilles, turn right on the **D94** to Bordeaux-en-Gâtinais. After 2km, turn left on the **D165**, towards Gondreville and Egry. At the **D975**, turn right. Then take the second left, the **D165** to Egry. Continue through Barville-en-Gâtinais and Boynes. 4km beyond Boynes, at Reigneville take the road to Yèvre-le-Châtel. Leave on

the **D923** to Yèvre-la-Ville. On rejoining the **D950**, turn right and continue into Pithiviers.

Leave Pithiviers on the **D921**, heading south towards Jargeau. Follow the road into the forest of Orléans, then turn left on to the **D243** at la Cour-Dieu to Ingrannes, and continue on the **D343** and **D143** to Vitry-aux-Loges. In Vitry, turn right and left towards Combreux just before crossing the Canal d'Orléans. At Etang de la Vallée turn right, then right again to Combreux.

From Combreux take the **D909** towards Sury-aux-Bois. After Sury follow the road to a junction with the **N60**, and turn left to Bellegarde.

Leave Bellegarde by the same road, bearing left on the **D44** immediately after leaving town. Continue through Beauchamps-sur-Huillard to Lorris. Leave Lorris on the **D961** to Thimory and Lombreuil and follow the road back to Montargis.

PLACES OF INTEREST

FERRIERES
Ferrières grew up around an abbey founded here in the 6th century, and which remained a flourishing religious community until the 18th century. The abbey church, built in the 12–13th centuries, remains. Near by is the château built by the Rothschild family in the 19th century to house their fabulous art collection, and owned by them until 1977. The château

and park were designed by Joseph Paxton, and the interior was lavishly decorated by Eugène Lami.

YEVRE-LE-CHATEL
On the main square of Yèvre-le-Châtel stand the ruins of its 13th-century fortress. The main gate leads through to the bailey, and viewing platforms in its north-west and south towers provide extensive views over the Gâtinais country to the east and the Beauce to the west. A wander through the narrow streets reveals ancient houses and pretty gardens hidden away behind high walls. The Romanesque church of St-Gault was built in the 12th century.

COMBREUX
See page 75.

BELLEGARDE
At the heart of the colourful village of Bellegarde, surrounded by a large moat, are the remains of the keep of the original 14th-century château. It

was extensively rebuilt in the 17th century, at which time windows and a slate roof were added. The doorway of the Romanesque church is decorated with fantastic carvings of foliage and animals. The interior houses 17th-century paintings by Annibale Carrachi, Pierre Mignard and Charles Lebrun.

LORRIS
Lorris, once at the heart of a royal hunting area, was granted a charter of freedom in 1122 by Louis VI. The 12th–13th century church of Notre-Dame exemplifies many periods and styles, having a Romanesque doorway, a Gothic nave, 15th-century choir stalls and a 16th-century organ loft. The town hall dates back to the 16th century, and the covered market, built in 1542, has an oak roof.

The local markets are full of a wide array of colourful produce

LE THOUREIL

There are many echoes of the Loire's former importance as a major navigation channel, notably the old river ports. An attractive example is le Thoureil, 20km north-west of Saumur.

As the seasons change, the fields spreading southwards across the hill that line the Loire are filled with sun-flowers, maize, soft fruit, apples and grapes. The same crops used to be shipped to Paris from le Thoureil when it was a flourishing port in the 17th and 18th centuries. A legacy of those days are the handsome stone houses that line the waterfront. Some, with fine carved architectural details and hidden gardens, were built by Dutch wine merchants.

At the village's western end is the pretty 12th-century church with its extremely unusual bell-tower, doubling as a lighthouse. The church contains notable woodwork, originally from the abbey of St-Maur-de-Glanfeuil.

TROO

Troglodyte dwellings are not uncommon in this region, and the picturesque village of Troo has some of the finest examples. 7km north-west of Montoire.

There are really two villages at Troo, the first a conventionally attractive place built up the steep northern bank of the meandering Loir, and the second a farming village. High above the river is the mound on which a château once stood, and near by is the Romanesque collegiate church of St-Martin, built in 1050. All around are the old houses, and at their heart is a musical well, so-called because of its fine echo.

Linking the two parts of the village are a series of precipitous paths and stairways, and narrow rocky passages that form the entrances to an astonishing variety of underground and cave dwellings. Some are ruined, some still inhabited, and some are only revealed by their chimneys, rising apparently from the ground. It is a secret and private world, continuing a tradition of troglodyte dwelling unbroken since prehistory.

Cave dwellings in Troo with all the trappings of picturesque cottages

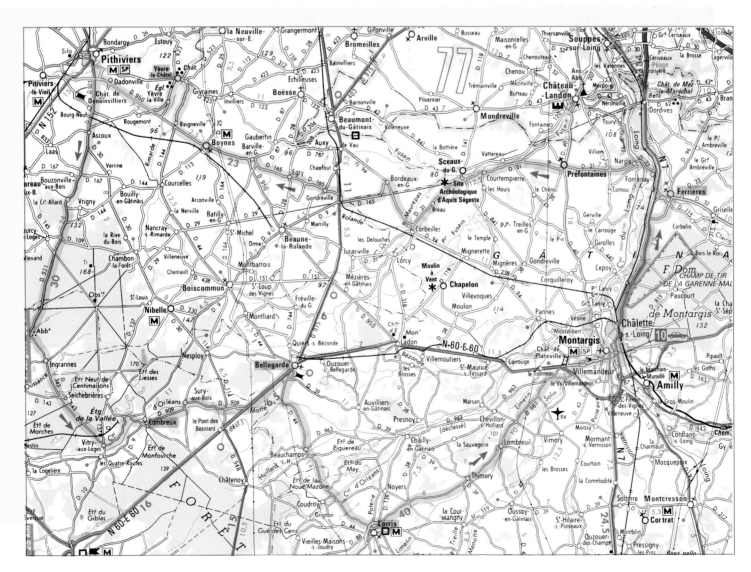

SECRET FRANCE
ILE DE FRANCE

Despite the widespread changes that have taken place across the face of the region during the 20th century, the Ile de France still retains much of its original charm and attraction for the visitor. Away from the bustle and turmoil of urban Paris, and within a comparatively short distance, vast expanses of countryside and woodlands continue to flourish, relatively unspoiled, in what is now one of the most densely populated areas of France.

This was the country's ancient heartland, the point from which the old kings gradually extended their power and influence over their rebellious nobles and subjects, and within its borders the Ile de France possesses an extraordinary wealth of historical castles and châteaux, along with great cathedrals and churches. Ranged alongside these are the small villages and hamlets whose former inhabitants once toiled in the fields and forests, served in the great houses and stables, and fought alongside their appointed lords in the many battles that punctuated past centuries. With the coming of the Revolution this way of life was to undergo a dramatic change. The end of the feudal system of government, the enfranchisement of the peasant population, and increasing wealth brought about by the Industrial Revolution gradually encouraged a movement away from these rural communities.

Once occupied by workers engaged in the local agriculture and crafts, many village houses are now the residences of those who commute daily to and from Paris, or who retreat here at weekends or for holidays. Although this change has had a major sociological and economic impact on life in the villages, the historic buildings and churches serve as a reminder of a past way of life.

Intersected by the River Seine and its major tributaries and dotted with outcrops of alluvial sand, the region displays a remarkable variety of scenery within its boundaries. By virtue of its long history of human settlement dating back over 5,000 years, it also offers a wealth of hidden treasures. Even those who believe they are already fully familiar with the attractions of Paris can still find that a casual stroll through its streets reveals some hitherto unnoticed and unexpected detail in the architecture of a building, or the fleeting glimpse of a concealed courtyard.

chêne d'Ile de France

Left, the confident 18th-century architecture of the Place St-Sulpice is an indication of the bold style so typical of Paris buildings

Above, an ancient windmill, marooned in a sea of corn in the fertile lands of the Ile de France, and, below left, agriculture on a smaller scale
Below, the Ile de France was traditionally the hunting and holiday ground for the Parisian nobility, and many magnificent palaces and estates remain

BARBIZON

The inspiration of the Barbizon school of landscape painters, this little village and its surrounding landscapes have retained all the atmosphere that attracted the great 19th-century painters. Barbizon lies 9km north-east of Fontainebleau.

Before it became an artistic colony, Barbizon was a village of wood-cutters who worked in the forest. Now the long, straight main street is a string of hotels, restaurants and art galleries, nearly all of which bear plaques commemorating their earlier distinguished inhabitants.

The uniquely wild landscapes of this area, and the proximity of both the dense forest of Fontainebleau and the open arable countryside of the Bière plain proved irresistible to the distinguished founders of the Barbizon school of painting. Devoted to landscape scenes and rural life, Théodore Rousseau and Jean-François Millet both came here in the mid-19th century, to be followed by a galaxy of other painters.

DAMPIERRE-EN-YVELINES

Dampierre's magnificent 17th-century château and park, the combined work of Mansart and the landscape gardener Le Nôtre, together make one of the most delightful domaines in France. 20km south-west of Versailles.

Standing at the heart of Dampierre is Mansart's superb moated and turreted château, its elegant frontage of red-brick architraves and honey-coloured stone rising from among beautifully maintained formal gardens. Built for the Duc de Luynes et de Chevreuse between 1675 and 1683, the château and its huge estate have remained in the hands of the Luynes family. Having survived the Revolution thanks to their good standing among the local population, the family was able to return to Dampierre after the fall of Robespierre. Both the château and the park are open to visitors.

The approach to the village of Dampierre itself is along a broad, poplar-lined avenue. The main street,

Many buildings in Barbizon boast their connections with the famous artists who have been inspired by the area

by contrast, is winding and narrow, meandering its way through the traditional stone-built, steep-roofed houses of this attractive village.

FLAGY

A medieval village laid out on a grid pattern, on the banks of the River Orvanne, Flagy is remarkable for its seven bridges and its ancient mill. It lies 10km south of Montereau-Faut-Yonne.

This unusual village with its incongruously urban grid-iron plan was laid out in the 12th century at the command of Louis VII, in order to mark the frontier between the crown lands and those of the Counts of Champagne.

The most intriguing consequence of this rigid plan can be seen beside the main communal wash-house, which gives an uninterrupted view of the seven little bridges by which as many

FRENCH BREAD

However loudly they lament the decay of their national cuisine, the French still take fresh and locally baked bread for granted. Even in places too small to support a bakery, you will find a *dépôt du pain* (a shop to which the nearest baker delivers) or, failing that, meet the baker's van on its round. In the bakeries themselves the shelves are still filled with sticks of white bread, crusty on the outside and airy inside, in the traditional shapes and sizes: the simple *pain*, the *baguette*, the *baton*, the *flûte* and the *ficelle*. Supplies are renewed several times a day, since French bread should be eaten within a few hours of baking: never keep it overnight unless you are willing to stoop to the old trick of dampening it and warming it in the oven. If you want something longer-lasting, try the darker, close-grained *pain de campagne*. And if you want something more substantial than a *croissant* with morning coffee, try a *brioche*, part-bread and part-cake, and what Marie Antoinette would have had in mind if she really said 'Let them eat cake'.

parallel streets cross the river. Two of them have their own wash-houses placed conveniently beside them. Beside the river on the main street stands Flagy's most remarkable building: the half-timbered 13th-century mill, surmounted by a roof of delicately shaded brown tiles, which is a rare example of traditional vernacular architecture. On the main square stands the 12th-century church with its distinctive turreted bell-tower.

GALLARDON

Standing on the edge of the area of plateaux and lakes known as the Hurepoix, Gallardon stands at the confluence of the rivers Ocre and Voise. 19km north-east of Chartres.

Viewed from across the Beauce plain, Gallardon is remarkable for two eye-catching structures. One is the ruin of a 12th-century circular keep, partly demolished in 1443, and now apparently leaning at a precarious angle. Its top-heavy silhouette, 38m high, earned it the nickname of the '*épaule*', from its resemblance to a shoulder of mutton.

The other is the remarkable church, built in the 12th and 13th centuries as part of a wealthy priory, and modified in the 15th and 16th centuries. Its severe Romanesque west façade offers a surprising contrast to the interior, which owes much to the architectural innovations of Chartres and St-Denis. The vast nave features a marvellous painted, barrel-vaulted roof with carved centre posts and tie-beams.

A charming oriental folly to be discovered in the park at l'Isle-Adam

GRISY-LES-PLATRES

Overlooking the arable lands of the Vexin and dominated, like all the villages of the Vexin, by its fine church, Grisy-les-Plâtres lies 18km north of Pontoise.

Grisy derives its curious name from the gypsum quarries that have been worked here since the Middle Ages. Until 1948 the village was served by a light steam railway, but this nod in the direction of industrialisation seems to have left its deeply rural atmosphere untouched.

In the Middle Ages Grisy was ruled by no fewer than 12 lords of the manor, one of whom has left behind a fine 10th-century farmhouse with traditional dovecot. The houses of the village, equally traditional, display a satisfying architectural unity. Above their tiled roofs towers the unusual and graceful bell-tower of the church of St-Caprais. Villages of the Vexin prided themselves on their churches, and St-Caprais is a fine example of 13th-century Gothic.

L'ISLE-ADAM

CHINESE PAGODA

The attractive town of l'Isle-Adam lies north-east of Paris.

In the landscaped park of the former Cassan estate, just off the Rue de Beaumont, stands a brightly decorated Chinese pagoda. During the 18th century, the estate was acquired by a financier, Monsieur Bergeret, who was an enthusiastic art-collector and patron of Fragonard. They travelled together to Italy in 1778, and the painter was subsequently commissioned to design this quaint and intricate building, which rises from the edge of a lake in the grounds.

TOUR 11 – 120KM
CHANTILLY AND THE ROYAL ABBEYS

The tour passes through the remnants of four forests to the north of Paris that are so far successfully resisting the pressures of the growing metropolis. In spite of their proximity to the centre of this urban mass, there are still substantial pockets of tranquillity to be savoured, particularly at the former religious centres of Royaumont and Chaâlis. Similarly, the elegant château at Chantilly and the medieval peace of Senlis both convey the spirit of a less frenetic period of history.

ROUTE DIRECTIONS

Follow the **N1** from Paris via St-Denis, signposted for Beauvais, and after 20km take the sliproad on to the **D64** which leads to the centre of l'Isle-Adam.

Leave l'Isle-Adam on the **N322**, which, after 3km, changes classification at the junction with the **N1** into the **D922**. Follow signs for Beaumont-sur-Oise. From Beaumont continue along the **D322** for 6.5km to the crossroads with the **D909**. Turn left, following signs for Chantilly and the Abbaye de Royaumont, and after another 1.5km turn right along the small side-road leading to the entrance to the abbey.

On leaving the abbey, rejoin the **D909** and continue along this road for 10km, following the signs for the town of Chantilly and the parking area adjacent to the château.

Return along the road leading back to the centre of Chantilly (1.5km) and turn left on to the **D924**, towards Senlis, and continue into Senlis (10km).

Leave Senlis on the **D330**, towards Mont-l'Evêque, and after passing through the centre of the village turn right on to the **N330**. This road cuts through the Forêt d'Ermenonville and after 6km, take the small turning on the left that leads to the parking area in front of the Abbaye de Châalis and its château museum.

On departure turn left to continue along the **N330** for 3km to reach the château and gardens of Ermenonville.

Fontainebleau forest stretches to the horizon

Take the **D922**, following signs for Luzarches and Beaumont-sur-Oise, and travel for 24km to Luzarches.

From Luzarches the **N16** leads back to the centre of Paris, 17km distant. Alternatively, continue along the **D922** through Beaumont-sur-Oise for 14.5km to the junction with the **N1** on the outskirts of l'Isle-Adam, near the start of the tour.

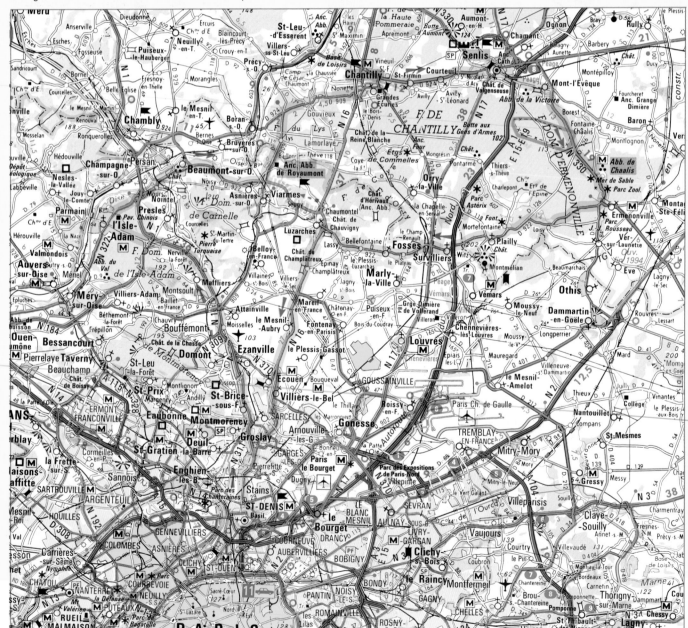

Left, The late Flamboyant south front of Notre-Dame, Senlis
Above, the château of Chantilly appears to float on the surrounding lake

PLACES OF INTEREST

ABBAYE DE ROYAUMONT

Founded in 1228, the abbey and its gardens still exude an atmosphere of retreat from the hurly-burly of the surrounding world, even though it is no longer used for religious purposes. The surviving buildings are now used as an international cultural centre.

The foundations of the original church, which was dismantled in 1791, can be seen on the lawn, with one of the staircase turrets still standing to give an indication of the building's former elevation.

CHANTILLY

One of the most graceful and splendid structures in the north of France, the combined 16th-century Petit Château and the 19th-century Grand Château resemble a fairy-tale palace rising from the waters of the surrounding lake. The former houses the magnificent library of manuscripts and brevaries assembled by the Duc d'Aumale, including the treasured 15th-century illuminated work, *Les Très Riches Heures du Duc de Berry*. The Grand Château displays some superb paintings, including Raphael's 'The Three Graces' along with the enormous pink diamond known as Le Grand Condé.

SENLIS

The whole of this venerable town is classified as an historic monument.

The 12th-century cathedral of Notre-Dame was built around the same time as the basilica of St-Denis in Paris, but was augmented in the following century with a slender 78m spire. The adjacent Château Royal, now in ruins, was once a main residence of the Merovingian and Carolingian monarchs, and England's Henry V and Catherine of France were married here in 1420.

ABBAYE DE CHAALIS

Originally founded as a Cistercian abbey by Louis VI in1136, this religious community thrived until the 18th century. The greater part of the original church and cloisters was destroyed during the Revolution, but in 1850 the ruins and grounds were purchased by Madame de Vatry, who transformed the 18th-century structure into a château. It now houses a museum of furniture, pictures and *objets d'art*.

GUIRY-EN-VEXIN

An archaeological centre for the whole of the Vexin, Guiry also boasts a fine château. It lies 19km north-west of Pontoise.

Archaeologists have found substantial evidence of human settlements in the area of Guiry as far back as the Neolithic age. Many of the wealth of artefacts discovered here (including a Neolithic tomb and three Merovingian burial grounds) and throughout the Val-d'Oise are now displayed in the museum in the village centre.

The splendid château was reputedly designed and built by Françoise Mansart in 1665, but bears no resemblance to his other work. In the grounds are the ruins of the original 15th-century castle, known as the Cabin. The present church, completed in the 16th century, stands on 13th-century foundations.

MAUPERTHUIS

Tucked away in the valley of the River Aubetin, between the woodlands and dairy pastures of Brie, this is a peaceful village with some surprisingly impressive buildings. 30km north-west of Provins.

Mauperthuis was the village where Théophile Gautier wrote *Mademoiselle de Maupin*, and his descriptions of it in the 19th century still find many echoes today. Elegant 18th-and 19th-century houses line the main street as you enter the village from Coulommiers. After a graceful square fronted by a semi-circle of houses, a road leads to the church with its unusual neo-classical façade. The houses are rich in little details, and it is a delight to wander the streets, spotting a dovecot here or a characteristic curved dormer window there.

NESLES-LA-VALLEE

Winding up the pretty valley of the Sausseron from Valmondois, the delightful D151 road reaches picturesque Nesles-la-Vallée at a point where the valley opens out. 15km north-east of Pontoise.

With its substantial farmhouses surrounded by high stone walls, Nesles-la-Vallée retains the tranquil, rural atmosphere of earlier centuries. A particularly fine farmhouse stands beside the church – two solid buildings forming a right angle, and a 16th-century dovecot in the courtyard. The fine Romanesque bell-tower of the church of St-Symphorien, originally free-standing, was linked to the rest of the building in the 12th century. Most of the remainder of the building dates from the early 13th century, a time when the influence of the building of great cathedrals like Notre-Dame was beginning to have its impact on the smaller churches of the region. The building was subjected to some less thoughtful restoration work at the end of the last century.

LA ROCHE-GUYON

Lying on the north bank of a great meander in the Seine this pleasant little village straggles along the road from Mantes-la-Jolie to Vernon, 12km to the west.

On the crest of a hill several hundred metres above la Roche-Guyon stand the menacing ruins of the massive 12th-century stronghold that controlled this part of the Seine valley and the neighbouring Epte to the west.

Below, at the foot of the cliff and linked to the great keep by steps hollowed out of the rock, is the graceful château, based on a 15th-century building but with a three-storey wing on the eastern side and a set of stables.

Set back from the main road in the middle of the village is the 15th-and 16th-century church of St-Samson, which houses the tomb of François de Silly, first Duc de la Roche-Guyon.

Further west, as the road to Gasny ascends to the escarpment, are some of the area's famous caves and troglodytic stables, carved into the soft chalk of the cliff face.

ROCHEFORT-EN-YVELINES

Lying in the shadow of the ruins of its 11th-century castle, Rochefort has retained much of its medieval heritage in its narrow streets and ancient houses, despite the proximity of the A10 and TGV line to Bordeaux. It lies 15km south-east of Rambouillet.

During the Hundred Years War Rochefort was witness to fierce fighting between the forces of Charles de Rivière, Lord of Rochefort and a faithful supporter of the French king, and Thomas Montague, Earl of Salisbury. Below the castle lies the church of the Assumption, with its Romanesque doorway and imposing bell-tower. Inside is the Renaissance Chapelle des Princes. Time-worn steps lead up to the church from the village, and from here and the castle ruins there is a good view back over Rochefort and its wooded surroundings.

At the heart of the peaceful village of Nesles-la-Vallée is the church with its fine Romanesque tower

TRIEL-SUR-SEINE

THE COCKEREL OF ST-MARTIN

Triel-sur-Seine lies south-west of Cergy-Pontoise.

One of the 16th-century windows in the church of St-Martin relates the legend of the Cock of Santo Domingo. A young pilgrim attracted the amorous attentions of a young lady who, when spurned, hid money in his boots and then accused him of theft. The young man was hanged, but, while passing the gallows, her father was hailed by the corpse and told the true story. When the father told the notary, who was eating a roast fowl at the time, the official refused to believe the tale unless his dinner came to life. The cockerel immediately sprouted feathers and sprang from the plate.

A tale told in a window of treachery revealed – by a corpse...

St-Loup-de-Naud

Standing on a hill which has been a sacred site for many centuries, St-Loup-de-Naud is celebrated for its remarkable church. The village lies 9km south-west of Provins.

The village of St-Loup-de-Naud is crowned by one of the best-preserved Romanesque churches in the Ile de France. Dedicated to St-Loup during the early 11th-century, it was completed in the 12th. The west portal, in the style of the one at Chartres cathedral, is the most outstanding feature of this remarkable building. Among its exceptionally expressive carved figures, St-Loup himself occupies pride of place, while the tympanum contains Christ in Majesty surrounded by the symbols of the apostles. The interior of the church is generally pure Romanesque and early Gothic, and the choir retains vestiges of 12th-century murals, poorly restored in the 19th century.

Other remains of the old priory can also be seen in the village, along with a number of medieval houses and, in front of the church, an elegant 18th-century mansion.

Vetheuil

With its picturesque setting on a graceful curve of the Seine and its attractive pale-yellow stone houses clustering around a Renaissance church, Vétheuil was a favourite subject of the Impressionists. It lies 18km east of Vernon.

Vétheuil's exceptionally attractive setting, the soft colours of the stone of its houses and tall church, and the changing quality and luminosity of its light reflected by the broad, smooth waters of the Seine made it irresistible to the early Impressionists. Monet lived here for several years, painting a number of studies of the church and its surroundings.

Built on a terrace overlooking the river, the church was started in the 12th century, and sarcophagi dating back to the Meringovian era were found beneath the present nave at the start of this century. Most of the building dates from the 16th century.

Of the fortified castle destroyed by Bertrand du Guesclin in 1364 only some of the underground passages remain.

Royal Parks

Visitors to the Palace of Versailles who tire of the glittering splendour can always escape to the cool greenery of its vast surrounding gardens and splendid parkland, landscaped by Le Nôtre.

Kings hunted in the forest of Fontainebleau long before they discovered the Loire valley. A royal castle stood here in the early 12th century, and in the 16th, François I imported Italian craftsmen to turn it into a palace. Visitors today, however, are as likely to be drawn by the forest as by the château: about 24,000ha, still unspoilt and most of it now owned by the state. A mixture of limestone and sandstone supports conifers, beeches and oaks as well as creating sandy wastes. The Route Ronde follows a hunting route established by Henri IV, but the best way to see the forest is by the 150km network of smaller trails and paths.

SECRET PARIS

1, RUE DE LA BANQUE

LUCIEN LEGRAND

A renowned grocery and wine shop that has been run by the Legrand family for more than three generations.

The bright-red façade dates from the Belle Epoque and is augmented by the glass jars of sweets that are displayed on the pavement. Inside, the entire ceiling is studded with corks from wine bottles.

19, RUE DE LA MONNAIE

LA SAMARITAINE

While the lovingly cared-for Art Nouveau interior of this huge department store, along with its wrought-iron balustrades, attract many visitors, the spectacular panoramic

cherchez le vignoble à Paris...

views across Paris from the ninth-floor open-air terrace cafeteria in Store No. 2 are relatively unknown.

A staircase leads up from here to a circular viewing platform where a ceramic legend indicates points of interest.

PLACE VENDOME

VENDOME COLUMN

Originally an equestrian statue of Louis XIV stood here, before Napoleon replaced it with a 43.5m bronze column to commemorate his military victories in Germany.

It is faced by 378 spiralling sheets of bronze obtained from melting down 1,200 cannons captured from the Russian and Austrian armies following the battle of Austerlitz. After the emperor's defeat at Waterloo, the Bourbons mounted their symbol of a fleur-de-lys atop the column. This, in turn, was replaced by a small statue of Napoleon in 1863.

During the Communard Insurrection of 1871 a mob led by the painter Gustave Courbet, who disliked the column for aesthetic reasons, brought the entire structure crashing to the ground. The Third Republic ordered Courbet to restore the monument at his own expense (the cost of which bankrupted him) and it was then crowned with the present statue of Napoleon dressed as Julius Caesar.

RUE DES ARCHIVES

A MACABRE LEGEND

The lower section of this street, leading to rue Rambuteau, formerly bore the curious name of 'The Street Where God Was Boiled'.

This unusual title derived from the anti-semitic legend of a moneylender, who reputedly lived here. He was alleged to have stolen a communion wafer, stabbed it with a knife and thrown it into a pot of boiling water, where to his astonishment and horror it began to bleed.

QUARTIER DES HORLOGES
(CLOSE TO RAMBUTEAU METRO)

THE DEFENDER OF TIME

Tucked away in a small courtyard, this sculpture in oxidised brass by Jacques Monestier, was inspired by the Rathaus clock in Munich.

As every hour strikes a majestic sword-wielding knight does battle with either a bird, a crab or a dragon (representing the elements of air, water and earth). At noon, 6 and 10pm, he is obliged to fight all three, but inevitably emerges victorious.

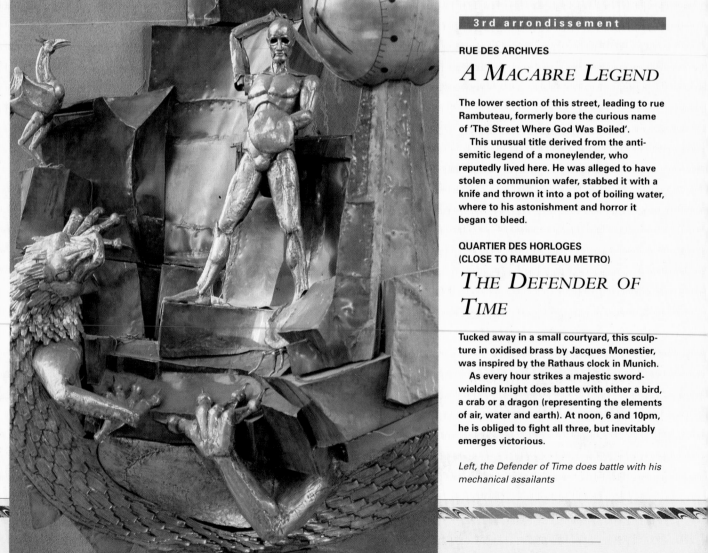

Left, the Defender of Time does battle with his mechanical assailants

8, RUE ELZEVIR

MUSEE COGNACQ-JAY

Ernest Cognacq, the founder of the Samaritaine chain of stores, and his wife Louise Jay first opened their collection of 18th century paintings, Meissen ornaments and jewellery to the public in 1920.

Paradoxically, Cognacq was not an art lover and boasted that he had never entered the Louvre in his life, but his collection contains some outstanding works by Boucher, Reynolds and Tiepolo. Watteau, Fragonard, Rembrandt and Gainsborough are among other artists represented.

Until recently, the collection was housed on three floors of the couple's townhouse but has now been moved to its present address. In spite of its attractions the museum remains off the familiar tourist route in Paris, and the collection can therefore be appreciated in relative privacy.

4th arrondissement

NOTRE-DAME

POINT ZERO

A simple, brass plaque embedded in the paved forecourt in front of the west door of Notre-Dame cathedral is, more often than not, overlooked by the many hundreds of thousands of tourists who visit the great cathedral each year.

All distances in France are measured from this compass star and throughout the entire country, roadside signs indicate in kilometres how far the traveller is from this specific point.

9–11 QUAI AUX FLEURS

The sculpted heads on the façade of this 19th-century building commemorate two of history's most famous lovers, Abélard and Héloïse.

In 1118, the young theologian Pierre Abélard, who had helped to found the University of Paris, fell passionately in love with one of his students, Héloïse. She was the niece of Fulbert, a canon of nearby Notre-Dame. Incensed by their affair and the resulting birth of an illegitimate son, Fulbert arranged for Abélard to be brutally attacked and castrated. In shame, Abélard entered monastic life at the royal abbey of Saint-Denis, while Héloïse became a nun at Argenteuil. But the lovers were reunited in death and now lie buried together in a grave at the Père-Lachaise cemetery in the 20th *arrondissement*.

Above, the oldest tree in Paris, now in need of artificial support
Right, all distances in France are measured from this unobtrusive point in front of the cathedral of Notre-Dame

45, RUE DES FRANCS-BOURGEOIS

A L'IMAGE DU GRENIER SUR L'EAU

A picture-palace of postcards, for the enthusiast or browser, on a historic street of grand houses.

More than 10 years of effort by the brothers Yves and Sylvain di Maria have gone into assembling this extraordinary collection of around one million vintage postcards of places in France and around the world. All of these are for sale, along with French publicity photos from the 1950s and reproductions of illustrations dating from the turn of the century.

5th arrondissement

SQUARE RENE-VIVIANI

THE OLDEST TREE IN PARIS

The false acacia (or *Robinia*) that dominates these pleasant gardens within sight of Nôtre-Dame was originally brought here as a seedling from French Guyana in 1680.

Now with the weight of its lower branches supported by crutches, it is surrounded by the remnants of statuary that originally adorned the nearby cathedral.

The attractive little René Viviani square itself (to be found just off the Quai de Montebello) also has one of the finest views in Paris of the cathedral of Notre-Dame, which can be seen standing on the Ile de la Cité, across the river.

47, QUAI DE LA TOURNELLE

MUSEE DE L'ASSISTANCE PUBLIQUE

After the Revolution, this 17th-century mansion became the central pharmacy for the city's hospitals, but now houses an unusual museum devoted to artefacts of French medicine and the hospital system, dating back to Roman times. Among the extraordinary exhibits, there are pewter syringes, copper basins, and a novel device invented by nuns in the last century to accommodate abandoned babies.

JARDIN DES PLANTES

Just inside the entrance to the gardens on the Rue Geoffroy-St-Hilaire is a small hillock, upon which stands a 19th-century bronze statue of a lion by Jacquemart.

Seen from below, the animal merely appears to have its head lowered to the ground, but closer inspection from the path that winds its way to the top of the mound reveals that it is, in a macabre depiction, sniffing at a disembodied human foot. Less than 30 years after the statue was installed here, however, the animals in the adjoining zoo were themselves slaughtered to satisfy the hunger of the starving population during the Siege of Paris.

6th arrondissement

PLACE ST-SULPICE

CHURCH OF ST-SULPICE

This 18th-century church not only boasts one of the largest organs in the world, with more than 6,500 pipes, but also a novel scientific device set in the floor of the aisle of the north–south transept.

A bronze meridian line set into the floor and running from the north to the south transept, catches any sunlight that percolates into the building through a blind window in the south transept on the three days of the equinoxes and the winter solstice, and reflects it upwards on to a obelisk and globe, and from there on to a crucifix. The obelisk bears the inscription 'Two scientists with God's help'.

PLACE DE FURSTENBERG

Tucked away off the bustling Rue Jacob, this small, tranquil square is named after a 17th-century abbot of St-Germain-des-Prés, and has been featured as a scenic backdrop in many French films.

At its centre, a white-globed lamp-post is surrounded by four paulownia trees, whose heavily scented blossoms perfume the air in springtime. For street-musicians, however, it is the remarkable acoustics of the square that provide a year-round attraction, allowing softer-sounding instruments like the guitar, harp and flute to be heard at their best.

JARDINS DE LUXEMBOURG

At the heart of the Left Bank, a stroll through these 24-hectare gardens never fails to provide some small spectacle of human idiosyncrasy.

Above, Luxembourg Gardens on a Sunday
Above left, a now-silent witness to the taxidermist's art

The dancer Isadora Duncan once danced across the lawns at dawn, while the writer Ernest Hemingway used to catch and strangle pigeons here for food when he was living in the capital and was destitute. Nowadays, the local bird-lovers vie with each other in persuading the semi-tame feathered inhabitants to take food from their outstretched hands. In one corner of the grounds is an apiary run by an Esperanto-speaking Dominican friar, who twice a week, gives practical lessons in bee-keeping.

7th arrondissement

45, RUE DE BAC

DEYROLLE

This astonishing shop has been dedicated to the art of taxidermy for more than 150 years.

Its two floors are packed with an incredible range of specimens, stuffed baby elephants, polar bears, lions and tigers intermingling with snakes and domestic pets. There are also displays of rare butterflies and collections of minerals from countries all around the world.

PONT DE L'ALMA

STATUE OF A ZOUAVE

The stern sculpted figure of an Algerian light-infantry soldier adorns the foot of the pier nearest to the right bank of the Seine. Facing upstream, the statue has long served as an indicator of the river's flood level. In 1910, the waters reached the soldier's chin.

8th arrondissement

RUE DE PENTHIEVRE AND AVENUE DELCASSE

TROMPE L'OEIL MURAL

Although the practice of concealing building constructions behind specially designed paintings is now commonplace, this permanent mural painted by Rieti in 1985 displays greater originality and success than most in deceiving the viewer's eye. Its main feature is the figure of a man looking from his balcony at a bronze nude while two doves fly away from him, casting their shadows on the wall.

296, RUE ST-HONORE

CHURCH OF ST-ROCH

The façade of this fine baroque church still bears the evidence of a Revolutionary skirmish in October 1795.

The bullet holes in the plaster and stonework were made during a brief battle between Royalist troops and other forces led by an unknown general named Napoleon Bonaparte. Ten days after his success in this action, which had threatened the Convention then sitting in the nearby Tuileries Palace, the 27-year-old Napoleon was appointed commander-in-chief of the home forces.

5, RUE CRESPIN-DU-GAST

EDITH PIAF MUSEUM

Not far from her grave at the Père-Lachaise cemetery is a modest museum commemorating the life and career of this internationally renowned French cabaret singer and entertainer.

Housed in a simple two-room private apartment, the exhibits include her birth certificate, autographed letters, photographs and clothes. Recordings by the 'little sparrow' provide a constant background accompaniment.

from the basement offices of the local Mairie. The occasion of the grape harvest in October provides the excuse for a local festival.

PLACE EMILE-GOUDEAU

FOUR GRACES FOUNTAIN

Standing modestly on a tree-shaded terrace halfway up the steep slope of the Montmartre hill, is this green-painted fountain; one of a hundred identical structures originally dotted around Paris.

They were the gift of the English art collec-

Left, La Marseillaise
Above, the city-centre vineyard, a strange sight in a modern city

tor and devoted Francophile, Richard Wallace, who, toward the end of the 19th-century, lamented that it was impossible to obtain a glass of water in the capital without paying for it in a café. A further example of his public-spirited generosity still stands near the oldest tree in the capital in the Square René-Viviani.

PLACE CHARLES DU GAULLE

ARC DE TRIOMPHE

The sculpture of *La Marseillaise*, or more properly *The Departure of the Volunteers*, by Rude (on a plinth at the right hand of the arch) includes a figure representing the Republic and brandishing a sword.

On the eve of the Battle of Verdun in 1916, the sword fractured and fell to the ground, The authorities immediately concealed the sculpture from view to avoid superstitious citizens regarding the incident as a bad omen.

RUE DES SAULES

MONTMARTRE VINEYARD

One of the last two remaining vineyards within the city, this small expanse of carefully tended vines yields an annual harvest of grapes that, in a good year, enables the production of 500 bottles of red Clos Montmartre wine.

The labels are designed by local artists and although the wine is not particularly memorable, the bottles are subsequently sold

ABBESSES METRO

This, at 100m below road level, is the deepest metro station in Paris and stands on the site of a medieval abbey.

The Art Deco exterior, with its green wrought-iron arches and amber lighting, was designed by Hector Guimard in 1900, and is one of the last surviving examples of his work. It was moved here in its entirety from the Hôtel de Ville station by Jacques Chirac when the central plaza there was remodelled.

SECRET FRANCE

BURGUNDY

A large region more or less in the middle of France, Burgundy is known by remarkably few people. Its wines may be well known, and one of France's busiest motorways passes through, but the people who come for the wine tend to stay within the comparatively small wine-producing areas, while those who travel the motorway are generally on their way to somewhere else. Consequently, there are vast areas of Burgundy that rarely see visitors, and many of its quiet by-ways and ancient, unspoilt villages become known to only a handful of visitors.

Burgundy's turbulent past has been a major influence on the shape of its villages, many of which had their origins as fortified places. During the Hundred Years War, the Wars of Religion, the Revolution and countless other lesser skirmishes such villages came into their own, often providing shelter for people living in outlying farming communities. While large numbers of these fortifications have been lost over the years, through either war or depredation, many others have survived more or less intact, retaining their strongly medieval character. Some are perched on hilltops complete with their castles, others nestle in peaceful river valleys, an age away from their troubled pasts.

If war played a significant part in shaping the history of Burgundy, so did religion, for in the Middle Ages the province became one of the major centres of Christianity in Europe. Abbeys, priories and churches sprang up all over the region, and although many later suffered terrible destruction, particularly during the Wars of Religion and the Revolution, many others survived or have been restored to their earlier glory.

That Burgundy is full of attractive corners there can be no doubt: any drive along a little-used by-way is almost certain to reveal something special. Isolated churches and chapels – some out of sight, others in more exposed positions but difficult to reach – are everywhere, not surprisingly in such an ecclesiastical region. It is not short of famous natural sights either, and there are many lesser-known ones that are just as beautiful in their own ways.

vigne de Bourgogne

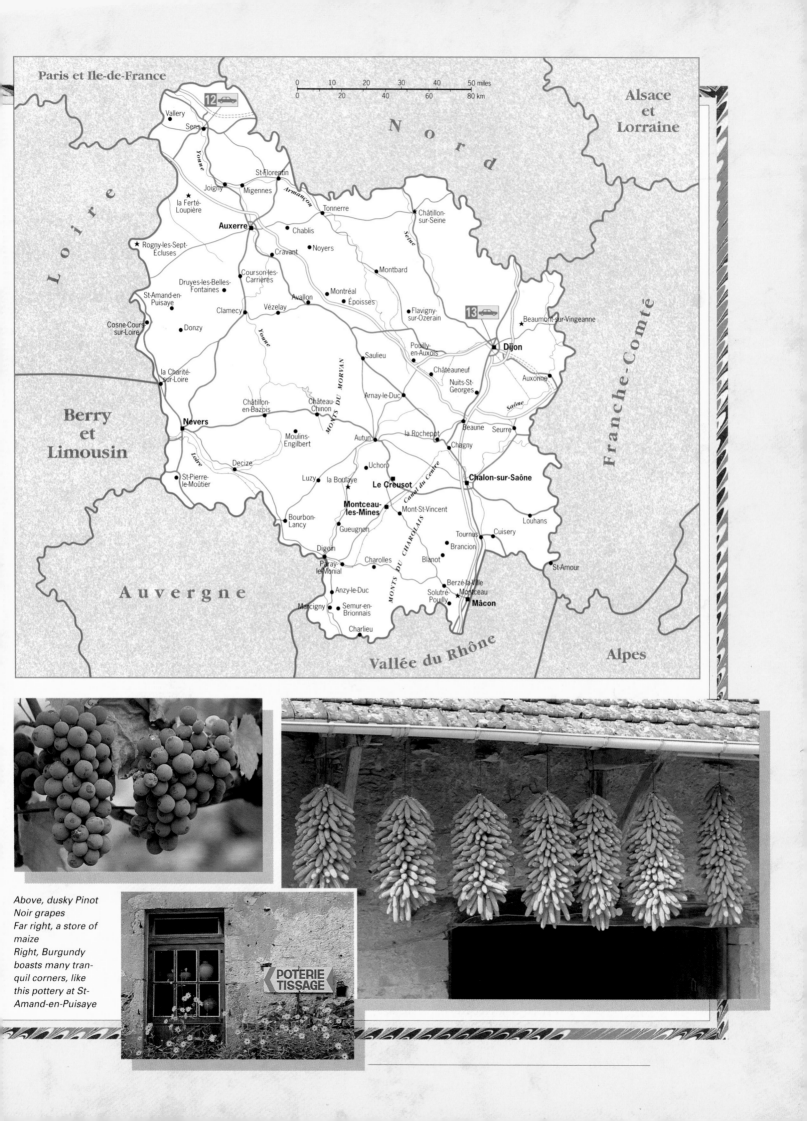

Paris et Ile-de-France

Alsace
et
Lorraine

N o r d

Vallery
Sens
Yonne
St-Florentin
Joigny
Migennes
la Ferté-
Loupière
Auxerre
Chablis
Tonnerre
Châtillon-
sur-Seine
Rogny-les-Sept-
Écluses
Cravant
Noyers
Seine
Courson-les-
Carrières
Montbard
Druyes-les-Belles-
Fontaines
Montréal
St-Amand-en-
Puisaye
Avallon
Époisses
Flavigny-
sur-Ozerain
Clamecy
Vézelay
Beaumont-sur-Vingeanne
Cosne-Cours-
sur-Loire
Donzy
Yonne
Pouilly-
en-Auxois
Dijon
Saulieu
Auxonne
la Charité-
sur-Loire
Châteauneuf
Nuits-St-
Georges
Châtillon-
en-Bazois
Château-
Chinon
Arnay-le-Duc
Saône
Nevers
la Rochepot
Beaune
Seurre
Berry
et
Limousin
Moulins-
Engilbert
Autun
Chagny
Decize
Uchon
Le Creusot
Chalon-sur-Saône
Loire
Luzy
la Boulaye
St-Pierre-
le-Moûtier
**Montceau-
les-Mines**
Mont-St-Vincent
Louhans
Bourbon-
Lancy
Canal du Centre
Cuisery
Gueugnon
Tournus
Digoin
Brancion
Charolles
Blanot
Paray-
le-Monial
St-Amour
Auvergne
Anzy-le-Duc
Berzé-la-Ville
Montceau
Marcigny
Semur-en-
Brionnais
Solutré-
Pouilly
Mâcon
Charlieu

MONTS DU MORVAN
MONTS DU CHAROLAIS
Armançon

0   10   20   30   40   50 miles
0   20   40   60   80 km

12
13

Vallée du Rhône
Alpes

Franche-Comté

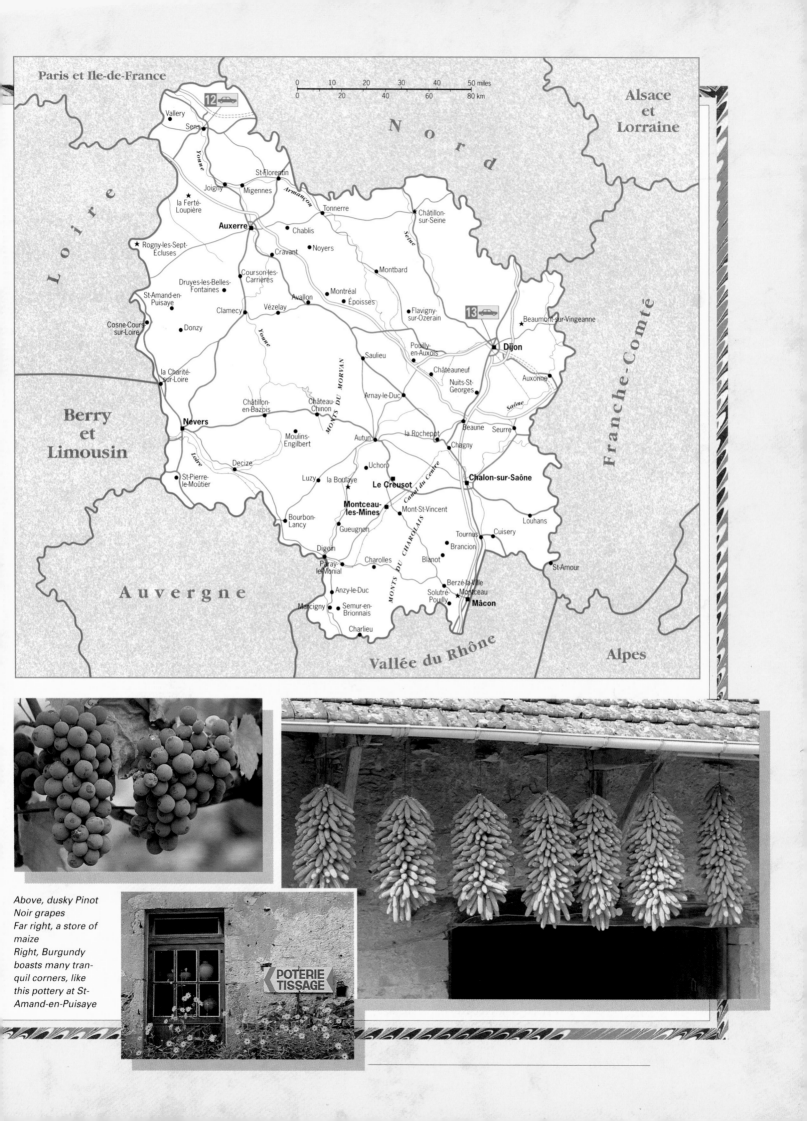

*Above, dusky Pinot
Noir grapes
Far right, a store of
maize
Right, Burgundy
boasts many tran-
quil corners, like
this pottery at St-
Amand-en-Puisaye*

POTERIE
TISSAGE

ANZY-LE-DUC

Set amid the rural landscape of the cattle-rearing Brionnais country close to the River Loire, this quiet village is best known for its Romanesque church. 22km south of Digoin.

Anzy's 11th-century church is one of the most beautiful in southern Burgundy, its superb Romanesque architecture heightened by the wonderful golden stone, and topped by red pantile roofs. Just off the main road through the village, its Lombardian three-tiered octagonal tower is thought to have provided the inspiration for the builders of the basilica at Vézelay. Especially notable are the sculpted capitals, which show biblical and allegorical scenes, the frescos on the ceiling and the tympanum above the superb west portal.

This is a village in which to linger among the quiet streets and typically Burgundian houses, or to follow the waymarked walks from the church along the Arconce valley.

ARNAY-LE-DUC

A long history has left a number of attractions to delay the traveller at this big, bustling village at the crossroads of the N6 and N81, 28km north-east of Autun.

Its position on two major highways has had a marked influence on Arnay-le-Duc's development through history. During the Wars of Religion the village changed hands several times between the Catholic and Protestant sides, and all that remains of the castle

that was destroyed in the process is the 15th-century Tour de la Motte-Forte, which stands behind the church.

There are a number of medieval town houses, probably the most attractive being the Maison Bourgogne in a corner of the Place Bonaventure des Périers, decorated with Renaissance turrets and sculpted heads. Not to be missed is the Maison Régionale des Arts de la Table, a museum of gastronomy, with displays of the specialities of the region and promotions of local products.

BERZE-LA-VILLE

A simple Romanesque chapel with some of the best wall paintings in France make this colourful village worth a stop. 12km north-west of Mâcon.

Berzé-la-Ville is a village of extremely attractive houses, some of them modern and most quite large, spread along the slope beneath a limestone escarpment. Beautifully decorated with floral displays, it has an 11th-century church in the lower village, near le Moustier, and a top-quality restaurant with a walled garden.

The village is best known, however, for its Romanesque Chapelle des Moines (monks' chapel). Formerly part of a priory, the chapel is in the upper village. It contains remarkable 12th-century frescos after those of St-Savin in Vienne, the most important collection of Romanesque paintings in France.

BLANOT

This typical little village of the Haut Mâconnais is picturesquely set at the foot of Mont St-Romain, its pink and red pantiled roofs clustering around its medieval church and priory. 10km north-east of Cluny.

Blanot's rustic 12th-century church, roofed in stone slabs, has a tall, square bell-tower which rises like a landmark above the surrounding houses. It was built on the site of a Merovingian necropolis, and several tombs have been unearthed. The priory, dating from the 14th century, was a daughter house of the abbey at Cluny.

This is still a farming community, but some craftspeople, mainly potters,

SECRET PLACES

ROGNY-LES-SEPT-ECLUSES

LOCK SYSTEM

Rogny-les-Sept-Ecluses lies south-east of Montargis.

It was the countryside around this tiny village which caused problems in the late 16th century, when the Briare Canal was planned to link the Seine and Loire, and ultimately the English Channel with the Mediterranean. At Rogny a large hill blocked the way, and a staircase of seven locks with a drop of 34m was proposed. Troops

had to quell opposition from local landowners, but construction started in 1605 and the first boat passed through in 1642.

The locks remained in continual use until 1887, when an alternative system was opened, taking the canal on a longer route over a more gentle gradient. The originals now stand, lined by fir trees, as a monument to a great engineering feat.

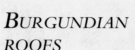

also work from the village's attractive houses with their wooden galleries enclosing ivy-covered terraces, typical of the Mâconnais.

A short distance from the village, at the foot of Mont St-Romain, are the Grottes de Blanot, the largest network of caves in Burgundy, which extend for about 1km and show signs of habitation by early man.

BRANCION

A superb example of a medieval fortified village of great charm and character, with outstanding views from its high position. 13km west of Tournus.

Brancion is a delightfully atmospheric medieval hilltop village built in the 10th century on the site of an ancient Gallo-Roman settlement. Inside the ancient walls are a superb Romanesque church, a feudal fortress, a 15th-century covered market, and a tangle of charming streets lined with medieval houses. The castle, originally 10th century, was rebuilt in the 14th century to become a residence of the Dukes of Burgundy.

The 12th-century church of St-Pierre, standing on the tip of the promontory with wonderful views over the valley of the River Grosne, would alone justify a visit to the village. A masterpiece of late Romanesque art, it has very pure lines, and inside, superb 14th-century frescoes and the

Above left, a shuttered window at Berzé-la-Ville, and right, magnificent Châteauneuf

magnificent recumbent figure of Josserand, the last lord of Brancion, who died during the Crusades in 1250.

CHATEAUNEUF

Another atmospheric hilltop village, renowned for its magnificent castle and its picturesque eagle's nest setting above the Vandenesse valley. 30km north-west of Beaune.

With its castle and its pepperpot towers, Châteauneuf presents an impressive sight from the D18 beside the Canal de Bourgogne. The castle was originally built in the 12th century by the lords of Chaudenay, and part of the walls and the great square keep survive. Succeeding centuries added the layers of fortifications, making this an exceptional example of Burgundian military architecture. In the 15th century it became the elegant Renaissance dwelling of Philippe Pot, seneschal to the Duke of Burgundy.

The village itself is small, and its lovely turreted and ivy-covered houses, built in the 14th–16th centuries by rich merchants, are well preserved. One of them, at the castle entrance, is now a respected hotel, the Hostellerie du Château.

BURGUNDIAN ROOFS

As a *lieu de transition* between northern and southern France, Burgundy can boast architecture as richly varied as any region, and this is reflected in its different roofing styles. They range from the severe grey slate seen around Sens in the north to the warm clay pantiles that announce the proximity of the south around Mâcon. But the most distinctive Burgundian style, a product of Flamboyant Gothic and the great days of the Valois dukes, is found on the *hôtels particuliers* and public buildings of Dijon, and the châteaux and churches that punctuate the vineyards of the Côte d'Or on its way down to Beaune. Here the roofs are made of tiles in white, yellow and blue as well as red, arranged in complicated geometrical patterns, and they bring a touch of wit to the humblest or the grandest architecture. At Beaune's 15th-century Hôtel-Dieu, which has the the most elaborate roof in Burgundy, the effect is openly fantastic – like an oriental carpet draped over a building which, dedicated as it was to the care of the sick and the poor, could otherwise have looked glumly functional.

TOUR 12 – 130KM
SENS AND THE YONNE VALLEY

Tucked in the north-west corner of Burgundy, Sens is the first town travellers from Paris come to when they reach the region, and the area, known as the Sénonais, is steeped in history. The tour, through a peaceful landscape of gently rolling hills and vast fields of cereal crops, punctuated here and there with small woods, takes in a former royal château, unspoilt towns and villages, the remains of an ancient village, and the old village of Chablis, renowned for its wine. Through it all runs the River Yonne, carrying commercial and holiday traffic.

ROUTE DIRECTIONS

Leave Sens on the **N60** for Montargis. At Paron turn left on the **D72** towards Etigny. After about 13km you will reach Villeneuve-sur-Yonne. Turn left across the Yonne into the town centre.

Re-cross the Yonne and turn left onto the **D15** towards Bussy-le-Repos, but in a short distance fork

Sixteenth-century carving stands out on the pillar of a house at Joigny

left on the **D3** for St-Julien-de-Sault. At St-Julien continue towards Joigny on the **D3**, which at Thèmes becomes the **D182**. At the junction with the **D943** turn left towards Joigny and at the **N6** turn left into the town.

Leave Joigny on the **N6** for Auxerre and in about 7km turn left, in Epineau-les-Voves, onto the **D181**, almost immediately branching right on to the **D477** towards Migennes. Pass the railway station and head for Cheny and Chablis.

At les Cités on the outskirts of Migennes turn left again, and follow signs for Cheny and Ormoy. Continue into Cheny, and from there head for Beaumont and Chablis. Within 1km fork left on the **D91** and drive through Hauterive and les Baudières to Pontigny.

Leave Pontigny on the **N77** to St-Florentin then turn left on the **D905** towards Sens and Joigny. Just beyond Avrolles turn right on the **D905** towards Sens. Continue for 29km through Champlost,

Arces-Dilo, Cerisiers and Theil-sur-Vanne, then turn left onto the **N60** and follow the signs to Sens centre.

PLACES OF INTEREST

VILLENEUVE-SUR-YONNE

Villeneuve has a history going back to 1163, when King Louis VII decided to build a royal residence on the banks of the Yonne. Only a tower remains of the château. Grouped around its 13th-century church, the old town was contained within ramparts, and the two 13th-century fortified gates, situated at each end of the Rue Carnot, have been restored. The Rue Carnot also has a number of 18th-century houses. The Porte de Joigny, at the southern end of the town, contains a small museum.

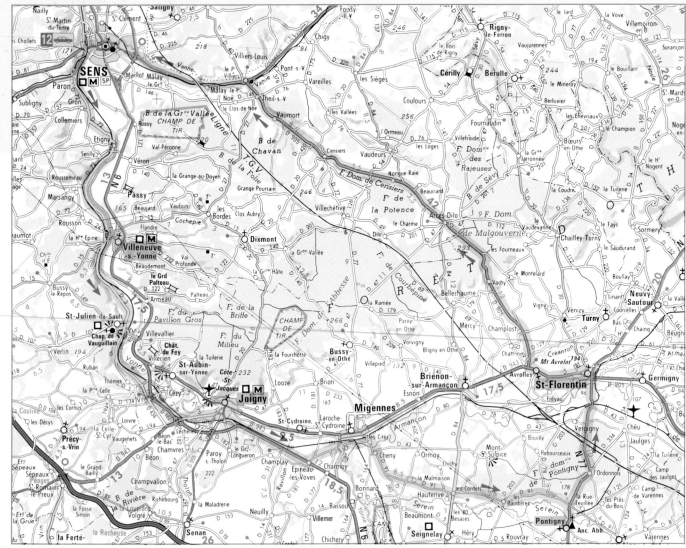

BURGUNDY

JOIGNY

Despite the volume of traffic that passes through Joigny on the N6, the town has retained much of its medieval character. Known as the Gateway to Burgundy, its network of narrow streets, covered passageways and court-yards includes some fine examples of 15th- and 16th-century timber houses, and three churches – the 14th-century St-Thibault, St-Jean and St-Andrew.

ABBAYE DE PONTIGNY

Lying like an upturned boat surrounded by fields of wheat, the 12th–13th-century abbey church of Pontigny is the largest Cistercian church conserved in France and is the only part of the original monas-tery to have survived. A number of famous people have sheltered here, among them three arch-bishops of Canterbury, Thomas à Becket, Stephen Langton and Edmund Rich, all of whom fell out with their monarch. Abandoned during the Revolution, the church was restored at the start of the 20th century.

ST-FLORENTIN

Overlooked by its largely 16th–17th-century church, famous for the quality of its stained-glass windows, St-Florentin stands on a terraced hill above the Armance River and the Canal de Bourgogne.

The town has given its name to one of Burgundy's best-known cheeses, which is made in the local area.

CHABLIS

About 13km south-east of Pontigny on the D131, Chablis is a pretty little town on the River Serein, surrounded by vineyards that are renowned world-wide for their light, dry white wines. The 12th-cen-tury church contains a number of 13th-century paintings. There are sever-al welcoming restaurants in the town and an attrac-tive tree-lined riverside walk.

Right, Chablis grapes, and below, serene arches span the river at Joigny

CHATILLON-EN-BAZOIS

One of Burgundy's most important centres of inland navigation, this sizeable village has other important attractions to offer, including a château, close to the canal on which it lies. 25km west of Château-Chinon.

Standing on both the Nivernais Canal and the River Aron, Châtillon-en-Bazois has developed into one of the busiest boating holiday centres of Burgundy. Overlooking both the river and the canal is the château, built as a powerful fortress on its rocky outcrop during the 13th century, and greatly altered between the 15th and 17th centuries. Privately owned, it can only be visited with a guide on afternoons during July and August.

The best view of the exterior is from the canal towpath, which also offers good walks. The old houses and mills lining the river and canal add a particular charm to the tangle of narrow streets that forms the heart of the village.

The main road through the village which links Château-Chinon and Nevers, has several shops, bars and hotels.

CRAVANT

This fortified village with its Renaissance church tower dominating the confluence of the Yonne and the Cure is of considerable historical significance and has retained its medieval atmosphere. 18km south-east of Auxerre.

Cravant proved of enormous impor-tance during the Hundred Years War, when in 1423 the Anglo-Burgundian army defeated a large French and Scottish force that had besieged the village for five weeks. Today, it still has a medieval feel to it.

The narrow street winds up through the village past one or two shops and bars and many old houses, including a half-timbered house built in 1328. Next to the grand-looking Mairie, the Rue de la Poterne leads to another of the old gates and the Tour du Guet, a 14th-century belfry that was once part of the fortifications.

The nearby church dates mostly from the 15th century and has a Renaissance choir and bell-tower. In the Rue de l'Eglise, which leads to the church, is a good hotel and restaurant, Les Hortensias.

BURGUNDY

THE WINES OF BURGUNDY

The Côte d'Or, or 'gold hillside' between Dijon and Beaune is ideal terrain for vineyards. Facing the morning sun, the soil is protected from cold and frost by the hills above, and enriched by minerals washed down in the watercourses that break up the hills. Nobody knows when these conditions first encouraged wine-making, but monks from Bèze were cultivating Gevrey-Chambertin grapes by the 7th century, and the Cistercians began developing the Clos de Vougeot in the 12th century. Since then, the Côte vineyards have survived to achieve a status that makes little places like Chambolle-Musigny, Vosne-Romanée or Aloxe-Corton internationally famous. This is not Burgundy's only great wine region. South of Beaune are the Chalonnais and the Mâconnais. The lands around Auxerre are famous for Chablis, but should also be explored for the local wines – and don't miss the wines of Tannay and Vézelay.

DONZY

A powerful centre and seat of the Counts of Nevers during the Middle Ages, this large village has retained its castle keep and a number of attractive 17th- and 18th-century houses. 17km east of Cosne-Cours-sur-Loire.

Lying in an agricultural and forested region of western Burgundy, at the confluence of the Nohain and Talvanne rivers, Donzy is a lovely old village with a history dating as far back in history as Gallo-Roman times.

It has several half-timbered and Renaissance houses of note, mostly clustered around the Gothic church of St-Caradeuc in the Rue de l'Etape. In the same street is the charming

SARCTUS VINCENTIUS

DONNÉ PAR MM. BABIN ET GDEFERT. 1868

Hôtel du Grand Monarque, which has an excellent and reasonably priced restaurant. At the entrance to the village from the crest is an attractive group of 18th-century houses, once part of a convent, laid out around the shaded Place de l'Hôtel de Ville. Nearer the centre of the village along Rue Général Leclerc, are some fine *hôtels particulars* from the same period.

To the south-west, at nearby Donzy-le-Pré, is what little remains of a priory church dating from the early 12th century, including a tympanum considered a masterpiece of Burgundian sculpture.

DRUYES-LES-BELLES-FONTAINES

This pretty village is built in two parts, the lower village around clear springs, the upper part beside the ruins of a clifftop fortress. 10km south-west of Courson-les-Carrières.

The picturesque lower part of Druyes-les-Belles-Fontaines, grouped around the transparently clear springs of the Druyes stream, from which it takes its name, has a 12th-century Romanesque church with some fine capitals and a beautiful portal, as well as some lovely old ivy-covered houses. One of these, near the church, was the birthplace in 1776 of Captain Jean-Roch Coignet, the first soldier to receive the *Légion d'honneur*.

The upper village, reached through a 14th-century gateway in the castle's outer wall, consists of a single street of medieval cottages on the summit of the rocky hill dominating the valley. Built in the 12th century for the Counts of Auxerre and Nevers, the castle was unusual in not having a keep, and was more a fortified palace than a military fortress.

Today it continues to lend the village an air of majesty, even though only the walls and the impressive gateway are intact. There are guided visits at weekends and on public holidays from July to September.

SECRET PLACES

LA FERTÉ-LOUPIERE

DANSE MACABRE

The church in la Ferté-Loupière, south-west of Joigny, contains a 15th-century masterpiece of religious art.

Only cleaned of the distemper covering it in 1910, the 25m long painting adorning one wall of the nave depicts a vivid *danse macabre*, or dance of death. Beginning with three hunters on horseback meeting three skeletal representatives of Death, it then shows a figure writing in a book who leads to the dance itself. Three musicians, all skeletons, play to 19 couples from all walks of life, from emperor to labourer, each led by a skeleton.

Look for the pillar showing St Michael and the dragon

102

EPOISSES

A château of great strategic importance has ensured this village's fame since the 6th century, while today a favourite Burgundian cheese continues its renown. 12km west of Semur-en-Auxois.

The château at Epoisses has seen many changes since Queen Brunehaut, once the most powerful woman in France, made frequent visits there in the 6th century. Always recognised for its strategic value, the Dukes of Burgundy and later the Kings of France for centuries ensured that it lay in trusted hands. Within its walls stand the 12th-century village church, some houses used by villagers in times of unrest, and an imposing 16th-century dovecote.

Most of the château as seen today was constructed in the 15th century, with a number of earlier towers. Though half demolished in the Revolution, it still makes a majestic sight beside its *cour-d'honneur* with its elaborate Renaissance well-head.

Epoisses also makes one of Burgundy's best-known cheeses, as it has done for 500 years.

FLAVIGNY-SUR-OZERAIN

A walled village perched above the valley of the Ozerain, which has retained many lovely old buildings and an air of dignity that recall its ancient role as the capital of Burgundy. 9km south-east of Venarey-les-Laumes.

Picturesquely sited on a rocky outcrop above wooded valleys, the village is entered by the 15th-century machicolated Porte du Bourg, one of the three gates of the well-preserved medieval ramparts. Narrow streets lined with Gothic and Renaissance mansions, some of them turreted, as well as restored stone cottages, lead up the hill to the focal point of the village: the church of St-Genest. Built in the 13th century and altered in the 15th and 16th centuries, it has some attractive carved stalls, sadly damaged by thieves in 1978.

Also within the massive walls are the ancient remains of the Abbaye-St-Pierre, which contain the 8th-century

Stretching as far as the eye can see: the view from Mont-St-Vincent

tomb of Ste-Reine and the recently uncovered chapel of Notre-Dame-des-Piliers, thought to be of similar age.

MONT-ST-VINCENT

An exceptional view is the chief attraction of this small and ancient village, perched at 610m on one of the highest points in the Saône-et-Loire. 12km south-east of Monceau-les-Mines.

On a clear day you can see as far as Mont Blanc from Mont-St-Vincent, and the village itself is a beacon clearly visible from many kilometres in all directions. A viewpoint with a telescope and orientation table has been set up on the spot where the ancient Gauls used to light fires in order to communicate with settlements at Bibracte and Suin.

Exposed on their hilltop, the grey stone houses of the village huddle closely together to protect themselves against the weather, while the 11th-century granite church, stands at the end of the promontory as if to give additional protection.

Among the maze of streets and squares, lined with houses from the 16th to the 18th centuries that form the village, are now a number of artists' workshops.

TOUR 13 – 150KM
DIJON AND THE CÔTE D'OR

Burgundy has a reputation as the land of great art and good living and this tour provides the evidence. Dijon and Beaune are two of the great artistic centres, not just in Burgundy but in the whole of France, while a drive through the Côte de Nuits, part of the Côte d'Or, takes you through village after village bearing names that rank among the most esteemed in the wine world. In addition, there are medieval castles and villages, a great religious centre, and countryside varying from wide plains to huge limestone escarpments.

ROUTE DIRECTIONS

Take the **N74** out of Dijon towards Beaune, and after 1km fork right onto the **D122** to Chenôve. Follow signs for the Route des Grands Crus through Marsannay-la-Côte, Gevrey-Chambertin and Chambolle-Musigny, to arrive at the famous vineyards of Vougeot.

From Vougeot take the road towards Beaune and shortly join the **N74** to Nuits-St-Georges. Turn left onto the **D8** towards Agencourt.

On reaching the A31 motorway, follow the **D8** and continue for 11km to the **D996**, and turn left to Abbeye de Cîteaux.

From the abbey turn right onto the **D996** towards Seurre and just after Auvillars-sur-Saône turn right onto the **D20** to Bagnot. There, turn left onto the **D35e**, following the signs to Montmain, then turn right onto the **D115** to Villy le Brûlé. Continue to Villy-le-Moutier and then follow signs to Beaune via **D115**.

From the centre of Beaune, take the **D18** towards Savigny les Beaune. Follow the **D2** through Savigny to Bouilland, then turn left on the **D18** through le Pont d'Ouche and Crugey. Take the **D18a** to Châteauneuf.

Continue through Châteauneuf on the **D977bis** to Commarin, and at Sombernon turn right towards Dijon. Within 100m fork left to Sombernon centre and follow signs towards St-Seine-l'Abbaye, first on the **D9** then on the **D7**. Where the **D7** branches left, carry straight on along the **D16** towards St-Seine-l'Abbaye and after 1km turn right onto the **V2** to Savigny-sur-Mâlain.

In Savigny take the **D104c** to Mâlain, and then the **D104c** to Ancey and Lantenay, then follow signs for Dijon, turning right onto the **D10** to Plombières, and from there into Dijon.

PLACES OF INTEREST

CLOS DE VOUGEOT

The Clos de Vougeot is one of the most famous of the Côte de Nuits vineyards, founded in the 12th century by the monks of Cîteaux and owned by them until the Revolution. It is now the headquarters of the Confrèrie des Chevaliers du Tastevin, who meet regularly at the elegant Renaissance château in the midst of the vines. Tours of the château are possible, to view the massive 13th-century Cyresses and the Romanesque-style, vaulted cellars.

NUITS-ST-GEORGES

Nuits-St-Georges, a busy little town on the N74, has given its name to one of the best-known wines of the Côte d'Or, popularised by Louis XIV who was prescribed a few glasses each day as a tonic by his doctor. The town's bustling market is overlooked by a lovely 17th-century ivy-covered belfry, while the 13th-century St-Symphorien is one of the most beautiful Romanesque churches in the region.

The spectacular Hôtel Dieu at Beaune is dominated by its magnificent patterned roof, the ornament echoed in the balcony below

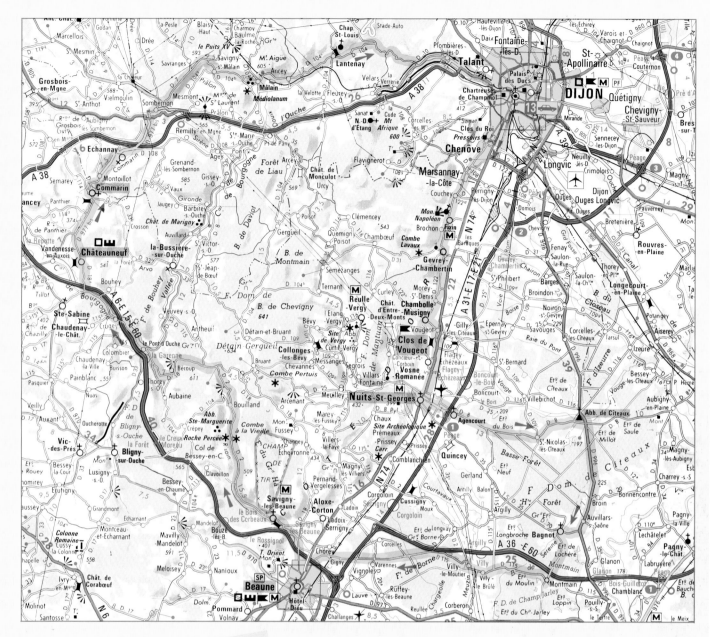

Fûts de Chêne

BOURGOGNE
...UTES-CÔTES-DE-BEAUNE
«GRANDE CUVÉE»
...TION BOURGOGNE HAUTES-CÔTES-DE-BEAUNE CONTRÔLÉE

12,5% vol

＊

Mis en bouteilles à la propriété par

LES CAVES DES HAUTES-CÔTES
...ENT DE PROPRIÉTAIRES-RÉCOLTANTS, ROUTE DE POMMARD A BEAUNE, CÔTE-D'OR

Produce of France

ABBAYE DE CITEAUX

Although much of the original Cistercian abbey at Cîteaux, founded in 1098, was destroyed in the Revolution, leaving only the library and a few 17th- and 18th-century buildings, new buildings were erected during the 19th century, and in 1898 Cistercian monks returned to their mother abbey to live and work in austerity. No longer involved in producing wine, they do have a small farm and make a well-regarded cheese. The abbey is not open to the public, but there is an audio-visual display and shop at the gatehouse.

BEAUNE

Enclosed within its ramparts, Beaune has been bequeathed some beautiful treasures by the dukes of Burgundy who made it their second home. The most outstanding is the Hôtel-Dieu, a beautiful 15th-century building which served as a hospital for more than 500 years. The 14th-century church of Notre-Dame contains 15th-century frescos, and tapestries illustrating the life of the Virgin.

Beaune is the Côte d'Or's wine centre, and it is worth seeing the Musée du Vin de Bourgogne, housed in the former ducal palace.

CHATEAUNEUF

See page 99.

COMMARIN

The little village of Commarin possesses a château, once owned by the Comte de Vienne, and regarded as one of the finest in Burgundy. Combining two 14th-century towers with 17th- and 18th-century buildings and a Romanesque chapel, it makes an unusual sight. The château houses some fine works of art, including four armorial tapestries. The church has an interesting 16th-century reredos.

MONTREAL

This fortified hilltop village in its strategic position overlooking the Serein valley was considered impregnable in the Middle Ages and has kept its medieval atmosphere. It is also celebrated for the outstanding furnishings of its church. 12km north-east of Avallon.

Montréal's history stretches back to the 6th century, when Queen Brunehaut is supposed to have built a manor here. The church, which occupies the highest point in the village and is all that remains of a Cluniac priory, has wonderful panoramas over the rolling Burgundy countryside. Built in the 11th and 12th centuries, it is a mixture of Romanesque and Gothic styles, and was restored after the Revolution by Viollet-le-Duc.

The most outstanding features of the church are the magnificent early 16th-century carved stalls and alabaster reredos inside. The latter, made in Nottingham in the 15th century, originally had seven panels; four were destroyed when the piece was stolen in 1971.

MOULINS-ENGILBERT

Lying on the edge of the Parc Naturel Regional de Morvan, at the confluence of the rivers Guignon and Garat, this historic village is named after the many watermills that used to line the two rivers. 16km south-west of Château-Chinon.

Moulins-Engilbert grew up around a Roman camp, and now consists of two rings of houses encircling the church of St-Jean. Originally built around 1350 and destroyed by fire in 1509, the church was rebuilt in the late Gothic style. A stained-glass window of the Last Judgement behind the choir has been classified a historic monument. Among the houses surrounding the church are some well-preserved buildings from the 14th, 16th and 17th centuries including the 17th-century Hôtel de Ville.

Overlooking the village, on the site of the Roman encampment, are the sorry remains of a château that was once a residence of the Counts of Nevers.

NOYERS

Occupying a beautiful position in a bend of the River Serein and overlooked by the modest Montagne St-Georges, this is a wonderful and well-preserved example of a medieval village. 22km south of Tonnerre.

Still protected by its horseshoe-shaped medieval defensive walls studded with 16 fortified gateways, Noyers seems to have been preserved intact, virtually as it was in the Middle Ages. Yet it has witnessed much strife over the centuries. Many times its walls have sheltered its citizens from war – from

Left, sunlight reflects off the old glazed tiles of the château at La Rochepot

LA BOULAYE

BUDDHIST MONASTERY

Just outside the tiny village of la Boulaye, south of Autun, Eastern religion appears in all its colours.

The Burgundy countryside is perhaps the last place you would expect to find a Tibetan Buddhist monastery, but there, in the grounds of the Château de Plaige near la Boulaye, it stands in all its incongruous splendour. The monastery of Kagyu-Ling was founded at the château in 1974 and the temple, the largest of its kind in Europe and built in traditional Tibetan style, opened in 1987. Ritualistic banners flutter from poles in front of the temple and nearby stands a *stupa* to ward off evil spirits.

which Burgundy is so famous. Yet only a century ago the castle was in a state of ruin: built in the 12th century by Philippe Pot, counsellor to Charles the Bold, in the 19th century it was plundered for building stone. It was only when the family of Sadi Carnot, a former president of France, bought it that this remarkable building was restored to its former glory.

In the village itself, the 12th-century priory church has a timber-framed roof covered with lava-stone and some interesting decorations.

SEMUR-EN-BRIONNAIS

Standing at the summit of a low hill, this village has an imposing medieval keep and one of the loveliest churches in Burgundy. 4.5km south-east of Marcigny.

The ancient heart of Semur-en-Brionnais, reached by followings signs for the castle and the church, is a delightful ensemble laid out around a dusty square. Among the picturesque old buildings are the former priory, an 18th-century courtroom that now serves as the *mairie*, and a former salt warehouse, Le Grenier de Sel, now used as a craft gallery.

The castle, of which only the keep and two towers remain on their artificial motte, was the birthplace in 1024 of Hugues de Semur, later St-Hugues, founder of the abbey at Cluny and the most influential of its abbots. The 12th-century church is one of the loveliest of all Cluniac buildings, its two-tier tower and apse forming a beautifully harmonious whole.

siege by Blanche of Castile in the 13th century to assault by Catholic forces in the 16th – but it has survived remarkably well. The fine Flamboyant Gothic church dates from the late 15th century.

Half-timbered houses, some displaying beautifully carved beams, lean crazily over the streets, while here and there Renaissance façades indicate the homes of rich merchants. Only the Hôtel du Ville, dating from 1765, adds a classical note. At Whitsun, the village is the scene of a medieval parade.

LA ROCHEPOT

This quiet village set in the rolling countryside at the southern end of the wine-producing Côte d'Or has one of the most celebrated and picturesque castles in Burgundy. 5km east of Nolay.

La Rochepot huddles at the foot of a rocky tree-covered outcrop on which stands its feudal castle, bristling with spires and pepperpot towers and roofed with the colourful glazed tiles for

---

Visitors are welcome to the temple most afternoons of the year, but only to the upper gallery, which looks down on the ground floor, used by participants in religious ceremonies. Here stands a 7m-high statue of Buddha in traditional pose, flanked by the figures of Padma Sambava, who developed

Buddhism in Tibet in the 9th century, and Tara, mother of Buddha. The walls are brightly decorated with frescos representing the life of Buddha. While the monastery is principally a centre of prayer and meditation, it also has a museum and a shop selling craft items and books.

BEAUMONT-SUR-VINGEANNE

FANCIFUL CHATEAU

Beaumont-sur-Vingeanne, north-east of Dijon, has an unusual château of a type rarely found in France.

The château is a rare French example of an architectural folly. A cross between a château and an *hôtel particulier*, it was built in 1724 by Claude Jolyot, the king's chaplain. Though small, the building

is well proportioned, and has a short double staircase sweeping up to the entrance. The roof of coloured tiles has a balustrade at the front, topped with sculptured figures and vases.

A rustic folly of a château.

SOLUTRÉ-POUILLY

This typical little village in the heart of the Burgundy vineyards lies in the shadow of a dramatic rocky escarpment, the scene of events thousands of years ago that have made Solutré famous. 9km west of Mâcon.

A quiet, pretty village, Solutré at first seems attractive but unexceptional. It is just outside the village that its unique feature is to be found: the tall, spectacular Roche de Solutré dominates the area. It has taken its name from the Solutrean period, some 20,000 years ago when the Upper Palaeolithic people who colonised the area perfected the art of making dressed flint weapons and tools. More dramatic still, the remains of tens of thousands of horses were found here, and it has been suggested that Palaeolithic hunters tracked massive herds of wild horses and drove them over the cliff to kill them for food.

Nowadays the cliff-face is popular with rock-climbers, but for the less adventurous a footpath offers an easier route to the top.

ST-AMAND-EN-PUISAYE

The little-known and intensely rural Puisaye region has been producing pottery for hundreds of years, a local tradition maintained in the many workshops of this village. 13km south of St-Fargeau.

Built on clay beds in the Vrille valley, St-Amand has been at the centre of the Puisaye pottery industry since 1316. It was not until the 17th century,

Fields full of vines encroach the base of the dramatic Roche de Solutré

MONCEAU
'LA SOLITUDE'

Monceau lies just off the N79, west of Mâcon. 'La Solitude' is reached along a track to the left just before the château.

The area around Mâcon is where the great romantic writer and politician, Alphonse de Lamartine, spent much of his life, and he did some of his most brilliant work while stay-

ing at the 17th-century Château Monceau, which he inherited from his aunt in 1833. However, much of his writing was done, not in the château itself, but in a small octagonal lodge named 'La Solitude', built of branches on a base of rocks, some 300m from the château. From there he could look out across his

however, that the trade really developed and the techniques and styles still used today came into being. As well as a school of pottery, the village has some 20 workshops and showrooms producing ceramics – simple for domestic needs and more decorative for ornamental use.

Unusually for Burgundy, all the village buildings are of red brick, including the château, built on the north bank of the river in the reign of François I and now open only for art exhibitions. The church, around which the village developed in the 12th and 13th centuries, has been destroyed three times in its turbulent history.

UCHON

From its lofty and spectacularly wild site this pretty village in miniature, known as the pearl of the Morvan, enjoys delightful views as far as the Massif Central. 23km south of Autun.

Tiny Uchon is a strange and compelling place occupying a wild mountain top scattered with extravagantly contorted granite boulders with names like the Devil's Claw and the Tottering Stone. Many a legend has been inspired by their weird shapes.

On a rocky mound stands a small and simple 14th-century church, and just below it a curious granite oratory to St-Sebastian, built to supplicate divine protection from the plague that ravaged the area in the 16th century. In the woods opposite are the remains of a feudal château, as well as an Orthodox monastery, which is open most afternoons for visits to the chapel and for the purchase of icons and aromatic plants.

There is superb walking in the area, with plenty of footpaths leading through the surrounding forest.

VALLERY

Two châteaux, one a feudal fortress, the other a Renaissance dwelling once owned by the famous Princes of Condé, distinguish this little village on the fringes of the Gâtine. 19km west of Sens.

Tucked away in a wooded valley, Vallery was home to the Condé family until the 18th century. The lords of Vallery lived in a medieval fortress for centuries, then, in the 16th century, they built the present château, a rather severe-looking Renaissance building in brick and stone. A daughter of the family gave the château to Louis I of Bourbon in the expectation that he would marry her in return. While he accepted her gift, however, he declined her hand, and was killed in battle at Jarnac in 1569 before he had made much use of his new home.

His great-grandson, Louis II, was brought up at the château and had a mausoleum built at the village church. Only the château grounds are open to the public.

VEZELAY

Dominated by its marvellous basilica, this beautiful village at the edge of the Morvan is one of the crowning glories of Burgundy – and of France – and draws pilgrims and tourists in large numbers. 15km south-west of Avallon.

Its pink ochre and white stone glowing warmly in the sunshine, Vézelay's 12th-century basilica of St Madeleine is a masterpiece of Romanesque art, protected by UNESCO as part of the world's heritage.

The abbey housing the relics of St Mary Magdalene became one of the most important pilgrimage centres in Christendom as early as the 11th century. It was in 1146 that St Bernard preached the Second Crusade at Vézelay, and 50 years later the armies of the Third Crusade gathered there. The 12th-century basilica is awe-inspiring, its great height and tall

Stylised carving over a doorway at the Basilica of St Madeleine

windows lending the light stone of the interior a magical radiance. Already in decline by the 14th century, the basilica was damaged during the Revolution and restored by Viollet-le-Duc.

The lovely village of closely terraced medieval houses spills down the hillside in front of the basilica.

beloved vineyards to the jagged profile of Solutré. Lamartine loved the isolation of the place and while there wrote *Journey to the East*, *The Story of the Girondins* and *Verses to the Count of Orsay*. The château is now an old people's home and is not open to the public, but the grounds can be visited.

Alphonse de Lamartine, poet, statesman and historian, born 1790 and died 1869, buried in the chapel at St-Point, near his favourite château.

SECRET FRANCE
FRANCHE-COMTÉ

Franche-Comté, the region to the south of Alsace, is one of widely varying countryside from the flat plains of the Haute Saône to the rugged and dramatic Jura mountains that run diagonally across the region in a series of stepped plateaux. As you travel across Franche-Comté, through the limestone valleys and cirques of the French Jura and along the meanders of the River Doubs, it is probably the churches that change most from neighbouring Alsace and Burgundy, the domes above their square or octagonal towers becoming almost onion-shaped. Churches and municipal buildings both have the multi-coloured tile designs in red, black, gold and green that are so typical of nearby Burgundy.

The northern part of the region is the Haute Saône, an extensive area of gently rolling farmland. A distinctive feature of many Haute Saone villages is the *lavoir*, or communal washing place. Some are plain shelters with stone slabs on which to beat the clothes. Others, designed to enhance the village, are truly elegant expressions of local pride.

Up on the high plateaux the houses take on an alpine character, with wide roofs and over-hanging eaves under which the firewood is kept dry. The *tuyé* is a feature of Haut Doubs farms. A huge fireplace with an equally wide chimney, it once served not only as the focus of family life on winter evenings, but was also used to smoke beef, hams and sausages. In the event of heavy snow blocking doors and windows, it provided a useful way out as well.

The region has a rich architectural heritage dating from many different periods, including medieval abbeys and châteaux, a gem of French 18th-centry industrial architecture at Arc-et-Senans, and a poignant chapel in memory of the war dead designed by Le Corbusier. Roman remains, impregnable fortresses perched on cliff tops and elegant spa towns all await those touring round the region.

However, it is for the thrilling scenery of the French Jura that Franche-Comté is best known. Craggy limestone escarpments overhanging clear sparkling rivers that cut through deep gorges and in places thunder down long cascades, are just some of the features to look out for, and high lakes and colourful caves can all be explored from the quiet mountain roads of the Haut Jura.

genièvre de Franche-Comté

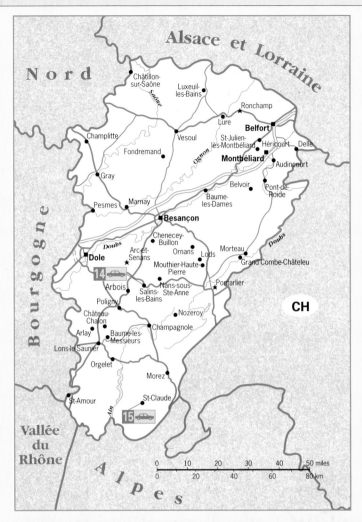

Above, limestone crags in
the Jura overhang peaceful
traditional farms
Right the local charcutier

Above, in the picturesque Jura village of
Arbois, precarious-looking houses are built
out from the rock face and overhang the
River Cuisance below
Right, a popular French tipple

ARLAY

An ancient site on the banks of the Seille, celebrated for its two châteaux, its noble park and its fine wines. 10km north of Lons-le-Saunier.

The ancient castle of the Comte de Chalon-Arlay, Prince of Orange, now lies in impressive ruins, a testimony to the power of this important family.

Arlay is now better known for its other château, an 18th-century building on the site of a former abbey, erected by the Comtesse de Lauraguais and altered in the 19th century by Prince d'Arenberg. The Prince's apartments can be visited, and contain some attractive furniture by local craftspeople.

At rest in the peaceful village of Arlay

The village itself is a quiet agricultural settlement, where the major *vigneron* has an interesting selection of Côtes du Jura wines, some bottles dating from before the Revolution.

BAUME-LES-MESSIEURS

In a lovely setting where three valleys meet, the village boasts an ancient and famous abbey as well as the natural beauties of the Grottes de Baume, with their remarkable stalactites. 11km north-east of Lons-le-Saunier.

The approach to Baume from the north passes sheer bluffs with scree slopes at their feet, several kilometres of hairpin bends and a waterfall, its rounded rocks covered with moss and ferns. Baume-les-Moines was reputedly founded by the Irish saint, Colomban, in the 6th century. Later it became a Benedictine house.

By the 14th century, as monastic life became less ascetic, monks were only accepted if they were of the nobility, and Baume-les-Moines became Baume-les-Messieurs. Of the 'Messieurs', Jean de Watteville, who became Abbot in 1659 was undoubtedly the most notorious and colourful. He died in the Abbey in

1702, at the age of 84, and his tomb is in the north wall of the nave just before the transept. The church itself has the most magnificent Flemish retable behind the high altar, a present from the city of Ghent in 1525.

BELVOIR

A tiny agricultural community clinging to a ridge top and dominated by its château, which has watched over the Plateau de Sancy for seven centuries. 42km south-west of Montbéliard

The imposing castle, originally built in the 13th century, has had a chequered history. Laid waste in the 15th century, it was rebuilt in the Renaissance before going into a long period of decline, and earlier this century it was in a state of dereliction. Then it was bought by the painter Pierre Jouffroy and his wife who, despite severe setbacks and a fire, have worked over many years to restore it. Beautifully furnished, it contains paintings by the Ornans painter Courbet as well as a Vandyke portrait.

The village contains some lovely old stone houses arranged round a square with a central fountain. Some houses were even built on top of the formidable old ramparts, parts of which can still be seen today.

ARC-ET-SENANS

SALINE ROYAL

Arc-et-Senans lies north of Salins-les-Bains. From the D32 follow the long entrance driveway to a Palladian-style portico.

The Saline Royal de Chaux (Royal Salt Works) were built in the 18th century by the architect Claude Ledoux, who was also inspector of salt works. Briny water from the springs at Salins was channelled off to Arc-et-Senans through a system of wooden pipes.

Most of the 14 buildings that make up the salt works are arranged in a semi-circle facing the Director's house, an imposing classical-style building.

Ledoux dreamed of building a 'model town' with the works at its heart, but this was never fulfilled.

In the beginning salt production went well, but gradually the wooden pipes disintegrated, production fell, and the works closed by the end of the 19th century. The buildings now house a Centre for Studies of the Future.

Displays relating to Ledoux may be seen at the Centre for Studies of the Future

CHAMPLITTE

An ancient fortified village in the lush valley of the Salon, notable for its Renaissance *vigneron* houses and its annual festival dedicated to the patron saint of *vignerons*. 20km north of Gray.

The château on its rocky spur dominates the village and the surrounding countryside. Imposing wrought-iron gates and a long gravel drive lead up to the fine Renaissance façade and its 18th-century wings. It now houses a museum of the history of the ordinary people of the region, the astonishing achievement of

The village street curves away under the cliffs at Baume-les-Messieurs

Albert Demard, the father of the present curator.

The village streets descend in stately fashion to the Salon, lined with rather austere 16th-and 17th-century houses and dominated by the severe 14th-century bell-tower of the church. Here and there are interesting squares, such as the Place des Halles and Place des Grenouilles, and remains of the old fortifications. On 22 January each year the village and château come to vivid life for the festival of St-Vincent, patron saint of vignerons, which has been celebrated here since 1719.

THE JURA AND ITS CAVES

The great limestone range of the Jura rises above the flat countryside of the Bresse and the Saône plain to straddle the border with Switzerland. The highest point is in the south-east, at the Crêt de la Neige (1718m). To the north and west are undulating plateaux carved out by glaciers and now dotted with forests, rivers, lakes, waterfalls and *reculées* – steep-sided gorges ending in a *cirque*, or rock amphitheatre, from which water gushes. Some of these *sources* are actually rivers resurfacing, as the Lison does near the Grotte Sarrazine. The caves perforating the limestone rocks can be vast, like the Grottes de Baume, near Baume-les-Messieurs. As well as their underground streams and prehistoric remains, they are rich in geological interest, with stalagmites and stalactites at the Gouffre de Poudrey, and columns at the Grottes d'Osselle, both near Besançon. Ice remains unfrozen all year round at the Grotte de la Glacière, south of Baume-les-Dames.

CHATEAU-CHALON

A hilltop wine village rising above its celebrated vineyards, with some fine old vigneron houses and an ancient church. 11km north-east of Lons-le Saunier.

Château-Chalon's ancient fortress, of which only ruins remain, from the 7th century protected a convent of Benedictine nuns. It was the nuns who first planted the vines for which the village is now famous. Many of the fine, tall vigneron houses in the village, dating from the 18th and 19th centuries, offer tastings in their deep cellars. Little trace remains of the fortifications, or of the Benedictine nunnery, but the 10th century church of St-Pierre still dominates the village, roofed, like many of the houses, in thin slabs of the local limestone. From the belvedere at the end of the village street is a magnificent view across the plain, and from the terrace by the church you can look across to the 15th-century Château du Pin, recently restored and well worth a visit.

Vineyards stripe the lanscape below Château-Chalon, as though it had been combed with a giant rake

SECRET PLACES

PONTARLIER

JOUX CHATEAU

The château lies 4km south-east of Pontarlier.

Joux château, standing on a rocky bluff overlooking the River Doubs, is a fascinating example of the development of military fortifications, having been improved and expanded over six centuries since it was first built.

The original castle, including the towers, was built in the 11th century. It was enlarged under Charles Quint, and in 1678 Vauban carried out further additions to strengthen its defences. In the 19th century an underground fort was added. Altogether, there are five lines of fortifications, one inside another, separated by open ditches and linked by three drawbridges. Within its walls, also, is one of the deepest wells in Europe.

During the Empire, the château was used as a prison for military and political prisoners. It now houses a fascinating military museum – with items including weapons, uniforms and headgear ranging from the 18th to 20th centuries – in the old dungeons.

There is a good view of the Doubs valley from the artillery terrace.

A breathtaking site, heavily fortified.

CHATILLON-SUR-SAONE

A treasure-house of vernacular 17th-century architecture, tucked away behind the main road and miraculously preserved down the centuries. 11km east of Bourbonne-les-Bains.

A fortress was built here, at the confluence of the Saône and the Apance, in the 13th century. In the 14th century the village was fortified, and in the 15th century it was destroyed by the Duke of Burgundy. It is the village as it was rebuilt from 1540 that has survived, and in 1985 a local *association* Saône-Lorraine was formed to retain and restore as much as can be saved of this little Renaissance jewel. In one of the old houses a school is being established, in which stonemasons and carpenters will be instructed in the skills and tools of their Renaissance forbears.

The Grenier à Sel, the first of the old buildings to be restored, is now an exhibition centre and there are guided tours of the village.

CHENECEY-BUILLON

A peaceful, secluded village on a quiet-flowing trout stream reputed to be one of the best in France and crossed by a magnificent bridge. 17km south-west of Besançon.

The village of Chenecey-Buillon, lying peacefully among green meadows and wooded hills on the banks of the Loue, takes its name from the Chenecey family castle, which stood here in 1124 and around which the village first clustered. The ruins of the Abbey of Buillon, founded by Cistercians in 1133, can still be seen. A superb 17th-century stone bridge crosses the river, a small hotel stands on the water's edge, and there is a small, four-square 14th-century church, much restored in 1734. An old forge that stands just up-river is a fine example of traditional industrial architectural and a reminder of the local importance of the iron industry. The first records of iron being worked here go back to 1500, and the last forge closed as recently as 1950.

A quiet, unassuming little village, Chenecey-Buillon is recommended for its fishing and its total peace.

FONDREMAND

A picturesque village with a bubbling spring and a powerful medieval keep, which hosts a popular festival of traditional crafts every Bastille Day. 24km south-west of Vesoul.

The imposing medieval keep that dominates the village is an indication of the former importance of this site, inhabited as early as Merovingian times. Of the original fortress only the 11th-century keep and its deep dungeons remain, with a short stretch of the bailey wall that used to encompass the whole village. From this wall one can look down on to the stone-lined basin and *lavoir* into which the emerging river Romaine has been channelled. Houses from the 15th to the 19th century line the narrow streets of the village, and in the château itself the village *curé* has set up a wonderfully haphazard museum of local artefacts. For three days around 14 July each year Fondremand holds an extremely popular festival of traditional local crafts.

GRAND'COMBE-CHATELEU

A mountain village renowned for its beautifully preserved farmhouses, complete with traditional interiors. 6km south-west of Morteau.

Like many a Haut Doubs village Grand'Combe-Châteleu is built in two small valleys, or *combes*. The Doubs, coming from nearby Remonot, runs along one, and a more capricious torrent, the Théverot, along the other.

Top, a colourful display at Fondremand Below, an old, weathered roof at Grand'Combe-Chateleu

The origins of the village go back to the 12th century; in the 15th century it was a thriving community, but later it suffered great destruction. An outbreak of the plague left the village virtually deserted, and like many nearby communities it was largely repopulated from neighbouring Savoie.

Most of the scattered farmhouses are set in meadowland, facing south, and backed by the communal forest. Typical of the region, they consist of two or more storeys, combining living quarters, kitchens, stabling and cattle byres, barn, grain and fodder storage around one or more *tuyé* chimneys: large fireplaces designed for both heating and smoking food.

Left, the tranquil river at Arbois
Above, lush greenery at the beautiful source of the River Lison

TOUR 14 – 100KM
THE NORTHERN JURA: SALT, CAVERNS AND WINE.

The northern Jura was once fought over and coveted for its salt, extracted from the briny springs around Salins since Celtic times. As salt production declined in the 19th century, however, the Jura wines have taken over as the region's main source of wealth. The area is also rich in Celtic and Roman remains, and in the natural wonders for which the whole Jura region is renowned. The tour takes in all these aspects of the area, visiting towns once famous for their salt springs, caves and underground rivers, and the wine capital of the Jura.

ROUTE DIRECTIONS

Leave Salins-les-Bains by the **D492** to Nans-sous-Ste-Anne. From here a small road is marked to the Source du Lison. After visiting the source and the Grotte Sarrazine, take the **D295** to Labergement-du-Navois and then the **D9** to Levier. Leave Levier on the **D452**, signposted to Villers-sur-Chalamont and

from there follow the old Roman road, the Route du Scay, through the Forêt de la Joux. From the arboretum, carry on along the **D66** to Onglières. Crossing the **D21e/D471**, the road leads into Nozeroy.

From Nozeroy, take the **D119** heading towards Charbonny and then the **D21** to St-Germain-en-Montagne. At the Pont de Gratteroche, take the **N5** signposted to Poligny, and

fork right on to the **D469** just after Montrond. This leads to the Cirque de Fer à Cheval and the Reculée des Planches. The **D469** continues towards Arbois, passing l'Ermitage d'Arbois before entering the town.

Take the **N83** north out of Arbois, signposted towards Besançon, and turn right after 2km on to the **D105**, through Aiglepierre and back into Salins-des-Bains.

PLACES OF INTEREST

SALINS-LES-BAINS
Salins was one of the centres of the Celtic 'La Tene' civilisation. Here also, the Romans exploited the salt springs. Because of the importance of its salt production to the economy of France, Salins was defended by two forts – Mont Belin and Fort St-André – built by Vauban in the 17th century on the high bluffs above the valley.

A vivid idea of the processes of extraction and evaporation of salt from the briny water of the local springs can be had from a visit to what remains of the underground workings. These closed, after 1,000 years of production, in 1962, no longer able to compete with Lorraine's salt mines or the salt pans of the Mediterranean.

SOURCE DU LISON – GROTTE SARRAZINE
In this limestone country, water often disappears to re-appear again somewhere nearby – as here where the Lison cascades down two picturesque falls and along its short course before becoming a tributary of the Loue. On the D477 the source is within sight of the small car park. Equipped with well-soled boots and a torch, one can penetrate some way into the cavern from which the river flows.

A two-minute walk from the source, across a footbridge is the Grotte Sarrazine. A huge 90m-high cave reaches back into the rock face and a small stream flows out to join the Lison.

Further up the gorge is the Creux Billard, where after heavy rain a waterfall appears at this point, evidence of the Lison flowing underground. At other times, the water flows underground to the regular source downstream.

LODS

A picturesque riverside village with fine old vigneron houses and watermills overlooking the weirs and waterfalls of the Loue. 12km south-east of Ornans.

The village clings to the right bank of the River Loue as it tumbles down the valley from its source a few kilometres upstream. Only the rush of the river over the rapids disturbs the peace it shares with the other tiny hamlets along the river. Steep narrow streets climb up to the church, lined with imposing vigneron houses that indicate the importance of the vine in the village's past. Beneath them are large and impressive cellars dating from the 16th and 17th centuries.

One stone arch of an old medieval packbridge can still be seen, just by the weir over which the River Loue rushes in the centre of the village. It is over-looked by a number of old watermills and a forge.

MARNAY

An ancient fortified river crossing clustered under its fortress, now a peaceful agricultural settlement offering fine water-sports and a nature reserve. 20km west of Besançon.

A fortified river crossing since Roman times, Marnay grew up as two villages, Marnay-la-Ville around the 12th-century church, and Marnay-le-Bourg around the fortress on a spur overlooking the Ognon river. They formed one community in Year VIII after the Revolution. Repeatedly burned and besieged in the turbulent 15th, 16th and 17th centuries, Marnay nevertheless retains a surprising number of fine houses from the 15th and 16th centuries. The finest building in Marnay is the Hôtel Terrier de Santans, recently restored to its Renaissance splendour and now housing the Hôtel de Ville. St-Symporien church, originally built in the 11th to 13th centuries, has been restored many times. Used as stables by occupying troops in 1595, it was reconsecrated in 1613.

The Ognon river divides into several branches to the south-east, a favourite spot for canoe and kayak enthusiasts.

NOZEROY

See page 118.

CIRQUE DU FER A CHEVAL

The main source of the River Cuisance, which flows through Arbois before joining the Loue, is a cascade in a cavern in the 245m-high cliff of the Reculée des Planches. A lower gallery – *galerie des gours* – is the bed of the river, a series of basins connected by waterfalls, with a lake over 130m long at the end. An upper gallery, an abandoned river bed, is full of stalagmites and stalactites.

ARBOIS

On the banks of the Cuisance, surrounded by over 700 hectares of vineyards, Arbois is the wine capital of the Jura. Its wine, made from Poulsard grapes, has a unique bouquet and tang. It also has a notorious reputation for liquefying the legs of immoderate drinkers.

The 64m-high, ochre-coloured tower of the church of St-Just dominates the town and surrounding vineyards. From the walk around the church there are views of the river, and to hear the church bells ringing out down the valley is a special experience

The house and the laboratory where the great scientist Louis Pasteur worked on fermentation, is now a museum, for the town is justly proud of its best-known son.

A sign to tempt all comers at Arbois

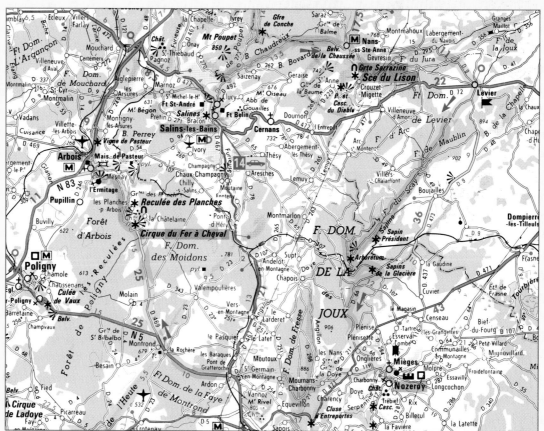

MOUTHIER-HAUTE-PIERRE

Set in the spectacular scenery of the upper reaches of the Loue valley, this picturesque and substantial village, famous for its kirsch, is prettiest at cherry-blossom time. 20km north-west of Pontarlier.

An abbey was founded on a hill in the middle of this rocky amphitheatre in the 9th century.

Originally made up of two villages, Mouthier and Haute-Pierre, Mouthier today still divides into two parts: Mouthier-Bas on the bank of the river beside the old bridge, and Mouthier-Haut on the hilltop, its imposing vigneron houses, dating from the Renaissance to the 18th century, clustered round the church. Built in the 15th century, the church was transformed into a Flamboyant Gothic masterpiece at the beginning of the next century. The soaring octagonal spire was added in the same century by Cardinal de Granvelle. Inside the church are fine 13th- and 14th-century statues and woodwork.

NANS-SOUS-STE-ANNE

A charming secluded little village on the banks of the Lison, noted for its remarkable old water-powered forge. 20km north-east of Salins-les-Bains.

Until 1969 there was a flourishing tool-making industry at Nans, making scythes, sickles, pruning hooks and other agricultural implements. The waters of the Arcange, a tributary of the Lison, powered the bellows and the huge oak beams of the drop-hammers and at the height of its activity, in the years before World War I, the workshop produced up to 20,000 scythes annually. Now the 19th-century workshops have been preserved as a living museum of local craftsmanship and traditions.

Above the village stand the ruins of a medieval castle, and below are the vestiges of an abbey. Five kilometres to the south is the Grotte Sarrazine, the magnificent natural limestone amphitheatre which is the source of the Lison.

The pretty village of Nans-sous-Ste-Anne, surrounded by greenery

NOZEROY

A fortified village in a picturesque setting, this medieval capital of the Jura has retained much of its historic fabric and charm. 11km north-east of Champagnole.

Set on a hummock in a shallow saucer-shaped bowl, the site of Nozeroy was both easily defensible and fertile enough to allow the peasants to feed the lord's family. The first castle was built in about 1250, by Jean l'Antique de Chalon. In the 16th century Philibert de Chalon, held sumptuous court here in the Renaissance palace that had replaced the medieval fortress, which was in turn reduced to ruins in the Revolution.

The road leads through the castellated Porte de l'Horloge, entrance to the fortified village since 1450. Some of the 17th- and 18th-century houses still have doorways and carvings bearing witness to past grandeur, and here and there carvings and stonework from the old castle are incorporated into a wall or doorway. The 15th-century church

SECRET PLACES

RONCHAMP

CHAPEL OF NOTRE-DAME-DU-HAUT

The chapel lies 1.5km north of Ronchamp, up a steep, twisting road.

Notre-Dame-du-Haut, perched on a hill overlooking the town of Ronchamp, was built in 1955 by the architect Le Corbusier to commemorate French soldiers killed here in 1944, replacing an earlier chapel destroyed in the fighting.

The chapel was constructed entirely from concrete, which was used to create a building of great simplicity and grace, its clean lines and inflated roof blending in beautifully with the surrounding countryside and echoing the peaks and valleys in the Jura and Vosges mountains that can be seen from the hilltop.

However, it is the interior that is particularly striking. Small, irregular windows set into the thick walls create strong, dramatic contrasts of light and shadow, giving the interior an expansive quality created by a feeling of light and space, while the sloping walls disguise the solidity and rigidity of the concrete.

'J'ai voulu créer un lieu de silence, de prière, de paix, de joie intérieure...' – Le Corbusier

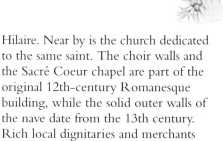

FRANCHE-COMTE

PESMES

Flowers blossom outside a wood store in Nans-sous-Ste-Anne

with its typical Franche-Comté bell-tower contains a notable 15th-century pulpit and some fine choir stalls, as well as a 15th-century polychrome stone statue of the Virgin and Child.

A turbulent history has not destroyed the historic atmosphere and architectural treasures of this village, perched above the River Ognon on the borders of Burgundy and Franche-Comté. 22km north of Dole.

A settlement has existed here since Roman times to protect the road from Dole to Gray. The little town was burned by Saracens in 736 and again by Huns 200 years later. Decimated by plague in the Middle Ages it then lay in the front line in the disputes between France and the Empire until the end of the Thirty Years War, in 1678.

The Grand'Rue, a wide street with yew trees and rose bushes down the middle, runs down from the topmost part of the old town to one of the two remaining town gates, the Porte St-Hilaire. Near by is the church dedicated to the same saint. The choir walls and the Sacré Coeur chapel are part of the original 12th-century Romanesque building, while the solid outer walls of the nave date from the 13th century. Rich local dignitaries and merchants continually added to and embellished the church in the 16th century. As well as its fine Gothic 13th-century vaulting, it has 16th-century lierne vaulting and other beautiful Renaissance work, including coloured marble balusters and ornaments and a marble pulpit.

The Ognon river washes the foot of the old castle walls, making a splendid setting for the *son et lumière* programmes in July and August, which vividly recall a tumultuous past. Fishing, canoeing, riding and walking are some of the country pursuits possible around Pesmes today.

The meandering Ognon, from Pesmes

TOUR 15 - 130 KM.
THE HAUT JURA NATIONAL PARK

The Haut Jura is a region of wild, wooded mountains, rolling farmland, rivers cutting deep gorges through limestone cliffs, spectacular caves and dramatic waterfalls. Hill farms are grouped around the two pivots of the community – the church tower, in times past a place of physical as well as spiritual refuge, and the *fruitière* to which the milk is brought to be turned into Comté, the local Gruyére-type cheese. The route travels through heavily wooded limestone cliffs, with plenty of picnic spots and quiet side roads that provide good stopping places.

Below, original casts in ¼ scale at the Pipe Museum, St-Claude

ROUTE DIRECTIONS

Leave St-Claude by the **D436** towards Oyonnax. At Lavans-lès-St-Claude turn right on to the **D118** to St-Lupicin. Continue through les Crozets and Etival into Clairvaux-les-Lacs. The **D144** leads from here to la Frasnée. Return to Clairvaux and turn right onto the **N78** towards the Hérisson Falls.

From the falls, head north on the **D75** to La Frasnois and Narlay. Cross the **N5** at Pont de la Chaux and continue along the **D16** towards les Planches and Gorges de la Langouette.

Continue to Foncine-le-Bas, and then turn right onto the **D437** to St-Laurent-en-Grandvaux. Leave St-Laurent on the **N5**, following signs to Geneve and Morez. Pass through Morez and les Rousses, and 3km out of les Rousses, turn on to the **D29** and join the **D25**, following signs for Crêt Pela. Near a small lake at the end of the valley, turn into Lamoura. Once through Lamoura, follow the **D436** through the Gorges du Flumen, past the Chapeau de Gendarme and the Saute du Chien viewpoint, back into St Claude.

PLACES OF INTEREST

ST-CLAUDE
St-Claude is France's acknowledged centre of pipe-making, and several of the workshops encourage visitors. There is an exhibition of pipe-making and of another St-Claude industry – diamond-cutting – close to the cathedral.

The 14th-century cathedral has splendidly carved choir stalls displaying a puckish sense of humour on the part of the craftsmen, although unfortunately, 200 carvings along the south side were destroyed in a smouldering fire in 1983.

LA FRASNÉE
This tiny village just off the D144 has a small church and a café conveniently situated beside cascades that tumble down moss-covered rocks.

You can scramble up the side of the stream, a little way up the narow cirque of limestone cliffs. Or you can take the path signposted to the Belvedere, from which there is a view right down the valley.

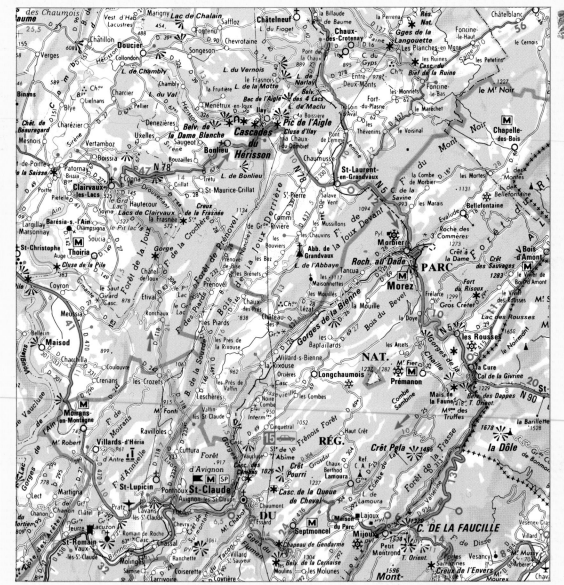

CLAIRVAUX LES LACS

There is a glimpse of the two lakes from the D118 as it dips down into Clairvaux. A minor road leads down to the lakeside, where the earliest lake dwellings in France were discovered over a hundred years ago.

CASCADES DU HERISSON

Five hundred metres from the car park are the Eventail Falls, a spectacular 65m cascade where the River Hérisson enters a narrow gorge. A narrow path crosses the river and after 300m re-crosses it over the Lacuzon foot-bridge. The best view of the Grand Saut, a sheer drop of 60m, is from the bottom. The river tumbles down a number of lime-stone lintels and steps, as you continue upstream to the Saut de la Forge, a 12m drop into a small shallow basin.

GORGES DU FLUMEN

The River Flumen, a tributary of the Tacon, has carved itself a 10km gorge through sheer limestone

Above, the holiday centre of les Rousses is beautifully set on the lakeside, with a view to the Swiss Alps Right, the spectacular falls at Herisson

cliffs. The most extraordinary formation is the Chapeau du Gendarme, a huge slab of sedimentary limestone which has been folded upwards by incredible internal forces.

There is a stopping place at the Dog's Leap (Saut du Chien) to allow a longer look at the valley and rock formations.

ST-JULIEN-LES-MONTBELIARD

A tiny and historic village set in a forest, which has managed to keep its identity despite its proximity to a large town. 5km west of Montbéliard.

Set in forest, the village has always had close links with its larger neighbour Montbéliard, but nevertheless has a long history, being first mentioned in 1150, and remains a village, having resisted urban sprawl and developments.

The 18th-century *lavoir* still has its hooks and ladders to be used in case of fire, to pull burning thatch off roofs and to rescue people from upper floors. The church tower has the typical Franche-Comté bulbous four-sided dome, but is in the red sandstone of the Vosges instead of the usual pale local stone.

One of the oldest and most interesting houses, its lintel dated 1675, was once the hunting lodge of the Princes of Würtemberg. Later it was turned into the presbytery, which it remained until 1950.

SECRET FRANCE

ATLANTIC COAST

France's Atlantic coast covers a vast area of hugely varied landscapes, from the salt marshes and luminous coastline in the north to famous wine villages and pine forests in the south, and it also boasts some of the country's best beaches. The villages are as varied as the landscapes, reflecting the traditional ways of life of the various regions.

Along the northern coast, mussels and oysters are still cultivated as they have been for centuries and the march of time seems to have made little impact on rural life. Inland, the villages that dot the mysterious salt marshes of Marais Poitevin are unspoilt. Generally they are still dominated by solid-looking Romanesque churches, often with little boats hanging from the rafters, as a reminder of the importance to this vulnerable land of the sea.

Further south, the wealthy cognac-growing region of the Charente around Angoulême and Cognac itself is noticeably more prosperous (though no less sleepy). Then perhaps comes the biggest and most welcome surprise for the traveller in this region: the area around Bordeaux and its coast. The names of the villages may be famous throughout the world for their wines, but they are surprisingly unspoilt and not too crowded even in the height of summer.

The Bay of Arcachon has served as an elegant playground for the wealthy of Bordeaux for almost a century now, but for all its *chic*, it remains less crowded and considerably less developed than the more popular Riviera, and therefore more rewarding for those who take the trouble to explore it. Below the bay is the vast forest of the Landes. This area was a huge swamp edged by dunes until the end of the 19th century, when it was fixed in place by the planting of thousands of pine trees.

One of the joys of driving through France is sampling the regional cuisine. In this respect, the Atlantic coast certainly lives up to expectations. It is particularly famous for its oysters and mussels. If it's history you're interested in, you won't be disappointed. *En route* you'll find churches and châteaux, and interesting museums ranging from the military to the amusing and the natural. But for many, the real joy of travelling in this area lies in visiting the sleepy, sun-kissed villages where time seems to have stood still, or walking along deserted beaches at sunset, where there's still enough space to get away from it all.

moules de Côte Atlantique

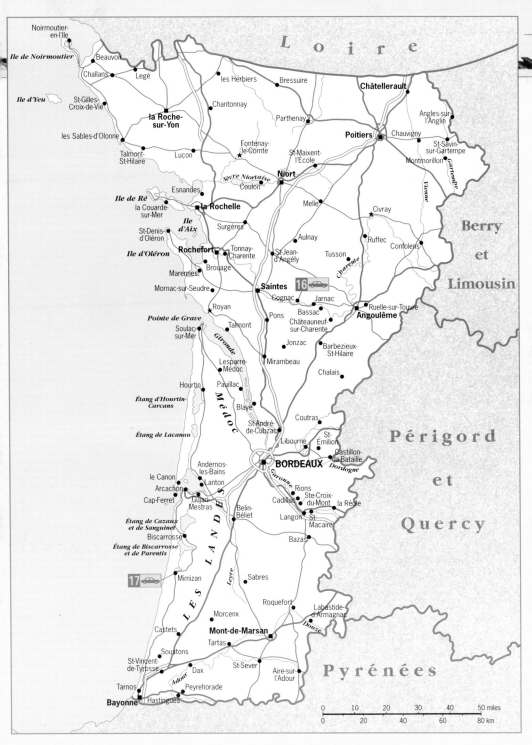

Loire

Noirmoutier-en-l'Ile
Ile de Noirmoutier
Beauvoir
Challans
Legé
les Herbiers
Bressuire
Châtellerault
Ile d'Yeu
St-Gilles-Croix-de-Vie
Chantonnay
Parthenay
Angles-sur-l'Anglin
la Roche-sur-Yon
Poitiers
Chauvigny
St-Savin-sur-Gartempe
Talmont-St-Hilaire
les Sables-d'Olonne
Fontenay-le-Comte
St-Maixent-l'École
Montmorillon
Luçon
Sèvre Niortaise
Niort
Esnandes
Coulon
Melle
Civray
Ile de Ré
la Couarde-sur-Mer
la Rochelle
Surgères
Aulnay
Ruffec
Confolens
Ile d'Aix
St-Denis-d'Oléron
Rochefort
Tonnay-Charente
St-Jean-d'Angély
Tusson
Charente
Ile d'Oléron
Marennes
Brouage
16
Mornac-sur-Seudre
Saintes
Cognac
Jarnac
Ruelle-sur-Touvre
Royan
Bassac
Angoulême
Pons
Châteauneuf-sur-Charente
Pointe de Grave
Soulac-sur-Mer
Talmont
Jonzac
Barbezieux-St-Hilaire
Gironde
Lesparre-Médoc
Mirambeau
Chalais
Hourtin
Pauillac
Étang d'Hourtin-Carcans
Médoc
Blaye
Coutras
Étang de Lacanau
St-André-de-Cubzac
Libourne
St-Émilion
Andernos-les-Bains
BORDEAUX
Castillon-la-Bataille
le Canon
Lanton
Dordogne
Arcachon
Garonne
Rions
Ste-Croix-du-Mont
Cap-Ferret
Gujan-Mestras
Cadillac
la Réole
Étang de Cazaux et de Sanguinet
Belin-Béliet
Langon
St-Macaire
Biscarrosse
Bazas
Étang de Biscarrosse et de Parentis
LES LANDES
Leyre
17
Mimizan
Sabres
Morcenx
Roquefort
Labastide-d'Armagnac
Castets
Mont-de-Marsan
Douze
Soustons
Tartas
St-Vincent-de-Tyrosse
St-Sever
Aire-sur-l'Adour
Tarnos
Adour
Dax
Peyrehorade
Bayonne
Hastingues

Berry et Limousin

Périgord et Quercy

Pyrénées

0 10 20 30 40 50 miles
0 20 40 60 80 km

The Marais Poitevin is a mysterious region that is well worth quiet exploration

Below left, life proceeds at a quiet pace in the forest region of the Landes
Below, the Atlantic coast around Bordeaux boasts mile upon mile of uncrowded golden beaches

ANGLES-SUR-L'ANGLIN

Perched on the banks of the River Anglin, this historic village offers considerable architectural interest, as well as perpetuating the art of drawn threadwork. 34km south-east of Châtellerault.

A stone bridge with an old watermill beside it crosses the river at Angles-sur-l'Anglin, linking the upper and lower parts of the village.

The upper village is dominated by the ruins of a 12th-century fortress and the tall Romanesque bell-tower of the church. From here there is a delightful view down to the tranquil river Anglin with its stone bridge, and across to the lower village, known as Ste-Croix, huddled around its venerable old 11th-century abbey church.

The well-preserved houses which surround the two churches, many of them dating from the Renaissance, are attractive and distinctive examples of the traditional building style of the Poitou.

Since the days of Napoleon III Angles-sur-l'Anglin has been famous for its delicate drawn threadwork. The craft is still practised today, and some of the finest examples can be seen at the fête which takes place here on the first Sunday of every August.

BASSAC

This tiny village, situated on the River Charente and surrounded by Cognac vineyards, is celebrated for its remarkable 1,000-year-old abbey. 3km south-east of Jarnac.

It was at the dawn of the 11th century that Benedictine monks founded a monastery here above the meandering Charente. A little stone bridge below the church gives a good view of the abbey buildings, dating from the

Water sports are popular on the lagoon on which Biscarosse is built

11th century to the 18th. The most handsome is undoubtedly the abbey church, with its Romanesque façade with defences added in the 15th century and its magnificent four-storey square bell-tower. Inside, the Gothic nave shelters a 13th-century statue of St Nicolas, its feet worn away by generations of girls praying for husbands. The 18th-century choir contains some beautifully sculpted stalls.

SECRET PLACES

FONTENAY-LE-COMTE

CHATEAU DE TERRE NEUVE

Fontenay-le-Comte is an old market town lying at the foot of hills astride the River Vendée and is the capital of the Bas-Poitou.

During the Renaissance period the town was very prosperous, becoming the home of poets and writers and as a result displays a considerable amount of

The pretty village that clusters round the abbey has narrow streets lined with high stone walls sheltering substantial old farmhouses, with lovely gardens stretching down to the river.

BISCAROSSE

Lying at the point where the beaches of the Gironde meet those of the Landes, Biscarosse and its surroundings form a fascinating microcosm of life and landscapes of the Landes. 40km south of Arcachon.

The beach at Biscarosse-Plage is one of the longest unbroken strips of sand and dune on the Côte d'Argent, swept by salt breezes mingled evocatively with the scent of pine trees. For a long time a base for sea-planes and hydro-aeronautics, it now also has a museum of hydro-aviation. The village of Biscarosse lies some 3km inland through the forest from the beach, on the edge of a freshwater lagoon where there is a choice of water sports. The village has a 15th-century Gothic church, restored in 1929, and the Château de Montrun, built from the 12th to the 16th centuries (not open to the public). During July and August there is also a nature museum with displays of the flora and fauna in which the Landes are so rich.

BROUAGE

Once the chief trading port for salt on the Atlantic coast and a jewel of naval defensive architecture, this landlocked village and its silted-up

Looking through the Porte-de-la-Mer along one the the old streets of Cadillac

harbour are now pervaded by an air of nostalgic melancholy. 18km south-west of Rochefort.

In the Middle Ages Brouage was an important trading centre for salt from the salt pans of the Saintonge. In the 17th century, after the siege of la Rochelle, Cardinal Richelieu ordered that it should be fortified, and the *bastide* was constructed.

At the height of its glory Brouage was the strong point of France's Atlantic defences. By the end of the

17th century, however, it was already in decline: the harbour silted up, the salt marshes became pestilential and the *bastide* was virtually abandoned. Today it has a population of some 200, and is still entered through the magnificent Porte de France. The gridiron layout of the *bastide*, the church, the governor's residence, the powder magazine and the ramparts are all intact and can be visited.

CADILLAC

This 700-year-old hilltop bastide, still surrounded by its 14th-century ramparts, lies at the heart of a region renowned for its sweet white wines. 40km south-east of Bordeaux.

Founded in 1280, Cadillac is dominated by the somewhat forbidding outlines of the château of the Duc d'Epernon, positioned on a limestone spur overlooking the River Garonne. There has been a castle on this site since the 13th century, but the powerful Duc d'Epernon, a favourite of Henri III, Henri IV and Louis XIII, demolished it in order to build a more splendid dwelling. Constructed between 1598 and 1620, the château was badly damaged during the Revolution and later became a prison. The interior, now classified as a historic monument, is beautifully decorated with tapestries, and contains some sumptuously carved marble fireplaces dating from 1606. The unusually well-preserved ramparts of the *bastide* retain two of their original fortified gateways, the Porte de Mer and the Port de l'Horloge.

Renaissance architecture. A splendid example is the Château de Terre Neuve, which lies at the end of a long avenue of chestnut trees and is reached from the Pont Neuf.

This charming building was constructed in the 16th century by architect Jean Morisson for his friend, the poet Nicholas Rapin, and was subsequently altered and restored in 1850. Richly decorated in the taste of the time, its façade features nine magnificent terracotta figures of the Muses and various inscriptions by Rapin himself. One of the porches origi-

nates from the Château de Coulonges, located 9km to the east. The interior boasts some fine fireplaces decorated with alchemists' symbols and griffins, ornate ceilings, notable 16th-century panelling and Louis XV and Louis XVI furniture. Also on view are collections of

costumes, ivories and weapons. The château is open to visitors during the summer months.

A charming 18th-century château that was built for a poet.

TOUR 16 – 125KM
COGNAC COUNTRY

The region of Charente is an area of flat country with wide horizons, full of rolling vineyards and quiet sleepy villages. The river itself, once described as the 'most beautiful river of the French kingdom' was responsible for the region's wealth, and there are fine river views along the route. The tour starts at Cognac, renowned the world over for its fine brandy, and travels through cognac vineyeards and cornfields, quiet hamlets and medieval riverside towns, to the fine old cities of Angoulême and Châteauneuf-sur-Charente. It returns through the Petite Champagne region, past medieval hilltop towns that were once resting places for pilgrims on the way to Santiago de Compestela.

PLACES OF INTEREST

COGNAC
A town famous for its old centre – and its brandy.

JARNAC
Jarnac's fame is owed to a duel fought there on July 10 1547. La Chateignerie, a friend of the king, had insulted Guy Chabot, Lord of Jarnac, and the duel was fought before Henri II, the Queen and all the court. Chabot made a surprise attack on his opponent and cut his leg off at the shin, giving rise to the expression 'coup de Jarnac'. The old abbey church dates back to the 11th century, and has a richly decorated tower.

BASSAC
See page 124.

CHATEAUNEUF-SUR-CHARENTE
On the left bank of the River Charente,

Châteauneuf was an important river crossing during the Middle Ages and was constantly fought over during the Hundred Years War, finally being captured by the French in 1380. The 12th-century Romanesque church of St-Pierre, which was damaged during fighting between the French and English in the 14th century, and between Catholics and Protestants during the 16th century, has wonderful carvings of human figures and animals over the main doorway.

BARBEZIEUX-ST-HILAIRE
Barbezieux is the capital of the Petite Champagne region. Only this area and the Grande Champagne (a small area south-east of Cognac) may call their brandy Fine Champagne. It is a tranquil town made up of old houses and narrow streets that twist up the hill to the summit, where there is an imposing 15th-

Hilaire. Follow the **D14** for 9.5km, and then turn right on to the **N10** into Barbezieux-St-Hilaire.

Leave Barbezieux on the **D731** following signs to Archiac (14km). From Archiac take the **D700** to Pons.

Leave Pons on the **D732** and continue through Pérignac and back into Cognac (23km).

Glorious golden fields of sunflowers carpet the rolling hills of the Charente valley in regimented lines for as far as the eye can see

ROUTE DIRECTIONS

Follow signs out of Cognac for Saintes, old Cognac and Boutiers. Almost immediately after crossing the River Charente turn right on the **D48** towards St-Trojan and St-Brice, driving alongside the river.

When the road meets the **D15** cross straight over on to the **D157** following signs to Jarnac. Pass through St-Brice, and stay on the **D157** to Jarnac (8km).

Follow the '*toutes directions*' signs through Jarnac and then turn on to the **N141** towards Hiersac.

Just outside Jarnac, turn right on to the **D22** for Triac-Lautrait and Bassac. Continue on the **D22** through St-Simon and Vibrac.

After Vibrac, turn right, then sharp left, staying on the **D22**, and continue into Châteauneauf-sur-Charente (5km).

Leave Châteauneuf by the road you came in on,

and turn on to the **D84** towards St-Simeux just outside the town.

Pass through St-Simeux and keep on the **D84** towards Champmillon. At Champmillon take a sharp right on to the **D7** to Sireuil.

Just after Sireuil, turn left and then bear left at the fork onto the **D53**. In about 1.5km turn right towards Trois Palis.

Pass Trois Palis and take the **D72** into the town of Angoulême.

Leave Angoulême following signs for la Couronne, on a road running parallel to the **N10**.

After 5km, and just after passing two large factories on opposite sides of the road, take a right turn towards Nersac, and cross over the N10.

Bear left at the fork and left again a short way on. On reaching the **D699**, turn left and continue into the centre of Châteauneuf (9km).

From the centre of Châteauneuf take the **D14** for Barbezieux-St-

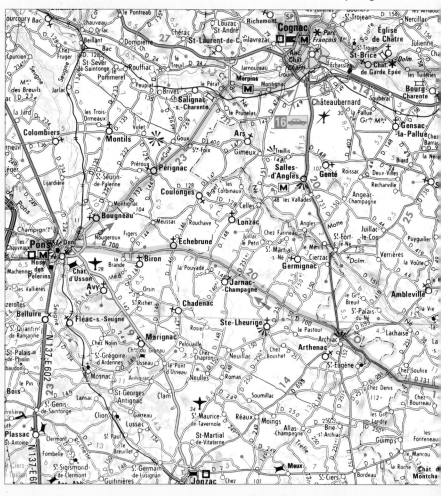

century château with an old gateway supported by two round towers, containing a small museum.

Barbezieux is famous for its preserved chestnuts and crystallized fruit.

PONS

A small hilltop town on the River Seugne, Pons was once a stop on the pilgrim route to Santiago de Compostela. Part of the pilgrim's hospice still remains, built outside the town's walls to receive those pilgrims who arrived late at night, after the town gates had been shut. The hospice is linked to the church of St Martin by an unusual 12th-century vaulted passage. Most of the castle at Pons has disappeared, but its keep and 12th-century dungeon remain.

Left, Angouleme cathedral dates back to the 12th-century
Below, St-Simeux is dominated by its church

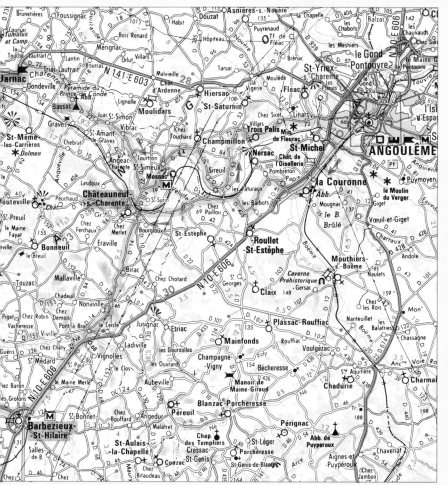

LE CANON

Overlooking the bay of Arcachon, this traditional little fishing village of colourful wooden huts lives almost exclusively by oyster-farming. 6km north of Cap Ferret.

The Cap Ferret peninsular is a long coastal strip that protects the Arcachon basin from the Atlantic. The road from Arès to Cap Ferret leads through a string of attractive fishing hamlets that have remained largely unspoilt, despite the increasing development of tourism. Sleepy in the sun, they spring to life every now and then as the fishermen land in the tiny harbours on their return from the oyster beds. Under a statute unique to this village, the wooden huts that fringe the bay are reserved for the fishermen to do their work.

Le Canon was named after the cannon that still stands there, a relic of the sea battles that took place with the English in the 17th and 18th centuries. Today it is a peaceful village of pretty wooden houses with green-shuttered windows and flower-decked verandas.

BIRDLIFE OF THE MARAIS-POITEVIN

Criss-crossed by a network of canals and dykes, the coastal marshlands of the Marais Poitevin are a haven for wetland birds. Visit in spring and early summer, when migrant wildfowl and waders, including garganey, spotted redshank and whimbrel, stop off to feed and rest alongside breeding species. Among the latter are groups of ruff, which gather to display at communal leks, black-winged stilts, and whiskered and black terns. If exploring the area by boat, watch for kingfishers perched on the waterside vegetation; also yellow wagtails and reed warblers, which are prey to marsh and Montagu's harriers. Listen out, too, for the fluty song of the golden oriole.

LA COUARDE-SUR-MER

Lying in the middle of the Ile de Ré, between le Bois-Plage-en-Ré and Ars-en-Ré, this village is built on the western edge of the largest of the two outcrops of jurassic limestone that formed the island. 29km west of la Rochelle.

The Ile de Ré, known locally as the white island bathed in light, is a unique community lying just off la Rochelle which has managed to retain much of its traditional character. La Couarde-sur-Mer became popular at the beginning of the century with writers and artists, attracted by the quality of the light and the seemingly infinite horizon of sea and sky.

A very picturesque settlement of small white houses with green-painted shutters, surrounded in summer by hollyhocks, it also has a fine sandy beach backed by a beautiful forest. The

ILE D'AIX

NAPOLEON'S HOUSE

The little flat, wooded island of Aix is a 25-minute boat journey from the mainland.

The main village (Aix) was once fortified by Vauban, but its fame is due to a famous guest, Napoleon Bonaparte. After visiting the island in 1808, he had a fine residence built here.

Following his defeat at Waterloo in 1815, Napoleon returned to the island, intendng to escape to America. His stay was brief, however, and proved to be

his last hours on French soil, for the English fleet forced him to surrender, and he was conveyed to Portsmouth, before being exiled on St Helena.

Napoleon is still an attraction on Aix, and his former residence is now the Musée Napoléon. Ten rooms are crammed with memorabilia, including portraits, furniture, arms, clothing and documents, and his bedroom, from where he watched the advancing British ships, is just as he left it.

Esnandes has four sandy beaches, and there are boat trips from here to the islands of Ré, Aix and Oléron. Peaceful as the village is, it also has a cinema, discotheque and piano bar, and sports facilities include tennis, fishing, *boules*, riding, water-skiing and walking.

GUJAN-MESTRAS

One of the busy little ports along the shore of the bay of Arcachon, Gujan-Mestras is an important centre of the centuries-old oyster-farming industry. 10km east of Arcachon.

The coastal village of Esnandes is famous for its mussel farming

little parish church, Notre Dame-de-l'Assomption, was built in 1865 to replace the original church which was decaying.

There are many tourist facilities, including plenty of seafood restaurants. Boat trips can also be taken from here to other islands.

The charming canal-side village of Coulon is typical of marsh villages of the Marais Poitevin

houses, a Romanesque and Gothic church, an interesting museum of local history and a number of good restaurants serving specialities of the region.

With its ramshackle clapboard huts along the sea wall, Gujan-Mestras is famous for its oysters. They have been farmed here since Roman times and their quality was celebrated by Rabelais. The bay of Arcachon is now one of the most important centres of oyster-production in Europe. When the local oysters were ravaged by disease in 1922 they were virtually replaced by Portuguese and later Japanese stock. Gujan has a museum and a school of marine trades, and just outside, is a water-sports amusement park.

Every August it holds a celebrated oyster fair when, for three days, thousands of oyster-lovers descend on the little seaside village to sample its produce.

COULON

Capital of 'la Venise verte' (green Venice), this intriguing village is the perfect centre from which to explore the waterways of the mysterious Marais Poitevin. 11km west of Niort.

Until they were reclaimed from the sea by the labours of the Benedictine monks from the abbey at Maillezais in the 11th century, the marshes of this region, known as the Marais Poitevin, lay under the waters of the ancient gulf of Poitou. The dense network of canals that the monks dug to drain the waters into the River Sèvre Niortaise were for centuries the region's only highways, navigated by local people in flat-bottomed punts. Many farmers still rely on these punts, even using them to transport their livestock.

Coulon is a charming and typical marsh village, with pretty stone-built

ESNANDES

This pretty little coastal village with its unusual church is devoted to the traditional culture of mussels. 12km north of la Rochelle.

With its little streets of low, whitewashed cottages, Esnandes is a typical coastal village of the marshes. Its church is far from typical, however, as the original Romanesque building was turned into a veritable fortress against Norman incursions in the 14th century.

But the most remarkable feature of Esnandes is its kilometres of mussel pens planted in the open sea, on which mussel broods stick and grow. Mussel-farming is explained in the Musée de la Mytiliculture, staffed by local enthusiasts. The museum is also a good introduction to the history of the area and also the mysterious marshland that lies inland.

The open-air museum at Sabres documents the life of the Landes region

With its arcaded walkways and fine Romanesque church, the large central square of Labastide, the Place Royale, has survived almost unchanged since the *bastide* was founded in 1284 by Bernard IV, Comte d'Armagnac, and Edward I of England. The lovely stone, brick and timber façades of the square are supposed to have inspired Henri IV in the building of the Place des Vosges in Paris. A 17th-century chapel houses an exhibition explaining the background to the *bastides* which are such a feature of the region.

The Syndicat d'Initiative has a small costume museum and a display of Armagnac brandy.

LANTON

One of the 'pearls of the Arcachon basin', this little fishing port was once an important stopping place for pilgrims on the way to Santiago de Compostela. 12km south-east of Andernos-les-Bains.

This little fishing port on the eastern side of the sheltered Arcachon basin has a surprisingly grand and long history, stretching far back beyond the days when the area became fashionable for its elegant resorts.

When Santiago de Compostela was the greatest pilgrimage centre in Christendom, Lanton was a major resting place for the large numbers of pilgrims who toiled down the Atlantic

HASTINGUES

An English *bastide* founded in the 13th century overlooking the River Gave, this tiny village retains its fortifications, its old houses and a great deal of charm. 38km east of Bayonne.

Hastingues is named after John Hastings, seneschal of Gascony, who – on behalf of Edward I, King of England and Duke of Aquitaine – signed the treaty under which it was founded in 1289. Less rigid in its layout than most *bastides*, the little village consists of two main streets crossed by minor ones. The medieval houses that line them – whitewashed with coloured shutters – are delightful in their simplicity, with some interesting details. The church stands on a charming leafy square, flanked by the Mairie and houses from the 15th and 16th centuries. The south-western fortified gateway is still standing, though now bereft of its original earth ramparts. Nearby are the ruins of a house with a fine Gothic doorway.

LABASTIDE-D'ARMAGNAC

One of the most picturesque and best-preserved bastides in the whole of France, this remarkable village lies on the edge of the pine forests of the Landes, 28km east of Mont-de-Marsan.

ROYAN

AN UNUSUAL CHURCH

Royan, a modern sea-side resort at the mouth of the Gironde, was substantially rebuilt after World War II, and its church of Notre-Dame, in the Place Notre-Dame, is a particularly striking piece of modern architecture.

Built between 1955 and 1958 to a dramatic, up-swept design, its structure is of reinforced concrete, the surface of which is coated with a shiny protective layer of resin.

The interior is even more dramatic, light and spacious, with a soaring nave. Narrow windows seem to stretch up to the sky. Catch, if you can, an organ recital here – the instrument is a fine one.

A striking example of modern architecture

route to the Pyrenees. Now the only indication of its former glory is its 11th-century Romanesque church.

In the 16th century, falcons were bred and trained here for the kings of England. The area is still celebrated for its birds: on a clear day you can see across the bay to the Ile aux Oiseaux, whose area varies from 300ha at high tide to 1,000 at low tide.

MORNAC-SUR-SEUDRE

This pretty village on the bank of the Seudre, in an area famous for its pottery since the Middle Ages, has become a magnet for craftworkers. 12km north of Royan.

Mornac's picturesque narrow streets are now crowded with leather, enamel and sewing workshops, as well as studios devoted to the pottery for which this area of the Saintonge has been celebrated since the Middle Ages. The nearby village of la Poterie was shipping its wares to England as far back as the 14th century.

The village, with its network of little streets leading down to the harbour, its priory and small castle, is best explored on foot.

Mornac also offers the visitor a surprisingly large number of sporting activities, and a little steam-train ride across the *marais* of Saujon and la Tremblade. In addition it has several restaurants serving the seafood for which the region is famous.

RIONS

An impressive miniature citadel perched on the vine-covered slope above the River Garonne, Rions is still encircled by its medieval ramparts. 30km south of Bordeaux.

The entrance to Rions is still through the massive 14th-century Porte de Lhyan, which has retained an imposing armoury of medieval fortifications. The ramparts, with their defensive towers and a 14th-and 15th-century fortress, are still remarkably complete. Within them lies a charming maze of narrow streets lined with old stone houses and punctuated by little leafy squares. In the centre is the lovely church of St-Seuvin, with its 12th-

century apse and 14th-century nave. Street names such as Rue de Normands and Rue Sarrazine are reminders of the waves of invaders which made the impressive fortifications of this now tranquil village so necessary.

SABRES

A tiny hamlet that grew up long before the Landes were planted with their immense pine forests, Sabres is now the gateway to a fascinating open-air museum of rural life. 38km north-west of Mont-de-Marsan.

Until the 19th century, the region of the Landes was a huge swamp edged by dunes. Then the land was fixed in place by the planting of hundreds of thousands of trees, mainly pine. Tiny Sabres, with its half-timbered houses and old church, was one of the few settlements of the Landes before the forest was planted. Its chief attraction is the tiny station, from which a steam train takes visitors to the Ecomusée de Marquèze, an open-air museum documenting the life of the Landes. Examples of traditional building types – many of them raised on stilts – have been painstakingly reconstructed, and there are demonstrations of local crafts such as stilt-making and bread-making.

LES LANDES AND THE ECOMUSEE

Les Landes is a region stretching down the Atlantic coast from the mouth of the Gironde to Capbreton, just north of Bayonne. It consists of about 14,000 square kilometres of sandy soil planted, since the 18th century, with pine trees. Lagoons (*étangs*) dot the coastline, and most of this country is now part of the Parc Naturel Régional des Landes de Gascogne. The Ecomusée de la Grande Lande (an *écomusée* is a museum of the environment) occupies three separate locations round Sabres, in the heart of the park. The forest clearing at Marquèze has traditional buildings in the local style, generous in their use of timber and sometimes with earth walls. Some have been specially moved and re-erected here. At Luxey an old workshop where resin was distilled into turpentine is preserved. At Moustey the former church of Notre-Dame houses an exhibition about the religious heritage of the region.

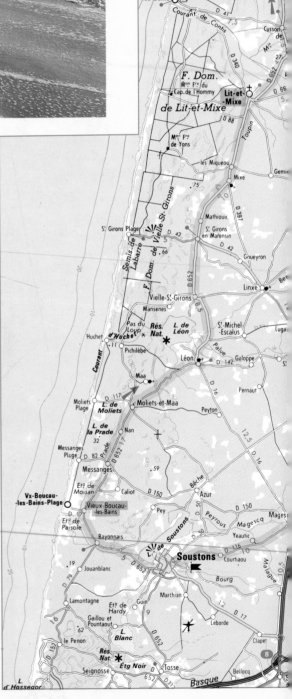

TOUR 17 – 190KM
LANDES AND SEA

Pine forests fringe the Atlantic coast while sandy beaches stretch for miles

It is hard to believe that the extensive forest covering the Landes is an environment created by man. The area was originally swampland, bordered on the west by dunes, until the 19th century the land was secured by planting thousands of pine groves to prevent the dunes encroaching further inland. The tour goes through the heart of the forest, along flat, straight roads, where the air is filled with the scent of eucalyptus. From the ancient spa town of Dax, the route then turns north and travels up the Atlantic coast, here fringed by long stretches of fine, sandy beaches and pine forest.

ROUTE DIRECTIONS

Leave Mimizan on the **D44** towards Escource (22km). After passing through Escource, continue on the **D44** to Cap de Pin, and then Sabres (18km).

Leave Sabres on the **D77**, following signs for Morcenx. On reaching the **D438**, turn left to Morcenx.

From Morcenx, take the **D38** and follow signs to Arjuzanx. After 2km, fork right on to the **D27** to Rion-des-Landes.

Follow the **D27** through Rions, following signs to Dax and Boos. Pass through Boos (8km) and carry on towards Laluque (5km). At the crossroads just before Laluque turn left on to the **D42** towards Laluque and Pontonx.

Drive through Laluque and take the right fork by

the cross back on to the **D27**, towards Dax. Cross the railway line at Buglose and turn right, staying on the **D27**. On reaching the **N124** turn right into Dax.

Leave Dax on the **D16**, following signs to Magescq (15km). From there, take the **D116** to Soustons, where you turn on to the **D652**, following signs to Vieux-Boucau-les-Bains.

From Vieux Boucau-les-Bains continue on the **D652**, through Messanges, until you reach Moliets-et-Maa (6km). At the crossroads continue straight on, staying on the **D652**, to Léon (6km). In the square take the left-hand fork towards Mimizan.

Continue on the **D652** to Vielle-St-Girons, and then St Girons en Marensin (9km). Pass through the hamlets of Mixe, les Miqueou and

Padaou. At Lit-et-Mixe (10km) the **D652** takes a right fork into the main square.

Follow the **D652** from Lit-et-Mixe to St-Julien-en-Born (3km), and from there back to Mimizan (17km).

PLACES OF INTEREST

MIMIZAN

Mimizan is a lively, seaside resort on the Atlantic coast. An important port in the Middle Ages, it was buried beneath the dunes in the 18th century. All that is left of the original town is the tower of a 13th-century church that was once part of a Benedictine monastery that sheltered pilgrims on their way to Santiago de Compostela.

SABRES

See page 131.

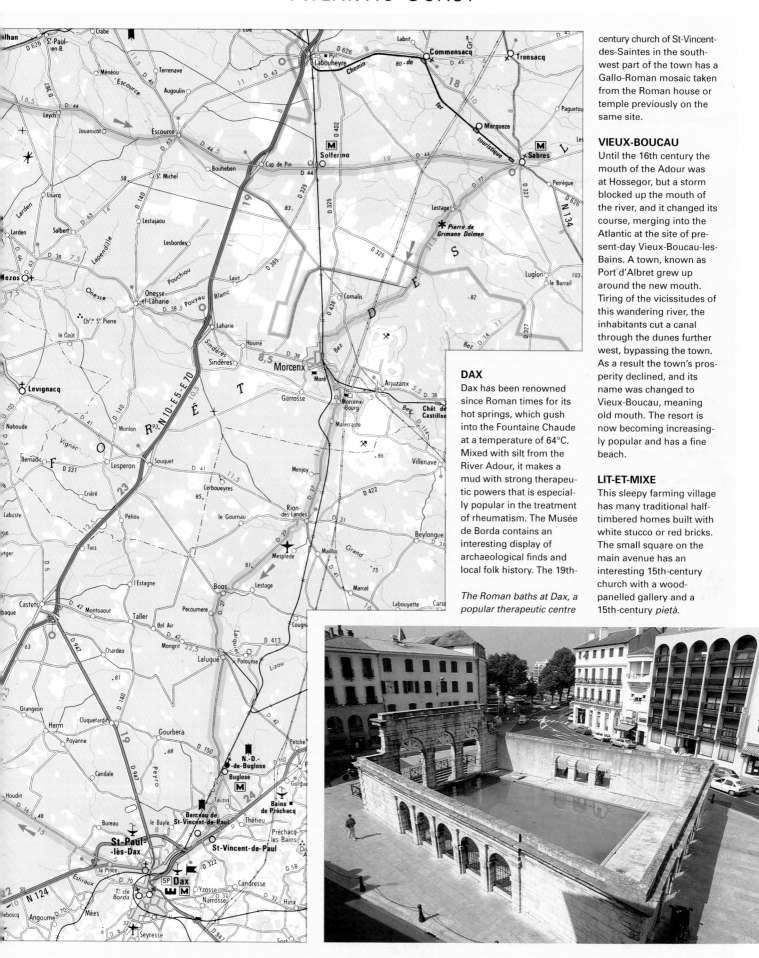

century church of St-Vincent-des-Saintes in the south-west part of the town has a Gallo-Roman mosaic taken from the Roman house or temple previously on the same site.

VIEUX-BOUCAU

Until the 16th century the mouth of the Adour was at Hossegor, but a storm blocked up the mouth of the river, and it changed its course, merging into the Atlantic at the site of present-day Vieux-Boucau-les-Bains. A town, known as Port d'Albret grew up around the new mouth. Tiring of the vicissitudes of this wandering river, the inhabitants cut a canal through the dunes further west, bypassing the town. As a result the town's prosperity declined, and its name was changed to Vieux-Boucau, meaning old mouth. The resort is now becoming increasingly popular and has a fine beach.

LIT-ET-MIXE

This sleepy farming village has many traditional half-timbered homes built with white stucco or red bricks. The small square on the main avenue has an interesting 15th-century church with a wood-panelled gallery and a 15th-century *pietà*.

DAX

Dax has been renowned since Roman times for its hot springs, which gush into the Fountaine Chaude at a temperature of 64°C. Mixed with silt from the River Adour, it makes a mud with strong therapeutic powers that is especially popular in the treatment of rheumatism. The Musée de Borda contains an interesting display of archaeological finds and local folk history. The 19th-

The Roman baths at Dax, a popular therapeutic centre

STE-CROIX-DU-MONT

This tiny village is on a hilltop surrounded by celebrated vineyards and offers spectacular views of the region. 5km north of Langon.

The road to Ste-Croix-du-Mont on a hill overlooking the River Garonne winds through vineyards producing the delicious sweet white wines of the region, which are somewhat cheaper than the better-known Sauternes. Dominating the village is the 15th-century château, an English fortress in the Hundred Years War, and beside it the church. From the shady square in front of the church there is a magnificent view over the Garonne valley and the famous vineyards of Sauternes on the other side of the river to the immense green of the forest of the Landes.

Near by is a wine information centre housed in caves hollowed out of rock consisting of layers of countless fossilized oyster shells, a geological curiosity of the region which is thought to contribute to the quality of its wines.

ST-EMILION

This golden village, one of the most beautiful in France, is famous throughout the world for its superb wines. 8km south-east of Libourne.

The village derives its name from the hermit Emilion, who settled in a cave here in the 8th century. The remarkable and extremely rare underground church was hollowed out of the rock over the following three centuries, and the village grew up around the Benedictine monastery which established itself here.

The lovely 13th-century Gothic Chapelle de la Trinité is built over the cave which is supposed to be St-Emilion's original hermitage, and next to it are some ancient catacombs.

The 13th-century Château du Roi has a massive square keep from the top of which, every autumn, members of

St-Emilion has many cafes where the famous wines of the area can be savoured, in the shadows of its ancient buildings

the brotherhood of la Jurade, which imposes strict quality controls on the wine, declare the official start of the grape harvest.

CIVRAY

CHURCH OF ST-NICHOLAS

West of the N10 between Poitiers and Angoulême, this pleasant little town nestles on the right bank of the River Charente and contains several attractive 15th- and 16th-century houses in its unspoilt heart.

The most remarkable building in the town, however, is the beautiful 12th-

ST-MACAIRE

A peaceful and atmospheric walled village of honey-coloured stone, this medieval bastide overlooks the River Garonne, 4km north-east of Langon.

Built on a limestone outcrop, over-looking the Garonne, the walled village of St-Macaire has retained its medieval layout and atmosphere. A typical *bastide*, it has the traditional arcaded market square, part of its 13th-century walls and three square fortified gateways, as well as a large number of Gothic and Renaissance houses. The 13th-century church of St-Sauveur has a fine Romanesque apse and Gothic nave, and from its terraces on the hill-top there are lovely views of the village and the valley of the Garonne.

On the main square is a postal museum, housed in a post-house dating from the reign of Henri IV. St-Macaire is also capital of the small wine appellation, Côte de Bordeaux St-Macaire.

TALMONT

This tiny fortified village, perched on the very edge of the Gironde estuary, is celebrated for its remarkable and powerfully moving church. 16km south-east of Royan.

Talmont's narrow streets and alleyways, lined with limewashed cottages and picturesquely sprinkled with hollyhocks in summer, all draw the eye towards the headland, the wide empty estuary, and the dramatically positioned church of Ste-Radegonde.

Built in the 11th century to replace a chapel that had grown too small to accommodate the growing stream of pilgrims to Santiago de Compostela,

the lovely Romanesque church stands completely isolated on the very edge of the cliffs, surrounded only by a tiny sailors' and fishermen's cemetery.

Part of the nave was claimed by the waters in the 15th century, and the cliff has had to be reinforced to prevent the rest of the building being undermined by the great tidal estuary. The church has a fine 12th-century portal, and offers poignant views over the vast spacious expanses of the Gironde estuary.

TUSSON

Now a centre of local arts and traditions, Tusson still preserves many reminders of its medieval heritage. 15km south-west of Ruffec.

Tusson grew up in the Middle Ages around the Abbaye des Dames, of which the 13th-and15th-century ruins can still be seen to the west of the village. The ancient church, badly damaged in the Hundred Years War, has had its great square tower restored. From the 13th century, local merchants grew rich on the commerce generated by the nunnery, and built themselves the fine stone houses that can still be seen here.

In the Place des Halles, the Conservatoire d'Art et Traditions Populaires encourages the preservation and revival of local arts and crafts. There is an agricultural fair every month, and the village fête takes place on the second Sunday of September.

THE ROYAL ROPE FACTORY

Rochefort's position on the Charente, coupled with the threat to the Atlantic coastline posed by the English in the 17th century, virtually guaranteed that Louis XIV's naval minister, Colbert, would develop it as a military port and arsenal. The result was a rather cheerless town with streets laid out on a grid system, yet it boasts a fascinating survival in the Corderie Royale, a slate-roofed building overlooking the river. From the 1670s until the Revolution the factory supplied the French navy with all its rope, finally closing in 1926. Hemp was brought from the Auvergne, spun and laid out at full stretch – hence the building's remarkable length of 370m. (For comparison, the Ropery at the former Royal Naval Dockyard in Chatham, built in 1785, is 347m long.)

---

century Romanesque church of St-Nicholas. Despite heavy restoration, the church is particularly noted for the beauty of its elaborate 12th-century façade. Rectangular, this has six semi-circular arches in two rows, separated by a cornice with corbels. The narrative includes Christ in Majesty, the Wise and Foolish Virgins, the Assumption, and the signs of the zodiac. The upper row preserves a mutilated Poitevan horseman, and is decorated with angels and musicians.

The nine statues on the right arches have been identified as St Nicholas (seated), three young girls and various apostles.

ST-MACAIRE

CHATEAU DE MALAGAR

The château lies in the hills on the right banks of the Garonne, north-east of St-Macaire.

This was the home of the novelist, Francois Mauriac (1885-1970), who used south-west France as the setting for many of his novels. He said of the place 'As long as there is at least one person who enjoys my books, Malagar will throb with muffled life'. The house is very beautiful and, from its terrace, there are wonderful views of the Garonne valley and the forest stretching west towards the Atlantic ocean.

Home of the famous novelist Mauriac

SECRET FRANCE

BERRY AND LIMOUSIN

These two quiet and deeply rural provinces are right in the centre of France. Surrounded by the great tourist regions of the Loire Valley, the Dordogne and the Auvergne, this is forgotten territory, unknown to many, dismissed by others. In their natives, however, they inspire passionate devotion and are considered close to paradise.

This is the empty quarter marked white in most tourist brochures. Few people stay here, except en route to the coast or the mountains. Off the national highways, however, these regions live on in peace, solitude, legend and tradition, offering enormous charm and a multitude of unexpected and fascinating sights.

Berry and Limousin can also make a strong case for being the real heart of artistic France. This is the home of Limoges porcelain and Aubusson tapestry, of exceptional Romanesque and Gothic churches and fairytale Renaissance châteaux. In the 14th century, the Duc de Berry created a magnificent artistic circle in Bourges that has left such lasting legacies as the Très Riches Heures du Duc de Berry, one of the finest illustrated manuscripts in existence, and the superb stained-glass windows of Bourges cathedral. In the 19th century, Monet, Rousseau and Rodin all came here to work, and George Sand turned her beloved Berry countryside into the Vallée Noire, a literary creation easily as powerful as Thomas Hardy's Wessex.

The landscapes of Berry and Limousin amply reward the visitor who takes the time and trouble to explore them. The great agricultural plains of northern Berry give way to gently rolling meadows through which the River Creuse cuts its way in splendid, tortuous gorges that are generally ignored by all but a few hardy cyclists. The Brenne – the 'land of a thousand lakes' – is one of the last great wetlands of Europe, and further south, the mountains of the Millevaches plateau and Haute Vienne offer views as dramatic as any in the Auvergne.

In these regions, a powerful style of naive art survived the Renaissance and Baroque periods to last until the 19th century. The tiny mountain villages still reek of mysticism, their legends alive and well. Even the very granite of the Limousin has a fascination, from dolmens and druidic circles to the work of the wandering stonemasons of the Middle Ages.

champignons de Berry

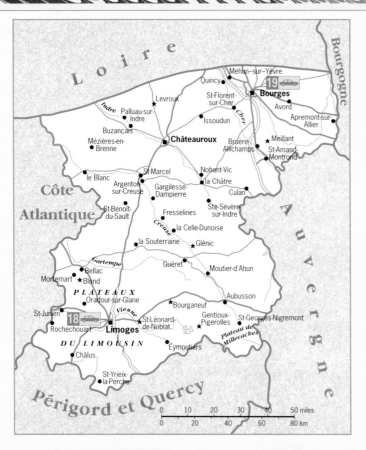

Brown Berry goats are famous for the cheeses produced from their milk

Above, small-scale farming thrives in this fertile region

Above, any shady corner will do for a game of boules, played in the dusty heat of a summer's day at Mortemart
Left, the shadow of a lamp falls beside a bright window box at Apremont-sur-Allier

WHERE IS THE CENTRE OF FRANCE?

Even a casual look at a map of France suggests that its centre must lie somewhere in this region, and in Berry three places – Bruère-Allichamps, Vesdun and Saulzais-le-Potier – put forward rival claims to be at the exact centre. Apart from local pride, however, why should it matter? One reason is that the French have always liked to regard their country as shaped, not randomly, but in fulfilment of a mathematical ideal. It is, so one favourite theory goes, a hexagon, neatly balancing three sides bounded by sea with three landward sides.

APREMONT-SUR-ALLIER

A picture-postcard village on the banks of the River Allier, dominated by its elegant Renaissance château, 17km north-east of Sancoins, on the border between Berry and Burgundy.

Strung out along a curve of the Allier at the foot of its great château, Apremont is so immaculately conserved and restored that it seems hardly to have changed since the Middle Ages. Its houses, with their picturesque turrets, external staircases and dormer windows, are all of the same golden sandstone, roofed in terracotta tiles. The earliest date from the 15th century, others were built in the 1930s in the medieval style. The château was virtually a ruin when the wealthy industrialist Eugène Schneider bought it at the end of the last century. He subsequently devoted much of his life and his fortune to restoring it to its present grandeur and filling it with magnificent furniture and tapestries. The château and the impressive flower gardens beside it are open to the public.

BRUERE-ALLICHAMPS

This village on its ancient site overlooking the River Cher is now famed chiefly for its curious monument symbolising the geographical heart of France. 8km north-west of St-Armand-Montrond.

At the centre of the main crossroads at the entrance to Bruère-Allichamps stands a Gallo-Roman milestone, found in 1757 and placed here in 1799 on what was believed to be the geographical centre of France. In 1865 this distinction was officially recognised, whereupon the villagers immediately erected a flag on the milestone and turned it into a monument. They then proceeded to name everything from the local garage to the café in honour of their unique position at the heart of France. Not surprisingly, perhaps, local villages, Vesdun and Saulzais-le-Potier, also claim the honour, and have also put up monuments.

The village, founded in the 12th century, is a pretty collection of old cottages and narrow lanes. It retains some vestiges of its medieval fortifications and some 14th- and 15th-century houses which tell of its former prosperity.

LA CELLE-DUNOISE

This pretty village tucked into a gentle curve of the River Creuse in the northern Limousin is a *station verte*, a centre for outdoor activities. 17km south of Aigurande.

Gently moulded into wooded hills, la Celle-Dunoise is a perfect place to stop for a lazy afternoon. There are plenty of shady picnic spots and a small swimming beach on the far bank, with a view of one of the region's rare fortified churches. Built originally in the 12th century, the church of St Pierre-lès-Liens was fortified in the 14th and 15th centuries. A Roman stone beside the main door is known locally as 'the death stone', for coffins have traditionally been rested here before funerals. The pretty stone bridge across the river was completely rebuilt in 1891 in the style of the Romanesque original.

There are good views of the village, which also has a good hôtel-restaurant, from the opposite bank of the river as well as from the hill above, on the road to Bonnat.

SECRET PLACES

MEILLANT
GOTHIC CHATEAU

Meillant lies north of St-Amand-Montrond.

The château in the pretty village of Meillant is a masterpiece of late Gothic architecture, one of the finest examples south of the Loire valley. On first impressions, this is a rather austere, 4th-century moated fortress. Continue

CULAN

The spectacular medieval fortress that glowers over the gorges of the River Arnon is the chief attraction of this pleasant old village, 33km north-west of Montluçon.

Although there has been a château on this vertiginous clifftop site since the 11th century, the massive rectangular fortress that stands there today dates from the 13th to the 15th century. Only the cliff wall still exists in its original form; a formidable expanse of grey stone complete with circular corner towers. The rest of the château was heavily altered in the 15th and 17th centuries, when it was turned into an elegant and comfortable stately residence, restored in the 1960s. Inside are some fine furnishings, tapestries and armour.

The oldest, prettiest part of the village, including the Romanesque and 15th-century church, lies just above the château, while steps lead down into the river valley past a splendidly overgrown aqueduct.

FRESSELINES

Perched up high above the confluence of the Creuse and the Petite Creuse, on the borders of Berry and Limousin, this village is best known as an artists' colony with an illustrious pedigree. 30km south of Argenton-sur-Creuse.

Maurice Rollinat, poet and musician, moved to Fresselines in 1884, and

The impressive medieval fortress at Culan overlooks the River Arnon

stayed until his death in 1903. Among the many artists who visited him were Rousseau, Rodin and Monet, who was so inspired that he completed over 20 paintings of the local scenery. There are still a number of studios dotted round the village, as well as two memorials to Rollinat – a bas-relief by Rodin in the back wall of the church, and a bust by Paul Surtel in the park.

At the centre of the village stands the 12th-century church of St Julien-de-Brioude. Behind it, a footpath leads down the cliff through the woods to the confluence of the Creuse and Petite Creuse rivers, a lovely, lazy spot well patronised by the local fishermen. The walk takes about an hour.

round to the east façade, however and you are struck by a riot of decoration, exuberant, intricate and of a quality to rival the châteaux of the Loire. In the late 15th century the Amboise family, lords of Meilliant, demolished much of the rampart wall of the old château, and incorporated the rest into the new château, a small but near-perfect example of late Gothic architecture. Particularly remarkable is the high Gothic Tour du Lion designed by Giocondo, a colleague of Michelangelo.

Inside, equally spectacular decorations cover every surface. Especially noteworthy are the dining-room, where every surface, from the painted ceiling to the stained-glass windows, is ablaze with colour, and the formidable medieval great hall, with its massive wooden ceiling and vast bosses depicting knights in armour.

An ornamental extravaganza of the Late Gothic period, where Italianate decoration can be seen in all its splendour, set in a fine park.

GARGILESSE-DAMPIERRE

One of the prettiest villages in Berry, in a delightful setting, with a remarkable church that houses some magnificent medieval frescos. The village lies 13km south of Argenton-sur-Creuse, on the confluence of the Dampierre and Creuse rivers.

Medieval frescoes adorn the crypt of Gargilesse-Dampierre's church

Gargilesse is a charming maze of narrow, picturesque streets lined with geranium-decked stone cottages that wind their way up the hill from the river. Off to one side, down an alley, is 'Algira', a tiny cottage used by George Sand as a writing retreat and now a museum

dedicated to the area's most famous author.

Set in the walls of the old medieval castle, rebuilt in the 18th century, is the lovely Romanesque church of Notre Dame-de-Gargilesse, built between the 12th and the 15th centuries. It has superb carved capitals, all different and well preserved, and the crypt is virtually covered in magnificent frescos dating from the 13th and 15th centuries.

MÉZIÈRES-EN-BRENNE

This small, bustling market town on the edge of the remote Brenne marshes has recently come back into its own as a centre for activity holidays. 40km west of Châteauroux.

Capital of the mysterious Brenne marshes, first cleared by monks in the 13th century, Mézières is a pretty, lively place built over a number of small canals. The remains of the château contain a small museum, and the village also has a heavily restored 14th-century collegiate church. A Syndicate d'Initiative provides tourist information on the walks and rides laid out across the marshes. 6km to the south is the 145-hectare Réserve Naturelle de Chérine. Its fascinating variety of habitats, including lakes, reedbeds, marsh, meadow and woodland, is host to over 150 species of bird, 40 species of amphibians and reptiles, 21 species of mammal and about 350 species of plants, as well as rare herds of Castor cows and Camargue horses.

BOURGANEUF

TOUR ZIZIM

Bourganeuf lies in hilly and well-wooded countryside, 35km south-west of Guéret.

The Tour Zizim is an old stone tower, situated adjacent to formal gardens and an ancient priory founded by the Knights Hospitallers in 1195. The priory was their headquarters

between 1427 and 1750 and now houses the town hall.

A romantic tower which once imprisoned a Prince with exotic tastes

MORTEMART

A charming little village on the northern edge of the Monts de Blond, with a remarkable variety of historic buildings. 15km south of Bellac.

Once the home of the powerful Mortemart family, the moated château on its low mound is now in ruins. The minute hamlet that it once protected is enchanting, with several cottages festooned with roses and geraniums, a few grander secular houses and two large, elegant monasteries, one Augustine, the other Carmelite. The simple, rectangular Augustine chapel, which dates from the 14th century, now serves as the village church. It has an unusual, slate-covered onion-domed bell-tower and a fine Baroque retable. Best of all, however, are the extraordinarily lively and inventive misericords in the 15th-century choir stalls.

A Sunday market is held in the 17th-century covered market hall in the square.

MOUTIER-D'AHUN

A charming village nestling among the trees beside the Creuse, it grew up around an ancient monastery celebrated for the carvings in its church. 20km south-east of Guéret.

Now a delightful tiny hamlet, in Roman times Moutier-d'Ahun was a major centre at the junction of four main roads. The bridge, with its solid piers, dates from the 11th century.

The first abbey was founded in the early 11th century by Benedictine monks. It was later taken over by the Cistercians, almost destroyed during the Wars of Religion, then became a Cluniac house until the Revolution.

The present church was started in the 12th century, fortified in the 14th, and substantially rebuilt in the 15th. Most dramatic, however, are the superb wooden carvings inside, created by Simon Bauer between 1673 and 1681, and covering the entire altar, rood screen and choir. There are guided tours in summer, at other times the key is available from the nearest house.

NOHANT-VIC

The village where George Sand lived, wrote and died using the surrounding countryside as her inspiration for a series of pastoral romances about the Vallée Noire. 6km north of la Châtre.

Nohant-Vic consists of two separate villages, about 2km apart. Vic has little exceptional about it except for the interior of its Romanesque church, which has some remarkably fine frescos discovered in 1849.

Nohant is the village of George Sand (Aurore Dupin) who came here at the age of four, in 1808, to live with her grandfather in the little château that makes up one side of the village green. The elegant, rather faded 18th-century château is fascinating for its authentic period atmosphere, for little has changed since George Sand's death here in 1876: even the dining table is still set with place cards for one of her dinners.

At the centre of the village green is a pretty and neglected little Romanesque church, and on the other side is a charming restaurant.

LES TRES RICHES HEURES

This illuminated medieval book of hours was the jewel in the collection of Jean, Duc de Berry, and vibrant blue and gold dominate its pages. Angels' wings are portrayed with the same calm, observant eyes that have also left an invaluable record of ordinary life. The pages faithfully depict the Duke's properties, but fill the foreground with humble activities that mark the seasons – fuel-gathering, ploughing, haymaking, harvesting and hunting.

The tower was used in 1484 by Pierre d'Aubusson, Grand Master of the Order, as a prison for an exiled Ottoman prince, Zizim, the brother of Sultan Bajazet II. During his internment in the tower he equipped it with every refinement of that time, including Turkish baths, elegant tapestries and a harem.

Less glamorous exhibits fill the five floors today: it is now a museum featuring, among other items, collections of Gallo-Roman artefacts found locally. The top floor commands fine views across the town and surrounding countryside.

BLOND
THE ROCHERS DE PUYCHAUD

A track leads off to the left, 2km south of Blond, near Limoges, on the D3.

One of a number of groups of standing stones, dolmens and balancing rocks in this area, the Rochers de Puychaud are a set of massive granite boulders that have quite naturally, formed a circle, they are thought to have been used by druids in pre-Christian times, but today they have been turned into a monument to one Fréderic Mistral who devoted his life to the Limousine language, The small memorial plaque is written in this ancient, and almost forgotten tongue.

TOUR 18 – 115KM

THE PAYS DES FEUILLARDIERS

The route travels through the area west of Limoges, where the River Vienne threads its way gently through the edge of the Limousin to the Charente border. Around it the countryside flows smoothly into lush, low, rolling plains, thick with chestnut woods and dairy farms. On the edge of Aquitaine, this region has traditionally looked west, the architecture more Perigordian than Limousine in style, its history that of a battleground between the Plantagenet kings of England and France. It is also the site of the greatest atrocity in France during World War II, the massacre at Oradour-sur-Glane. Plenty of time is allowed for sights that encompass the entire history of the region, from prehistory to the modern day.

ROUTE DIRECTIONS

Leave Limoges on the **D79**, which leads through the industrial area to Aixe-sur-Vienne. From Aixe, head due west along the **D10** for 28km to Rochechouart.

In the centre of Rochechouart, turn right onto the **D675**, heading north to St-Junien. From here, take the **N141** north for about 3km, then turn left, back onto the **D675** towards Bellac. Follow this for about 17.5km through Chêne Pignier to Mortemart.

At Mortemart, turn right on to the **D5** to Blond, then right again in the village on to the **D3** towards Cieux. The Rochers de Puychaud can be found up a short footpath off the **D3** about 2km from Blond. Continue along the **D3** to Cieux.

Go through the village, still on the **D3**, heading towards Oradour-sur-Glane.

From here take the **D9** heading south-east towards Limoges. After about 8km, turn left onto the main **N141** for the last stretch back into Limoges.

PLACES OF INTEREST

AIXE-SUR-VIENNE

Once a peaceful little town on the River Vienne, Aixe has virtually been swallowed up by the industrial suburbs of Limoges. It has a 13th-century Romanesque church, dedicated to Ste-Croix, with some fine stained-glass windows, and there are several attractive old houses in the town centre. This is also the site of several Limoges porcelain factories.

One of the biggest, La

Maison de la Porcelaine, runs hourly tours, and all have shops selling both heavily discounted seconds and the very finest hand-crafted works of art.

Above, Oradour-sur-Glane, monument to a massacre
Below, sweet chestnuts

ROCHECHOUART

This small town is completely dominated by its imposing château, constructed in the late 15th century on the site of an earlier building. Inside, on the ground floor are some fine early 16th century frescos, while the upper

ORADOUR-SUR-GLANE

This ruined village, site of a notorious massacre, is one of France's most chilling reminders of the horrors of World War II. 20km north-west of Limoges.

On the afternoon of 10 June 1944, the élite Das Reich SS detachment swept into Oradour-sur-Glane and rounded up the entire population in the market square. The women and children of the village were then imprisoned in the church, the men in barns and garages. Grenades were tossed in followed by sub-machine-gun fire, and 642 people died. Only five people escaped. The entire village was then set alight, and 328 buildings were destroyed.

After the war a new town was built next door, and a wall was thrown around the village, which has been left exactly as it was after the massacre as a monument to those who died.

The cemetery is a mass of flowers, with photos of the victims on the gravestones. A memorial stands behind, and off to one side a memorial museum houses many small objects from a collection of stopped watches to children's toys.

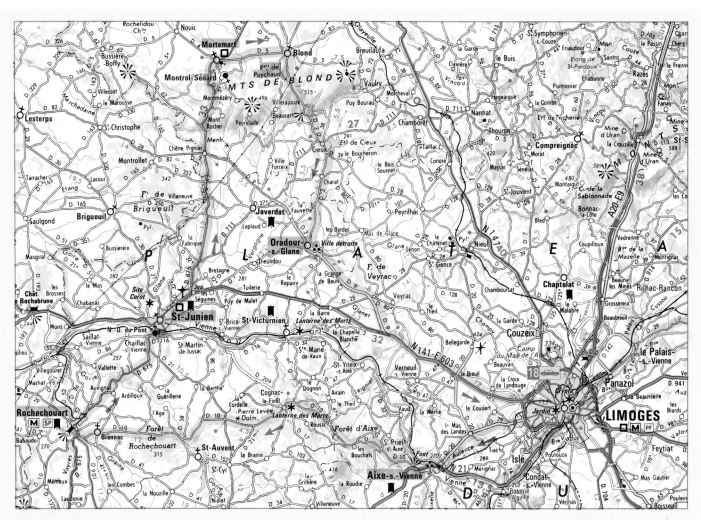

floors house the municipal museum.

The ancient parish church of St-Sauveur, dating back to 1067, houses a 12th-century tomb and several interesting modern paintings, and is most remarkable for the twisted spire added in the 18th century.

CHALUS

Twenty-five kilometres south-east of Rochechouart, on the D901.

The splendid medieval château of Châlus-Chabrol, best known as the place where Richard the Lionheart, King of England and Lord of Western France, received the fatal wound from a crossbow arrow while besieging the château in 1199. Housed in the château are informative displays on the Plantagenets, local crafts and archaeology.

ST-JUNIEN

The massive 11th-century collegiate church is a magnificent example of Limousine romanesque architecture, filled with wonderful art. There are several fine old houses in the town and two 13th-century bridges across the River Vienne. Beside one of them stands the 15th-century Gothic chapel of Notre Dame du Pont, with a stone statue of the Virgin that has been the centre of a pilgrimage cult since the 13th century.

MORTEMART

See page 141.

THE ROCHERS DE PUYCHAUD

See page 141.

ORADOUR-SUR GLANE

See above.

CHESTNUTS

Chestnuts used to be the staple food of this region and they are still the local passion. Almost every road is lined by chestnut trees and the spiky green balls rain down onto the passing cars. The nuts are boiled, roasted, puréed and turned into liqueurs, while one of the great local specialities is *boudin de châtaigne*, a blood sausage with chestnut. Many towns and villages even have a special chestnut festival during the harvest.

The *feuillardiers* after whom the district is named lived out in the forest all summer, in shacks made of chestnut branches, creating, from chestnut wood, the thin strips which bind together an oak barrel.

Palluau-sur-Indre

This elegant hillside village in its picturesque setting above the River Indre is crowned by a massive medieval fortress, 35km north-west of Châteauroux.

From the other side of the river Palluau looks like an image from a fairytale. Its streets wind up the hill, past the Hôtel de Ville to the château,

the houses getting older all the way. Dating from the 11th to the 16th centuries, the château has had a turbulent history, especially during the Wars of Religion. The collegiate church just below the castle has some fine 15th-century choir stalls and a wonderful collection of painted wooden polychrome statues from the 15th and 16th centuries.

On the Rue Basse, at the bottom of the hill, is the

Pallau-sur-Indre lies beside the River Indre, dominated by its medieval fortress

minute Romanesque chapel of St Laurent. The key is kept next door, The Romanesque frescos, a thoroughly romantic and rather jolly vision of the Apocalypse, are magnificent.

ST-LEONARD DE NOBLAT

Church of St-Leonard

30km east of Limoges.

Standing on a hill above rolling Limoges countryside, this small picturesque market town contains a number of attractive medieval houses, clustering around the beautiful Romanesque church of St-Léonard.

Dating from the 11th, 12th and 13th centuries it has a graceful bell tower – one of the finest in the

Limousin – standing six storeys above the north porch. Between the porch and the north transept is an unusual restored round

A striking old church with a particularly fine bell tower

QUINCY

This village dedicated entirely to the grape, is an essential stop for those seeking out local specialities. It lies on the south bank of the Cher, 12km south-east of Vierzon.

On the southern edge of the great wine regions of the Loire and Sancerre, Quincy has a tiny population but at least a dozen wine cellars, all of which are happy to offer tastings. The village has only 150 hectares of vineyards, run as a cooperative, producing a light, dry, white wine. It cannot compare in quality to those of its northern neighbours, it is extremely drinkable and is sold only in the Berry region.

Some 6km north is the village of Brinay, where the tiny early Romanesque church has some remarkably fine 12th-century frescos, uncovered in 1911 and currently undergoing restoration.

ST-BENOIT-DU-SAULT

Once an important medieval Renaissance town, St Benoît is virtually untouched, making it one of the most charming villages in the region. 26km south-west of Argenton-sur-Creuse.

In the 10th century a Benedictine priory was founded on this rocky promontory above the River Portefeuille. Later a small area around the priory was fortified. Then a second ring of defences was thrown around the growing town in the 15th century. Traces of both walls are still visible, The priory church, begun in the 11th century, is mainly Romanesque with a 14th-century bell-tower.

Best of all, though, is the maze of steep, narrow alleys and tiny lopsided old cottages that make up the heart of the old village. A road suddenly opens out into a cobbled square bright with flower shops or market stalls, and eccentric rooflines plunge down the hill into neat kitchen gardens

ST-GEORGES-NIGREMONT

A tiny hilltop hamlet on a Gallo-Roman site on the road to nowhere, this has some of the finest views in the Limousin. 12km south-east of Felletin.

The narrow twisting mountain roads seem to take forever to reach this minute hamlet hovering on the edge of the Plateau de Millevaches at a height of 750 metres. It consists of little more than about three houses, a war memorial, and a church, built in the 13th and 14th centuries and heavily restored. The massive square bell-tower is a later addition., A terrace by the church, however, looks out over a superb panorama that stretches eastwards halfway across the Auvergne.

The granite Plateau de Millevaches is the main regional watershed, a high, bleak, remote, stunningly beautiful area, most of which is now used by the army as a firing range. For this reason it is wise to see if the roads are closed before setting out to drive across it.

A CRAFTS REVIVAL

Nowadays you can find a pottery in just about every French town and village – a striking return to the way things were several hundred years ago, for today's potters use local clay and follow an ancient craft. The Burgundian region of the Puisaye is particularly known for its *grès*, or stoneware. Limoges has long been a centre for porcelain and enamel, and the oldest and finest piece to survive is the enamelled reliquary shrine in the church at Ambazac. The potteries are signs of a general revival in traditional crafts from basket-weaving to silk-weaving and musical instrument-making. Visitors to the Massif Central town of le Puy-en-Velay can see lace still being made by hand, and study its history at the local Musée Crozatier.

chapel – la Chapelle du Sépulcre – that was probably a baptistery. Inside, the 12th-century choir (restored in 1603) has an elegant and light ambulatory and contains some 15th-century oak stalls and the tomb of St-Léonard, who died in 559.

Léonard was a nobleman of the court of Clovis before being converted by St-Rémy, and he became the patron saint of prisoners. The town is known locally for the 'Quintaine' ceremony which takes place each November in memory of St-Léonard, and entails horsemen demolishing a wooden castle, symbol of a prison.

GLENIC

PRIMITIVE CHURCH ART

Glénic is north of Guéret, just off the D940.

The massive 12th-century church in this tiny village was substantially rebuilt and fortified in the 14th and 15th centuries. Its dour, brooding walls enclose some of the finest examples of primitive art in the region. Outside, above the west portal, squats an Eskimo-like Madonna and child, while in a side

chapel stands another, black Madonna (but the face of the infant Jesus is pink) – an example of the strong pagan streak in the religious art of this area, which has merged the Christian Virgin with a primitive Earth Mother figure. Opposite the main door, in the nave, are 14th-15th century frescoes, again in the primitive style, of the story of Adam and Eve.

TOUR 19 – 115KM
ALONG THE JACQUES COEUR TRAIL

This tour through the gentle farming country of Berry starts in Bourges, birthplace of a man named Jacques Coeur. He became an exceedingly successful trader, and was appointed Master of the Mint by King Charles VII, making him one of the most powerful men in France. In 1451, he fell from favour and was exiled, and the king promptly seized his vast fortune. One of the region's most famous inhabitants, Jacques Coeur's name has been used to link together loosely a selection of the finest historic sights, including a medieval abbey, a 17th-century château and unspoilt old towns, in the region of the River Cher.

ROUTE DIRECTIONS

Although relatively short stretches of this route are on major roads, all of the roads used are good, well-maintained and across flat country. The driving therefore is extremely easy.

Leave Bourges, heading east on the major **D976** towards Nevers. At Avord, turn right on to the **D36** and continue to Jussy-Champagne. Turn left in the centre of the village and follow signs to the château.

From Jussy-Champagne, continue south along the **D36**. Cross over the main **N76** and keep going to Dun-sur-Auron.

From Dun-sur-Auron, take the **D10** south to Meillant. Follow the road around until you come to the château gate, on the edge of the old part of the village.

Take the **D92** and on reaching la Celle, turn left on to the **D92E**. This acts as a slip road on to the main **N144**. Turn left towards St-Amand-Montrond and follow the road until you reach signs for the Abbaye de Noirlac, about 4km on the right.

Return to the **N144** and proceed to Bruères-Allichamps. Leave the village on the **N144** and after 1km turn left onto the **D35**, which follows the Cher valley to Châteauneuf-sur-Cher.

From the château, turn left onto the **D940** towards Levet and Bourges. At Levet, turn left and follow the **N144** north to Lissay-Lochy. Turn right here onto the **D27** to Plaimpied-Givaudins. Go through the village and turn left again onto the **D106** which leads back into Bourges.

The clean lines of the original Romanesque building of Plaimpied abbey are still clearly distinguishable

PLACES OF INTEREST

CHATEAU DE JUSSY-CHAMPAGNE

This charming red-brick château, built in the early 17th century, has a simplicity of design and a cosy family atmosphere. The house surrounds three sides of a central courtyard with an arcaded gallery, while a formal staircase leads up to the entrance hall. The furnishings, which belong to the Louis XIII, Louis XIV, and Regency periods, are exceptionally fine.

CHATEAUNEUF-SUR-CHER

Only two towers and the foundations remain of the original 11th-century fortress, but the château still hangs broodily above the Cher River valley. Substantial rebuilding in 1581 created the existing château with its extravaganza of Gothic decoration, panelling in the main rooms dates from the time of Louis XIV, while further additions were made in the 17th and 18th centuries. The sumptuous furniture collection and magnificent Flemish and Gobelin tapestries are mainly 18th century.

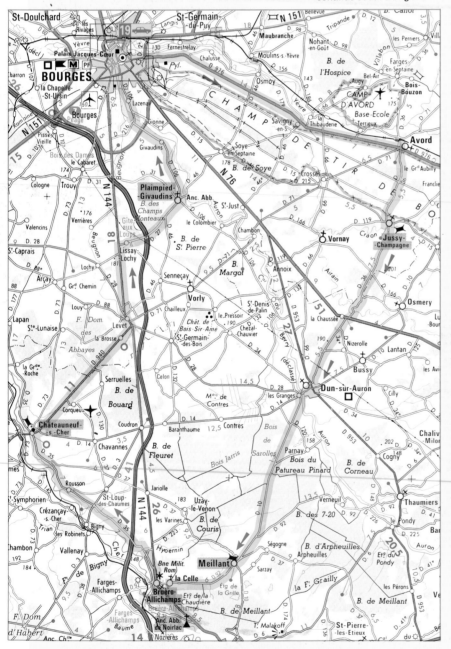

PLAIMPIED-GIVAUDINS
Founded in 1080 by a colony of Augustine canons, the abbey church took 100 years to build, and the original Romanesque building had flying buttresses and a tower or two added to it.

The interior, built of a creamy yellow stone, is light and airy, and soars gracefully upwards. The marvellous capitals of the nave and apse, many of them still in perfect condition, show biblical scenes. The vault of the small crypt was painted in the 13th century.

CHATEAU DE MEILLANT
See page 138.

ABBAYE DE NOIRLAC
The only Cistercian abbey in France to have survived almost intact, Noirlac was founded in 1150 by Abbot Robert, a cousin of St-Bernard of Clairvaux.

The warm honey-coloured stone building is

Above, Bourges's streets are rich in history
Right, the cloisters of 12th-13th century Noirlac abbey

remarkably simple, with graceful arches, but no adornment. The only real decoration is in the 13th–14th-century cloister, one side of which was damaged during its time as a porcelain factory during the 19th century.

BRUERE-ALLICHAMPS
See page 138.

St-Marcel

This small walled village which grew from the ashes of the Roman town of Argentomagus retains its distinctive character, despite being almost swallowed up as a suburb. 2km north of Argenton-sur-Creuse.

The site of St-Marcel has been inhabited for some 15,000 years, first as an Iron Age hill-fort and then as a thriving Roman city with a population of some 30,000. The 15th-century walled village that stands there today is a quiet haven of stone houses and empty streets that grew up around the priory church.

The existing church was built by the Benedictines in the 13th century, above the Carolingian crypt, and was altered and added to until the 15th century. Among the relics in the treasury is the arm of the evangelist St Marcel.

Excavations are still uncovering the full extent of Roman Argentomagus, and the prehistoric settlements which preceded it. A superb site museum displays prehistoric and Roman artefacts found in the region. There are also remains of a Roman theatre, amphitheatre, monumental fountain and temples nearby.

Ste-Severe-sur-Indre

A lively village in a lovely setting, perched on a clifftop overlooking the Indre, with a fascinating history and an attractive central square. 15km south-east of la Châtre.

Ste-Sévère takes its name from a Merovingian abbess who founded a convent here in the year 630. Though the convent has long disappeared, the town that grew up around it survived and was fortified in the 14th century. It has been sacked twice in its long history, the first time in the 13th century to remove its brigand lords who were terrorising the area, the second in 1372, to recapture it from the English during the Hundred Years War.

The central square is lovely with a 15th-century fortified gateway, a 16th-century stone pilgrim cross and an open-sided 17th-century market hall. The weekly market is on Wednesday morning.

In the grounds of the 18th-century château are the ruins of the old keep, and from the terrace there are good views over the river valley.

SECRET FRANCE

AUVERGNE

The Auvergne is an area of striking contrasts, from the Bourbonnais in the north, with its rich dairy pastures and unspoilt villages, to the mountainous Massif Central – the volcanic landscapes of Monts Dômes, with their rolling hills cloaked in forests and pitted with volcanic craters, and Monts Dore and Monts du Cantal, areas of lush farmland, broken intermittently by extraordinary volcanic outcrops. Close to Clermont-Ferrand, the area's chief town, is the Parc Natural Regional des Volcans d'Auvergne, with its range of ancient volcanic cones, one of which, Puy de Sancy, is the highest peak of the Massif. The region is often passed over by those heading for the more dramatic mountain areas such as the Alps or the Pyrenees, yet for those who enjoy exploring along quiet roads, or sitting in the sun in a quiet village square, the region has much to offer.

The Massif Central, the best-known part of the Auvergne, was formed by a series of volcanic eruptions that created lakes and mountains, and high plateaux that have subsequently been eroded over many centuries.

Rivers have cut their way through the soft rock, creating deep, narrow gorges, a dramatic landscape that is now cloaked in forests, with green valleys and sparkling rivers, its highest peaks often lost in the clouds. Cutting through the plateaux are numerous underground streams and rivers that have carved out extensive and fantastic cave systems, for which the region is famous.

The unspoilt countryside is dotted with little medieval towns and villages. There is also a wealth of medieval chateaux, some perched on volcanic outcrops, and which here tended to be baronial homes rather than fortresses. There is an abundance of Romanesque churches, the local style making good use of the soft volcanic rock.

Those touring in the region will find limitless opportunities for exploring off the beaten track, and for searching out tranquil villages and hidden beauty spots along roads that emerge above the clouds one minute and plunge down into a deep gorge the next. The Bourbonnais, in contrast, is a land of gently undulating, fertile dairy-farming country at the eastern end of the Loire valley, characterised by its oak forests and fortified villages.

maïs d'Auvergne

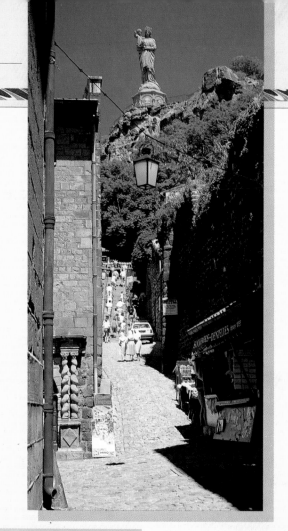

Above, a quiet, cobbled back-street recalls a peaceful time before the motor car
Below, schoolchildren bring history to life in a region that is steeped in a rich heritage of tradition

Left, the ancient, fortified settlement of Arlembes is set in an apparently ageless landscape, the result of volcanic action many centuries ago

BILLY

To the north-west of the Massif Central is the fine, fertile land of the Bourbonnais. This great château and fortified village were built to protect one of its main thoroughfares. 15km north of Vichy.

Although the surrounding land is relatively flat, the Bourbon dukes needed to hold the valley of the Allier and the Roman road that ran through it. Billy was their chosen site, and from the 12th century the village was progressively fortified. The 12th-century castle is still the focal point of the village. Entering what is now a shell through a massive gateway, visitors can walk the ramparts; as well as being the best way of seeing the village, these also offer a superb view of the Allier valley and the Monts Dômes to the south-west.

The best of the village can be discovered by strolling along rue Chabotin, where there are a number of very fine medieval buildings offering an appealing visual history of the local domestic architecture.

CHATELDON

Superbly set in a slight hollow at the foot of the Bois Noirs hills, the lovely fortified village of Châteldon is approached through vineyards or along an avenue of limes. 20km south of Vichy.

This lovely old village was fortified in the 14th century, though all that remains of the fortifications is the Tour de l'Horloge. It is chiefly remarkable now for its beautiful and well-preserved 15th-and 16th-century *vignerons'* houses, with their delightful wooden balconies.

There are also some fine half-timbered shop-fronts to be seen, dating from the same period. The Vieux Logis (now a pharmacy), on the main square, is perhaps the best.

Dominating the village still is the

The ancient and unspoilt village of Billy is entered through the remains of its medieval fortified walls

château on its hill, built in the 13th and 15th centuries. The best view of it is from the road to Thiers.

The village church was started in the 12th century and enlarged in the 15th. Inside are a fine early 16th-century Crucifixion, a 17th-century *pietà*, and a Virgin and Child dating from the 16th century.

HÉRISSON

North of Montluçon lie the pretty valley of the Aumance and the Forêt de Tronçais, claimed by many to be the finest in Europe – because of its collection of ancient oaks. At its southern edge is Hérisson. 24km north-east of Montluçon.

Hérisson sits on the right bank of the Aumance, beneath a hillock on which the Dukes of Bourbon built a

PAPERMAKING IN THE TRADITIONAL WAY

The pleasant little town of Ambert, in the valley of the River Dore on the western edge of the Monts du Forez, is today known for the Fourme d'Ambert, a cylindrical blue cheese with a dark grey rind. From the 14th century onwards, however, the region round Ambert was famous as a papermaking centre, and by the 17th century it boasted about 300 paper mills. (One local papermaking family, the Montgolfiers, migrated to Annonay, where their descendants achieved international fame by inventing the hydrogen balloon – see page 165.) At Ambert nature assisted the industry by providing a plentiful and powerful supply of clear water flowing from the heights above. In the Val de Laga, east of the town, several of the old *papeterie* buildings survive. One, the Moulin Richard de Bas, has been lovingly preserved as a working museum. It traces the history of the craft and its connection with the region, and allows visitors to see paper being made by hand in the traditional manner.

fortress as early as the 11th century. The present imposing ruins are all that survive of the work of Louis II of Bourbon, their red-brown towers and walls dating from the 14th century. When this new castle was built the village was also heavily fortified, and some of the 22 towers of its ramparts and two ancient gateways, Porte de Gatoeil and the Porte d'Enfer, still remain.

The village houses, many of them built with stone from the old castle, are strung out along a series of narrow interweaving alleyways that are a pleasure to explore.

LAVAUDIEU

At the south-western edge of the Parc Regional du Livradois-Forez, lie the attractive village and abbey of Lavaudieu. 10km southeast of Brioude.

Lavaudieu consists of a picturesque clutch of old houses built by *vignerons* in past centuries, winding down to a little bridge over the stream. In the old *boulangerie* on the main square is the Maison des Arts et Traditions Populaire de la Haute Loire, with fascinating displays on all aspects of local life.

The village's outstanding feature is the remains of the Benedictine abbey that was founded in this secluded spot in the 11th century. Inside, a superb series of 14th-century frescoes decorate the nave. Only rediscovered in 1967, these are astonishingly well preserved.

The abbey cloister is the only surviving Romanesque cloister in the whole of the Auvergne, and one of the best to be found anywhere in France, with slender twinned columns supporting a first-floor wooden gallery. It has been restored, but the work was so lovingly carried out that it is virtually impossible to detect.

SECRET PLACES

ST-NECTAIRE

THE PETRIFYING FALLS

An extraordinary water source which turns everyday artefacts to stone

St-Nectaire – which is divided into two distinct halves, St-Nectaire-le-Haut and St-Nectaire-le-Bas – lies south of Clermont-Ferrand.

St-Nectaire-le-Bas is a spa with a thermal station at the northern end of the village, and the waters that rise here are rich in minerals and calcium carbonate, or lime. While the water is moving rapidly its lime burden stays in solution, but if it slows to a trickle the lime is deposited, and in time it hardens into beautiful opalescent stone.

At St-Nectaire, this has been put to an extraordinary use at the Petrifying

Falls. In most places, the deposition rate is minimal, centuries being required to produce a reasonable piece of cave sculpture. At the Petrifying Falls, however, lime is laid down at a rate of up to 14cm each year. Everyday objects are placed on a staircase in the falls and, over a period of a few months, they become petrified. The end product is as hard as rock and every detail of the original remains clearly visible.

So good is the water-borne lime at reaching every nook and cranny that moulds are used to produce beautiful relief sculptures.

TOUR 20 – 110KM
LE PUY-EN-VELAY AND THE UPPER LOIRE VALLEY

The combination of the town of Le Puy and an early view of the Loire, the finest of French rivers, makes this a memorable tour. Le Puy occupies what is certainly the most dramatic site in the Massif Central and one of the most extraordinary sites in the whole of France, being built on a series of volcanic spires. In complete contrast to these angular remnants, the Loire valley is soft and pastoral, despite its closeness to the river's source on the flank of Gerbier de Jonc. The tour also passes through quiet villages grouped around fine Romanesque churches and beautiful châteaux that are the equals of those further west.

ROUTE DIRECTIONS

From the centre of le-Puy-en-Velay, follow signs for Valence. Go under a viaduct, and then turn left off the main street, following signs to Valence. Go straight over at the traffic lights, continuing to a roundabout. Exit left towards Valence. Follow the main road through Brives-Charensac, and beyond another viaduct turn right on to the **D535**, continuing through Arsac-en-Velay. At le Monastier-sur-Gazeille, ignore the right turn to the town centre, going along the bypass instead.
To visit le Monastier, go under a small bridge and then turn right into a square, where parking is available. Return to the bypass.

The route continues along the bypass: take the first right exit on to the **D49** towards Laussonne. In Laussonne go straight over a crossroads towards le Planchas. Bear left and cross a small bridge to leave Laussonne. The road climbs, and then drops into the next valley. Cross a bridge and continue on the **D49**. Just after le Betz and Bellernt, turn right at a junction on to the **D150**,

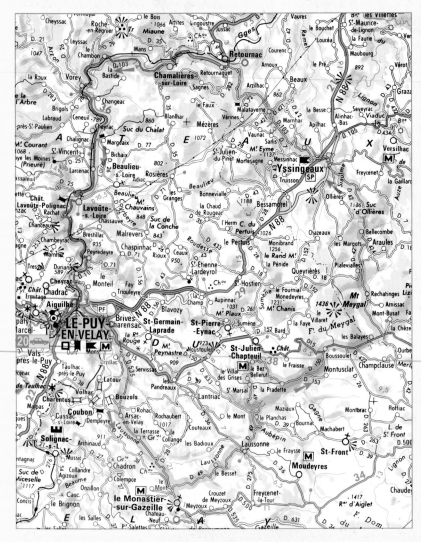

doubling back towards la Pradette. Go through la Pradette, and fork left to Boussoulet. At Boussoulet turn right on to the main road, the **D15,** through the village.
At the next crossroads, about 3km further on, turn left on to the **D42** to Recharinges. Continue on the **D42** to Yssingeaux. At a T-junction in Yssingeaux turn right, following '*Autres Directions*' signs. At the fountain in the town centre turn left, and left again at the next junction on to the **D103** towards Retournac. Cross a dual carriageway by bridge, and follow a lovely road into Retournac.
At the main road across the river from Retournac turn left down the Loire valley, and follow the **D103** all the way back to Le Puy.

Le Puy's streets are flanked by traditional buildings

PLACES OF INTEREST

LE-PUY-EN-VELAY
So dramatic is le Puy that all the roads into the town have numerous lay-bys in which the visitor can stop and wonder without endangering other road users. The town is built on a volcanic dome, on which are set several basalt stacks, one of which is topped by the 10–11th-century chapel of St-Michel d'Aiguilhe.
The Romanesque west front of le Puy's famous cathedral is a mass of arches and coloured geometric patterns but with a distinct Moorish influence. Inside, the main altar is

The chapel of St-Michel at le Puy perches on top of a volcanic dome

topped by a copy of the most famous of the Auvergne's Black Virgins, while the treasury includes the Bible of Théodulfe, a 600-page vellum bible illuminated in gold and silver, which dates from the reign of Charlemagne. The Crozatier is a museum to the history of the lace trade, as well as having other small collections.

RETOURNAC

The pretty village of Retournac has a Romanesque church (restored in the 15th century), constructed in delightful yellow-coloured stone beneath a slated roof. Inside it is airy and elegant. The Château de Chabanoles has some Louis XV furniture.

CHAMALIERES-SUR-LOIRE

The best Romanesque church in this part of the Loire valley is at Chamalières. A fine 11th–12th-century building, its pure Romanesque façade is squeezed by a flanking pair of rocket-like turrets. Inside there is a superb column carved with the figures of Old Testament prophets, as well as wall paintings and part of the original cloisters.

LAVOUTE-SUR-LOIRE

In the small Romanesque church is a remarkable carved wooden Christ. Close to the village is the fine Château de Lavoûte-Polignac, originally built in the 13th century, but almost completely rebuilt in the 17th century. What the visitor sees, however, is a late 19th-century restoration, in absolutely faithful and accurate style. It contains many mementoes of the Polignac family – who owned it since the 13th century – including tapestries, paintings and correspondence.

Traditional sights abound in the unspoilt Auvergne

Salers is an unspoilt medieval village of exceptional charm, with many fine buildings, set in the very heart of rich farming country

SALERS

To the south of the extinct volcanoes of the Auvergne are the regional peaks of the Monts du Cantal, the remnants of one massive volcano. West of the highest peaks is Salers, one of the finest villages of the whole Massif Central. 22km south-west of Mauriac.

One of the joys of Salers is its architectural harmony, for it has virtually no buildings from before the 15th century or after the 16th. The earliest houses date from the time when the village was a fortified refuge against bands of marauding English soldiers and bandits during the Hundred Years War, while the later houses were built during the period when it was a prosperous market town and seat of local government for the Haute Auvergne.

Among the fine houses in the Grande-Place are a reconstruction of the 15th century Hôtel de Ville, and just off to the east is the Maison de Bargues, a superb late 15th-century house with a surprising spiral staircase and a delightful courtyard. The interior is furnished in 17th-century style. The 15th-century church at the end of the Rue du Beffroi is entered through a fine 12th-century porch. Inside is a notable 15th-century polychrome Entombment.

ST-SATURNIN

Lying on an ancient volcanic ridge, this village, with its close-packed houses and narrow alleys set around a beautiful central square, has retained its authentic medieval atmosphere. 20km south of Clermont-Ferrand.

From the lovely central square with its fine Renaissance fountain, the best way of seeing this picturesque and ancient

SOUVIGNY

AN ANCIENT CALENDAR

Souvigny lies west of Moulins.

Opposite the north side of the priory church of St-Pierre is the venerable old church of St-Marc, now a museum, which contains a fascinating 12th-century calendar.

The calendar consists of an octagonal stone pillar about 1.8m high and weighing close to 1 tonne.

The faces of the pillar are covered with exquisite, vigorous and highly imaginative carvings. These depict the activities in which the monks of the priory would have been engaged during the months of the year, interspersed with floral designs, the signs of the zodiac, strange folk and mythical animals.

A carved octagonal pillar provides a pictorial clue to seasonal activities

village is to wander upwards towards the castle, built in the 13th century by the noble family of La Tour d'Auvergne, which gave France generations of cardinals, bishops and generals, as well as royal wives and mistresses. The castle has been carefully restored to give a true impression of medieval fortified architecture.

In the 11th century a Benedictine abbey was founded here, and the Romanesque chapel of the Madeleine was its original church. Near by stands the church of St-Saturnin, a fine example of Auvergnat Romanesque architecture.

TOURNEMIRE

Nestling among the peaks of the Monts du Cantal is the delightful valley of the Doire, which in medieval times was defended by the Château d'Anjony beside the village of Tournemire. 24km north of Aurillac.

Tournemire is a tiny village that straggles prettily along the valley of the Doire. At the end is the miniature 12th-century church, built of volcanic tufa. Inside, a reliquary holds one of the thorns from Christ's crown of thorns, brought back from the Holy Land by the local lord, Rigaud de Tournemire, in 1101.

The Château d'Anjony, built in the 15th century, is beautifully preserved and most imposing, consisting essentially of an austere square central keep flanked by four round corner towers. It has some remarkable interiors, including some fine 16th-century frescos. From the walls there are superb views of the valley of the Doire.

VOLCANOES OF THE AUVERGNE REGION

The Auvergne, the wildest part of the Massif Central, is still dominated by the violent geological activity that first gave it its shape. The most characteristic feature of this scenery of peaks and gorges are the *puys*, or cones, of the volcanoes which once thundered over the Auvergne and now stand eroded into strange and striking forms. The best preserved of them are in the Dômes, stretching west and south of Clermont-Ferrand. Of over 100 volcanic peaks, the Puy-de-Dôme reaches 1,465m. The older, more weathered Monts Dore to the south include the Mont Dore (1,050m) and the Puy de Sancy (1,885m). The rugged Cantal mountains include the Puy Mary (1,787m), the Puy Griou (1,694m) and the Plomb du Cantal (1,855m). Since 1967 about 362,000ha of the area has been registered as a Parc Naturel Régional; among other services provided, the park maintains some 200km of footpaths.

COL DE CUREBOURSE

The Col de Curebourse, at 997m quite a low mountain pass by Auvergne standards, is on the D54 south-east of Vic-sur-Cère.

This is the Pass of the Cutpurses. The name dates from the 18th or 19th century, when the pass was the favourite haunt of highwaymen, who would lie in wait and attack passing coaches, or even single travellers. The thefts that followed the arrival of a suitable victim had little in common with purse-cutting, however – that was an early form of pickpocketing, when a sharp knife was used to slit open a purse. The more usual form of crime at the pass of Curebourse was robbery – preceded by murder.

From the pass a 20-minute walk southward will bring you to the prominent Rocher des Pendus, which at 1,069m, provides superb views of the Cère valley, the Monts du Cantal to the north, and towards Aurillace in the west. It is doubtful that those whose name is actually associated with the rock enjoyed the view, however, for this is the Rock of the Hanged Men, named after those notorious highwaymen who were apprehended by the law and dispatched close to the scene of their crimes in order to discourage others.

SECRET FRANCE

RHONE VALLEY

The Rhône valley has always been a major thoroughfare for travellers heading north and south, as the flat plain of the valley made early route-finding simple. However, with mountainous areas to east and west, journeys from the Rhône towards the Pyrenees or the Alps were much more testing, both in plotting the path and in guarding travellers from attack. So once routes through the mountains became established, hilltop fortresses were built to provide the necessary protection.

These fortresses were the forerunners of many of the villages that can be seen in the area today. They not only provided protection for the route they were guarding, but also in times of turmoil sheltered people from the surrounding area, who would often build their houses close by so as to be able to reach the safety of the fortress walls quickly. Whatever their appearance or condition, the villages of the Rhône valley have an authentic charm, each with its own personality, which for visitors invariably provides a fascinating link between an eventful past and an ever-changing present.

Travellers should take their time driving along this narrow corridor, because there is plenty to see. Many sections of the Rhône take on a majestic beauty, especially where the hills crowd close. Venture away from the immediate valley to these high points and some of the

views of the river are astounding. Wander further still along the panoramic detours and you'll discover another, totally different world.

Because of its position, the Rhône valley has been heavily involved in events in the nation's history. The Romans established several towns along the river's course. It was a stronghold of the Protestant faith during the Wars of Religion, and the Revolution left its many marks. All these, and smaller events too, have left the region with a wealth of treasures that are often overlooked.

Some of the region's secrets take a little seeking out. There are 'lost' villages that, despite their isolation, have not been untouched by history, and the region is not without its eccentrics and legends. Unusual museums abound, and when it comes to natural attributes, the Rhône itself takes pride of place.

tournesols de Rhône

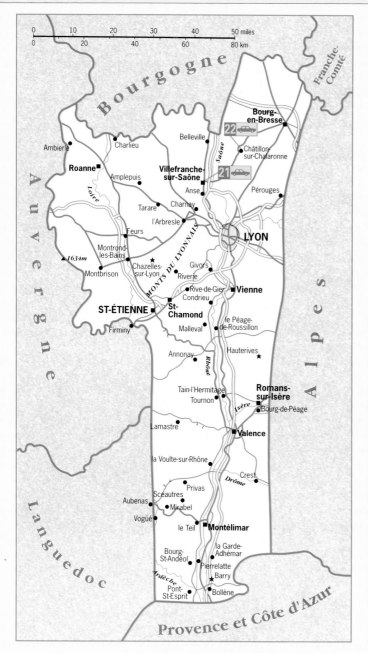

The Rhône Valley is famous for its rich red wines

The charm of the Rhône villages is enhanced by the abundance of flowers that decorate them

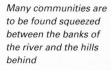

Many communities are to be found squeezed between the banks of the river and the hills behind

TOUR 21 – 115KM.
VILLEFRANCHE AND THE BEAUJOLAIS

Set between the Rhône and the Loire, the Beaujolais region is well known for its wine, but has many other attractions as well. The vineyards cover only the eastern slopes of this mountain area. Further west, the landscape is much more rugged, rising to a height of 1009m at Mt St-Rigaud, with roads climbing into and out of picturesque valleys, switching from forests to *bocage* scenery and back again. This is a tour you won't be able to hurry as the winding roads of the west will slow you down, while the *dégustations* of the east will prove tempting distractions. The finest Beaujolias wines (Supérieurs) come from the area directly east of Villefranche; the area north of this produces the Beaujolais Villages.

ROUTE DIRECTIONS

Leave Villefranche on the **D43** for Arnas and after 2km turn left on to the **D35** to Blacé.

Follow the signs to Blacé and then continue on the **D19** to St-Etienne-des-

Oullières. At the crossroads in the village turn left on to the **D43** to Odenas. Turn right at the T-junction with the **D37** and continue to Cercié. At the traffic lights in the village turn left on the D68 to Villié-Morgon.

In the centre of Villié-Morgon fork right (no

signs) on the **D68** and drive to Fleurie. Continue on the **D68** following signs to Chénas and Jullié. When the **D68** meets the **D17** turn left to Moulin Aujas and then follow signs to la Siberie.

After the Col de la Siberie bear left on the **D23** to St-Jacques-des-

Arrêts, then descend to the **D18**, turning left in St-Mamert and still following the **D23**. In 1km fork right at le Razay on to the **D23** to the Col de Crie, then at the col turn left on to the **D43** signposted to les Dépots and Beaujeu. At les Dépots turn left onto the **D37** and drive 3km to Beaujeu.

Return to les Dépots and turn left on to the **D129** towards Claveisolles. Descend from the Col de Casse Froide and at Claveisolles turn left on to the **D23** signposted to Pont Gaillard.

At Pont Gaillard turn right on to the **D9** to le Gravier, then left onto the **D485** through Lamure-sur-Azergues. Turn left at Chambost-Allières on to the **D504** signposted to Villefranche, which is reached in 24km.

PLACES OF INTEREST

SALLES-ARBUISSONNAS-EN-BEAUJOLAIS
A small village on the east-facing escarpment of the Beaujolais mountains, Salles-Arbuissonnas has several buildings remaining from a priory founded by monks from Cluny in the 10th century. These include the church with its beautiful Romanesque doorway, the cloisters surrounding a former cemetery, and a *salle capitulaire*, an elegantly decorated and vaulted chamber with some, unfortunately badly damaged, frescoes.

MT BROUILLY
Mt Brouilly, a prominent hill beside the road near

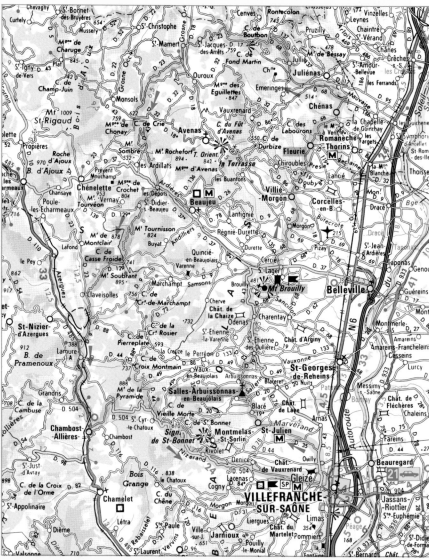

Above, Fleurie, snug amidst its famous vineyards
Right, the caveau below the museum at Beaujeu

Cercié, is well worth the short drive to the top. The narrow road runs through the vineyards of the Côte de Brouilly (the most southerly in the Beaujolais) to the chapel at the summit (484m), from where there are superb and extensive panoramas over the Saône plain to the east and into the hilly Beaujolais region to the west. A wine-growers' pilgrimage takes place at the chapel on the first Sunday in September each year.

FLEURIE

The village of Fleurie, at the foot of vine-covered

slopes offering extensive views over the Saône plain and beyond, produces the most popular of the Beaujolais *crus*.

The lively and welcoming restaurants in the village, frequented by large and ruddy-faced vineyard workers as well as visitors, provide entertaining opportunities for tasting the wine together with other local specialities.

BEAUJEU

The small town of Beaujeu, squeezed along a narrow valley between vine-clad hills, was once the most important town in the Beaujolais and gives its name to the region. Among its sights are the 12th-century church of St-Nicolas, and the Musée des Traditions Populaires

Marius-Audin. This has a fine collection of 19th-century dolls and an interesting section on folk-lore that includes a reconstructed 19th-century home interior and a display of craftsworkers' tools. In the Temple of Bacchus beneath the museum, visitors can taste the wines of Beaujolais-Villages, which are generally thought to be of superior quality to basic Beaujolais.

COL DE CASSE FROIDE

At an altitude of 740m, the Col de Casse Froide is the highest point on the tour. Like much of the western Beaujolais, this is a well wooded area, but there are superb views south through the trees towards Lamure-sur-Azergues.

COUNTRY FESTIVALS

In France almost any excuse
will serve for a festival – a patron
saint, the harvest, even the change
of the seasons. Bonfires and
fireworks celebrate summer on
the Night of St-Jean (23/24
June), with particularly spectacular
displays at Brançion and Mont-St-
Vincent in Burgundy and Lyons-la-
Forêt in Normandy. Widespread,
too, in country regions are the
fêtes de la batteuse, or threshing
festivals, where the labourers
wear traditional costumes. The
most important day in the vintners'
calendar is the January Festival of
St-Vincent. Licques holds a turkey
festival just before Christmas, and
Rouffignac in the Périgord has
a goose fair at the end of July.

AMBIERLE

With its old streets coiled around
the former abbey, this attractive village
is now best known for its lovely
Gothic church with fine furnishings
inside. 18km north-west of Roanne.

Even from a distance, when it is still
a pinkish blur on the hillside, Ambierle,
dominated by the remains of its 10th-
century Cluniac priory, has all the
appearance of something special. Its
15th-century church, in Flamboyant
Gothic style, has an unusual roof of the
coloured glazed tiles that are
more normally associated with
Burgundy. The elegant interior
has very tall 15th-century
stained-glass windows,
considerd the most beautiful
in the Rhône-Alpes, and a
lovely retable depicting the
Passion, thought to be the work of
Roger van der Weyden.

The village itself is a collection
of attractive old houses arranged con-
centrically around the old abbey. The
clock tower now serves as a *caveau* selling Côte Roannaise red and rosé wine.

CHARNAY

Built of warm golden stone, this
pretty wine-producing village in the
extreme south of the Beaujolais, is
still dominated by its château. 9km
south-west of Anse.

Charnay, built on a ridge separating
the valleys of the Azergues and the
Saône, is an attractive village of golden
stone and red pantiled roofs. These
warm materials impart a soft glow to
its old streets, especially around the
central square, where the 17th-century
slate-roofed château, the 12th-century
Romanesque church and some lovely
15th- and 16th-century houses are
grouped harmoniously together.
Sometimes the courtyards of the
houses can be glimpsed, filled with
flowers in summer.

The château, with its great courtyard and square towers, was inspired
by the architecture of Versailles. Since
the Revolution it has served the
municipality as Hôtel de Ville, library

HAUTERIVES

PALAIS IDEAL

The Palais Idéal in
Hauterives, 28km north of
Romans-sur-Isère, is a
remarkable monument to
one man's energy and
determination.

From 1869 until he
retired in 1896, Ferdinand
Cheval worked as the
postman in Hauterives.
But in 1879 he took on a
much greater task and set
about using his spare time
to build his dream palace
in the garden of his home.
Called the Palais Idéal, and

combining aspects of a
mosque, a Hindu sanctu-
ary, a feudal castle and the
manger in Bethlehem, it is
built of cement, pebbles
and shells. Surreal turrets
and spires are linked by
inner passages, stairways
and terraces decorated
with animals, serpents and
birds. Cheval had no previ-
ous building experience

*An eccentric and
individual
labour of love.*

and school canteen. The church has a superb Romanesque apse, and inside is a beautiful 13th-century polychrome stone statue of St Christopher.

LA GARDE-ADHEMAR

High on its rocky promontory above the Rhône valley, this medieval fortified village offers magnificent views as far as the hills of the Ardèche. 6km east of Pierrelatte.

A fortress belonging to the Adhémar family in the Middle Ages, la Garde-Adhémar retains little of its ancient fortifications except the traces of its ramparts and an arched gateway. The old streets of the village – extensively restored – wind and twist their way up the hill to the superb view. At the end of the main street stand the remains of the 16th-century Renaissance château,

and on the edge of the steep limestone promontory stands the lovely 12th-century church of St-Michel, an extremely fine example of Provençal Romanesque with a high nave and two apses. Nearby is a small and ancient chapel, which in the 17th century became a place of worship for the White Penitents. Hooded members are depicted in a fresco in the nave.

MALLEVAL

Only a short distance from the main Rhône Valley, this fortified village, hidden away in its exceptional location, could be in a different world. 10km south of Condrien.

Occupying a rocky spur in the wooded Gorge de Malleval, this fortified village was originally built in the 10th century to guard one of the

The old village of Malleval blends into its rocky landscape setting

treacherous routes between the Rhône and the Loire. It grew to its greatest prosperity in the 14th century, and never fully recovered from the damage inflicted on it during the Wars of Religion. Signs of its more glorious past can be seen in a number of impressive 16th-century houses. The church has chapels dating from the 15th and 16th centuries, and from the viewpoint in front of the cemetery there is a breathtaking view of the Rhône Valley and even the Alps.

Several footpaths radiate from the village, one leading past the cemetery to the site of the old fortress of the archbishops of Vienne. Another, the Flore footpath links the village with the Parc Naturel Régional du Mont-Pilat some 22km away.

---

and had not even used a trowel before, but he was undaunted by the project and worked with vigour until he finished it in 1912, at the age of 76.

The following year he started building his own vault, a mini version of the Palais Idéal, in the village cemetery. He was finally interred there in 1924. The Palais Idéal is open daily to visitors and Cheval's vault can be seen at the entrance to the cemetery.

CHAZELLES-SUR-LYON

HAT MUSEUM

Chazelles-sur-Lyon, north of St-Etienne, has a unique museum that gives an interesting insight into the town's former glories.

Chazelles' hat industry, which first became famous in the 16th century and flourished up until World War II, gained a world-wide reputation for quality and earned it the title of 'capital of the hat'.

The industry has since declined, leaving only one factory in the town.

However, there is also the Musée de Chapeau, the only one in France, where visitors can discover how hats were made. This fascinating museum takes one through the whole process, from the carving of wooden moulds to the final embellishment.

There are mock-ups of shops and workshops, old juke-boxes playing French songs with hat themes, advertising posters from the 1920s and 30s and

interesting old photographs of crowds where everyone on view was wearing a hat. Fashions from 1830 to 1970 are on display, as well as traditional hats from the regions of France and around the world, plus hats worn by famous people. A nice touch at the end of the tour is the big chest of hats through which visitors can rummage to try on various styles in front of a mirror.

TOUR 22 – 160KM

PEROUGES AND THE REGION OF LA DOMBES

La Dombes, a marshy area of lakes straddling the N83 between Lyon and Bourg-en-Bresse, has particular appeal for lovers of wildlife. Birds, especially waterfowl, abound here and the grassy shores are alive with frogs. There are several interesting places to stop at *en route* too, with Pérouges, one of the best-preserved medieval villages in France, standing atop a vantage point overlooking the plains. Though fairly long, the tour follows quiet secondary roads through easy driving country, so each leg between stops should be reasonably quick.

ROUTE DIRECTIONS

Leave Châtillon-sur-Chalaronne on the **D2** to Villars-les-Dombes. Follow '*autres directions*' signs through Villars, and at the **N83** turn right to the Parc Ornithologique on the left as you leave the town.

Return to Villars and turn right on the **D904** towards Chalamont, forking right after 500m on to the **D2** and following signs to Montluel. Turn right at the T-junction in Montluel, follow '*toutes directions*' signs to the **N84**, then turn left in the direction of Genève. In a few metres, where the **N84** bears left, carry on towards the Pont de Jons.

After the Pont de Jons turn left on the **D55** to Chavanoz, then follow the signs to Crémieu. Leave Crémieu on the **D65** in the

Above, peaceful Pérouges Below right, the bird park at Villars-les-Dombes

direction of Lagnieu and immediately bear right on the **D52** to Optevoz. From there follow signs to Charette. Just beyond the village turn left towards Lyon. Follow this road, the **D52c**, to the **D65** and turn right to la Balme-les-Grottes. In 1km fork right to the caves (les Grottes de la Balme), pass through the village and rejoin the **D65** towards Lagnieu. At the **N75** turn left towards Lagnieu. Immediately after crossing the Rhône, turn left on the **D20** to St-Vulbas and from there follow the signs to Meximieux. On the outskirts of Meximieux turn right on to the **N84** and immediately turn left on to the **D4** into Pérouges.

Return to the **N84**, turn left towards Genève and in Meximieux fork left on the **D22a** to Chalamont. In Chalamont turn left on the **D904** and follow the **D7** back to Châtillon-sur-Chalaronne.

PLACES OF INTEREST

CHATILLON-SUR-CHALARONNE

Just north of la Dombes, this floral town has several medieval buildings at its centre. The walls of the

MIRABEL

This medieval village occupies a sheltered and formerly extremely strategic position beneath the strange black basalt cliffs that break out from wild country at the edge of the Coiron plateau. 16km east of Aubenas.

The magnificent square keep that stands at the edge of the cliff, towering over the village and visible for miles around, is a reminder of the great strategic importance that Mirabel formerly had, and all that is left of the great fortress. Guarding the main route between the Rhône and the Cévennes, for centuries it played a major part in the history of the region.

The village itself clusters at the foot of the cliff, still almost entirely surrounded by its arcaded ramparts, now partly turned into houses. On the

Tucked dramatically under the black cliff, Mirabel was a fortress village of great strategic importance

main square are some fine 15th- and 16th-century houses, built in the unusual mixture of pale limestone and dark basalt that characterises the village.

A vaulted passageway beside the church leads up to the tip of the promontory, from where there are superb views of the surrounding land.

12th–13th century fortress look down on the Place des Halles, where the unusual brick-built 14th-century church of St-André stands next to the huge 17th-century timber market hall, scene of a colourful flower market every Saturday. Nearby is the Porte de Villars, a 14th-century gateway, while the former hospital and apothecary form an attractive grouping in the Place St-Vincent-de-Paul.

LA DOMBES
La Dombes, midway between Bourg-en-Bresse and Lyon, is a strange plateau made up of approximately 1,000 shallow man-made lakes. For 600 years local farmers have been taking carp, roach, tench and pike from the lakes, which are drained by rotation after a few years, leaving fertile land that is ploughed up for crops while new lakes are created elsewhere.

VILLARS-LES-DOMBES
In the middle of la Dombes, Villars-les-Dombes is famous for the ornithological park just outside the town. France's largest bird park, it is based on one of the lakes of la Dombes, which is on a main migratory route across Europe and so attracts many passing species.

Some 2,000 exotic birds from all over the world are kept there, including wildfowl, birds of prey, flamingos, ostriches, pelicans and parrots.

There is also a display showing what life is like beneath the surface of the region's lakes.

LA BALME-LES-GROTTES
La Balme-les-Grottes is best known for the caves, known as les Grottes de la Balme, located in the limestone cliffs behind the village. Beyond the massive entrance, which

shelters a small chapel, is a huge chamber with smaller galleries leading off it, complete with stalactites, stalagmites, pools and lakes.

One of the galleries is decorated with a fresco of François I, a famous visitor to the caves.

PEROUGES
See page 164.

CHALAMONT
Chalamont, standing at 334m, is at the highest point of la Dombes. Among its attractions is a renovated old district with several half-timbered houses, which won a prize in a national competition for the environment.

PÉROUGES

With its maze of cobbled streets and old houses enclosed within ancient ramparts, this is one of the finest examples of a medieval hilltop village to be seen anywhere in the whole of France. 27km north-east of Lyon.

In a state of seemingly terminal decay early this century, Pérouges has undergone careful and loving restoration and now thrives on its past. Such is the authentically medieval flavour of the village that it has been used on several occasions as a backdrop for films needing a historical setting.

The village is entered by the Porte d'En Haut, the street passing in front of a fortified church built in the 15th century and then winding past magnificent old houses, including the Maison des Princes de Savoie, to the Place du Tilleul, the village's picturesque central square.

There are more beautiful buildings here, some with exposed timber beams and broad overhanging eaves, others with mullioned windows. Among them are the Ostellerie de Vieux Pérouges and the Maison du Vieux-St-Georges.

RIVERIE

A background of war, turmoil and recovery makes this historic village with extensive panoramas a fascinating place to visit. 34km south-west of Lyon.

Much of the original medieval village was destroyed and its population massacred in 1590 during the Wars of Religion. In 1595 Antoine Camus, Baron of Riverie, rebuilt the château and the houses of the village.

The château, a large square building of golden stone, now serves as the Mairie and a *gite-d'etape*. From here there is a lovely view down over the terracotta roofs of the village. The Grande-Rue, the narrow main street of the village, lined with tall houses, has kept its medieval atmosphere. It is possible to walk around the old ramparts, following signs for the Chemin de Ronde, from which there are some superb views, especially down to St-Didier-sous-Riverie and beyond to Lyon and as far as the Alps.

SCEAUTRES

A tiny, virtually unknown village huddled in an isolated wind-swept position high up the weird and wild landscape at the edge of the Coiron plateau. 22km north-west of Montélimar.

A narrow road leads along a valley at the edge of the Coiron plateau to reach Sceautres, a tiny village sheltering beneath a strange, brooding basalt outcrop. Few tourists visit this blustery spot where the gently sloping pantiled roofs have boulders on top to stop the tiles blowing away.

A small fortified gate, part of the medieval fortifications that are still fairly well preserved, gives access to the main part of the village, where narrow alleyways wind between simple traditional houses built of pale limestone and dark basalt. Dusty tracks crossed here and

Sceutres is a little-known village, off the beaten tourist track but well worth an exploratory visit

there by vaulted passageways, serve as streets, while behind the village a steep and rocky path leads up to the outcrop's summit.

VOGUE

Occupying a narrow shelf beneath limestone cliffs and a massive Renaissance château, this village, a popular spot in summer, spreads along the banks of the River Ardèche. 9km south of Aubenas.

A maze of charming little alleyways

BARRY

DESERTED CAVE VILLAGE

Barry is 5km north of Bollène. Turn off the D158A at St Pierre and wind up the hill until the road ends. Park the car and continue on foot along a dusty track to the village.

This strange, cave-dwellers' village overlooking the Rhône and all

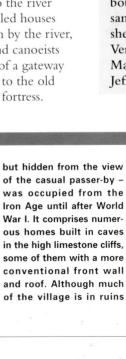

runs behind Vogüé's main street along the river bank, giving tantalising glimpses of the river. The best view, though, is from the hanging gardens beside the château. Owned by the Melchior de Vogüé family since the 17th century, the château is a handsome, almost square building with round towers at each corner, built in the 16th century. It has a fine monumental staircase, a notable state room and a tiny 12th-century chapel with a retable taken from the church at nearby Rochecolombe.

The way back down to the river winds past medieval pantiled houses and arcaded streets. Down by the river, which is full of bathers and canoeists in summer, are the ruins of a gateway to the old fortress.

THE HISTORY OF THE BALLOON

The Montgolfiers were the largest paper mill-owners in the hilly town of Annonay in the 17th century, but their name is most famous for the contribution to aeronautics by the brothers Joseph and Etienne. After a modest start, experimenting with heated paper bags, they launched the world's first successful balloon flight, albeit unmanned, from the Place des Cordeliers at Annonay in June 1783.

The achievement caught the imagination of an age that found science both an adventure and a fashionable entertainment. By September of the same year a vast crowd was watching a Montgolfier balloon, with a sheep, a duck and a rooster in its basket, float over the palace at Versailles. The first manned balloon flight, by Pilâtre de Rozier and the Marquis d'Arlandes, followed in November, and in 1785 Blanchard and Jeffries made the first crossing of the English Channel by balloon.

but hidden from the view of the casual passer-by – was occupied from the Iron Age until after World War I. It comprises numerous homes built in caves in the high limestone cliffs, some of them with a more conventional front wall and roof. Although much of the village is in ruins and no longer inhabited, it has undergone some recent restoration and many of the caves have separate rooms with fireplaces and chimneys. Among the buildings is a chapel, Notre-Dame de l'Espérance, dating from 1682 and restored in 1906, while a recent addition is a statue of a cave-dweller.

Steep tracks lead past the dwellings and climb to the few remains of a 12th-century château that stood at the top of the cliffs.

From here there are tremendous views over the Pierrelatte plain and Tricastin nuclear complex to the Vivarais hills.

A curious and secretive location, with dwellings and even a chapel built straight into the rock.

THE ALPS

The French Alps cover a truly vast area, being bounded by Franche-Comte in the north and Provence in the south, the Rhône valley in the west, Switzerland to the east and Italy to the south-east. For many people this high mountain region means the opportunity to get away from the crowds into an atmosphere of clean air, unusual wildlife, stunning views, hidden lakes, carpets of alpine flowers in the spring, and unspoilt and sometimes isolated villages in spectacular mountain settings where time seems to have stood still. There are also two national parks in the region, the Parc National des Ecrins south-east of Grenoble and the Parc National de la Vanoise in the south, both well-known for their chamois, marmots, ibex and mountain hares and opportunities to see rare bird species such as golden eagles, eagle owls and bearded vultures.

The true scale of the Alps is increased as a result of the hundreds of valleys that slice deeply into the mountains. The sheer scale and diversity of the landscape means that even on a busy summer's day it will be possible to find a quiet corner, even in the most heavily used parts of the region. Out of season things are different, and visitors in autumn and spring will have little difficulty in finding peace and tranquillity.

In the north of the region is Lac Léman, where old lakeside villages cluster around ancient quays. South of this are the Savoie Alps, bordering Switzerland. Deep valleys divide mountain slopes cloaked in lush alpine pastures and evergreen woods, topped by snowfields. South of here, bordering on Provence, are the Dauphiné Alps, which appear impressively harsh and forbidding, with high, isolated valleys where villages appear to be heaped higgledy-piggledy up the mountainsides in spectacular settings, reached by high-level passes that are often blocked by snow in winter.

Although many traditional old villages have been developed for winter sports, great care has been taken to blend the new with the old, thus retaining their charm, and much from the past remains to be explored.

For those touring in the region, the Alps offer some of the most spectacular roads and cliff scenery in Europe. However, quite often the real jewels are left to the visitor to discover on foot, as some of the best views and the most ancient villages cannot be reached by car.

gentiane des Alpes

Below, given the right weather, the Alps are an outdoor paradise at any time of the year, with a great variety of sports in winter and summer

Left, the Alpine landscape is vast

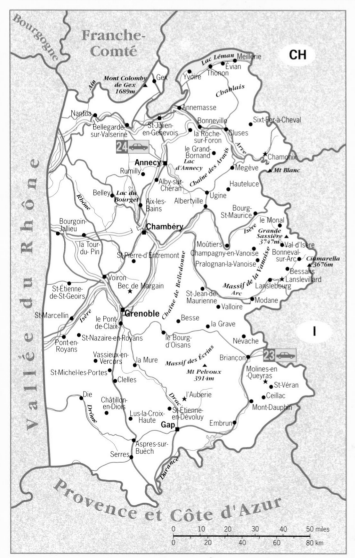

Map labels:

Bourgogne
Franche-Comté
CH
Lac Léman Meillerie
Évian
Thonon
Yvoire
Chablais
Mont Colomby de Gex 1689m Gex
Nantua
Annemasse
Bellegarde-sur-Valserine
St-Julien-en-Genevois
la Roche-sur-Foron
Bonneville
Cluses
Sixt-Fer-à-Cheval
24
le Grand-Bornand
Arve
Chamonix
Annecy
Chaîne des Aravis
Mt Blanc
Rumilly
Lac d'Annecy
Megève
Alby-sur-Chéran
Hauteluce
Belley
Lac du Bourget
Aix-les-Bains
Albertville
Ugine
Bourg-St-Maurice
le Monal
Bourgoin-Jallieu
Chambéry
Isère
Grande Sassière 3747m
Val-d'Isère
la Tour-du-Pin
Moûtiers
Champagny-en-Vanoise
Bonneval-sur-Arc
St-Pierre-d'Entremont
Pralognan-la-Vanoise
Ciamarella 3676m
Voiron
Bec de Margain
Massif de la Vanoise
Bessans
Lanslevillard
St-Étienne-de-St-Geoirs
Chaîne de Belledonne
St-Jean-de-Maurienne
Lanslebourg
Arc
St-Marcellin
Grenoble
Besse
Modane
le Pont-de-Claix
Valloire
Isère
St-Nazaire-en-Royans
le Bourg-d'Oisans
la Grave
Névache
Pont-en-Royans
I
Vassieux-en-Vercors
la Mure
Massif des Écrins
Briançon
23
St-Michel-les-Portes
Clelles
Mt Pelvoux 3914m
Molines-en-Queyras
St-Véran
Die
Châtillon-en-Diois
Drac
l'Auberie
Ceillac
Lus-la-Croix-Haute
St-Étienne-en-Dévoluy
Mont-Dauphin
Drôme
Gap
Embrun
Aspres-sur-Buëch
Serres
Durance
vallée du Rhône
Rhône
Provence et Côte d'Azur

Scale:
0 10 20 30 40 50 miles
0 20 40 60 80 km

Above, the Alps have plenty of other attractions, including pleasant locations such as Pont en Royens, and, left, the strange rock formations of the Parc de Queyras

WINTER SPORTS

There are few places on earth better suited to such a wide variety of sports and pastimes as the Alps. Each Alpine region seems tailor-made for a variety of activities. The limestone of the Vercors and the Chartreuse provides dazzling white rock faces to climb, and in winter the high plateaux are supreme Nordic and cross-country ski areas. The areas around Lac d'Annecy and Lac du Bourget are suited to more regular, leisurely pursuits, but cater for climbers and paragliders too. The Tarentaise and Vanoise offer exciting downhill skiing, with everything for the energetic Alpinist from glacier walks to more arduous mountain climbing routes.

ALBY-SUR-CHERAN

Lying close to but just escaping the effects of a busy autoroute, this old medieval market town lies at the foot of the Semnoz peaks and the Crêt de Châtillon. 14km south-west of Annecy.

Alby-sur-Chéran was formerly surrounded by ancient châteaux, but only the Château de Montpon remains in good condition. The old, single-span stone bridge over the River Chéran provides an excellent view of the village, which stretches out along both banks of the river.

The old sector of the village is well worth exploring with its fountain and charming old buildings, and old arcaded square. It is one of very few places in the Alps which has a modern church, this one built in 1954 and featuring a splendid stained-glass window by Manessier.

BESSANS

Bessans occupies an austere high mountain setting, surrounded by sheer peaks with their attendant gullies, waterfalls, snowfields and glaciers, and encircled by peaks over 3,000m. 36km south of Val d'Isère.

Bessans is the first village in a little community of four hamlets; the other three, running up the Avérole valley, are la Goula, Vincendières and Avérole. Of these, Vincendières is perhaps the most attractive.

Though developed as a winter resort and well-known for its cross-country skiing, Bessans retains a traditional feel, and local costumes are still worn during festivities. The chapel of St-Antoine, originally built in the 14th

century, and restored in the 19th, has murals on its exterior walls depicting 'Virtues and Vices'. Inside it houses paintings and carvings, and a series of 15th-century frescos which are in good condition.

Bessans is solated from the rest of France to the north and from Italy to the south by exposed, high-level passes which are frequently blocked by winter snows. The route west via Lanslebourg provides the only year-round access.

BESSE

The charming old village of Besse, with its traditional houses arranged higgledy-piggledy on the hillside, lies at the foot of the Grandes Rousses, a short way from the Alpe d'Huez ski area. 21km east of Bourg-d'Oisans.

The route to the village is somewhat bewildering, with so many dramatic changes of direction that you are left wondering whether you will find it. At last, however, the village reveals itself, small and compact, surrounded by traditional, terraced meadows. Everything here faces to the south taking maximum advantage of the sun to help compensate for the high altitude.

The most striking feature of the village is the nature of the houses themselves. Their attractive stonework is usually a combination of flat schists and rounded quartz, giving a neat yet random-looking finish. Many of the older buildings exhibit the traditional style of architecture with over-hanging eaves, intricately carved balustrades, and roofs sometimes pitched with *lauzes*, the traditional larch tiles.

CHAMONIX

THE BOSSONS GLACIER

This long tongue of ice stretches down almost into the town of Chamonix, Haute Savoie's world capital of alpinism.

Immediately above the south end of the town is the madcap jumble of ice called the Bossons. Fed by the eternal snows of Mont Blanc, the last 1,000m of the glacier's descent is

BONNEVAL-SUR-ARC

At 1,825m above sea level, in the midst of 3,000m peaks of unrelenting steepness, Bonneval's sturdy, rust-coloured houses huddle together as if seeking mutual shelter from the harsh climate, 34km south-east of Val d'Isère.

Bonneval has been carefully maintained in order to preserve its unique character. There are no visible telephone or electricity lines (they are all buried underground) and aerials are banned. In addition to this, visitors are prohibited from taking their cars into the village. The result of these measures is that Bonneval retains a peaceful and authentic atmosphere that is accentuated by the rustic buildings and the full use of natural materials.

The old stone roofs are masterpieces of design, and though the buildings are squat, stout and solid, they possess a peculiar grace and beauty of their own, which is enhanced by the subtle oranges and browns of the granite. The heavy roof tiles, or *lauzes*, often projecting over balconies and entrances, provide some shelter from the winter snows.

In the centre of the town is the Grande Maison, an ancient chalet that now houses a butcher's shop, a bakery and information centre.

The stone roofs of Bonneval-sur-Arc are an outstanding feature of this peaceful and unspoilt village

down very steep slopes that allow the ice to become increasingly crevassed and split. In winter, its appearance changes to a uniform creamy white, but the higher temperatures of summer soon burn off the softer snow, leaving the steely blue glacier of ice exposed.

Excellent views of the glacier can be obtained from the slopes just above Chamonix, but the mouth of the glacier can be seen much more closely. A short chairlift gives access to its left-hand (true) bank, from where its power and majesty can be fully appreciated. A path also leads to it through the woods from a point near the entrance to the Mont Blanc tunnel, but advice on this route should be sought locally.

Close inspection reveals the textures and formations that can only be guessed at from a distance. Huge slopes of boulder-embedded moraine line its sides – obvious danger areas – while the glacier rises in a kaleidoscopic jumble of ice fins and blocks.

The Bossons glacier is at its most spectacular in summertime, when the sun's warmth melts the top covering of snow, and its light illumines the ancient blue ice

CEILLAC

Although now a small winter resort, Ceillac, with its beautifully decorated traditional chalets and old churches, is a typical Alpine village. 50km south-east of Briançon.

Access to Ceillac is from the Combe du Queyras via a steep, narrow and winding road which hugs the side of a pine and fir covered canyon. The route levels out on to a high plateau, on which the village is spread out.

A traditional wooden chalet of the Haute Alpes, with its typical summer decoration

Although many of the outlying buildings are quite new, the old heart of the village contains many ancient wooden chalets that exhibit beautiful woodwork, some intricately carved. The building housing the town hall dates back to 1558. Also in the centre is the church of St-Sebastien, dominated by its unusual 18th-century five-faceted clock. The interior is decorated with, among other things, some 16th-century murals. Adjoining the church, the Chapelle des Pénitents houses a museum of religious art where the treasures of the area are displayed.

CHAMPAGNY-EN-VANOISE

Nestling in the Doron de Champagny – a narrow valley that splits the area between la Plagne and Tigne – and access point for the Parc National de la Vanoise, Champagny-en-Vanoise has many typical old alpine houses and an ancient church. 18km south-east of Moûtiers.

Champagny is very much a sporting centre, though not overdeveloped – new buildings having been carefully blended with old. It is made up of a collection of hamlets spread across the forested hillsides. The lower village of Champagny-le-Bas has a beautifully situated church, standing proudly on a rocky bluff overlooking the valley. Originally built in 1250, then rebuilt in 1648, it houses a superb altar by the sculptor, Clérant de Chambéry.

CHATILLON-EN-DIOIS

On the boundary of the Parc Natural Regional du Vercors, its backdrop one of forests and cliffs, Châtillon-en-Diois is a delightful jumble of ancient streets, on the site of a settlement dating back to Roman times. 14km south-east of Die.

It may appear to the visitor on first acquaintance that the village is composed of just one long main street. It soon becomes apparent, however, that there is considerably more of interest to see on the north side of the road.

Built around a long-gone fortress, from which the village originally took its name, is the medieval quarter, which has changed little over the years. Behind the church is the small Place Reviron with a central, circular water trough. On one side, the road leads enticingly beneath an 18th-century clock tower, beside a beautiful 16th-century building now housing the town hall, into the oldest part of the village. Running off the Rue des Rostangs, the main street, are several delightful narrow alleys, such as the Viol du Temple. The name Viol – a derivative of Via – reveals the village's Roman origins.

LE GRAND-BORNAND

Tucked in behind the Aravis mountains is a wide, sunny valley that hosts le Grand-Bornand and its satellite hamlets. Surrounded by a pleasant mixture of forests and pastures, studded with chalets old and new, the village is spacious and relaxed. 35km east of Annecy.

On the southern approach to the village are some wonderful old wooden chalets. Though surrounded by newer chalets of similar designs, their weather-worn and gnarled woodwork oozes charm and character. Their roofs slope gently to avoid sudden avalanches after a heavy snowfall, their eaves overhanging considerably for shelter. Only the lower sections are constructed from stone, and these are set into the hillside, while the huge upper parts are magnificently constructed in timber.

Along with neighbouring le Chinaillon, le Grand-Bornand is now a major resort both in summer and

SECRET PLACES

LA GRAVE

THE HIGH ROMANCHE

A magnificent spot for a picnic on a clear day

This spectacular valley leads into the Ecrins massif from the foot of the Col du Lauteret near la Grave. East of la Grave, turn right for le Pied du Col, then right again to pass the Refuge de la Lochette. Continue for another 2km along a rough track to a remote parking area.

Though this wild setting is splendid in itself, it takes relatively little effort to gain access to the Refuge de l'Alpe, set in a vast, high valley beneath a cirque of 3,000m peaks. A well-marked path leads along the river, climbing past some fine waterfalls before levelling out on the approach to the hut, with its majestic views.

Though this magnificent spot can be gained comparatively easily, it should be noted that the path is rough and steep in places, and appropriate footwear and clothing must be worn.

La Grave huddles below the spectacular La Meije glacier

winter, offering a bewildering array of activities from golf to fencing and from paragliding to trampolining. It is also well known as the originator of that famous cheese, Reblochon.

LA GRAVE

At the bottom of the Col de Lautaret and overshadowed by the glaciers of la Meije lies la Grave, which, although now a major skiing and mountaineering centre, has successfully retained its old buildings and character. 39km north-west of Briançon.

Although la Grave's main street is attractive with several small bars overlooking the magnificent snowfields, to its rear, on the steep, south-facing slope lies old la Grave, a mixture of stone-faced and rendered houses and narrow roads that lead towards the 12th-century Romanesque church. This squat structure with its strong tower and short but attractive spire, occupies one of the most dramatic positions in the Alps. The tiny cemetery in front recalls many victims of the mountains, and there is also a monument to the local guides in front of the *Guides Bureau* on the main street. Beside the church is the 17th-century Chapelle des Pénitents, with a ceiling decorated with frescos.

A spectacular cablecar ride takes climbers, skiers and tourists alike to the Col des Ruillans, 3,200m high on the north-west flank of the Rateau, from where the views are quite simply magnificent.

TOUR 23 – 120KM

BRIANÇON AND THE QUEYRAS

A relatively short tour, but one packed with splendidly varied scenery and a wide range of cultural and architectural interest. Surrounded by peaks and passes, Briançon is undoubtedly the principal centre of the Queyras region, the strategic significance of its position having long been recognised. To the south is the magnificent Queyras Regional Park, famous for its summer flowers and year-round beauty.

Roads on this tour are generally good, the Col d'Izoard being probably the most memorable section by virtue of its altitude (2,360m) and exceptional views, and the journey through the Queyras is charming.

From Guillestre take the **D902A** towards Briançon. This leads in 4km to a junction with the main **N94**. Turn right towards Briançon, then left after about 1km on to the **D37**.

To reach Mont-Dauphin continue a little further along the **N94** and turn right. Retrace the route back to the **N94** and take the turn off it on to the **D37**.

Cross the river and bear right to reach a junction. Bear right here on to the **D38** and follow the narrow road for 4.5km, continuing beside the river to Chanteloube. Follow this road for a further 17km, passing le Gouffre de Gourfouran on the right, to reach l'Argentière-la-Bessée, and there turn right through the town to rejoin the **N94**. Turn left towards Briançon and after 7km pass through St-Martin-de-Queyrières and continue to Briançon.

Alternatively, you can turn right after a further 1.5km along the **D136** to Villard-St-Pancrace (an attractive village with superb views), and from there follow a well-marked descent in to Briançon.

PLACES OF INTEREST

COL D'IZOARD AND THE CASSE DESERTE

One of the highest Alpine passes at 2,360m, the Col is well known as one of the toughest routes taken by the Tour de France. The names of famous riders are painted on the road,

Briancon, the capital of the Queyras region, encircled by snow-capped peaks

ROUTE DIRECTIONS

From Briançon, take the **D902**, heading for Col d'Izoard. After 6km, and past the village of Cervières, the climb up to this classic col starts in earnest.

From the top, descend through the wilderness of the Casse Déserte and pass through the village of Arvieux to reach a junction with the **D947**. Turn left here, signposted Château Queyras, which is reached after 2km.

From here, continue for 2.5km, and then take a right turn along the **D5**, signposted St-Véran (11km).

From St-Véran retrace the route back through Château Queyras to the junction with the **D902**. Bear left here along the **D902** towards Guillestre and descend the Combe du Queyras for 17km to reach this busy little town.

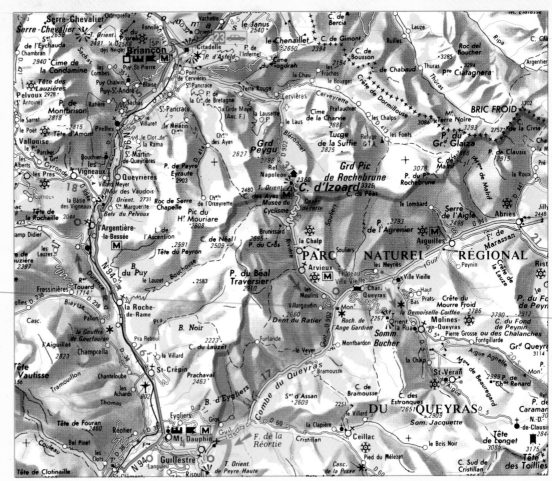

and there is a Tour de France information centre on the summit.

One of the most impressive sights on the descent from the Col d'Izoard to Arvieux is the Casse Déserte, a huge mountainside of grey scree slopes, out of which sprout dozens of rocky pinnacles left behind as the softer rock has eroded.

CHATEAU-QUEYRAS
Fortifications on this magnificent glacial vantage point date back to the Middle Ages, though the present buildings were instigated by Vauban at the turn of the 17th century. Further additions were made during the 18th and 19th century.

Beneath the watchful eye of the fort lies the small village of Ville Vieille, many of whose tightly gathered houses are roofed with the iron sheets common throughout the region. It is possible to drive up a rough track from the village to one of the region's finest viewpoints at Sommet-Bucher. St-Véran and Mont Viso

Above, the Queyras Regional Park looks spectacular at all times of the year
Right, old farmhouses at St-Veran – the upper floors are used in summer

are easily recognisable to the south-east. Particularly eye-catching is the semi-circle of peaks that form the boundary with Italy, stretching from Briançon in the north to Guillestre in the south.

ST-VERAN
See page 180.

GUILLESTRE
At the foot of the wild and rocky Combe du Queyras lies Guillestre, a small but busy market town with pretty medieval streets and a 16th-century church built in rose marble, with fine Renaissance door panels.

Towards Mont-Dauphin is the Rotunda of the Plan de Phazy, which houses an exhibition next to the warm thermal waters, which have been used since Roman times.

MONT-DAUPHIN
See page 175.

LE GOUFFRE DE GOURFOURAN
The waterfalls that feed down into the Freissinières valley culminate in a spectacular gorge over 100m deep. Easily reached with care, it is an awesome and powerful spectacle.

HAUTELUCE

The deep, enchanting valley of Hauteluce provides a perfect background for the delightful farming village of Hauteluce, which has features dating back to the 12th century, and one of the most beautiful clock towers in the region. 25km north-east of Albertville.

Sunny and open, yet sheltered from the cold northerly winds of winter, Hauteluce is surrounded by Alpine meadows and sporadic forest cover that provides shelter for the many small clusters of chalets.

The name seems to originate from Roman times, when the Beaufortain valley belonged to a Roman, Lucius, who called it 'the valley of Luce'. The present-day valley of Hauteluce was indeed higher than the valley of Luce, hence the original name of Alta Lucia.

In the village centre is an *ecomusée*, which organises exhibitions of both traditional ways of life and of future plans for the development of the Beaufortain area.

Dominating the village and the surrounding countryside is the 55m high tower of the 17th-century church. Its façade is decorated with a particularly striking mural of the Grim Reaper. The many and varied treasures on display inside are also of great interest.

At the top end of the main street of Hauteluce is a *table d' orientation* from where it is possible to pick out all the major physical landmarks of the area.

ALPINE FLORA

At any time from May to August in the Alps you will find colourful meadows full of flowers on the sheltered slopes and hollows, while rocky outcrops and scree slopes harbour the more resilient plants. Depending on soil type and altitude, one of the most abundant Alpine meadow flowers is the familiar dandelion. Look closer, however, and among clumps of equally well-known hedge bedstraw and bladder campion will be black vanilla orchids, bird's-eye primroses, louseworts, alpine pasqueflowers and even edelweiss, all restricted to high altitude habitats. Further up the slopes where the vegetation is sparse, clumps of spring gentians and trumpet gentians adorn the turf. Saxifrages seem to grow out of the bare rock.

LUS-LA-CROIX-HAUTE

In a magnificent setting, backed by sheer-sided peaks, Lus-la-Croix-Haute is a typical, quiet Alpine village with a sunny, relaxed atmosphere. It lies 40km south of Monestier-de-Clermont.

Situated on a high, level plateau between the south-west side of the Vercors and the more spectacular peaks of the Grand Ferrand and the Rocher Rond, the village of Lus-la-Croix-Haute is most definitely on the sunny side of the Alps, enjoying a kind and healthy climate. This is a popular centre for level walking and cross-country skiing.

It is a busy village, hotch-potch in layout and more Provençal than Alpine in character. The higher sector has a small square, where a 146-year-old Italian black poplar tree proudly boasts to be the 'Arbre de la Liberté'. This part is also noticeable for its traditional houses with attractive pantiled roofs.

Lower down the village is a street named after Daniel Pavier, who was shot by the Gestapo in July 1944.

MEILLERIE

The enchanting village of Meillerie, with its picturesque little port, lies sandwiched between the tranquil eastern end of Lac Léman and the lofty calcarious cliffs and forest behind it, 10km east of Evian.

The location of this little fishing village is one of the finest on Lac Léman. The shore is lined with plane and acacia trees, the waters a clear marine blue. The views across to the other side of the lake are equally impressive, the terraced cultivation on the south-facing slopes being very obvious, and the beginnings of the Swiss Alps are also identifiable.

The houses are mostly built of stone, neat and tidy, with attractive red/bronze tiled roofs. They hug the contours of the hillside from the lake shore right up to the church at the top of the village, which has a 13th-century steeple.

It was in Mellierie that Rousseau set certain parts of *La Nouvelle Héloïse*.

LE MONAL

Perched high among steep Alpine pastures and forests way above the valley floor, le Monal has some of the finest examples of traditional architecture in the region and exceptional views of the surrounding countryside. 15km south-east of Bourg-St-Maurice.

Those not deterred by the approach to le Monal – the twisting, narrow road, the rough track and the walk – will be rewarded with some of the best views in the northern Alps, to the Gurra glacier, and below it the village of Gurra, opposite the glacier tongues that spill down from Mount Pourri, 3,779m high. Indeed, the village seems to be at the same height as the glaciers, though its south-facing position guarantees it a kinder climate.

In the past le Monal would have

SECRET PLACES

THE QUEYRAS

MOLINES-EN-QUEYRAS

Set in the heart of the Queyras, the peaceful, old settlement of Molines can be reached from Château-Queyras by following the road to St-Véran.

There are many fine examples here of the early architectural styles of the Queyras Region. The upper sections of many of the older chalets are made from seasoned timbers. Their typical, massively overhanging eaves form spacious balconies on which the harvest can be ripened. The harshness of the climate at this altitude means that little produce

The traditional Alpine village of Le Monal

been a summer base for farmers grazing their stock, and though it was no doubt lived in year-round at some stage, the village is now inhabited only during the summer months, the road being closed between November and May.

The buildings themselves are very special, many exhibiting original construction methods. Although some of the roofs have been replaced, the older roofs still have the traditional stone tiles. A close look at the buildings reveals the size and strength of the beams that support the immense weight of the roof, and the ways in which they interlock for maximum strength. The small windows and low doors of the houses give the inhabitants maximum protection from the remorseless winters up here.

MONT-DAUPHIN

Perched on top of a huge, natural fortress of steep, pock-marked conglomerate rock, the fort and village of Mont-Dauphin represent one of the finest examples of military architecture of its time. 30km south of Briançon.

Though the faint-hearted can reach Mont-Dauphin by turning right just north of Mont-Dauphin Gare, to savour the real atmosphere the village is best approached by following the narrow, twisting road that climbs steeply through the guardian cliffs from Guillestre.

On instructions from Louis XIV, Vauban chose Mont-Dauphin as the site for one of several fortresses to defend France's south-east frontier following invasion by the Duke of Savoy. Building started in 1693 and continued for almost 100 years.

The present-day fortress is almost unchanged from that time, and many of the military constructions such as the powder house, arsenal, officers' mess and specially designed fortifications are intact and in fine condition.

Above the main gate is the Pavillon de l'Horloge. This clever device allowed swift opening and closing of the gate and drawbridge, while the main pillars of the portcullis-like gate were replaceable as individual units, enabling any damage to be repaired promptly.

A fine example of classical military architecture and evidence of Louis XIV's great power, this dramatic stronghold is now a protected site, and guided tours are available in summer.

has the opportunity to ripen in the fields, so it is brought under cover until ready to use.

A traditional old settlement where time appears to have stood still

L'AUBERIE

LA CHAPELLE DES PETETES

The chapel can be found in tiny l'Auberie, near la Motte-en-Champsaur, which is 45km towards Gap from la Mure.

Built between 1730 and 1741 by a shepherd who dedicated his life to the service of his faith and his village, the chapel has one outstanding feature. Its exterior is punctuated with recesses containing statues and faces, known as *pététes*, carved in the 18th century.

The leather-covered altar originates from the chapel of the old château of Lesdiguières.

NÉVACHE

Flanked by hillsides coated sometimes with thick forests, elsewhere with barren scree and rock, Névache, with its well-preserved traditional architecture and splendid church occupies the best position of the villages in the beautiful Clarée valley. 20km north of Briançon.

The village's name is probably descended from the Latin, *Annavasca*, which underwent a series of changes before reaching its present form: in 1118, Nevasca, in 1330 Nevaschia, in 1568 Navayasse, then Neuvache, which later gave way to Névache.

The village is most attractive, and well worth leisurely exploration, especially as a small car park on the outskirts keeps the centre mostly car-free.

The church was built in the 15th century and incorporates an 11th-century tower from a château that

Pont-en-Royans climbs up the mountain in tiers from the banks of the River Bourne

previously occupied the site. Its basic wooden pews, ancient balcony and doors carved with scenes from the Descent from the Cross, form a dramatic contrast to the highly ornate baroque altar, with its gilded décor.

PONT-EN-ROYANS

Lying at the western end of the Gorges de la Bourne, the mellow riverside village of Pont-en-Royans is famous for its gravity-defying houses overhanging the River Bourne and its peaceful setting. 24km west of Villard-de-Lans.

Bleached and weathered limestone houses, bars and small shops line the narrow streets of Pont-en-Royans, mirroring the natural features of the Vercors whose narrow valleys are overlooked by foreboding crags.

One of the better known sights here are the *maisons suspendues*, terraces of sun-drenched houses seemingly built into and suspended from the cliff face above the town, above the River

Bourne. A good riverside walk is accessible down several narrow alleyways that descend from the Grande Rue. This is particularly pleasant around dusk, when the local fishermen are casting flies over the clear water, hoping to lure one of the many fine trout in the river, and the reflections of the first evening lights begin to dance on the fast-flowing water.

A walk up from the Place de la Porte de France leads to an excellent viewpoint. The path is steep, but the climb is rewarded with a superb panorama.

PRALOGNAN-LA-VANOISE

Lying on the edge of the Park National de la Vanoise in a dramatic and inspirational setting, the village of Pralognan-la-Vanoise has developed into an important centre for walking, climbing and skiing while preserving its sense of history. 28km south-east of Moûtiers.

Pralognan is surrounded by towering rock faces, steep pastures and forests topped with ribbons of snow, the whole crested with the menacing snouts of the Vanoise glaciers. Higher still are the peaks of le Grand Marchet, Mont Bochor, then the great summits of the Vanoise – the Grande Casse and the Grande Motte.

A small cablecar climbs from the village centre to the summit of Mont Bochor, where a short walk gives access to a *table d'orientation* and a short discovery walk. Information can be found here on a wide variety of subjects, including geology, conservation and history. The view to the Grande Casse is particularly spectacular, and there are several well-marked paths back down to the village.

Pralognan has a strong sense of history, and was first mentioned in church annals as early as the 10th century. Although parts of the village are new, an older quarter behind the cablecar station waits to be explored. The mid-1800s saw the area start to be developed for tourism, after Englishman Sir William Matthews came to climb the Grande Casse in 1860.

The latter route snakes alongside overhanging limestone cliffs until a final narrow bridge, beneath which is an awesome drop into the Souloise, and an abrupt descent on to gentler ground and the start of the village.

Popular as a summer resort, and also in winter as part of the Super-Dévoluy ski area, the village is rather scattered, its form matching the open, spacious nature of this high valley. Though it has a church dating from the 11th century and some attractive old chalets, its importance lies very much in its situation, and it makes a good base for touring the region.

The French Alps are a popular destination for climbers

ridges and forests, in which nestle several attractive villages. Of these, St-Michel-les-Portes is one of the most spectacularly sited. 12km south of Monestier-de-Clermont.

Situated on a steep hillside, overlooking a valley and in turn overlooked by Mont Aiguille, one of the most dramatic peaks in the Vercors, St-Michel is neat, perfectly poised and in immaculate proportion to its surroundings. Its mixture of old and new buildings exhibit an almost Bavarian smartness, though the architecture is unmistakably French.

The church is a simple, sturdy construction with a granite upper to its spire, while to its rear is a small area to sit and enjoy the mountain panorama to the full.

Impossible to ignore is the towering bulk of Mont Aiguille, first ascended in 1492 by what was recognised as the first ever technical Alpine climb.

ST-ETIENNE-EN-DEVOLUY

Set in a high-level valley near the source of the River Souloise, St-Etienne's situation is unrivalled throughout the French Alps. 46km north-west of Gap.

Access to the area is either via the excellent viewpoint of the Col du Noyer (closed November to mid-May), or, more dramatically, via the Défilé de la Souloise and the Défilé des Etroits.

ST-MICHEL-LES-PORTES

The main route south from Grenoble is overlooked by the preposterously steep and continuous cliffs that form the eastern rim of the Vercors plateau, below which is a complex system of valleys,

LANSLEVILLARD

CHAPEL OF ST-SEBASTIEN

The village of Lanslevillard lies at the foot of the Col du Mont Cenis, at its junction with the upper Arc valley.

The magnificent chapel of St-Sébastien stands in a superb position atop a knoll on the west side of the village, overlooking Val Cenis. Built in the 15th century by a local man, Sébastien Turbil, to fulfil a promise made before his miraculous recovery from the plague, the dull, weather-blasted exterior belies the riches inside. Most striking are the murals that adorn its walls. The colours remain strong and clear, the detail hardly affected by age, those sections depicting the life of Christ being particularly expressive.

TOUR 24 – 170KM

ANNECY AND THE EDGE OF THE ARAVIS

Bounded by the Aravis mountains to the east and Annecy to the west, this wandering tour merely brushes the edge of the main Alps, but stands firmly on its own merit as an outing of distinction. It includes the lac d'Annecy, reputed to be the purest in Europe with a wealth of sporting and cultural interest. The lake displays a range of tones, hues and moods as varied as the landscape that surrounds it. Annecy itself has one of the most interesting old quarters of any Alpine town, while away from the lake, the tour travels through some splendid limestone scenery and over several spectacular passes.

Left, the colourful old quarter of Annecy
Above, lac d'Annecy
Right, walking is a popular summer activity in the region

ROUTE DIRECTIONS

From Annecy centre, head for Sévrier on the **N508** lakeside road. On the outskirts of the town, turn right on to the **D41** towards Crêt de Châtillon. This road leads up through the forests, climbing steadily to the open area that marks the summit.

Continue on the same road, descending to the village of Leschaux, and on to the Col de Leschaux. At the col, cross the **D912**, and bear left following the **D10** towards la Chapelle-St-Maurice. Continue the descent on the **D10** through la Magne to Villard, and continue to a junction with the lakeside **N508**. Turn right and continue on the lakeside road to Duingt.

From Duingt continue to Faverges (17km). In Faverges centre turn left on to the **D12**, signposted Thônes and St-Ferréol, and follow it to Thônes.

From Thônes, retrace the route for 2km and turn left on to the **D16** towards Col de la Croix Fry (watch out for snow early and late in the season). Descend from the col and follow signs to la Clusaz (7km).

From here, follow the **D909** for 3km to St-Jean-de-Sixt and take a right turn on to the **D4** towards le Grand-Bornand. After 1km, turn left on to the **D12**, heading for Entremont and Bonneville and continue for 20km.

Just after passing through the village of St-Pierre-en-Faucigny is a main junction. Turn left on the **N205** towards Annecy and la-Roche-sur-Foron, which is 6km further on.

From here, rejoin the **N203** and follow it for 28km back to Annecy.

St-Nazaire-en-Royans

Beautifully situated on the southern bank of the River Isère, St-Nazaire-en-Royans developed on a site that has been inhabited since prehistoric times. 18km east of Romans-sur-Isère.

The descent into the village from the west suddenly reveals the vast aqueduct which carries water from the River Bourne to the plains of Valence, and near its foot, overlooking the smooth, pea-green water is the entrance to the Grotte de Thais. These spectacular caves have been explored for 4,200m, though public access is more limited. The spectacular forma-tions and natural sculpture make this one of the best caves in the region. Important remains have been found dating back to the Magdalenian period, including tools and evidence of a lunar calendar.

The village lies at different levels, much of the older part starting below the main road. Most of the buildings are made from limestone, and some

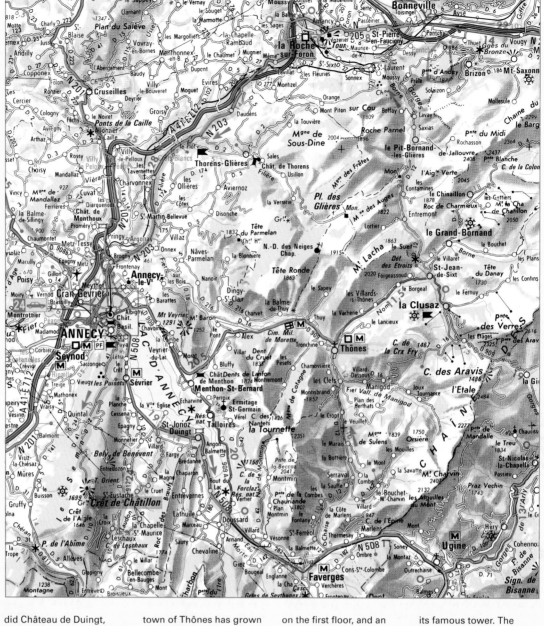

PLACES OF INTEREST

CRET DE CHATILLON

A 10-minute walk from the parking area leads to the summit cross. The walk is rewarded with a stunning panorama, a viewfinder aiding identification of Mont Blanc, the Chamonix Aiguilles, the Dents de Lanfon and many other peaks. The area is also a popular paragliding, walking and Nordic skiing centre.

DUINGT

Despite being on a main road, this lakeside village – with its ancient wooden houses, exterior stairways, and trellises overflowing with honeysuckle and wisteria – has some fine examples of Savoyard domestic architecture. On the lake front is the splen-

did Château de Duingt, originally built in the 11th century, and later restored. Owned by the de Sales family, it is best viewed from the small square named after St-François de Sales.

THONES

Sheltered by the surrounding tree-clad hillsides, the town of Thônes has grown up around its 17th-century church, which has a typically baroque interior. It boasts a series of solid yet elegant covered archways, behind which shelter an excellent selection of shops and bars.

The museum has a display devoted to the history of the Thônes area

on the first floor, and an interesting variety of artefacts, objects and information relating to local traditions and crafts on the second floor.

LA ROCHE-SUR-FORON

Perched above the plains of the Arve valley, this ancient city is named after the rock on which stands

its famous tower. The tower is all that remains of a mighty fortress built by the counts of Geneva.

The present church dates back to the 16th century. It was built to replace an earlier construction going back to the start of the 12th century, which was destroyed by fires in 1507 and 1530.

walls are constructed from the rounded river cobbles – an infinitely difficult task.

St-Pierre-d'Entremont

Nestling in spectacular mountain scenery and surrounded by excellent

walking country, the unspoilt Alpine village of St-Pierre-d'Entremont lies 21km south of Chambéry.

Lying in the middle of an area of deep gorges and high cliffs, forests and swift-flowing rivers, St-Pierre sits astride the boundary of Isère and Savoy, (once the frontier between France and Savoy). Particularly worth a visit are the Cirque de St-Même, with

its 400m high cliffs and striking waterfalls, and the caves and gorges at St-Christophe, reached through the equally impressive Gorges du Guiers Vif.

The village is attractive and neat, the buildings constructed in the traditional regional style from weather-worn limestone, and it makes a good walking centre.

ST-VERAN

At an altitude of 2,040m, making it the highest village in the Alps, the old streets of St-Véran, lined with traditional chalets, exude character and atmosphere like no other village in the Alps. 51km south-east of Briançon.

The local legend says that many years ago the bishop of the area, St-Véran, freed the area from a troublesome dragon, which was so surprised at being spoken to so sternly by the bishop that it flew into the hillside and was mortally wounded. The Queyras inhabitants then built a village on the spot, naming it after the saint.

The village is now a popular tourist centre, but still manages to retain its rough mountain character. One old chalet is preserved intact to demonstrate the ancient way of life of this high

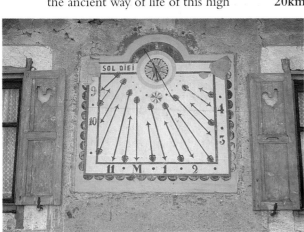

An ancient sundial decorating a house in St-Veran

Alpine region. The 17th-century church is one of the few entirely stone-built buildings in the village. The predominantely wooden chalets exhibit classical design features, the gnarled timbers weather-worn and warped by

the contrasts of the harsh climate. The stone-built ground floors were inhabited by peasant and animal alike during the hard winters, and above this the summer quarters often have a pleasant south-facing balcony. The roof will often project over the balcony and barn entrance, tough lengths of larch directing rainwater into wooden gutters that shed the water well clear of the building. Other, lower roofs are covered with large slabs of rock, pointed downslope to assist water run-off.

SIXT-FER-A-CHEVAL

In a truly fairy-tale setting, dwarfed by the scale of the mountains, whose slopes mirror the fir and spruce that thrive in such improbable situations, Sixt-Fer-à-Cheval lies 20km south-east of Morzine.

Through the centre of the village runs the River Giffre, fed by the dozens of waterfalls that plunge from the Cirque de Fer à Cheval at the head of the valley. Next to this is the large and sunny square, overlooked by an enormous old lime tree whose centre has rotted away.

Also in the square is a memorial to Jacques Balmat, first conqueror of Mont Blanc and famous crystal-hunter, who was killed on the Ruan glacier while searching for gold in September 1834. Below this is a list of the major walks available – Chamonix for example is a mere 12 hours away!

On the east side of the village are the remains of an old monastery, founded in 1144, around which the village developed. The nearby church has a Gothic nave and 13th-century

A typical high-altitude farm near Sixt-Fer-à-Cheval with the mountain peaks not far away

choir and the sacristy houses treasures from the 12th and 13th centuries.

VALLOIRE

A collection of traditional and modern buildings – including one of the most lavishly decorated churches in the Alps, spread around the slopes at the base of Col du Galibier – the winter resort of Valloire lies 30km south of St-Jean-de-Maurienne.

There are 17 hamlets and 16 chapels within its confines, dotted around the hillsides surrounding the main village. Although Valloire has less than 1,000 permanent residents, that figure can be increased twelvefold in the height of the winter season.

The village is very much a mixture of old and new buildings. Dominating the centre is its main architectural attraction, the 17th-century church. Above the main entrance are three frescos, depicting St-Pierre and Ste-Thècle, born at Valloire in the 6th century. The superb altar is decorated with gilded sculpture of the highest calibre. The cross above the vestry door dates from 1609, but it is the ornate decoration of the whole – the paintings, statues and decoration which

SECRET PLACES

ST-HILAIRE

BEC DE MARGAIN

The Bec de Margain is a stunning viewpoint overlooking the Isère valley to the north-east of Grenoble. Access is via the D30 to le Margain or the funicular to St-Hilaire.

Viewpoints as dramatic and wide ranging as the Bec de Margain are rarely gained so easily. Just

north of the tiny village of le Margain, take a track on the right, about 150m past the football pitch. This leads gently to a viewfinder, poised over 800m above the floor of the valley. The panorama extends from the Vercors to the south, right through to the Vanoise and eventu-

ally to Mont Blanc to the north-east.

Access is also possible via the steepest funicular in Europe, constructed in 1924, which has one section that climbs at an angle of 83°. It runs between the station at Montfort on the N90 down in the valley, and St-Hilaire

on the plateau. It is then a short walk from the funicular station to the Bec de Margain.

Take the funicular to a spectacular panoramic viewpoint

Just 3km to the south is the site of a prehistoric stone-axe 'workshop'. Extensive and varied displays demonstrate how the flint was quarried and cut to shape.

YVOIRE

Combining authentic medieval charm with a breathtaking setting at the western end of Lac Léman, the ancient walled village of Yvoire retains many traces of its past. 16km west of Thonon-les-Bains.

The old village was rebuilt between 1306 and 1316 on the site of an even older stronghold, and its strategic position allowed it to control navigation on the lake. It retains a considerable amount from this time, including its fortified walls and ramparts, castle, town gates, church belfry and old harbour.

Cars should be left outside the protective walls, and the old quarter explored on foot, where narrow streets lead around neat, flower-filled squares and down to the busy harbour.

Just above the harbour is the Garden of the Five Senses, an immaculately laid-out series of walkways through an immense variety of species, all enclosed by the original garden wall.

adorn ceilings and walls alike – that is most striking.

Recently a 'Centre Alpin de la Glisse' has been founded here, where research is carried out on competition equipment. A more recent activity is that of 'Snow Sculpture', and there is now an annual competition which results in some marvellous ice carvings.

VASSIEUX-EN-VERCORS

Scene of a major battle between the Maquisards – the Resistance fighters – and the German SS in July 1944, Vassieux occupies an ironically peaceful setting, on a high, wide plateau in the southern Vercors, 34km north of Die.

As part of a major assault on the Vercors, Vassieux was one of several villages decimated by the Germans during World War II, and it was completely reconstructed after the war. By the church is the Musée de la Résistance, which houses a vast and interesting collection of memorabilia, telling the story of both the struggle in the Vercors and the war in general. A

short way north of the village is the Cimetière National du Vercors.

Dwelling overmuch on the past can overshadow the attractions the area has to offer. There is a fine nature walk and excellent cross-country skiing to the north of the village, while it makes an ideal base for touring the region.

BIRDS OF THE ALPS

High above the tree line lives a community of species that have adapted to this harsh, high habitat. Perhaps most characteristic of this rarified group of birds is the Alpine chough. A bold scavenger, it is often found living alongside people, and haunts the higher ski-lift terminals; it is easily recognised by its yellow bill, dark plumage and tumbling flight. Smaller songbirds are comparatively scarce, but the Alpine accentor can be located by its rapid song, delivered from a rocky perch. The snow finch feeds unobtrusively along tracks and scree slopes; its most characteristic feature is the white wing patches, displayed to best effect in flight. Ptarmigan move slowly among the lichen-covered boulders in summer, their mottled, grey-brown plumage a perfect match for their surroundings.

SECRET FRANCE

PÉRIGORD AND QUERCY

Few regions of France have as much to offer the visitor as Périgord and Quercy. With their lovely and varied landscapes, their celebrated gastronomy, their rich history and wealth of châteaux and churches, and of course their exceptionally pretty villages, it is not surprising that every year they should attract tourists in their thousands. Yet a visit out of season or even only slightly off the beaten track will reap rich rewards, for in the sleepy backwaters of these two ancient provinces are many delightful places that time seems to have passed by. Even the more famous waterside villages dotted along the Dordogne are peaceful out of season, so that there is still a thrill of discovery in wandering through their lovely old streets.

The cliffs and caves of the northern part of the region, around les Eyzies, have become known as 'the cradle of mankind', for early man settled here and left more evidence of his habitation – in the form of cave paintings and other archeological remains – than almost anywhere else in the world.

Within the villages of Périgord and Quercy is some of the finest and most attractive rural architecture in France. The wooded plateaux and soft valleys of Périgord, to the west, are dotted with solid, four-square houses in golden limestone, their steeply pitched roofs covered in tiles or stone slabs, which weather beautifully to blend in with the surrounding countryside. In Périgord Noir, so called because of the deep shade of its forests, these fine houses

are often flanked by towers and dovecots. Périgord Blanc takes its name from the whiteness of its limestone, used to build lower houses with gently sloping roofs covered in terracotta tiles. The white limestone houses of Quercy, to the east, are among the most elegant and graceful of all French country buildings, with external staircases, turrets and gables combining in perfect harmony.

Almost every era of history, and every invader, has left its mark on the region. There are prehistoric dolmens, Roman villages, English *bastides*, medieval castles, beautiful churches, and remote caves and forests that provided good hiding places for refugees over the centuries, all set in some of the most dramatic scenery to be found anywhere in France.

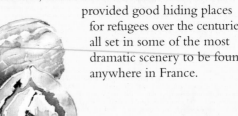

noix de Périgord et Quercy

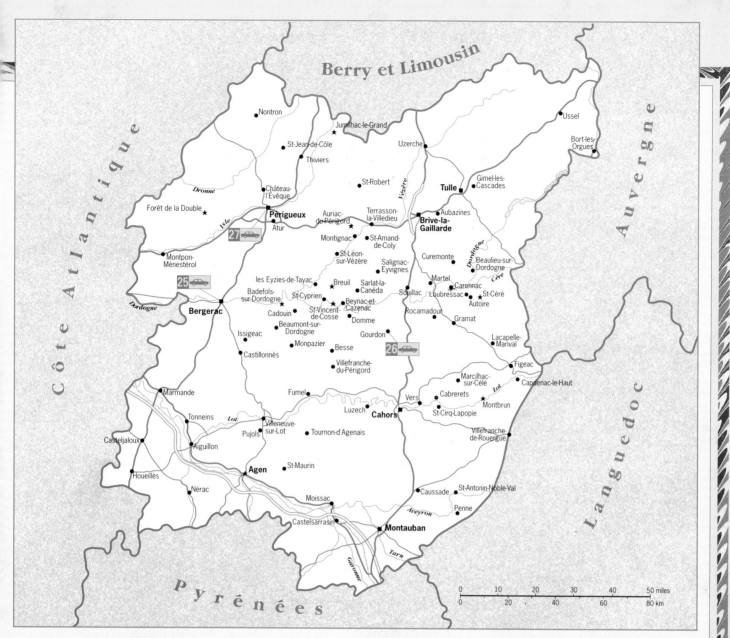

Berry et Limousin

Nontron
Jumilhac-le-Grand
St-Jean-de-Côle
Thiviers
Uzerche
Ussel
Bort-les-Orgues

Dronne
Château-l'Evêque
St-Robert
Gimel-les-Cascades
Tulle

Forêt de la Double ★
Périgueux
Auriac-du-Périgord
Terrasson-la-Villedieu
Brive-la-Gaillarde
Aubazines

Isle
Atur
27
Montignac
St-Amand-de-Coly

Montpon-Ménestérol
St-Léon-sur-Vézère
Curemonte
Beaulieu-sur-Dordogne
Salignac-Eyvignes
Martel
Carennac

25
les Eyzies-de-Tayac
Breuil
Sarlat-la-Canéda
Loubressac
St-Céré
Dordogne
Badefols-sur-Dordogne
St-Cyprien
Beynac-et-Cazenac
Souillac
Autoire

Bergerac
Cadouin
St-Vincent-de-Cosse
Domme
Rocamadour
Gramat

Beaumont-sur-Dordogne

Issigeac
Gourdon
Lacapelle-Marival

Monpazier
Besse
26

Castillonnès
Villefranche-du-Périgord
Figeac

Marcilhac-sur-Célé
Capdenac-le-Haut

Marmande
Fumel
Vers
Cabrerets
Lot

Tonneins
Lot
Luzech
Cahors
St-Cirq-Lapopie
Montbrun

Casteljaloux
Pujols
Villeneuve-sur-Lot
Villefranche-de-Rouergue

Aiguillon
Tournon-d'Agenais

Houeillès
Agen
St-Maurin

Nérac
Moissac
Caussade
St-Antonin-Noble-Val

Castelsarrasin
Montauban
Penne

Garonne
Aveyron
Tarn

Côte Atlantique

Auvergne

Languedoc

Pyrénées

| 0 | 10 | 20 | 30 | 40 | 50 miles |
| 0 | 20 | 40 | 60 | 80 km |

The famous quality of the light in this region, filtered through leaves and reflected from the pale stonework, left, has attracted numerous artists over the years Below and right, the region is also famous for its gastronomic pleasures

BOULANGERIE

183

INVADERS AT MONTCARET

The locals still sometimes refer to Montcaret as Montcaret Tête-Noir, for it was once the head-quarters of Geoffroy Tête-Noir, one of the most notorious *routiers* who ravaged France in the Hundred Years War. Its name is only the first evidence of the long history bequeathed to this little hamlet by its position in the Garonne valley, on the Gallo-Roman route from Bordeaux to Narbonne. The church stands amid the ruined foundations of a 4th-century villa, which include a bath with one of the best mosaic floors in the Dordogne, charmingly decorated with fish and an octopus. The site became a place of Christian worship in the 6th century.

ATUR

This sleepy little village is remarkable for its mysterious Lanterne des Morts, one of only three in the region. It lies in beautiful wooded countryside, 7km south of Périgueux.

This tiny village has an interesting Romanesque church, notable for its barrel-vaulted roof and its octagonal dome. But Atur's most remarkable building is its 12th-century Lanterne des Morts. These 'lanterns of the dead' (Sarlat has a more famous one) were funerary monuments of some kind, but their precise purpose remains shrouded in mystery. A tall, slender construction with a conical roof, the one at Atur stands in the former graveyard, silently guarding its mysterious secret.

AUBAZINE

Dominated by its 12th-century abbey church, this austere little village lies in lovely wooded country-side between the valleys of the Corrèze and the Coiroux, 10km east of Brive-la-Gaillarde.

It was here in the 12th century that the hermit St-Etienne (St Stephen) founded an abbey. Originally Benedictine, then Cistercian, the abbey grew and a sister convent was estab-lished in the gorges of the Coiroux.

The 12th-century abbey church is a fine example of the Cistercian style. The conspicuous exception is the superb Gothic tomb of St-Etienne, decorated with beautifully expressive sculptures showing the saint and his followers being received in heaven by the Virgin and Child. The face of St-Etienne's effigy has been worn away by centuries of scraping by the faithful, who believed the dust had miraculous properties. The vestiges of the monastery buildings, including the Romanesque chapterhouse, are now occupied by a convent and may be visited. There is also a most impressive stew-pond and water supply system built by the Cistercians.

AUTOIRE

Officially one of the most beautiful villages in France, Autoire is a magical confection of turrets and gables tumbling down the slopes of a wooded valley in the old province of Quercy. It lies 8km west of St-Céré.

The quarries of the nearby Causse de Gramat provided the creamy limestone for the houses of this lovely village, domi-

MONTBRUN

SAUT DE LA MOUNINE

A spectacular view-point with a curious name reveals a story

South-west of Figeac, Saut de la Mounine is a rocky spur overlooking a bend in the River Lot.

The view from the top of the cliff, even in an area renowned for its views, is spectacular – and like so many such spots there is a legend attached to it.

Almost opposite the spur, on the other side of the river, is the village of Montbrun, huddled around the ruins of a castle which was once owned by the powerful Cardaillac family. One of the lords of Mont-brun was unhappy with his daughter's friendship with a rival lord's son, and

ordered that she be thrown from the cliff at this point.

However, the hermit charged with carrying out the deed could not bring himself to do it. Instead, he dressed up a monkey in her clothes and flung it from the cliff, hoping his master would not be able to tell the difference.

When the lord saw the monkey hurtling down the cliff face, he regretted his rash decision. Over-whelmed with relief to dis-cover that his daughter was still alive, he then forgave her, but ever since the location has been known as 'Monkey's Leap'.

Above and left, turreted roofs and peaceful streets in Autoire, widely considered to be one of the prettiest villages in the whole of France

BEAULIEU-SUR-DORDOGNE

Named by a 9th-century monk after its beautiful setting, this historic market town boasts some of the finest carvings in south-western France to be found in its abbey church. 45km south-east of Brive.

The abbey at Beaulieu was founded in 850 by monks from Cluny. The abbey church of St-Pierre, a fine example of Limousin-Romanesque with characteristic barrel-vaulting in the aisles, went up in the 12th-century. Interesting as it is architecturally, it has one feature which elevates it to the rank of a masterpiece, its carved tympanum depicting the Last Judgement. Full of expression and movement, it is as moving and fresh now as it was when it was carved by the best master-carver in south-western France. An important centre of pilgrimage over the centuries, the church still possesses a richly endowed treasury. Around the church are a good number of Renaissance houses, built of pink or grey granite and ornamented with turrets and delicate mullions.

nated by the Château de Limargue, an extravagantly picturesque *gentilhommière* renovated in the 16th and 17th centuries. Surrounded by vines until the phylloxera epidemic in the 19th century, Autoire is endowed with numerous lovely houses dating from the Renaissance onwards, built by wealthy wine-growers in the style of tiny châteaux. Now the village is famous for its Reine-Claude plums: if you are fortunate enough to visit it in the second half of July you can enjoy the plum market.

On the cliffs above the village is the ruined Château des Anglais, said to have been built during the Hundred Years War.

BEAUMONT-SUR-DORDOGNE

Constructed on the orders of Edward I in 1272, this tiny village was one of the first English-built *bastides* that were to become so characteristic of this area. It lies 29km south-east of the town of Bergerac.

Although Beaumont is a place of great charm, little remains of the forti–fications that must have made it so impressive in the Middle Ages. Perfectly rectangular, it was surrounded by a double defensive wall, pierced at regular intervals by fortified gateways. One of these, Porte de Luzier,

Right, part of the ancient village of Beaumont-sur-Dordogne, heavily fortified during the Middle Ages

TOUR 25 – 110KM

ON THE TOBACCO TRAIL IN PURPLE PERIGORD

The attractive area of countryside around Bergerac has been named Périgord Pourpre, after thedeep, rich colour of its world-famous wines. These wines and the many hill-top *bastides* to be found in the area are two of the region's most significant attractions. Religion has also played an important role in the history of the area, and the many old churches along the route are a delight to explore. The tour begins at the old town and former river port of Bergerac, with its old quarter and tobacco museum, and runs through some wonderful countryside, passing tranquil villages, vineyards, châteaux and old churches. It takes in Beaumont, undoubtedly one of the most dramatic and best-preserved *bastide* towns in the region, and also includes one of the many fascinating sites of prehistoric art in the area.

Left, the old town of Bergerac

ROUTE DIRECTIONS

Leave Bergerac on the **D32** towards Ste-Alvère. Pass through Liorac-sur-Louyre and Ste-Foy-de-Longas, and continue into Ste-Alvère (29km).

Leave Ste-Alvère on the **D30**, following signs to Pezuls and Trémolat. Follow the **D30** for 11km, crossing the **D703**. Turn left into Trémolat and then left again on to the **D31** to Limeuil.

From Limeuil, continue on the **D31** towards le Bugue, passing the charm-ing chapel of St-Martin on your right. On reaching the **D703** turn right and follow the road, past the Caverne de Bara-Bahau on the left, into le Bugue.

Leave le Bugue by crossing over the River Vézère and taking the **D31e** to le Buisson-de-Cadouin. After 7km this road becomes the **D51**. Continue into le Buisson (3km).

Leave le Buisson on the **D25** for Beaumont. Stay on the **D25** through Cadouin and St-Avit-Sénieur, and continue into Beaumont.

From Beaumont take the **D660** through Bayac to Couze-et-St-Front (10km). Take a left turn on to the **D37e**, following signs to Varennes. Don't make the mistake of turning on to the **D37**, which comes just before it. Follow the **D37** for 12km back into Bergerac.

PLACES OF INTEREST

TREMOLAT

The Dordogne makes one of its many leisurely loops, known as the Cingle de Trémolat, around the village. In the village itself is an unusual fortress-like Romanesque church.

Just to the north, on the D31, is the Belvédère de Racamadou, from which there are good views of the river and the surround-ing countryside across a patchwork of farmland.

LIMEUIL

This fortified hilltop village stands where the Dordogne and the Vézère rivers meet, and owes its name to the Romans, who named it *Lemioalum*, meaning a place planted with elms. Two adjoining bridges, at right angles to survives, along with many of the stone houses of the 13th and 14th centuries.

The kernel of Beaumont's defences, however, and its people's last refuge in time of war, was the church of St-Front. A fortress as well as a place of worship, the church retains its fortified corner towers and its sentry walk.

In July and August every year a Syndicat d'Initiative opens to provide tourist information on Beaumont and the surrounding area.

BESSE

Nestling in the forest between the valleys of the Dordogne and the Lot, this beautiful medieval village lies 8km north of Villefranche-du-Périgord.

According to many, the parts of old Quercy that lie close to the River Lot are like Périgord used to be before the advent of tourism. With its sleepy, narrow streets lined by old houses,

radiating from a small market square, Besse is certainly reminiscent of a gentler age. It is best to explore its winding streets on foot, enjoying the view down the valley. The unusual fortified Romanesque church, with Renaissance additions, has remarkably spirited 11th-century carvings on its porch, depicting among other scenes the Garden of Eden. While in the village be sure to buy some of the famous St-Nectaire cheese.

each other, have been built across the two rivers and provide a wonderful view of Limeuil, with its old ivy-coverd houses and steep cobbled lanes, climbing up the woody hill. The castle, now in ruins, is 13th-century, and the heavily restored church has a 14th-century choir.

CHAPEL OF ST-MARTIN

This 12th-century chapel was built by Richard the Lionheart and dedicated to the martyr Thomas à Becket. Having been allowed to fall into disrepair, it is now being restored by Amis de St-Martin.

CAVERNE DE BARA-BAHAU

Just outside the village of

Bara-Bahau is the Caverne de Bara-Bahau, a very spectacular 100m-long cave.

Discovered in 1951, it is decorated with drawings of bison, wild oxen, bears and ibex from the Aurignacian culture that flourished in the area up to 40,000 years ago. It is one of the earliest decorated caves to have been discovered.

CADOUIN

See page 188.

BEAUMONT

See page 186.

A sample of the rich red wines for which this region, aptly known as Périgord Pourpre, is justly famous

BEYNAC-ET-CAZENAC

The Château de Beynac, one of the most impressive fortresses in the region, looms over this little group of houses clustered on a bend of the magnificent Dordogne. The village lies 10km south-west of Sarlat-la-Canéda.

It is hard to imagine this little village as the scene of bitter fighting. Yet the strategic position of its great castle has earned it a history as violent as any in the region. Razed to the ground by Simon de Montfort during the Albigensian Crusade, it was rebuilt to become a key stronghold in the Hundred Years War. When peace returned the lords of Beynac concentrated on embellishing their château, which has a magnificent interior.

Beneath its ramparts cluster the medieval houses and 12th-century church of Beynac-et-Cazenac, all built of the same golden stone. The village has a small museum of folklore and from its old quays the visitor can join boat trips along the Dordogne, or hire canoes and kayaks.

CABRERETS

Set in its rocky amphitheatre, Cabrerets has provided shelter for folk since prehistoric times. Overlooking the lovely valley of the River Célé, it lies 33km north-east of Cahors.

Hidden away among the winding roads of this exceptionally beautiful valley, Cabrerets is a pretty, sleepy little village which in 1922 revealed its spectacular secret. At Pech-Merle, 4km north of the village, two young boys discovered a cave decorated with hand prints and powerfully executed images of bison, mammoths and horses, all painted some 20,000 years ago.

In comparatively modern times the village was protected upstream and downstream by the medieval castles of Gontaut-Biron and le Diable (the ruins of which loom menacingly overhead). A little way upstream at the Fontaine de la Pescalerie a lovely waterfall gushes from the rock.

The village of Beynac huddles at the foot of its mighty fortress

CADOUIN

This medieval village clustered around its abbey is famous as the home of the controversial 'holy shroud'. It lies on the edge of the Forêt de la Bessède, 6km south of le Buisson on the D25.

Founded in the 12th-century, the Cistercian abbey quickly came to prominence as the repository of a 'holy shroud' that had covered the dead Christ's face, and which had been brought back from Antioch by a local priest. Pilgrims flocked to Cadouin until it came under threat from the English during the Hundred Years War.

Entrusted for safe keeping to the monks of Toulouse, the shroud subsequently became the object of an unbecoming wrangle as the abbey at Cadouin attempted by any means, fair or foul, to wrest it back again. The final ignominy was yet to come, however, for in the 1930s scientific tests showed that the shroud was an 11th-century fake, and scholars

Nothing could be prettier or more typical of Quercy than the turreted rooftops of Carennac, clustered around the old priory beside the river. This ancient foundation, which dates back to the 10th century, owes its fame to the gentle prelate and author François de Salignac de la Mothe-Fénelon, who was prior here from 1681 to 1685.

The Romanesque village church has a magnificent tympanum carved with figures in the fluid elegant style that reached its fullest expression in this region. The restored cloisters, part

revealed that it was embroidered with Islamic inscriptions. Pilgrimages ceased forthwith, and Cadouin lapsed into its present sleepy calm.

Above, the abbey at Cadouin lies beneath its sun-baked roofs, and right, watching the world go by near Beynac

CAPDENAC-LE-HAUT

Perched on a rocky crag high above a tight meander of the River Lot, this ancient village enjoys a position as dramatic as any in the area. It lies 7km south of Figeac.

Many people believe that the village of Capdenac-le-Haut lies on the site of Uxellodunum, the site of the Gauls' last stand against the Romans, and this view is supported by substantial Gaulish and Roman archeological finds here. Besieged no fewer than eleven times, Capdenac nevertheless remains surprisingly and delightfully complete.

Behind the 13th-century ramparts and Gothic gateways lie a massive 13th- and 14th-century keep and delightful steep, winding streets of medieval houses. The museum contains a cast of the famous neolithic statue known as the Venus of Capdenac, dating from about 3200BC (the original is at Cahors).

CARENNAC

One of the most irresistibly romantic spots on the Dordogne, this beautiful village of golden stone is also of considerable historic and literary interest. It lies 21km north-east of Rocamadour.

Romanesque, part Flamboyant Gothic, are a delightfully shady spot in which to sit and contemplate. Try to visit Carennac out of season, when its charms are not overwhelmed by crowds of tourists. In season, however, there is a great variety of watersports on the river.

SECRET PLACES

ST-VINCENT-DE-COSSE

'OWL DOORS'

An open invitation to these efficient night-hunters

The pretty, sleepy little village of St-Vincent-de-Cosse lies between St-Cyprien and Beynac-et-Cazenac.

This picturesque village is named after Vincent of Agen, an early Christian martyr who attempted to introduce Christianity to the area, and the roofs of its ancient houses hide an unusual feature. If you look carefully at the *lauze*

roofs you may spot some curious little triangular openings. These are not there just to keep the lofts ventilated. The holes are actually large enough to allow access for owls, and the wise birds feed off any stray rodents. These 'owl doors' may be seen on many old houses in the area.

BADEFOLS-SUR-DORDOGNE

CASTLE RUINS

Slow, flat-bottomed river craft, or 'gabares', made an easy target for robbers

The hamlet of Badefols lies east of Bergerac, on the left bank of the Dordogne.

On the cliffs above Badefols are the ruins of an old castle, once a hide-out for thieves and robbers who would ransack passing boats laden with valuable cargoes *en route* to Bergerac, Libourne or Bordeaux. As a result, the castle was demolished in 1794 by Joseph Lakanal.

CUREMONTE

With not one but two magnificent medieval châteaux within its ramparts, this completely unspoilt fortified hilltop village well repays the effort required to find it. It lies some 12km west of Beaulieu-sur-Dordogne on minor roads.

Its imposing position on a granite outcrop means that you can see the turreted skyline of Curemonte from as far away as the Causse de Martel, long before you reach it. A feudal dependance of the lords of Turenne since the 11th century, Curemonte, perched on its rocky eminence, has never been able to spread outside its ramparts. Within them are the 15th-century Château de St-Hilaire, with its great round towers, and the 16th-century Château des Plas, both protected not only by the same massive walls but also by the same watch-towers. Beneath the walls of the châteaux huddle picturesque old houses and a turreted Renaissance *manoir*, all in the warm colours of the local granite and mellow roof tiles.

DOMME

Founded on a dauntingly sheer rocky outcrop above the Dordogne in 1283, this is one of France's most spectacular and beautiful bastides. It lies 4.5km south of la Roque-Gageac.

Built for Philip the Bold on a site that offered such remarkable natural defences, Domme was never fortified on its most impregnable side.

Because of the shape of rock on which it is built, Domme does not follow the rectangular plan of the classic *bastide*, but instead is trapezoidal. Inside the massive walls, pierced by three impressive gateways, is a village of exceptional beauty, its straight streets lined with medieval and Renaissance houses. Place de la Halle contains the

Outside the caves at Les Eyzies

17th-century market building, under which there is access to the caves beneath the village, where the inhabitants used to shelter. The Musée Paul-Reclus has displays on the history of Domme, and there is a magnificent panorama over the Dordogne from the Belvédère de la Barre.

LES EYZIES-DE-TAYAC

The prehistoric centre of France, if not the world, this dramatic site below the limestone cliffs where the River Vézère meets the Beaune was known to humankind some 40,000 years ago. It lies 26km south-west of Montignac.

The tiny village of les Eyzies has come to prominence because it lies in the heart of a region – particularly the valley of the Vézère – which has an extraordinary wealth of prehistoric sites. The fascinating history of these is summed up in the Musée National de la Préhistoire, in the 13th-century Château de Beynac overlooking the village. In an area so rich in remarkable places to visit, priority must go to the caves at Font-de-Gaume, les Combarelles and the Grand Roc, and the deposits at la Laugerie Haute and la Laugerie Basse, inhabited by primitive man for some 20,000 years.

ISSIGEAC

Atmospheric and extremely picturesque, Issigeac is a place to explore at leisure. It lies in lovely countryside 19km south-east of Bergerac.

The best day to visit Issigeac is on a Sunday – market day in this medieval town, with its twisting cobbled lanes and half-timbered, cantilevered houses. Lapped by the waters of the River Banège and once completely surrounded by walls, this lovely spot was used by the bishops of Sarlat as a retreat. The 16th-century Gothic church was built by one of their number, Armand de Gontaut-Biron, and another built the imposing 17th-century Château des Eveques which now houses the Syndicat d'Initiative.

A meat market is held in its cellars on the third Sunday in January, and there is an antique/flea market and an agricultural show on the first Sunday in August. On the third Sunday in June the local rugby team holds its carnival, with a procession of flowered floats.

BREUIL

GAULISH VILLAGE

A curious prehistoric site near Beyssac

Breuil lies just outside Beyssac, south-east of les Eyzies-de-Tayac.

The whole of Périgord and Quercy is dotted with reminders of ancient habitation, one of which is the Gaulish village of Breuil, which consists of a small collection of ancient dwellings. These small stone huts are said to have remained unchanged since Neolithic times. However, they have not been left entirely untouched over the centuries – they were 'cleaned up' and restored somewhat during the 1960s, when the settlement was used as the authentic setting for a film.

GIMEL-LES-CASCADES

A natural fortress on a promontory above the River Montagne, this little village takes its name from its waterfalls, the highest in the Limousin. Gimel-les-Cascades lies 12km north-east of Tulle.

Left, the narrow streets of Issigeac belong to a time long before the motor car.
Above, the falls at Gimel-les-Cascades

Defended by the Château-Haut, the Château-Bas and its famous waterfalls, Gimel-les-Cascades knew prosperous times in the 16th and 17th centuries, as can be seen from its surviving Renaissance houses. The 15th-century church, built in typical Limousin style, houses a remarkable treasury.

Downstream, a little Romanesque chapel perches above the gorges of the Montagne and a dramatic series of waterfalls. The first, Grande Cascade or the Saut de Gimel, falls a steep 42m; in the next, la Redole, the rushing waters fall a further 25m; and lastly they are channelled down the 27m of the Queue de Cheval, or Gouthatière, into a maelstrom of impassible rapids aptly named the Gouffre d'Inferno.

TOUR 26 – 120KM
A JOURNEY INTO PREHISTORY

If you only have time to tour one section of the Dordogne region, many would argue that this part, Périgord Noir, so named by the writer Docteur Boissel for the 'blackness of its mushrooms, its truffles and the beautiful eyes of its Mesdemoiselles', is the one to choose. One of the joys of touring the area is the fact that so many of the original medieval buildings still remain, the best-preserved of all being found at Sarlat-la-Canéda. The route also takes in some of the most important prehistoric sites in France – indeed, in the world – and travels through countryside that is breathtakingly beautiful.

ROUTE DIRECTIONS

A cobbled side street winds its way between the houses and shops in the lovely old town of Sarlat

Head south-west out of Gourdon on the **D673** towards Salviac, Cazals and Fumel. 2km outside Gourdon look out for a turning to the right to la Fontade. Just beyond la Fontade (in about 2.5km)

turn right for Léobard. Come down the hill into Léobard, and bear right towards les Vitarolles and Payrignac.

Just after passing a cemetery on the left and after a sharp bend, take the left turn towards la Bastide. At the next junction, turn left for la Bastide and 1–2km later, turn right into la Bastide.

Pass through la Bastide and continue to meet the **D46**. Turn right on to the **D46** to St-Martial-de-Nabirat and continue into Domme (11km).

Head out of Domme on the **D46** over the river. Pass through Vitrac and continue along the **D46** into the medieval town of Sarlat-la-Canéda (6km).

Leave Sarlat on the **D704**, heading north towards Montignac. After passing through wonderful countryside for 15km you arrive in Montignac.

Leave Montignac on the **D65** for Sergeac. In 7km turn right, over the River Vézère to Thonac, then turn left on to the **D706** for St-Léon-sur-Vézère.

After passing through St-Leon-sur-Vézère, look out for the Roque St-Christophe to the left. Continue on the **D706** through Tursac and into les Eyzies-de-Tayac-Sireuil. Head out of les Eyzies on the **D47** signposted Sarlat-la-Canéda.

Follow the **D47**, passing Château du Roc and Château de Puymartin, into Sarlat (21km).

Leave Sarlat on the **D704** heading south towards Gourdon. The route passes through Carsac-Aillac, Groléjac and Nadaillac, back into Gourdon (26km).

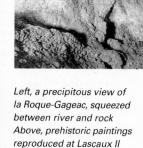

Left, a precipitous view of la Roque-Gageac, squeezed between river and rock Above, prehistoric paintings reproduced at Lascaux II

Place de la Liberté, in the centre of the town.

PLACES OF INTEREST

DOMME
See page 190.

LA ROQUE-GAGEAC
Steep, cobbled streets wind uphill past honey-coloured stone houses perched precariously on ledges in the cliffs overlooking the Dordogne. The remains of a little quay can been seen at the waterside.

The early-Renaissance Manoir-de-Tarde was, over several centuries, the home of the Tarde family, which included in the 16th century the historian and astronomer Jean Tarde of Sarlat, and in the 19th century the sociologist Gabriel Tarde. Above the village is a 16th-century church.

SARLAT-LA-CANEDA
A walk through the streets of this medieval and Renaissance gem of a

town, with its honey-coloured buildings with twisted towers, turrets and gables, alleyways and courtyards, is like a journey back in time. Especially charming among the many architectural jewels are the Renaissance-style Maison de la Boétie (built in the 16th century by a local magistrate, Etienne de la Boétie), the cathedral of St-Sacerdos, the 12th-century Lanterne des Morts with its conical tower, and the

MONTIGNAC
Montignac climbs in terraces up the hillside overlooking the River Vézère, and consists of a few houses grouped around a tower, the only surviving part of a fortress that was once owned by the Counts of Périgord. This small village was unknown until the discovery in 1940 of the nearby Lascaux cave, which contains the foremost prehistoric cave paintings in Europe. Unfortunately, thousands of tourists achieved what thousands of centuries did

not – the paintings started to be damaged by pollution. Since 1963 the original caves have been closed to all but a select few, although an authentic and painstaking reproduction has been created close by.

LA ROQUE ST-CHRISTOPHE
This exceptional troglodytic fort – five storeys high and 500m long – overlooks the Vézère valley. It consists of long natural terraces in the cliff face, and was inhabited as long as 20,000 years ago. A fortress was built on the terraces in the 10th century, but was destroyed in the 16th, with just a few remnants remaining.

LES EYZIES
See page 190.

LACAPELLE-MARIVAL

A comfortable market town set amid rolling hills, fertile farmlands and shady woods, Lacapelle-Marival was for six centuries under the sway of the great Cardaillac family. It lies 21km north-west of Figeac.

Southern and relaxed in feel, Lacapelle-Marival is built of the warm local sandstone, containing slivers of quartz that shimmer in the sunshine. The great, square 13th-century keep that dominates the village says everything about the considerable power of the Cardaillac family, lords of Quercy, whose fief it was from the 12th to the 18th century. The little 'pepperpot'

watchtowers are a typical Quercy touch. The living quarters with their heavy round towers are a 15th-century addition.

Near by are the Gothic church, the 15th-century market building and the attractive medieval quarter. A lively centre, rich in local events and specialities, Lacapelle-Marival hosts a beer festival on 14 July and a regional festival on 15 August every year.

LUZECH

This beautifully sited medieval village, virtually surrounded by a tight meander in the River Lot, has important Roman remains. It can be

found some 18km west of Cahors.

Shrouded by the steeply wooded banks of the Lot and standing virtually on its own peninsula, Luzech is dominated by the hill of the Impernal fortress. Reached up a steep track behind the village, the site is one of several believed to be where the Gauls made their last stand against Caesar. The hill has certainly been inhabited since prehistoric times and excavations have revealed Gaulish and Roman remains.

A good view of Luzech can be had from the Impernal. The old part of the village, near the 12th-century chapel, contains some ancient houses, one of which is now a museum displaying some of the findings of the excavations on the Impernal.

LOUBRESSAC

This tiny fortified medieval village enjoys one of the most dramatic and beautiful positions in the entire region, high above the valley of the Bave, 11km west of St-Céré.

Even in this region so rich in lovely villages Loubressac is exceptional. Perched high up on a rocky spur overlooking the Bave valley, it has always been valuable strategically for its commanding view over the confluence of the rivers Céré and Bave with the Dordogne, and to the great château of Castelnau, to St-Céré and on to St-Laurent les Tours. The twisting road up to Loubressac is lined with walnut and plum trees, two of the area's most important crops. Finally you reach the shady main square, from which narrow medieval streets lead off, tempting you to explore.

The church dates from the 12th and 16th centuries, and on the tip of the spur stands a beautiful 17th-century château, which sadly is not open to the public.

MARCILHAC-SUR-CELE

Nestling beneath the cliffs of the Célé valley, this picturesque little village clusters around the ruins of one of the most ancient of all Benedictine abbeys. 33km west of Figeac.

Deep in the lovely valley of the Célé, girded by high cliffs, the village of Marcilhac-sur-Célé – like so many in Quercy – grew up around its abbey.

The delightful village of Loubressac is perched high above the valley of the River Bave

Once one of the most powerful in the region, this ancient Benedictine foundation also controlled but neglected the sanctuary of Rocamadour in the 11th century. The abbey's gradual and inexorable decline began with the Hundred Years War and culminated during the Revolution.

The ruins of the abbey, part Romanesque and part-Gothic, now rise above the roofs of the village. With their fine vaulting, sculptures and frescos they retain a powerful atmosphere, and are well worth visiting.

A vertigious *corniche* leads to the Grotte de Bellevue, 1.5km to the north-west, with its intriguing stalagmites and stalactites.

MARTEL

Occupying a strategic position on the high limestone causse, this heavily fortified little town is known locally as the 'town of seven towers'. It lies 33km south of Brive-la-Gaillarde.

According to legend, Martel was founded by Charles Martel, 'hammer of the infidel' and grandfather of Charlemagne, after his defeat of the Saracens in the 8th century. The earliest reliable record of it, however, is from the 11th century, when the Viscounts of Turenne made it their capital. Martel's war-like past is recalled in the gateways and towers that remain of its medieval perimeter wall, and in the fortifications of its 14th-century church, with its striking 16th-century

ST-CERE

CHATEAU DE MONTAL

The Château de Montal is north-west of St-Céré on the hills overlooking the River Bave.

This beautiful château, which today is owned by the state, has one of the saddest and most romantic histories: its bricks were said to have been soaked in tears. The widow, Jeanne de Balsac d'Entraygues, built the castle as a present for her eldest son, who was then fighting in Italy. To do the

bell tower. All battlements and buttresses on the outside, the church contains some beautiful stained glass windows, paintings and statues.

Within the walls are some lovely medieval and Renaissance houses and mansions, and the Hôtel de la Raymondie is especially fine. The second floor houses the Musée Uxellodunum, which contains many Roman objects and an absorbing collection of old maps of Quercy.

MONPAZIER

The most perfectly preserved of all the *bastides* in Périgord, this fascinating little town was founded in 1284 by Edward I of England, Duke of Aquitaine. It lies 45km south-east of Bergerac.

Time seems to have stood still in Monpazier: its fortified gateways, its quiet streets laid out on a rectangular grid, its church and its beautiful market square – complete with covered arcades and its original measures – all remain remarkably intact, despite bitter fighting during the Hundred Years War and again in the 17th century.

One of the most important rights granted to *bastides* was that to hold a market or fair. Monpazier is still an important ,market town: local produce includes tobacco, chestnuts and strawberries, and pre-eminently mushrooms. There is a painting festival in June, a book festival in July and local fêtes and horse racing in May. There are guided tours of the old town, and swimmers can enjoy the nearby lake of Vérone.

MONTIGNAC

Standing at the head of the valley of the Vézère, this attractive little town is an important centre for the many local prehistoric sites. It can be found 48km south-east of Périgueux.

Once a fortress town belonging to the Counts of Périgord, Montignac is still centred on the fortified tower of its ruined château. No longer a sleepy village thanks to the discovery in 1940 of the famous painted caves of Lascaux on the hills above the town, it nevertheless retains a restful air. The caves have been closed to the public

since 1963 in order to protect the fragile paintings from atmospheric changes, but a remarkable exact replica has been constructed some 200m away. Tickets must be bought in Montignac, and in summer Lascaux II draws large numbers of visitors. Near by is Régourdou, where in 1954 the 70,000-year-old skeleton of a man was found. The town itself has some attractive medieval houses, a 17th-century priory church, a local folk museum and the Musée Eugène-Le-Roy, dedicated to the celebrated Périgord novelist.

Below, cheerful bunting indicates a holiday mood in the streets of Montignac

---

work, she recruited the finest architects and craftsmen from the Loire valley.

In 1534 the château was completed, and day after day she sat in a high turret watching for her son's return. Sadly, he never came back from the wars. Finally, his mother had the window from which she had watched for him sealed up, and around the window was carved the sad words, 'Hope no more'.

Soon afterwards, the castle was sold, and there were several more owners before an adventurer, Macaire, in 1879, who virtually stripped it and sold off all its treasures. In 1908 its fortunes took a turn for the better when it was bought by M. Fenaille, who restored the building and sought out its treasures from museums and collections around the world. In 1913, he donated the château to the nation.

AURIAC DU PERIGORD
CHAPEL OF ST-REMY

Nestling beneath the 14th-century Château de La Faye is the village of Auriac du Périgord, north of Montignac.

The Château de la Faye, perched on a clifftop to the north of the village, possesses a notable ecclesiastical building, the delicately vaulted chapel of St-Rémy, which was added to the keep and 14th-century towers of the château during the 15th century. It became the

object of pilgrimages as a rumour spread that the statue of the saint had healing powers, and the sick would come from far and wide to rub themselves with the effigy.

Pilgrims would travel for many miles to this peaceful chapel

PENNE

Clinging to the cliffs above the beautiful gorges of the Aveyron, this village with its skeletal château ruins is one of the most dramatic sights in the region. It lies 35km east of Montauban.

Above, a colourful corner of Penne, and right, Rocamadour, a regional highlight

From a distance, along the gorges from St-Antonin Noble-Val, the ruined walls of the château at Penne, rising sheer from the cliff face, look like a dizzily fragile rock formation. As you draw nearer, the massive stonework of the fortress becomes even more impressive, etched against the skyline with the medieval houses of the village huddled beneath. The narrow streets, alleys and stairways of the village are lined with medieval houses and often terminate abruptly in spectacular views over the valley. The best views are to

FORET DE LA DOUBLE

A remote corner of a popular region

Between the rivers Dronne and Isle, west of Périgueux, the mysterious forest of the Double is the Dordogne's least populated region.

For centuries this land of forests and marshy lakes was plagued with malaria and only a few hardy souls lived here, eking out a meagre living from forestry and fishing. Because the area was so remote and wild, few dared penetrate it, and it became a favourite hiding place for outlaws and others escaping their enemies. This, coupled with disease, gave the land its menacing atmosphere.

At the end of the 19th century Trappist monks established the monastry of Bonne-Esperance near Echourgnac, and things began to improve. The monks drained and cultivated the land and introduced cattle. Pine trees were also planted, replacing some of the traditional white and black oak, to improve drainage and produce resin. When the monks left the abbey in 1910, they were replaced by nuns, who today make the excellent La Trappe cheese. Despite the recent development of the area, it still has a slightly mysterious and forbidding atmosphere.

be had from the château ruins, reached up a steeply climbing street flanked by some of the finest houses and leading past the 12th-century church.

PUJOLS

Time seems to have passed by this medieval, fortified white-walled village, with its 13th-century ramparts and two fine churches. 2km south of Villeneuve-sur-Lot.

You enter this lovely, crumbling, walled village through a gateway in the bell-tower of the 14th- and 15th-century church of St-Nicolas, which brings you into a small square with a beautifully timbered covered market. Sunday morning is the best time to visit, when this shelters the bustling local market. Of Pujols' original three lines of defences only one remains, sheltering the stone-built medieval houses squeezed together along the narrow streets. From the walls there are fine views along the valley of the Lot. The other church in the village, the 16th-century Ste-Foy, has good frescos.

ROCAMADOUR

This spectacular village and pilgrimage centre, dramatically sited on a steep rock face in the gorge of the Alzou, is now the second most important tourist centre of France. It lies 48km north-west of Figeac.

All the crowds and the tawdry souvenirs sold from its narrow streets cannot take away the magic of Rocamadour and its breathtaking position. The village consists of a single medieval street at the foot of a precipitous limestone cliff, lined with fine houses, and dominated by a 14th-century castle. This is reached from the village by a steep flight of 233 steps, climbed since the 12th century by generations of pilgrims on their knees. For between the village and the château lies the religious heart of Rocamadour: the shrines, chapels and basilicas dedicated to its twin miracle-working relics, the remains of St-Amadour and the mysterious Black Virgin, crudely carved in local walnut.

Try to visit Rocamadour early or late in the day, when the light is at its most atmospheric and the crowds at their lightest.

SALIGNAC-EYVIGUES

Narrow streets lined with fine medieval and Renaissance houses lead up to a magnificent château. Salignac-Eyvigues lies 20km north-east of Sarlat-la-Canéda.

This lovely and substantial village in the heart of Périgord Noir has a typical covered market, attractive narrow streets and a 14th-century Gothic church. However, it is the medieval castle, built between the 12th and 17th centuries, which dominates the village. Within its 12th-century ramparts it retains three great towers – two round and one square – and all roofed in beautiful stone *lauzes*. Inside, the armoury hall has 15th-and 16th-century fireplaces, and up a spiral Renaissance staircase are rooms furnished with Louis XIII pieces. The castle still belongs to the family that produced the great writer François de Salignac de la Mothe-Fénelon, who became Archbishop of Cambrai, and is open to visitors. Both the castle and the village, which huddles around its feet, are built of the warm local stone, which seems to turn golden in the sunlight,

BASTIDES

Bastides (from the *langue d'oc* word 'bastidas') are the fortified towns that were built from the 13th century onwards throughout the south-west of France, in the region stretching from the Dordogne valley to the foothills of the Pyrenees. During the Hundred Years War they took on particular importance in Périgord, where the French and the English (who held Aquitaine) confronted each other across the Dordogne. Typically, a church, perhaps an earlier castle and a grid-plan of streets are enclosed within a square or rectangular wall, with a tower at each corner. Monpazier, Domme, Eymet and Vianne are probably the best preserved, but a fuller tour of *bastides* might also take in Castelsagrat, Labastide-Murat, Libourne, Monségur and Villefranche-du-Périgord.

AGEN

MUSEE DES BEAUX-ARTS

Agen is a modern town situated between Bordeaux and Toulouse.

Despite its attractive riverside setting most tourists rush through Agen, preferring to explore the more historic towns and villages near by. Art lovers, however, will stay to enjoy its wonderful museum, which occupies several buildings dating from the 16th and 17th centuries. The museum's collection covers a wide range of subjects, including archeological finds from prehistoric times, medieval carvings and tapestries and a collection of ceramics. An impressive display of 19th-century French art includes work by Corot, Courbet, and the Impressionists Sisley and Caillebotte. A highlight of the collection is a group of paintings by Goya, including a particularly expressive self-portrait, and the small, curious painting called 'Caprichos', of a bull, a' donkey and an elephant flying over an astonished crowd of people, which is believed by some to mark the beginning of surrealism.

A modern town is home to priceless treasures of the past

TOUR 27 – 115KM
PERIGORD VERT

The northern part of the Dordogne, christened Périgord Vert by Jules Verne, is indeed lusciously green. Watered by several rivers, and having a humid climate, the landscape remains green all year round, and even through the driest summers. Starting from Périgueux, the route passes through pretty riverside villages such as St-Jean-de-Côle, rolling green farmland, and Brantôme, sometimes called the Venice of the Dordogne. This golden-stoned village is dominated by its ancient abbey, and with its prehistoric caves typifies the charm of the region. As you drive through the gentle countryside, dotted with farms selling local produce, nuts, cheeses, and *foie gras*, it is tempting to linger awhile.

ROUTE DIRECTIONS

Leave Périgueux by the **D939** towards Angoulême and look out for a right turn on to the **D3** for Agonac almost immediately outside the town. Just under 2km along the **D3**, at a roundabout, turn left towards le Godet. At the junction bear left to pass through le Godet heading for Château-l'Evêque.

A jumble of buildings in the attractive old quarter of Périgueux

At the end of the road turn right, then right again on to the **D939** to go through Château-l'Evêque. After passing through the town, turn right on to the **D3e** for Agonac. Pass through Preyssac d'Agonac to arrive in Agonac.

Turn left in the centre of Agonac on to the **D69** towards Puyblanc and Brantôme then left on to the **D106** for Puy-de-Fourches.

After 4.5km pass a cross at the crossroads. Keep bearing left, then take the second right on to a narrow road for la Besse and Lasserre. Just 2km later, pass the tiny hamlet of la Besse on the left. Another 2km after that turn right on to the **D939** for Brantôme and carry on to a large roundabout. Take the first exit into Brantôme.

Leave Brantôme on the **D78** heading east towards St-Jean-de-Côle and Thiviers. Continue for

19km on the **D78** from Brantôme, passing la Chapelle-Faucher and St-Pierre-de-Côle to reach St-Jean-de-Côle.

Leave St-Jean by the same road, and just outside the town take a left turn to St-Clément and Thiviers.

Leave Thiviers on the **N21** followings signs for Périgueux. Just outside the town, look out for the left turn on to the **D76** for Eyzerac and Corgnac-sur-l'Isle. Continue on the **D76**, and after passing through St-Jory-las-Bloux turn right on to the **D73e** for Coulaures.

After driving through some wonderful countryside for 6km, turn left and cross the River Isle into Coulaures.

Drive straight through Coulaures, leaving on the **D73** for Tourtoirac. Just after passing the tiny hamlet of Terrier, turn right off the **D73** on to a narrow road towards Exorbepey and St-Pantaly-d'Ans. At the end of this road turn right to Exorbepey, and continue into Ste-Eulalie-d'Ans.

Turn left and cross the river and then turn right on to the **D5** for St-Pardoux-d'Ans and Cubjac. From here cross back over the River Auvézère and follow the **D5**, bypassing Cubjac.

Continue on the **D5**, which crosses the river twice and passes through le Change and Blanzac. After passing Blanzac turn left on to the **D6** and then right, back on to the **D5** at la Roquette towards Bassillac. Stay on the **D5** back into Périgueux.

PLACES OF INTEREST

CHATEAU-L'EVEQUE
The 14th-century church in Château-l'Evêque was the place where St-Vincent de Paul, at the tender age of 20, was ordained by Monsignor François de Bourdeille in September 1600. The castle, originally built in the 14th century, has been altered many times in the years since.

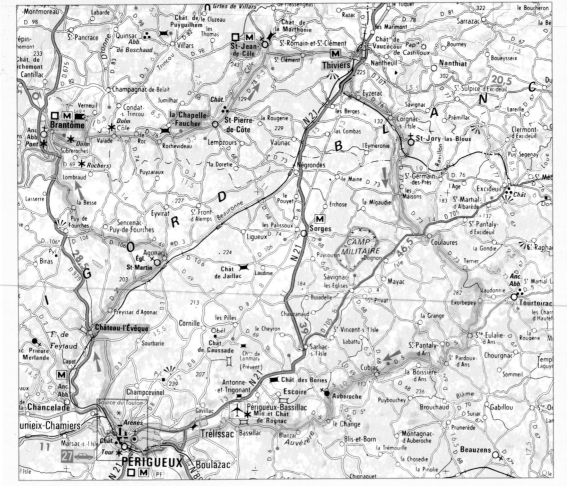

Vert, Thiviers was once a Gallic fort, then a Roman camp. Later, it was a resting place for pilgrims on the route to Santiago de Compostela. The 12th-century church has some fine Romanesque capitals. The Renaissance-Gothic Château de Vaucorour has been heavily restored. It is now best known for its markets and fairs, special-ising in *foie gras* and truf-fles. There is also a Duck and Goose Museum, these birds being central to the region's cuisine.

Left, shopping at the local market, Périgueux, and below, ancient sculptures behind the abbey, Brantôme

BRANTOME

Known as the Venice of Périgord, and surrounded by the River Dronne, Brantôme is one of the most picturesque towns in the area. Its honey-coloured, flower-decked houses are overshadowed by steep cliffs and the massive Benedictine abbey, built into the cliff face. The original abbey was founded in the 11th century by Charlemagne, and the present building has undergone many changes. Signs of much earlier human habitation can be found in the many cave dwellings near by, and those carved out of the rocks beneath the abbey, including the dramatic 'Cave of the Last Judgement' can be toured.

LA CHAPELLE-FAUCHER

This superb château looks down on the River Côle from its perch on the cliff top. The history of la Chapelle-Faucher dates back to the 15th century, and parts of the original building, such as the main gate and the curtain wall, still survive. During the Wars of Religion, the Huguenot leader, Admiral de Coligny, locked 300 peasants into the building and set it alight. Chapelle-Faucher is now rather more peaceful. The two battlemented towers are still inhabited.

ST-JEAN-DE-COLE

See page 200.

THIVIERS

Situated on the border of Limousin and the Périgord

ST-AMAND-DE-COLY

This tiny village boasts an awe-inspiring 12th-century fortified church, the mightiest in Périgord, and one of the most unusual in France. It lies 7km east of Montignac.

St-Armand-de-Coly's massive fortress-church stands as an enduring testimony to the dangers and uncertainties of life in medieval Périgord. The astonishing west front is built like a castle keep, with walls 4m thick. Once inside, the villagers were provided with high-level walkways from which to bombard marauders, and a labyrinthine network of concealed staircases and passageways and hollow pillars in which to hide should the defences be breached – as indeed happened in the 16th century during the Wars of Religion. At the same time, with its fine proportions and the simplicity of its architecture, the church still retains the dignity of a place of worship. In the former pres-bytery opposite the church, les Amis de St-Amand-de-Coly show audio-visual presentations on the history of the village and its church.

ST-ANTONIN-NOBLE-VAL

Among the delights that this ancient Gallo-Roman spa town has to offer are a spectacular site, a wealth of medieval architecture, and a variety of holiday activities. It lies 19km east of Caussade.

St-Antonin-Noble-Val nestles on the right bank of the River Aveyron, opposite a high sheer cliff known as the Rochers d'Anglars. This impressive feature, combined with the existing Gallo-Roman settlement's position at the confluence of the Rivers Aveyron and Bonnette, made this the perfect site for the founding of an abbey in the eighth century.

Present-day St-Antonin is a delightful labyrinth of narrow streets lined by superb pantiled houses of the 13th–15th-centuries, which bear witness to the town's prosperity in the Middle Ages. Most remarkable of all is the 12th-century former town hall, the oldest civic building in France. Romanesque in style, it is dominated by a great machicolated belfry, which was restored during the 19th century by Viollet-le-Duc. Almost opposite is the solidly built 14th-century covered market, which is still the focus of St-Antonin's lively Sunday-morning market.

St-Cirq, basking in sunshine in its tranquil setting on the River Lot

ST-CIRQ-LAPOPIE

In its dramatically picturesque setting, half-hidden in the hills overlooking the Lot, this is indisputably one of the most beautiful villages in France. 35km east of Cahors.

The cobbled, steeply sloping medieval lanes and timber-framed houses of St-Cirq-Lapopie, clinging perilously to the side of this rugged cliff above the Lot, are a sheer delight to wander through, admiring the tumbling confusion of soft-coloured roofs and the wealth of Renaissance and Gothic details on the ancient façades. The village is crowned by the 15th-century church with its squat fortified bell-tower, standing on a terrace from which there are more good views. The Syndicat d'Initiative is located in the Château de la Gardette, which also houses a small furniture museum. The traditional craft of St-Cirq, going back to the Middle Ages, was wood-turning. Now its old houses have been taken over and faithfully restored by artists and craftspeople attracted here by the exceptional beauty of the village and its setting.

ST-JEAN-DE-COLE

A remarkable church and castle, fine old houses and a Gothic bridge combine to make this one of the prettiest villages in Périgord. 7km west of Thiviers.

The lovely main square of St-Jean-de-Côle is flanked on one side by the Château de la Marthonie, with a 12th-century tower and some fine additions from the 15th and 16th centuries. Classified as a historical monument and open to visitors in July and August, it has a gallery of publicity posters and an exhibition of old handmade papers. Near by is the church, the chapel of a 12th-century priory that used to stand here. This powerful building has an astonishingly high and rather short nave with an unusual bell-tower. Inside it has some good 17th-century woodwork, and it gives access to a lovely Renaissance cloister.

The old houses that cluster along the narrow streets radiating from the square are extremely picturesque; indeed the roofs of St-Jean are said to be the finest in France.

SECRET PLACES

JUMILHAC-LE-GRAND

LEGEND OF THE SPINNER'S BEDCHAMBER

Jumilhac-le-Grand is a small village overlooking the River Isle, north-east of Thiviers.

The château at Jumilhac was originally built in the 14th century by the Knights Templar, but was later given by Henry IV to Antoine Chapelle, an ironmonger and arms manufacturer. A study of the towers and turrets of the castle reveals the family handiwork, in the decorative form of iron birds, suns and moons. Naturally, a château with such a fairytale appearance has to have a legend to match.

A room on the first floor is called the 'spinner's bedchamber'. Here, it was said, Antoine II locked up his wife, Louise, when he went off to war, for he suspected her of having an affair with a courtier. Louise spent her time spinning, and the walls are decorated with her handiwork. However, she was also able to keep in touch with her lover, using a shuttle to wind a thread down the castle wall. In another version of the story, her lover dressed up as a shepherd and managed to enter her bedroom while pretending to deliver wool to her.

Above, a reflective view of lovely St-Jean-de-Côle

St-Leon-sur-Vezere

A lovely village in a pretty riverside setting, with two castles and one of the finest Romanesque churches in the region. 15km north-east of les Eyzies.

This sleepy village, lying on a tree-lined loop of the lovely valley of the River Vézère, close to the region's centres of prehistory, is exceptionally picturesque.

Its remarkable church is one of the best Romanesque churches in Périgord. Built in the 12th century as part of a Benedictine priory, it is laid out on a basilica plan, with a magnificent round apse flanked by two smaller ones. Traces of Romanesque frescos can be seen inside the apse. Above the perfectly proportioned building rises a two-storey bell-tower, roofed like the rest of the church in stone slabs or *lauzes*.

Just to the north is the imposing Château de Belcaire, standing proudly on a limestone outcrop overlooking the river, and all along the river valley are the exceptional sites which have made this area a world capital of prehistory.

St-Maurin

This very old, atmospheric village is unusually situated within the ruins of an 11th-century Benedictine abbey. It is situated some 30km east of Agen.

The abbey that once stood at St-Maurin was a Cluniac foundation, a daughter house of Moissac. The original foundation stone, recording the dedication of the church in 1097, can still be seen beneath the bell-tower. The abbey was destroyed and rebuilt several times. The most recent restoration took place during the 17th century, since when little appears to have changed in the village.

The fortified Mairie occupies what once was the abbot's palace, and some very old houses with unusual round tiles stand in the transept. The village retains the old covered market typical of the region.

Ten kilometres to the south-east is the picturesque 13th-century *bastide* of Castelsagrat, originally built by Alphonse de Poitiers, Count of Toulouse, to protect the land between the Séoune and Barguelonne streams.

Villefranche-du-Perigord

A 13th-century *bastide* overlooking a tributary of the River Lémance, in a beautiful setting surrounded by woods. 27km north-west of Fumel.

Founded by Alphonse de Poitiers in 1260, Villefranche has had a troubled history owing to its strategic position on the borders of Périgord and Quercy. Although consequently not as well preserved as its neighbour and one-time rival Monpazier, it still has its arcaded square and covered market complete with grain measures – throughout the year, the market is a good place to shop for local delicacies, and antique fairs are held here in August. The village also retains the original grid pattern of its streets, and many 12th- and 13th-century houses.

In the centre of the *bastide*, one of the oldest medieval buildings houses a museum of chestnuts and mushrooms, with displays explaining the history of these two important local products. It also demonstrates the importance of the surrounding pine, oak and chestnut forests to the local economy.

Geese, Ducks and Foie Gras

In the Dordogne, if ducks are not trooping in single file across the narrow lane ahead of you, then geese are honking from the neighbouring field as vigorously as they ever did when the Romans used them to guard the Capitol. Together, these birds form the basic ingredients of the local cuisine. Goose fat replaces butter in the cook's repertoire and gives texture to a *cassoulet* or a thick vegetable soup (*garbure*). *Confits* consist of the meat potted and preserved in its own fat. *Foie gras* ('fat liver') is made by depriving geese and ducks of exercise during the last weeks of their life and force-feeding them with half-cooked maize three times a day. The liver swells to several times its natural weight. It can be potted and preserved whole, used to make pâté, terrine and mousse, or included in a *ballotine*.

SECRET FRANCE
LANGUEDOC

Languedoc, which takes in the southern section of the Massif Central, encompasses two areas that are particularly stunning for their landscapes and natural features. The mountainous Haut Languedoc region and the Cévennes, a national park, has always been sparsely populated, but with its extensive forests and sparkling, fast-flowing mountain streams it offers wonderful opportunities for activities such as walking, climbing and, in particular, trout fishing. The Grand Causse, making up the southern end of the Massif Central, is a huge, bleak plateau of raised limestone pavements cut through by deep canyons, the Gorge du Tarn being the most spectacular. The Causse is riddled with underground rivers and extensive cave systems.

The area saw little of the medieval conflicts, the consequences of both internal squabbling and sea-borne invasion, that neighbouring Provence had to bear, and so has fewer villages that were positioned for purely defensive purposes, though these do exist. Some also indicate the difficulties of policing such a vast, thinly populated region, having originally been established in medieval times to provide a base for groups of knights employed to protect travellers in the region.

Other villages show the remains of castles, but these were usually baronial homes rather than fortresses. Many other notable villages grew up around the pilgrim churches. The centre of the area was crossed by one of the main pilgrim routes to Santiago de Compostela, and many of the villages catered for the pilgrim traffic, offering both accommodation and the opportunity to pray at a local shrine.

The Cévennes is one of the emptiest regions in France, a country of exquisite wildlife and seemingly tailor-made for quiet, secret spots, while the Causse also has its share of curiosities. The haunted ruins of medieval castles, villages clinging to the sides of cliff faces, strange rock formations and areas strewn with fantastically shaped blocks of granite, and quiet roads through breath-taking scenery richly reward the traveller who enjoys seeking out the unusual.

ail de Languedoc

Ruggedness is a feature of this central region of France, whether in the survival of its people, left, or its breathtaking landscapes, below

Above and left, softer images may be seen in the villages of Languedoc, where half-timbering decorates the houses, and brilliant flowers adorn grey stone walls

AMBIALET

Downstream from its spectacular gorges, the Tarn flows through a beautiful pastoral landscape on its way to Albi. It passes through or close to a number of interesting villages, but none as extraordinary as Ambialet, 50km east of Albi.

The best view of Ambialet and its spectacular site is from the road up to the 11th-century Benedictine foundation on top of the ridge. The priory chapel, dedicated to Notre Dame de l'Auder, is Romanesque in design and very austere inside, with a fine 17th-century painted wooden statue of the Virgin. A room of the priory has been taken over as a museum of objects brought back by missionaries from Brazil. From the chapel the view of the village with its ruined château, and of the surrounding countryside with its chestnut and holm oak trees is exceptional. The other ecclesiastical-looking building that can be seen close to the village is, surprisingly, a hydro-electric power station.

BRASSAC

With its two châteaux, its picturesque bridges and its old houses, this village makes a charming centre for exploring the Sidobre, a high granite plateau strewn with fantastically distorted boulders. 24km east of Castres.

Brassac occupies both banks of the River Agout, which is spanned by a pair of lovely bridges, the older one in fine 12th-century Gothic style. On each bank is a château, the older one on the right bank, the Château de Castelnau, rising sheer from the waters of the river. Built of pale stone with granite facings, it rather dwarfs its more modest neighbour on the opposite bank.

The older part of the village lies around Place St-Georges, on which stands the church with its twin round towers. Rue du Moulin, with fine overhung houses and steps leading down to the river, is a reminder of the textile industry on which the village's prosperity was founded and which still survives.

CHATEAUNEUF-DE-RANDON

Spectacularly situated at 1286 metres on top of a granite hill at the edge of the Montagnes de la Margeride, this village enjoys superb views and is a haven for lovers of nature and wide open spaces. 28km north-east of Mende.

Renowned for the magnificence of its views and the purity of its air, Châteauneuf is surrounded by hills and heathland, woods and streams which are perfect for walking.

Châteauneuf's origins go back to Gallo-Roman times, and by the 10th century an imposing fortress stood on the site. It has gone down in history, however, as the place where the great military commander Bertrand du Guesclin died in 1380, while besieging the English forces who had occupied the castle. Over the centuries the

A trip the the baker in Châteauneuf-de-Randon

village has developed lengthways, following the contours of its site, and its houses – of granite and with stone roofs – are typical of this part of the Lozère.

SECRET PLACES

ST ALBAN-AURIOLLES

MAS DE LA VIGNASSE

This 17th-century farmhouse, 24km south of Aubenas, contains two unique museums.

Mas de la Vignasse was once the home of the Reynaud family, relatives of the 19th-century author, Alphonse Daudet. It now houses two museums, one dedicated to popular arts and traditions, the other to the life and works of Daudet himself.

The Reynauds, who built the farm, owed their prosperity to the production of silk and there are numerous reminders of that time. The courtyard is still shaded by mulberry trees, the leaves of which

were fed to the silkworms, and there is a 16th-century loom complete with a partially completed cloth from the period, said to be unique in France. There are many other examples of objects evoking life on the farm, including a 17th-century olive-oil press turned by a donkey, bread ovens, and an old still for making a type of brandy called 'Marc'.

Everything is provided, it would seem, for the needs of a simple life

CONQUES

This village with its exceptional abbey was one of the great pilgrimage centres of medieval Christendom. 38km north-west of Rodez.

From the 11th century to the 13th Conques was at the height of its glory, attracting countless pilgrims to worship before the reliquary of Ste-Foy, before toiling on their way to Santiago de Compostela. The present abbey church is a magnificent example of 12th-century architecture. The tympanum depicting the Last Judgement over the west portal is generally acknowledged to be the finest carved stonework from the Romanesque period in all of Europe.

The rest of the village is surprisingly unspoilt, its steep streets lined with 15th- and 16th-century houses with stone-tiled roofs. On a little square is the modest 16th-century Château d'Humières, with interesting wooden corbels. Close by is the Porte de Vinzelles, the last remaining 12th-century gateway into the village.

DOUCH

The Parc Naturel Régional du Haut Languedoc was created to preserve the region's superb natural scenery and wildlife. Nestling beneath Mont Caroux is the tiny hamlet of Douch. 26km west of Béderieux.

Lost in the middle of nowhere and over 1,000 metres high, Douch is little

Blending into the hillside behind it, the unspoilt village of Conques has buildings dating back to the 15th and 16th centuries

more than a huddle of traditional houses, all of the local stone and roofed with *lauzes*, the weighty split-stone tiles that are a feature of Massif Central villages. Wending their way between the houses are a little stream and a series of delightful alleys that lead the visitor to unexpected and impressive views of the local country, dotted with small farms, and of Mont Caroux. The tiny Romanesque church, set a little way from the centre of the village, is delightful.

From the village the view is superb, stretching east towards Provence's Mont Ventoux and west towards the Pyrenees.

TOUR 28 – 160KM
RODEZ AND THE GORGES DU LOT

The region of Midi-Pyrénées lies like a flat book between the Massif Central and the Pyrenees themselves. In the north of the region is the *département* of Aveyron, whose eastern edge is formed by the last of the Massif Central hills. The *département* is split by two rivers, the Lot and the Aveyron, both of which flow through beautiful gorges surrounded by delightful rural country. The Aveyron flows through Rodez, the starting point of the route. Heading north from Rodez, the town explores both the pastoral and the more rugged delights of the area, and then follows the Lot through a dramatic gorge.

ROUTE DIRECTIONS

From Rodez, go north on the **D988**, and follow it to Bazouls, then continue on the **D920** to Espalion. Go through Espalion, then turn left on to the **D920**

The River Lot is lined with limestone gorges

towards Estaing. Go through Estaing, and enter the Gorges du Lot.

Traverse the gorge to reach Entraygues-sur-Truyère. In the village turn left over the old bridge and turn left again onto the **D107**, following signs to Conques and Decazeville.

Go through Vieillevie, and 6.5km further on turn left at a junction towards

Rodez and Conques. The road goes downhill to reach a junction with a bridge on the left going over the river. Here, go straight on to the **D42**, towards the main road towards St-Parthem and Decazeville. After 16km turn left at a junction with the main road towards Flagnac and Decazeville. Continue to the outskirts

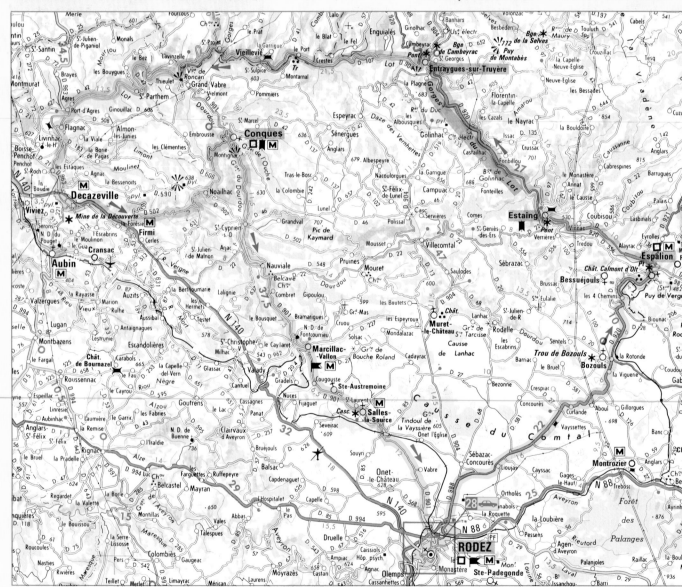

of Decazeville. Go through the town centre and leave on the **N140** towards Rodez and Firmi.

After 5km at a junction after the turning to Firmi, turn left off the main road on the **D502** towards Noailhac and St-Cyprien. The road bears left then right immediately, and climbs. It flattens when a valley is reached, and then climbs to a junction. Turn left along the main road towards Noailhac. Turn right at the next fork and continue into Noailhac. Turn left at the church towards Almon-les-Junies, Decazeville and Conques. Climb out of the

village and turn right, signposted Almon, Grand-Vabre, Conques-tourisme. Then right again at the next junction (signposted '*Conques tourisme*'). Drop down to a 2m-wide bridge over the river. Go up to the village if you wish to stop.

Leave Conques on the **D901** to St-Cyprien. Follow the road into St-Cyprien, going straight through the village following signs for Rodez and Marcillac-Vallon. When you reach Marcillac, follow the Rodez signs through the village. Go through Salles-la-Source and follow the road back into Rodez.

RODEZ

The chief attraction of Rodez is undoubtedly the huge cathedral of Nôtre-Dame. The interior is 170m long and 36m wide and was started in the 13th century, though not finished until the 16th.

Close to the cathedral are a number of very beautiful old houses. The Musée Fenaille occupies a Renaissance building and has a collection of local antiquities, furniture and pottery.

ESPALION

Set on the Lot, and with a fine 13th-century bridge, Espalion is a delightful place. Near the bridge, the château is a 16th-century mansion in fortified Renaissance style, now a folk museum. In the village centre old houses group around a church dedicated to St-Hilarion, with fine carvings and an arcaded belfry.

ESTAING
See below.

GORGES DU LOT
Between the villages of Estaing and Entraygues

A fine old 13th-century bridge spans the Lot at Espalion, and the tranquil river reflects the houses that line its banks

the Lot, which has been flowing in a wide valley, is cramped into a picturesque gorge. The Barrage de Golinhac, the 36m high dam that is passed along the way, feeds water to a hydro-electric station.

ENTRAYGUES-SUR-TRUYERE
See below.

CONQUES
See page 205.

ENTRAYGUES-SUR-TRUYERE

A picturesque village in a superb position at the confluence of the Lot and the Truyère, with lovely views and fine old streets. 27km north-west of Espalion.

It was in the 13th century that the counts of Rodez built their château here, dominating the two river valleys. The same century saw the construction of the beautiful Gothic bridge over the Truyère, with its heavily buttressed arches. The heart of the old village lies on the spur of land between the two rivers, behind the château. Place Albert Castanié is a good starting place; Rue Droite, which leads off it to the north, has some fine 16th-century doorways; Rue Basse, which leads to the west, is the best-preserved street in Entraygues, with some excellent half-timbered and corbelled houses from the 15th and 16th centuries. This was the era of

Entraygues' greatest prosperity, when river traffic laden with local produce would ply to Bordeaux and back.

ESTAING

Clustered at the foot of its château, at the opposite end of the wild and dramatic Lot gorges from Entraygues is Estaing. 10km north-west of Espalion.

Estaing is named after one of the Auvergne's noblest families. It was the d'Estaing family who built the château, largely in the 15th and 16th centuries, an eclectic collection of buildings in different styles and materials grouped around the keep, but lost it at the time of the

Revolution. The château is now occupied by a religious community who will give a guided tour to visitors who knock at their door. Opposite the château is the church, an interesting 15th-century building that houses the remains of St-Fleuret, a 7th-century saint who died near where Estaing now stands. The village at the foot of the château has a fine collection of old stone-built houses roofed in *lauzes*. The Lot is crossed by a fine Gothic bridge, close to which is the statue of François d'Estaing, Bishop of Rodez.

Above, a warm welcome is given to visitors to the ancient village of Estaing

LA GARDE-GUERIN

This imposing fortified village was built to protect medieval travellers on the road from Languedoc to the Auvergne. 43km south of Langogne.

The Romans forced a road across the Lozère plateau, and for 1,000 years this remained the only route for travellers heading north from Provence towards central France. Not surprisingly the road became notorious for the robberies and murders carried out along its length.

In the 12th century, Aldebert, Bishop of Mende, decided to combat the brigands by appointing 27 knights to act as armed escorts. La Garde-Guérin was to be their headquarters, and here he built 27 fortified houses for the knights. Many of the knights' houses still stand – imposing constructions of granite with mullioned windows. Only the keep and the Romanesque chapel remain of the castle.

LABEAUME

An isolated village lost in time, hidden from the 20th century in a deep gorge and little changed since it was built in the Middle Ages. 25km south of Aubenas.

Clinging to the side of the Beaume gorge, the stone houses and cobbled streets of Labeaume seem to merge into the rock as they tumble down between the limestone cliffs to the river. On the tiny dusty square stands the church, with its unusual belfry porch supported by two large columns, and the Mairie. Farther on, through

vaulted archways and past the old terracotta-roofed houses and little nooks and crannies, steep cobbled alleyways eventually lead down to the riverside and a broad, sandy esplanade shaded by plane trees. A primitive low stone bridge without a parapet spans the river with its 10 arches, and there is a good walk from here beneath the lofty cliffs of the Beaume gorges, sculpted into fantastic shapes over the centuries and reflected in the clear waters.

LAUTREC

This splendid fortified village overlooking the plain of Castres owes its name to the ancient feudal family of which the great 19th-century painter Toulouse-Lautrec was a late descendant. 30km south of Albi.

SECRET PLACES

CANTOBRE

HANGING VILLAGE

The dramatic cliff village of Cantobre lies north of Nant on the D991.

Cantobre is perched on the edge of a final section of the Causse where the Trèvezel joins the River Dourbie. What makes Cantobre special is that the final, jutting section of the plateau is undercut, so that the last houses of the village are perched on the edge of an overhang. In silhouette this part of the

village really does look cantilevered, and it is easy to understand why Cantobre is so called. The name is from the village's description in the Provencal language, deriving from 'quant ora' – such work!

A strange village, perched dramatically on an overhang

its elegant arcading supported on wooden pillars. The half-timbered houses, dating from the time of the village's fortification, overlook the old communal well. The church, started in the 15th century, has a fine pulpit and marble reredos.

The weekly market, every Friday, specialises in the high-quality garlic, for which Lautrec is one of the local centres. The garlic season lasts from July to April, and on the third Friday in August the village holds a *Fête de l'Ail rose*.

MEYRUEIS

Beautifully positioned at the confluence of the Bétuzon, the Brèze and the Jonte; this lovely old village is understandably popular with visitors. 35km south-west of Florac.

Standing as it does where two small streams, the Bétuzon and the Brèze, reach the Jonte, close to the entrance to the beautiful Jonte gorges, as well as lying on the borders of the Causse Noir and the Causse Méjean, and not far from Mont Aigonal, Meyrueis has long been an important village, despite its small size. Now a popular tourist centre, it has nevertheless kept its tranquil charm. The Maison Belon, with its elegant Renaissance windows, is particularly striking, and the Tour de l'Horloge is the last remnant of the medieval fortifications. Of the castle that used to dominate the village only ruins remain. Despite all its visitors Meyrueis is still a working village, its chief industry centring on the sawmills which are kept supplied with lumber from the slopes of Mont Aigoual.

The busy market is popular with visitors as well as locals in unspoilt Meyrueis, where there is much to see

Of its 13th-century fortifications Lautrec has retained part of its walls and the Porte de la Caussade, the last of its eight gates. Inside the walls are some fine streets lined with old houses and a lovely central square that retains

THE CEVENNES NATIONAL PARK

The Cévennes, at the south-eastern fringe of the Massif Central, form a rugged landscape of granite and limestone, chestnut forests and fast-flowing streams. Their remote heartland is the national park, whose information centre at Florac lies between Mont Lozère (1,702m) and Mont Aigoual (1,565m). Lacking major towns or roads, the region has traditionally nourished a defiant spirit. Its terrain offered refuge to heretics in the Middle Ages and *maquisards* in World War II. The bloodiest chapter of its history occurred in 1702–5, during the War of the Camisards, a Protestant rebellion against Catholic persecution which took its name from the occitan word for the blouses worn by the local peasantry. The Protestant leader, Pierre Laporte, is remembered at the Musée du Désert in Le Mas Soubeyran, near Alès.

LODEVE

PRIORY OF ST-MICHEL-DE-GRANDMONT

The ancient Priory of St-Michel-de-Grandmont lies 8km east of Lodève on the D153.

The Priory was originally a daughter house of the Grandmont order, which was founded in Limousin in 1076 and dissolved in 1772. St-Michel was founded in the early 12th century, though the building was not actually completed for almost 100 years.

Architecturally it is an important relic, with a unique cloister in Grandmont Romanesque style. The galleried cloister is superb, simple, yet dignified, and a contrast to the remainder of the building, which seems overly severe.

The priory is home to a further curiosity – dolmens may be discovered, standing in different parts of the grounds.

Spectacular natural rock formations dominate the site of this intriguing and exceptionally pretty village. 12km west of Clermont-l'Herault.

The Causses of the southern Massif Central – huge limestone plateaux split by gorges and frequently hollowed into lofty caves – are also remarkable for their cirques and erratic rock forma-

Built among great outcrops of rock, it is difficult to tell where the rocks end and the buildings begin in unusual Moureze

TOUR 29 – 120KM

THE SOUTHERN MASSIF

At the eastern end of the Massif Central is the last of the four limestone Causses. This, the Causse de Larzac, is the largest of all, covering over 1,000 square kilometres. It is a high, dry plateau, cut in several places by green valleys. One of the finest of these is the Hérault Valley, the valley that forms the southern end of the Causses and, therefore, the Massif Central itself.

The route does not follow the valley itself, though it does touch it in several places, but for the most part the tour stays on the Causse, sampling that most particular of landscapes.

ROUTE DIRECTIONS

Leave Ganges on the **D999**, heading north-west towards le Vigan. At Pont-d'Hérault bear left with the main road to reach the river, and continue into le Vigan. Go straight through the town, and on the other side turn left on to the **D48** towards Avèze and Montdardier. Go through Avèze and climb up to Montdardier.

Leave Montdardier and continue on the **D48** towards Rogues and Lodève. The road bypasses Rogues to reach the small hamlet of le Cros. From here, drop down through a number of hairpin bends into Madières. Turn right in the village and continue on the same road over a river and up to St-Maurice-Navacelles.

Keep on the main road through the village, and at the end of a straight section of road, 8km from St-Maurice-Navacelles, turn left on to the **D152** towards la Vacquerie-et-St-Martin-de-Castries. Go through this village, and continue on the **D9** through Arboras to Mont-peyroux. Here, turn left at the fork to reach the village centre. Go left in the centre, following signs to St-Jean-de-Fos, Gignac and Montpellier. Follow the road out of the village and turn left at a road fork to St-Jean-de-Fos. At St-Jean follows signs for St-Guilhem-le-Désert and Ganges. Turn left at the junction in the village centre.

Just outside St-Jean, turn right over a bridge across a splendid gorge of the Hérault towards Aniane and Montpellier on the **D27**. Just before reaching Aniane, turn left on the **D32** to Puéchabon.

Go through Puéchabon, bypass Viols-le-Fort, and continue to a junction at St-Martin-de-Londres. Turn left and follow the **D986** back into Ganges, passing the Grotte des Demoiselles on the way.

The eastern end of the Massif Central is famous for its strange and beautiful rock formations

PLACES OF INTEREST

LE VIGAN

Le Vigan is an excellent centre for touring both the Cévennes and the Causses, and is also a good place to stop, with its cafés and shady chestnut trees. The old bridge over the Arre is 13th century, and beside it, housed in an old silk mill, is the Musée Cevenol, a fine museum with a good collection of items from the history of village life in the Cévennes.

ST JEAN-DE-FOS

Close to where the route crosses the Hérault stands the Pont du Diable, an 11th-century bridge built by Guilhem's monks. The

tions known as *roches ruiniformes*. Mourèze stands in a spectacular cirque, surrounded by huge, twisted outcrops of rock. The old château emerges from the top of one great, buttressed dolomite tower in such a way that it is difficult to work out where one starts and the other finishes. The houses stand on picturesque narrow alleyways that thread their way between other outcrops, or occasionally appear from the towers. Only the village church, a much-restored 15th-century Romanesque building, seems to remain aloof from the game.

The cirque of Mourèze, covering some 240 hectares, lies to the north of the village, and should not be missed.

SAUVE

A pretty old village tumbling down the slopes of the Montagne du Coutach to the banks of the River Vidourle, overlooked by the ruins of its old château. 9km south-east of St-Hippolyte-du-Fort.

The best view of the village is from the medieval bridge over the Vidourle,

specially constructed to minimise the risk of flooding when the river is swollen. From here it is a delight to wander through the maze of narrow alleys that makes up Sauve – climbing steeply up the hill to where the oldest houses cluster beneath the château, blending into the rock on which they are built. Further down is the more spacious but equally attractive Place Jean-Astruc on the site of the cemetery of the Benedictine abbey that once stood here, and of which only a section of the cloisters survives, close to the Place de la Mairie.

---

more modern bridge offers a tremendous view of the Herault Gorge, and of the aqueduct that takes water to the local vineyards.

ST-MARTIN-DE-LONDRES
St-Martin is a delightful village with arcaded houses set around a three-sided main square. There are remains of fortified

walls dating from the 12th century, and a pleasant church, built in the 11th century by monks from nearby St-Guilhem, though much restored in the late 19th century.

GROTTE DES DEMOISELLES
The formations in this fine cave are magnificent, and the sheer size of the cave –

the main cavern, known as the Cathedral, is 120m long and almost 50m high – is little short of awesome. The visitor is transported in on a funicular

railway, which adds a touch of theatre to the visit. Many of the cave's formations have fanciful names – in the Cathedral is a stalagmite called the

Virgin and Child – but the occasional difficulties in matching the names with the reality of the shapes should not detract from their real beauty.

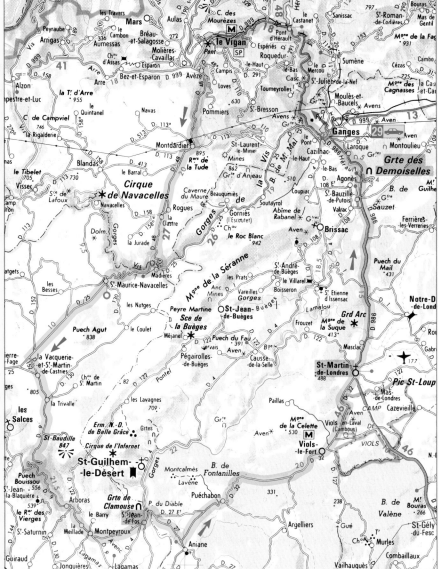

Languedoc langue d'oc

THE LANGUE D'OC

The name Languedoc recalls the medieval language of the South, the *langue d'oc*, so-called because its word for 'yes' was *oc*. North of a line roughly between Bordeaux and Geneva lay the territory of the *langue d'oïl*, whose word for 'yes' was *oïl*, later *oui*. Both languages were branches of the latinised tongue spoken after the collapse of the Roman Empire, and they developed along separate paths. Though it produced the work of the Provençal troubadours, the *langue d'oc* steadily lost prestige in the Middle Ages. The *langue d'oïl* became the official language of government, law and learning as successive kings unified France. The *langue d'oc* split into increasingly distinct dialectical forms, ranging from Gascon and Catalan to Languedocian and Provençal, but it never disappeared, and Southerners today prize it as a symbol of regional identity.

SAUVETERRE-DE-ROUERGUE

A 13th-century *bastide* with a superb central square, built to police the lawless and wild expanses of the Ségala. 42km south-east of Rodez.

The Ségala – once wild, infertile country on which only rye (*seigle*) would grow – was prey in the Middle Ages to bandits and over-powerful local lords. So it was that in 1281 Guillaume de Mâcon, governor of Rouergue, was empowered by Philippe III to build a fortified village. Sauveterre immediately became an important administrative and commercial centre, and today is remarkably well preserved. Guillaume laid out his village on the rectangular *bastide* plan, and placed at its centre a large and imposing square – lined by paved, arcaded walkways known locally as *chistats*. In the square is the communal well, and from it there branch off straight roads lined with half-timbered houses and leading to the towers and gateways of the defensive wall. The 14th-century church has some good furnishings and a fine 17th-century altarpiece.

STE-ENIMIE

One of the highlights of a visit to the Massif Central is a boat trip along the magnificent Gorges du Tarn. The most popular starting place is the picturesque and spectacularly positioned village of Ste-Énimie.

The village is beautifully positioned on both banks of the Tarn, linked by a magnificent medieval bridge. In the larger, northern part the old alleys are pure delight. The 12th-century church is much modified and contains some excellent statues from the early medieval period. Close by is the Vieux Logis, a tiny museum of local life. To the north of the museum is the lovely Place de Beurre, a delightful old square at the heart of the village. On it stands the old corn market.

Above the Place de Beurre is the Place de Plot, a large square in front of the old monastery, gutted by fire at the time of the Revolution and now partially restored. From here there are superb views, and the view downstream especially is magnificent.

STE-EULALIE-DE-CERNON

Seat of an important commandery built by the Knights Templar in the 12th century, this historic fortified village lies in the green Cernon valley on the great Causse du Larzac. 26km south-east of Millau.

Amid the aridity of the high Causse, the lush green Cernon valley is an oasis of orchards and cereal crops. In the 12th century the Knights Templar made it their headquarters, with dependencies at nearby la Cavalerie and la Couvertoirade, both well worth a visit. Their successors, the Knights Hospitaller, fortified the village in the 15th century and of those fortifications

---

SECRET PLACES

CASTELBOUC

THE CASTLE OF THE GOAT

Castelbouc lies about 8km south-east of Ste-Énimie on the D907B.

The Gorges du Tarn is one of the natural wonders of France, and many visitors who enter it drive quickly to Ste-Énimie and the spectacular narrow sections beyond. Few see, and even fewer stop, at Castelbouc, where the ruins of a medieval château overhang a tiny village. During the early Middle Ages the knight who owned the castle lived a life of extreme self-indulgence while his fellow nobles were off risking death in the Crusades. When he died during the course of yet another excess, his spirit, unable to rest in peace, was forced to roam the crags in the form of a huge billy goat. This ghastly presence scared off the château's next owners, and the place became known as the 'castle of the goat', the *castelbouc*. Later,

A haunted castle ruin with a marvellous view

The peacefulness of Ste-Eulalie's square belies the village's historical importance

Ste-Eulalie's 18th-century fountain is a popular attraction

the larger part are still intact, with fine walls, towers, gates and arches. The rest of the village, laid out around a pretty square with an old fountain, is equally interesting, with vaulted passages between rows of fine old houses.

STE-EULALIE-D'OLT

As it cuts its way between the Causse de Sévérac and the Monts d'Aubrac, the River Lot describes a series of tight meanders, on one of which cluster the steep roofs of Ste-Eulalie-d'Olt, 24km south-east of Espalion.

The village stands on the right bank of the Lot, and was at its most prosperous in the late medieval period, when it was a thriving centre for the making of woollen cloth. Most of the village houses date from that period, fine houses built of the local basalt with steep stone-tiled roofs, mostly with a little dormer window or two. A fascinating part of St-Eulalie's industrial heritage can be seen in its old mill, the only one with an overshot millwheel in the whole of the Rouergue. The village church also displays signs of local prosperity, with three naves added in the 16th century.

ST-GUILHEM-LE-DESERT

At the confluence of the Verdus and the Hérault, clustered around its Romanesque abbey, is one of the loveliest villages in France. 33km north-west of Montpellier.

The village is named after Guilhem, born in about 755 and trusted lieutenant of Charlemagne. At the end of his life, the courageous general decided to retire to this deserted valley and founded a monastery. Of the monastery founded by Guilhem only the crypt of the old church remains, the present abbey church dating from the 11th century. A fine Romanesque building, it has an interior of great simplicity and a fine vaulted roof.

The village of St-Guilhem is equally delightful, with house after house an architectural treasure. The Syndicat d'Initiative occupies a superb 16th-century house, near the Tour des Prisons, part of the former defences.

THE ROCKS OF SIDOBRE

exploiting local fear of the castle, and its impregnable position on top a 60m-high rock, a group of bandits used Castelbouc as a hideout. Eventually their terrorising of the neighbourhood became intolerable and they were forcibly evicted.

To prevent re-occupation the castle was partially destroyed. That was 400 years ago, and it has been in ruins ever since. If you are willing to risk meeting the billy goat, the view from the site is impressive.

East of Castres the D622 passes through a wonderland of huge perched boulders that stretches almost into Vialevert, and also continues on each side of the D30 north-west to Lacrouzette, and the D58 from Lacrouzette to Ricard.

Erosion of the granite rock in the area has created strangely shaped heaps of boulders that are stable, yet give the appearance of being completely unstable. In some cases the great boulders form *roches*

tremblantes: trembling rocks or logans. The most famous rocking assembly is the Rochers de Sept-Faux, to the north of the D622 about 2km west of Vialevert. This pair of boulders looks so unstable that many who visit do not dare approach them.

A fine legend is attached to the Peyro Clabado, which stands to the east of the D30, about 1.5km south-east of Lacrouzette. This extravagantly perched boulder has a flat, but angled top.

If it is visited by an engaged couple they should throw a stone on to the boulder; if it stays still, their marriage will be long and happy. If it falls off, the couple should, presumably, go home separately.

A special feature of the Parc naturel régional du Haut Languedoc.

SECRET FRANCE
THE PYRENEES

The Pyrenees form an impressive wall stretching from sea to ocean, effectively sealing north-western Europe from the sun-baked expanse of the Iberian peninsula. In France the mountain barrier falls steeply to the foothills, while the frontier crest mostly follows the watershed. There are anomalies, and the Garonne is one. The great river that becomes such an important waterway winding through the vineyards of Bordeaux is born in Spain, among glaciers draped from the highest Pyrenean summit. It then flows northward via a subterranean channel and down the Val d'Aran, a Spanish valley that really belongs geographically – although not politically – to France.

If there is one unifying factor among the many diverse villages spread across the region, it is their reliance on the land. These are villages that grew either as a direct response to the demands of an often inhospitable environment, or were sited in isolation at a time of regional or national unrest. The hill country that forms the universal backcloth is at once a protector and a threat, a source of employment and sustenance and an adversary.

From the white-walled houses of the Basque country to the soft-textured stone of Béarn, from the unfussy grey streets and rooftops of Haute Garonne to the mellow, cascading pyramids of sun-warmed houses in French Catalonia, Pyrenean villages cover a wide range of architectural styles. In religious architecture, the flowering of the Romanesque is reflected among the churches of certain tiny, little-known villages of the Cerdagne, in the eastern Pyrénées.

At the western end of the range there grew up a style of church architecture unique to the mysterious Basque country, the interiors of its churches having carved timber galleries – in places three high – and ornate ceilings hung with model sailing barques. Around them in the villages, ranks of sturdy, limewashed houses spread along a grid of streets, their exposed timbers painted rust-brown beneath the shallow-sloping roofs.

Most of the river valleys drain roughly northwards, so the traveller journeys across the grain of the land by way of sometimes narrow and demanding roads, over passes from whose viewpoints the spectacular landscape is revealed in all its dramatic detail. It is, as one traveller in an earlier century was inspired to remark, a very bumpy country.

aigle royal des Pyrénées

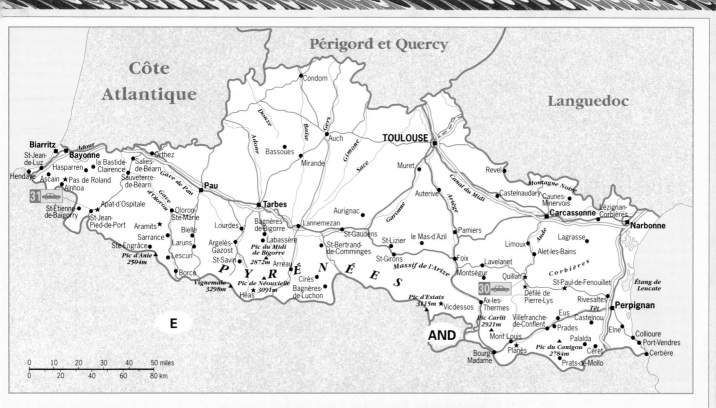

Côte
Atlantique

Périgord et Quercy

Languedoc

Condom

Douze

Adour

Baïse

Gers

Gimone

Auch

TOULOUSE

Biarritz
Adour
St-Jean-de-Luz
Bayonne
Hendaye
Hasparren
Ascain ★ Pas de Roland
Ainhoa
la Bastide-Clairence
Salies-de-Béarn
Sauveterre-de-Béarn
Orthez
Gave de Pau
Pau
Bassoues
Mirande
Sare
Muret
Revel
Montagne Noire
Castelnaudary
Caunes-Minervois
Lézignan-Corbières
St-Étienne-de-Baigorry
Apat-d'Ospitale
Oloron-Ste-Marie
Gave d'Oloron
Tarbes
Lannemezan
Auterive
Canal du Midi
Carcassonne
Narbonne
St-Jean-Pied-de-Port
Aramits ★
Bielle
Lourdes
Labassère
Aurignac
Garonne
Ariège
Pamiers
Aude
Lagrasse
Sarrance
Laruns
Argelès-Gazost
St-Savin
Pic du Midi de Bigorre 2872m
Bagnères-de-Bigorre
St-Bertrand-de-Comminges
St-Gaudens
le Mas-d'Azil
Limoux
Alet-les-Bains
Ste-Engrâce
Pic d'Anie 2504m
Lescun
Borce
Arreau
Cirès
St-Girons
St-Lizier
Foix
Lavelanet
P Y R É N É E S
Massif de l'Arize
Montségur
Corbières
St-Paul-de-Fenouillet
Étang de Leucate
Vignemale 3298m
Pic de Néouvielle 3091m
Héas
Bagnères-de-Luchon
Pic d'Estats 3115m ★
Vicdessos
Quillan
Défilé de Pierre-Lys
Rivesaltes
Tét
Perpignan
Ax-les-Thermes
Eus
Castelnou
E
Pic Carlit 2921m
Villefranche-de-Conflent
Prades
Palalda
Elne
Collioure
Port-Vendres
Cerbère
Mont Louis
Pic du Canigou 2784m ▲
Céret
AND
Bourg-Madame
Planès
Prats-de-Mollo

| 0 | 10 | 20 | 30 | 40 | 50 miles |
| 0 | 20 | 40 | 60 | 80 km |

Left, the rugged high country of the Pyrenees is lent a pleasantly domestic scale by fields and villages

Right, the great cowbells provide music to the ear, but are also highly practical tags to help find and identify beasts which stray

Far right, farming methods in remoter rural communities have changed little over the years, relying still on hard manual labour

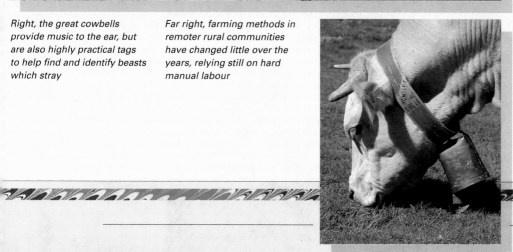

THE BASQUE PEOPLE

'Three plus four equals one'. So runs the slogan asserting the identity of a people now living on both the French and Spanish sides of the Pyrenees. In recent years the separatist claims of the terrorist group ETA and its political wing, Herri Batasuna, have again drawn attention to the curious status of the Basques. Their origins remain as much of a mystery as they were to the Roman historian, Livy, or to Esteban de Garibay, who in the 16th century tried to trace them back to the sons of Noah. The Basques do not belong to the Indo-European stock from which other folk of the European mainland spring. Hematological research reveals a disproportionately high percentage of Basques with blood group O: 55% as opposed to 40% in the rest of Spain and 43% in the rest of France. And a more immediate sign of difference is in the unique Basque language, Euzkadi.

AINHOA

Set in rolling countryside close to the Spanish border, the single broad street of whitewashed houses makes this one of the most attractive of all Basque villages. 14km south-west of Cambo-les-Bains.

Aïnhoa exemplifies the very best of rural Basque architecture. Most of the houses date from the 17th or 18th century and have traditional painted shutters and carved lintels.

Founded in the early 13th century as a stopping place for pilgrims on their way to Santiago de Compostela, Aïnhoa then came under English jurisdiction, and only returned to France in the mid-15th century.

Ravaged by fire during the Thirty Years War, the village was almost entirely rebuilt during the 17th and 18th centuries, when it became an important staging post for muleteers on the road between Pamplona and Bayonne, and prosperity returned once more.

The church, started in the 14th century, is notable for its typical Basque woodwork and galleries.

ALET-LES-BAINS

This historic and attractive thermal spa stands in a sheltered position on the right bank of the River Aude, 32km south of Carcassonne.

Entry to the village is by way of a 17th-century triple-arched bridge over the river. Just south of this stand the remains of the former 11th-century cathedral of Notre-Dame, which was partly destroyed by the Huguenots in 1577. Alet was already known for its waters in Gallo-Roman times; but it was the founding of the great abbey here in the 7th century that gave impetus to the settlement seen today.

The heart of the village is the Place de la République, with its arcaded Renaissance and classical buildings surrounding the square, and radiating from it narrow alleys with cantilevered upper storeys, their brown timbers against cream-coloured plaster showing their great age. A large portion of the ramparts that formerly enclosed the village remain intact, as do the old gateways.

ARREAU

The Neste d'Aure and Neste du Louron converge within the limits of this former capital of the Pays de Quatre Vallées, so that everywhere in the village is the constant sound of rushing water. 12km north of St-Lary-Soulan.

Strategically placed between the Col d'Aspin and the Col de Peyresourde, Arreau is a small market town that has prospered through lying on a main trading route with Spain. The covered wooden market hall on the left bank of the Louron stands

---

SECRET PLACES

HEAS

CHAPEL OF NOTRE-DAME

Héas lies east of Gavarnie, but must be approached via Gèdre.

In 1915 an avalanche devastated this tiny village, which sits beneath a steep wall of mountains in view of the Cirque de Troumouse. It consists of only a handful of houses and a pilgrimage chapel,

Notre-Dame de Héas, which was destroyed by the avalanche and subsequently rebuilt.

The chapel's simple but beautiful interior is lit by stained-glass windows added in the 1930s, depicting pastoral scenes of the mountains. One tells

the tale of the stonemasons who built the chapel. Every day, three goats and their kids came down from the mountains to provide the builders with milk. However, the masons decided that they would prefer goat meat to milk, and planned to

opposite the handsome 16th-century Maison des Lys, whose exposed timbers are adorned with numerous fleurs-de-lis. Backing the river, a row of old houses partially overhang the water, while on the right bank the 13th-century chapel of St-Exupère has an octagonal tower, an imposing Romanesque doorway and, inside the porch, a wooden corn bin formerly used to collect tithes.

ASCAIN

This prosperous village, with many well-maintained Basque houses, stands amid rich farmland in the valley of the Nivelle. 6km south of St-Jean-de-Luz.

The focal point of Ascain is the massive church, built in the 13th century and enlarged in the 17th. The interior bears all the hallmarks of a classic Basque place of worship. In the churchyard a number of traditional Basque discoidal gravestones are to be seen, some dating from the 17th century. Next to the church is perhaps the finest *fronton*, or *pelota* court, in all the Basque country, and this in turn is overlooked by other traditional Basque buildings and the 17th-century Mairie. During the 17th century a number of alleged witches and wizards, including the village priest were put to death in the square. While staying in the Hôtel de la Rhune near by, Pierre Loti wrote much of his novel *Ramuntcho*. Below the village an attractive bridge over the river is claimed to be of Roman origin.

AURIGNAC

This hilltop village bordering the Pyrenean foothills is celebrated for its prehistoric remains, which have given their name to the Aurignacian era, dating from 30,000

The old houses of Aurignac cluster on a hilltop, overlooked by the ruined keep and fine church

to 20,000 years ago. 25km northeast of St-Gaudens.

Houses of sand-coloured stone roofed in orange pantiles cluster round this low hill, topped by a ruined keep whose winding stairway reveals extensive views over the Pyrenees. The doorway to the church is notable for its four twisted pillars, which come from another church demolished during the Revolution. It is reached through a fortified gateway beneath the 16th-century bell-tower.

The village streets contain some fine Renaissance and medieval houses, notably in the Rue des Nobles. The Musée de la Préhistoire chronicles the remarkable story of the 19th-century discovery of Aurignac's famous cave shelter. The shelter itself lies on the outskirts of the village, towards Boulogne.

---

butcher one of the kids on their next visit. But the story continues that the goats disappeared, and were never seen again.

Several treasures from the original chapel were salvaged after the avalanche, including an 18th-century processional cross, a 17th-century clock, and a highly valued statue of Notre-Dame-de-Héas, which stands in the choir.

A tale of three wise goats, told in the stained glass of a chapel window

ARAMITS

THE DUMAS CONNECTION

Aramits lies south-west of Oloron-Ste-Marie.

The village of Aramits, one-time capital of the Barétous, found fame by way of Alexandre Dumas's great novel, *The Three Musketeers*. Henri d'Aramits (Aramis), who was lay abbot of the village, went to Paris to fight for Louis XIII. The character of Porthos was supposedly based on Isaac de Portau of Pau, while there are two Gascon villages named Athos and Artagnan, from which the remaining musketeers took their names.

BASSOUES

A 13th-century *bastide* in Armagnac country, Bassoues has kept its distinctive layout and arcaded houses, as well as its celebrated keep. 35km south-west of Auch.

The *bastide* at Bassoues was founded in 1279 by the Archbishop of Auch, but the village's history goes back beyond that, as testified by the 11th-century basilica of St-Fris, built by Benedictine monks and enlarged in 1520 by a later Archbishop of Auch.

The *bastide*, with its characteristic central square surrounded by half-timbered arcaded houses, is dominated by a massive butressed and machicolated keep, some 40m high. Beneath it lies the impressive remains of the former castle of the Archbishops of Auch. From here the straight main street leads to Bassoues' remarkable old market hall, which straddles this central highway.

LA BASTIDE-CLAIRENCE

A *bastide* built early in the 14th century to protect the north-western boundary of the kingdom

Traditional half-timbered Basque houses in la Bastide-Clairence retain many of their original features

of Navarre. 23km south-east of Bayonne.

The original plans on which the construction of the village were based in 1314 are preserved by the local authorities and are on public display. From these, one can recognise original features that have altered little, and sometimes not at all, over the passage of nearly 700 years.

Exploration is best begun in the centre, in the generous space of the square, lined with arcaded buildings that offer welcome shade on hot summer afternoons. Leading from it is the short Rue Jésus, whose houses have cantilevered upper storeys. This in turn leads into Rue St-Jean and Rue Passenillou, both with fine Basque houses. More Basque houses with red cross-timbers line Rue Notre-Dame, linking the square with the church. With its triple galleries, stone carvings, massive doorway and simple cloisters, the church is rather fine and typically Basque.

BIELLE

A number of 15th-and 16th-century houses, sturdy and simple, provide the essential character of this typical Béarnaise village, which sits below the Col de Marie-Blanque in the Ossau valley, 30km south of Pau.

Descending into Bielle, one's first impression is of a blending of grey slate rooftops, like a neat spread of playing cards in the valley below. Upon closer inspection this former capital of the valley and ancient Gallo-Roman settlement reveals its age, for its houses are pleasantly weathered by time and its streets show few concessions to the 20th century. The 500-year-old church, standing quietly away from the main road, is noted for its Flamboyant Gothic porch. At the entrance to the choir are six blue marble pillars, said to be from a Roman villa.

The 18th-century château on the left bank of the river contains some fine panelled rooms.

BORCE

Perched above the Aspe valley on a natural hillside shelf, this small medieval village comprises a number of stout-walled, unpretentious houses. 20km north of the Col du Somport.

If it were not for the fact that the GR10 trans-Pyrenean footpath passes through it, following the route of an ancient Roman road, Borce would remain little-visited. It lies off the beaten track, and is all the more charming for that, but in the Middle Ages it was an important stronghold by virtue of its strategic position. The single main street is lined with stone-built houses, many of which date from the period of Borce's heyday in the 15th or 16th century and have Gothic doors, mullioned windows and flowers at their window grilles. There is a fine church towards the southern end, and a single restaurant near by. For walkers there is a *gîte d'étape*, and a campsite lies just to the south. There are sweeping views over the Pyrenees of Béarn from the village.

CASTELNOU

This feudal complex of 10th-century castle and fortified village clustered beneath is a vision of timeless beauty. 16km south-west of Perpignan.

Outside the village's protective walls stands the church, with a spring near by and watchtower guarding a neigh-

bouring hillock. The village is entered through a fortified gateway, inside which a steep twist of narrow alleys, paved with cobbles or stepped with flagstones, leads unerringly to the feudal castle that has for so many centuries given Castlenou its reason for existence. It was built about 1,000 years ago by Bernard, Comte de Besalu, in the shadow of the Rocher de Majorque, but it was the looming presence of the rock that was to bring about its downfall in 1559, when a battery of artillery was taken on to the rock by a band of brigands, and the ensuing two days of cannon-fire destroyed much of the original fortress. It has since been partially restored, and from its battlements there is a magnificent view to the towering Pic du Canigou.

CAUNES-MINERVOIS

A historic fortified settlement of cream-coloured stone with a splendid abbey, this pretty village lies among the southern slopes of the Minervois. 20km north-east of Carcassonne.

Rising from the valley of the Argent-Double in the midst of wine-growing country, this former walled village of stout stone houses, founded in the 8th century, is a maze of charming streets

and cobbled alleyways. It is dominated by the buildings of the former abbey, in particular the church, with its Romanesque portal and pillared semi-circular apse flanked by square towers of conflicting styles. All around are fine examples of local medieval and Renaissance architecture. There are also numerous reminders of the ancient fortifications destroyed at the end of

the 16th century. Many of the old buildings include in their facings and details some of the celebrated pink marble from the local quarries, used in the building of the Paris Opéra and the Trianon Palace at Versailles.

The once-important mountain stronghold of Borce has many fine old houses dating back to the 15th and 16th centuries

SECRET PLACES

DEFILE DE PIERRE-LYS

The dramatic Défile de Pierre-Lys is reached by following the D117 south from Quillan (see Tour 31, below).

The defile, or gorge, of Pierre-Lys, is a dramatic gateway to the mountains of the eastern Pyrenees. A series of gorges carved out by the River Aude, some of whose walls overhang the narrow, twisting road, lead into the mountains, of which Pierre-Lys is the northernmost.

At the entrance, the road cuts through a tunnel known as the Trou du Curé, or Priest's Hole, in honour of Félix Armand, an 18th-century parish priest at St-Martin-Lys, the little hamlet at the bottom of the gorge. Armand is credited with being the driving-force behind this tunnel, which was cut out by hand to create a mule-track through the defile. Impressed by the work, Napolean declared it was 'a pity the man should be a priest'.

A remarkable tunnel, bored by hand, stands as a memorial to its creator

TOUR 30 – 195KM

IN THE SHADOW OF THE CANIGOU

Deep gorges scour the countryside south of Quillan, but climbing through them one emerges, first to the high Capcir, then into the broad sun-trap of the Cerdagne. Eastwards lies the Conflent, the valley of the Têt, which opens at Prades into a rich agricultural basin overlooked by the greatest Catalan mountain, Pic du Canigou. Nearby are the beautiful old abbeys of St-Michel-de-Cuxa and St-Martin-du-Canigou. The tour returns across the rolling Fenouillèdes district.

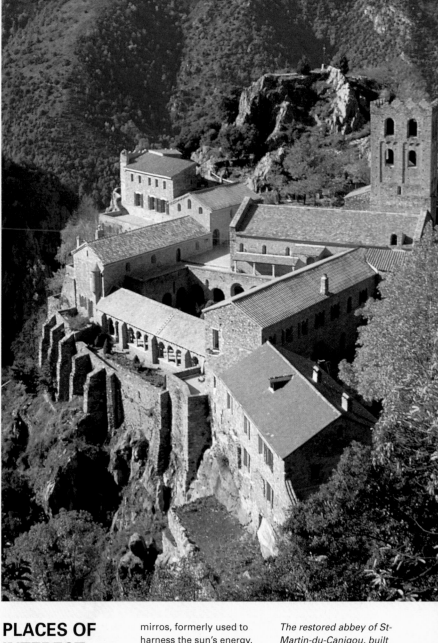

ROUTE DIRECTIONS

Sheep grazing and enjoying the sun in a mountain glade

Take the Perpignan road heading south from Quillan (the **D117**) and after 3km enter the Défilé de Pierre-Lys (see page 219). In 8km bear right on to the **D118** at a round-about, pass through Axat and the Gorges de l'Aude and come to Usson les Bains (19km). Cross the river to the left and continue on the **D118** through Carcanières-les-Bains and Escouloubre-les-Bains to the high open valley of Capcir.

Drive through Formiguères, past Lac de Matemale rising to Col de la Quillanne (1714m) and down to Mont-Louis (57km from Axat).

Leave Mont-Louis on the **N116** in the direction of Perpignan and Prades. Descend into the valley of the Têt and in 30km reach Villefranche-de-Conflent.

Turn right on the **D116** towards Vernet-les-Bains, passing the Grottes des Canalettes on the right. In 3km bear left into Corneilla-de-Conflent.

Continue along a narrow winding road to Fillols (4km). Turn left at a T-junction, and follow the **D27** north, passing St-Michel-de Cuxa on the right, and come to Prades (13km). Follow signs for Perpignan and at a round-about take the road for Molitg-les-Bains. Beyond Catllar the road climbs; in 1km bear right where it forks, towards Sournia, and wind up and over Col de Roque-Jalère (976m).

In Sournia (23km from Prades) turn right at a junction and shortly after, at the top of the village, bear right again, in the direction of Pézilla-de-Conflent.

Continue to Ansignan (14km), bear left and in 9km come to St-Paul-de-Fenouillet. Turn left and follow the **D117** west-wards. To visit the château of Puilaurens, turn left in Lapradelle and follow a winding road into the village of Puilaurens.

Return to the **D117** and follow it back to Quillan.

PLACES OF INTEREST

MONT-LOUIS
Vauban created this fortified village for Louis XIV following the Treaty of the Pyrenees (1659), and the streets, lined with solid-looking houses, still seem ready to repel all-comers, although the moat has become overgrown and its harshness is softened by trees. The citadel now houses a commando training centre, and there is a strange incongruity in the presence near by of large solar mirros, formerly used to harness the sun's energy.

From Mont-Louis fine views are to be had across the Cerdagne to the rolling Cambras d'Aze.

VILLEFRANCHE-DE-CONFLENT
See page 229.

GROTTES DES CANALETTES
These extensive limestone caves, whose entrance is through 160m of passage-way hollowed out by streams some 395 million years ago, were only discovered in 1951.

Impressive chambers

The restored abbey of St-Martin-du-Canigou, built on top of a tower of rock at an altitude of over 1,000 metres, dates back to the 11th century

are adorned with stalactites, stalagmites, ceiling fins and massive pillars like huge overflowing candles, their beautiful colours, shapes and textures picked out now by electric lights.

ST-MICHEL-DE CUXA
A succession of churches was built on this site over the years, the last having been consecrated in AD974.

The sight of its lofty bell-tower rising above the orchards is certainly an encouragement to stop for closer inspection. Sadly, however, much of the majesty of the abbey was destroyed during the Revolution, although the revitalised cloisters are worthy of study and are notable for their lion carvings. The abbey now houses a religious community, and a music festival, started by Pablo Casals, holds several concerts there each summer.

ANSIGNAN

Below this small village in the northern Fenouillèdes, a long, low, multi-arched aqueduct carries water across the valley of the Agly to irrigate vineyards. Some say it was of Roman construction, while others claim that it dates from the 13th century.

PUILAURENS

On its exposed, lofty crest of rock, the ruined Château de Puilaurens was another of the seemingly impregnable castles sacked by the anti-Cathar crusaders in the 13th century. The original fortress was enlarged and given ramparts in the 12th century, and there are some well-preserved remains, including sturdy towers, battlements and sections of outer wall.

CIRES

A small but picturesque village in a pastoral setting, with its houses rising in a distinctive pyramid shape to the church, which stands alone on its rocky pinnacle. 14km north-west of Bagnères-de-Luchon.

Like other villages in the valley, Cirès owes its existence to farming, and among the houses and barns that line the narrow alleys or precipitous streets one can sense a dependence on the land that has barely changed over the centuries. This, together with the 'lost world' atmosphere of the village, creates an appealing contrast with the sophistication of nearby Bagnères-de-Luchon. The steep climb to the church may be a struggle, but the views down over the cascade of houses and the valley spread below, are ample reward. The church itself has a square bell-tower with a slate-clad steeple, and a tympanum carved with three figures in naïve style.

COLLIOURE

Sometimes called 'the jewel of the Côte Vermeille', this attractive fishing port, artists' colony and popular seaside resort is situated 6km south of Argelès-sur-Mer.

It was the rich light of the Mediterranean that from 1910 brought an invasion of artists known as the *Fauves* (wild beasts) – Braque, Matisse and Picasso among them – and whole generations of painters have flocked here ever since.

There is a fine bay for bathing, and the tiny harbour is a delight. On one side it is protected by the 17th-century fortified church of Notre-Dame-des-Anges, whose bell-tower is the former lighthouse; on the other by the Château Royal, an imposing fortress dating from the 12th century but improved by the ubiquitous Vauban 500 years later. The old streets that used to cluster at the foot of the château were demolished by Vauban in order to make way for another belt of fortifications.

Behind the harbour rises the surviving old quarter of the Mouré, a charming maze of narrow shaded alleys lined with shops and cafés, the galleried houses used now as artists' studios.

EUS

Bathed in sunlight, the stone houses of the village clutch the hillside in layers, commanding a magnificent view across the valley from the Têt to the Canigou. Eus lies 4km north-east of Prades.

Rising in terraces from the rich husbandry of the Prades basin, Eus has long been famed for its situation. Originally, in the 9th century, it occupied a site in the valley itself, only moving on to the hillside in the 17th century. Now its carefully restored houses, all positioned to face the sun and the Canigou, are decked with flowers.

Cobbled alleyways wind steeply through the village, and tunnels and archways provide access from one part of it to the next. The hill from which Eus hangs is crowned with a fortified 17th-century church, built within the walls of the castle that used to defend the village from attacks by the Spanish and the French alike.

LABASSERE

A remote crest-top settlement dominated by the keep of a long-vanished castle, the village forms a protective western outrider to the spa town of Bagnères-de-Bigorre, 6km to the east.

For several decades in the late 18th and early 19th centuries, Jacques Pédefer (1756-1854) was *curé* of Labassère. Among this remarkable man's achievements was the discovery in October 1800 of the source of sulphur springs – now known as the Fontaine de Labassère – at the head of the nearby Ossouet valley. A bust of *curé* Pédefer, with a suitable inscription beneath, adorns the village square. His tall, grey church stands near by, its slender spire competing with the ruin of Labassère's old keep, topping a natural rocky knoll close by. From it

The rich light and colours of the old port of Collioure have drawn generations of artists

there is a view of a wide range of countryside: deep folding valleys walled by green ridge crests, and the substantial basin in which Bagnères-de-Bigorre has so liberally spread itself.

LAGRASSE

Standing on the banks of the Orbieu, this historic village boasts impressive defences and is celebrated for the remains of its magnificent abbey. 35km south-east of Carcassonne.

A lovely humpback 11th-century bridge links the old streets of Lagrasse with its abbey, founded in the 8th century and then an important cultural

---

SECRET PLACES

ST-PAUL-DE-FENOUILLET

GORGES DE GALAMUS

St-Paul-de-Fenouillet lies west of Perpignan. To reach the gorge, take the D7 north from St-Paul.

Situated on the southern edge of the Corbières district, the astonishing limestone cleft of the Gorges de Galamus presents one of the most remarkable natural sites of the eastern Pyrenees. The River Agly has carved out a deep but narrow slice through the ridge of mountains; the cliffs are

vertical or overhanging for much of the way, and the road has been engineered to provide a dramatic drive. Deep within the gorge stands the hermitage of St-Antoine de Galamus, reached by a stairway and twisting path.

The drive through a dramatic gorge leads to an isolated hermit's cell

outpost of Charlemagne's empire. The earliest surviving part is the 11th-century Romanesque transept of the otherwise 13th-century church. The monks' dormitory and the abbot's chapel also date from this time, and the imposing bell-tower and keep that still dominates the village was added in the 16th century. The ancient cloister was rebuilt in the 18th century.

The village itself contains a wealth of fine old stone and half-timbered houses, a Gothic church, an old covered market hall and the Tour de Plaisance, a survivor of the fortifications that once ringed Lagrasse. Its setting, in the beautiful Orbieu valley at the foot of the Corbières, surrounded by vine-yards, olive trees and forest, is superb.

LESCUN

On the edge of the Parc National des Pyrénées, this slate-roofed medieval village is dwarfed by one of the finest mountain panoramas in the whole of France. 32km south of Oloron-Ste-Marie.

A single historical event records the name of Lescun. On 6 September 1794, 1,000 peasants and volunteer militiamen confronted 6,000 Spanish troops in the Battle of Lescun, forcing the invaders to retreat. Apart from that one occasion, this otherwise peaceful, pastoral village owes its distinction to the magnificent cirque of mountains that makes such an enchanting backdrop.

Lescun's situation is everything. Snug amid sloping pastures high above the left bank of the Aspe valley, this Béarnais village of dark pitched roofs and unadorned grey walls clustered on a sunny shelf of hillside, with a few medieval houses, an old château, hay-barns and cattle byres, has made few concessions to tourism.

From the village itself there is an unparalleled view of the Cirque de Lescun. Rising above the village to the west are the twin Pics du Billare, while to the right of them is Pic d'Anie.

LE MAS-D'AZIL

A 13th-century *bastide* built around its Benedictine abbey, this village on the Arize is celebrated for the huge natural cave near by. 23km north-east of St-Girons.

On the approach to the village from the south along the D119, both the road and the River Arize are suddenly swallowed by a vast natural cavern, 65m high at its entrance and over 400m long. Inside, it is easy to see why it has been used as a refuge over countless centuries. In the 19th century they yielded abundant evidence of habitation in prehistoric times.

In the attractive village itself, the church of St-Etienne, surprisingly bare inside and firmly Protestant, is all that remains of the Benedictine abbey around which the *bastide* was founded in the 13th century.

PELOTA

Pelota (*pelote* in French and *pilota* in Basque) is to the Pays Basque what *boules* is to Provence: a local game likely to catch though perhaps to puzzle the visitor's eye. However, unlike *boules*, pelota does not tempt the unskilled and unathletic to join in. Like fives, squash and tennis, it is a court game played hard and fast. In one or other of its many variants, players strike a rubber-cored ball with hand, glove, racket, bat or, most distinctively, the *chistera*. This is a narrow, curved basket of the sort traditionally used for picking fruit and vegetables, adapted as an extension of the player's hand. *Rebot* is five-a-side pelota played against the wall of an open court. The walls in the main squares of many towns and villages still lend themselves to this purpose. *Grand chistera* is a popular form of *rebot*, with three players on each side. *Cesta punta* is a doubles game played in an open three-walled court called a *jaï-alaï* in Basque and a *fronton* in French. *Pasaka* uses an indoor court whose design suggests that pelota may have had its origins in 'real tennis'.

MONTSEGUR

One of the most historic and atmospheric sites on the edge of the Pyrenees, the seemingly impregnable ruined castle stands on the spot that was witness to the last terrible drama of the Cathars. 33km south-east of Foix.

In 1244, at the end of a 10-month siege by Catholic forces, over 200 Cathars climbed down from the fortress, and were burned on a communal pyre rather than surrender their faith. The present village, consists of a series of parallel terraces set steeply below the *pog* on which the fortress stands, most of the houses having been built in the 17th or 18th centuries. In the village is a museum devoted to the castle's history, and set into a wall of one of the houses is a decorated stone, said to have been brought down from it.

The ruins that crown the ridge above are the remains of a fortress built later in the 13th century to replace the Cathar stronghold. They are reached by a steep climb from a car park below the Col de Montségur, passing first through the meadow known as the Prats dels Cramats, where the Cathars were burned.

Vineyards spread out below the ancient Catalan village of Palalda

PALALDA

A lovely Catalan village consisting of a pair of ruined towers, a Roman-esque church and a cascade of orange-tiled roofs above colour-washed walls on the banks of the Tech, 3km north of Amélie-les-Bains.

Known as Palatinum Dani to the Romans, who discovered sulphur springs at the junction of the Mondony and Tech, Palalda is a historic Catalan village which enjoys a generous climate. At the top of the hill rise two round towers, all that remain of the 13th-century castle in which Charles V once lived. They are now incorporated into the Mairie. The 10th-century church, which has a door whose iron-work, according to legend, was fashioned from the shoes of Saracen horses brought back from the Holy Land, abuts one of them. Across the courtyard are the Musée de la Poste en Roussillon and the fascinating Musée des Traditions et Arts Populaires, which has displays of local crafts, as well as histori-cally furnished rooms.

PRATS-DE-MOLLO

This sturdy, handsome mountain village, close by the frontier with Spain and with an Iberian atmosphere, was fortified by Vauban. 23km south-west of Amélie-les-Bains.

Standing on the left bank of the Tech, most of Prats is enclosed within the security of its turreted ramparts: Vauban's

VICDESSOS

DOLMEN DE SEM

Vicdessos lies close to the head of the Vicdessos valley, south of Foix. The dolmen is signposted from a side road that breaks away from the western entrance to Vicdessos.

Prehistory haunts the Ariège where, down the valley from Vicdessos, the fabulous painted cave of Niaux is among the most remarkable sites to be found anywhere in Europe.

But above Vicdessos evidence of prehistoric life is shown in a very differ-ent form. The Dolmen de Sem, dating from around 5000BC, is a huge, balanced rock perched on an elevat-ed spur high above the valley. Although not as uniquely stunning as the painted caves, the wonder that prehistoric man could have raised such a mon-strous block, measuring about 4m long and 1.5m high, on a pair of smaller blocks on an exposed site 300m above the valley, is in itself a wonderful achievement.

The nearby village of Goulier, which lies to the south-west of the Dolmen de Sem, consists of a very long street lined with time-battered houses. Superb mountain panora-mas are to be enjoyed from the village entrance.

A region rich in prehistoric sites offers spectacular cave paintings and a mysterious dolmen

impressive fortifications, the lovely streets of the Catalan village within them and the mountain setting combine to give Prats its unique charm. The Porte de France, with its 17th-century Gothic church, gives access to the Ville Basse. Above looms Vauban's Fort Lagarde, built on a rocky outcrop at the end of the 17th century and containing the remains of a medieval castle. Numerous steps lead up from the Ville Basse to the Ville Haute, whose ancient streets rise parallel to the river with linking passageways; here the visitor leaves behind the austere atmosphere of the military fortress and enters the picturesque tumble of a Catalan mountain village.

SARRANCE

A fine monastery, a granite statue of Notre-Dame-de-Sarrance and a half-hidden calvary suggest the religious significance of this small village, 18km south of Oloron-Ste-Marie.

The typically Béarnais houses in Sarrance, dating mostly from the 17th century, lead in two parallel streets, one above the other, to the focal point: the church. Rebuilt in the 17th century, it has an elegant baroque octagonal bell-tower, and inside is the statue of the Virgin whose discovery led to Sarrance becoming a place of pilgrimage from the 14th century onwards. A church was built, followed by an abbey, and kings and noblemen came to pay homage.

A typical but hard form of local transport in mountain country

The Premonstratensian monastery buildings stand next to the church, and together they form two sides of the village square. During the religious strife of the 17th century, most of the village was burned to the ground, only to be rebuilt later in the century. The remarkable two-tier cloister of the monastery dates from this time.

Inevitably, since Sarrance is on the frontier of the Basque country, there is a *fronton* near by. From it a footpath climbs to the tree-shrouded calvary from which there are good views over the village and across the valley.

SAUVETERRE-DE-BEARN

A handsome and historic fortified village, beautifully positioned on an escarpment overlooking the Gave d'Oloron, with many buildings of interest. 40km north-west of Oloron-Ste-Marie.

One arch and a 12th-century gateway are all that remain of the Pont de la Légende, from where there is a lovely view up a steep slope to the village ramparts, its great keep and the massive church.

Fought over for centuries by the French, Spanish and Basques, Sauveterre had become a place of great strategic importance by the late 14th century. Of the great Château de Montréal, only the keep remains, overshadowed by the imposing bell-tower and keep of the 12th-century church of St-André. Started in the Romanesque style before the Crusades, it was finished afterwards in Gothic style, then rebuilt and subsequently ruined before being restored in the 19th century.

Colourful streets lead to the square dominated by the church, which stands against the escarpment edge and appears to form part of the village defences. Part of the medieval fortifications survive, including two gateways. Sections of the curtain wall of the Tour Montréal guard a corner of the square.

PAS DE ROLAND

A location linked with the legendary French hero-knight Roland

The pass lies south of Cambo-les-Bains, on a minor road, the D349, leading from Itxassou to Bidarray.

Nephew of the great Charlemagne, the paladin Roland is remembered in various legends throughout the Pyrenees, not least in the medieval epic Chanson de Roland, which recounts his adventures against the Saracens. The Pas de Roland is the curious site of one of these legends.

Below the narrow road that winds through a defile carved by the River Nive south of Itxassou, stands a large upright boulder with a man-sized hole in it. According to legend, Roland was fleeing the Vascons when his horse's hoof pierced the rock in flight.

TOUR 31 – 115KM
ST-JEAN-PIED-DE-PORT AND THE BASQUE HILLS

The heart of the Basque country beats with the pulse of mountain streams, and few are more insistent and powerful than the River Nive, whose valley flows between St-Jean-Pied-de-Port and Cambo-les-Bains. South of it, wooded hills grow in stature towards the Spanish frontier, and in the triangle of land to the north, green uplands form a last pretence of wilderness before folding into gentle pastures bright with villages and farms. Several long stretches of road on this tour are narrow, hilly and winding and demand steady concentration, but it's a fine circuit with a variety of landscapes.

Below, a walk along the old town walls of St-Jean is a good way to explore the town
Right, a typical Basque farmhouse

ROUTE DIRECTIONS

Leave St-Jean-Pied-de-Port on the **D933** in the direction St-Palais. After 1km turn left on to a minor road, **D22**, towards Jaxu. Bear left in Jaxu, rising to the crest of a hill.

Descending, come to a T-junction and head left, signposted Irissarry and Hasparren. After a few bends turn right on a narrow, unmarked road near a barn, soon descending

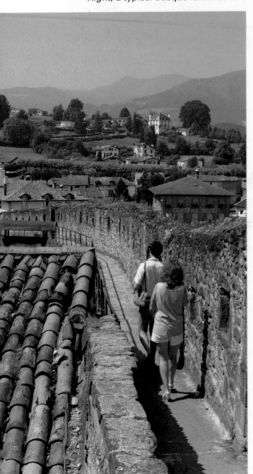

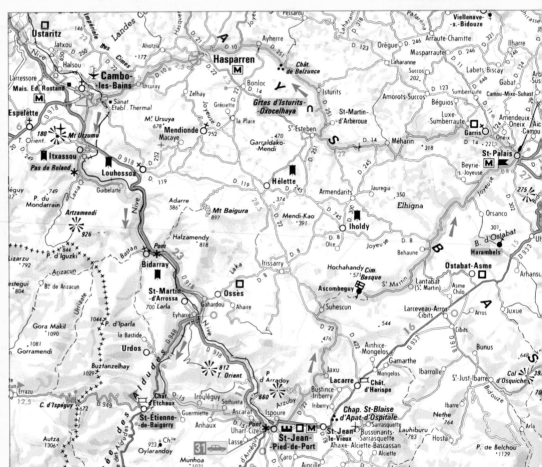

ST-BERTRAND-DE-COMMINGES

The great buttressed cathedral seems to overwhelm this fortified village, clustered below and encircled by protective ramparts. 9km south of Montréjeau.

Lugdunum Convenarum was a substantial Roman town of 50,000 inhabitants in the fertile valley of the Garonne, to which four years after the Crucifixion,

Herod Antipas and his wife Herodias were reputedly exiled by the Emperor Caligula. In the 4th or 5th centuries the town was virtually destroyed, while in the 6th century a combination of civil strife and plague more or less finished it completely. A few houses remained, but it was not until about 1120 that Bertrand de l'Isle-Jourdain, Bishop of Comminges, began work on a small cathedral on the beautiful hilltop site of the former town. The building that stands today, though enlarged and

greatly adorned under successive bishops, is a testament to the power of Bertrand's vision. The great west façade and portal are Romanesque in style, and the rest of this extraordinary building is Gothic. Perhaps the loveliest feature of the cathedral is the delicate 11th-and12th-century cloister, overlooking the peaceful meadows of the valley and the nearby hills.

Although it inevitably exists in the cathedral's shadow, the village has unquestionable charm and attraction of steeply to Suhescun.

At a three-way junction turn sharp right and take the track to Ascombeguy and the Col des Palombières (337m). Beyond the col descend steeply to St-Martin. At the next T-junction head left for about 11km to St-Palais. Turn left on the **D11** and 2km later fork left into Garris.

Continue on the **D14** for a little over 15km through Méharin, to take a right turn on a minor road (**D251**) to St-Martin-d'Arberoue and the Grottes d'Isturits-Oxocelhaya.

Leave the Grottes d'Isturits-Oxocelhaya on the **D251** towards Hasparren, passing through Isturits and Ayherre. Go straight ahead at cross-roads, following directions for Cambo-les-Bains. The **D22** (later the **D10**) leads for 10km into Cambo-les-Bains.

From the centre of town follow signs for St-Jean-Pied-de-Port. At a major road junction turn left on to the **D918**. In 3.5km pass a road on the right (signposted to Itxassou), and take the second road on the right after this. At a minor road junction by a convalescent home (La Nive), turn sharp right (signposted to the Pas de Roland) and at the next minor crossroads bear left. The road is narrow here and requires care. Follow the river to the edge of Bidarray.

Over the River Bastan turn left, and soon after left again to cross a bridge over the River Nive. Rejoin the **D918**, turn right and in 6km come to Osses.

Just beyond the village fork right and take the **D948** to St Etienne-de-Baïgorry.

On the northern outskirts of St-Etienne turn on to the **D15** and follow it back to St-Jean-Pied-de-Port.

PLACES OF INTEREST

ST-JEAN-PIED-DE-PORT
St-Jean is a handsome town situated below the pass of Roncevaux, which during the Middle Ages was crossed by millions of pilgrims on their way to the tomb of St James in Santiago de Compostela. St-Jean was a major regrouping centre, and today the scallop shell emblem of this pilgrimage is seen in various parts of the town. The pilgrims' route may be traced from the Porte St-Jacques to the Porte d'Espagne. Above the town is Vauban's citadel dating from the 17th century.

HARAMBELS
About 10km south of St-Palais, reached by way of a farm road off the D933, stands the 12th century Chapelle St-Nicolas, next to a farmhouse in a beautiful pastoral landscape. Once a pilgrims' chapel on the route to the Spanish shrine of St James in Santiago de Compostela, it has a Romanesque porch, curious bell-tower and a 15th century wooden altarpiece. In the small graveyard stand several discoidal tombstones.

St-Etienne-de-Baigorry has many fine houses

GROTTES D'ISTURITS AND OXOCELHAYA
Before about 8000BC Isturits and Oxocelhaya, one cave above the other, were continuously occupied by prehistoric people for thousands of years, during the palaeolithic period. The upper cave contains a remarkable reindeer carved in stone, while the chambers of Oxocelhaya, some 15m below, are decorated with stalactites, stalagmites and petrified cascades. Finds from the cave are displayed at the entrance.

CAMBO-LES-BAINS
Cambo comes in two parts: Bas Cambo, the old Basque village in the valley, and les-Bains, the spa town on a hill among trees overlooking the Nive. Cambo-les-Bains is a pleasant shady resort of hotels and villas, the finest of them all being Villa Arnaga, built by Edmond Rostand, author of *Cyrano de Bergerac*, who lived in Cambo from 1900 to 1918. Arnaga is now a Rostand museum open to the public. The gardens, with their ornamental pools and fountains, are justifiably famous.

ITXASSOU
Noted for its cherry trees, Itxassou is an old village with typical Basque features such as the *fronton*, against which *pelota* is played, and a church with triple galleries. In the graveyard, a collection of discoid tombstones is lined against the wall. From the village there are beautiful views along the valley of the Nive.

PAS DE ROLAND
See page 225.

ST-ETIENNE-DE-BAIGORRY
See page 228.

its own, with some exceptionally fine 15th-and-16th-century houses.

There are other places to see close by. Below St-Bertrand, 2km to the north-east, is the beautiful little Romanesque Valcabrère, along with excavations of the original Roman town. Two kilometres to the east of the village is the Romanesque masterpiece of St-Just, and 6km to the north-west are the prehistoric Grottes de Gargas with their mysterious rock paintings and engravings.

STE-ENGRÂCE

A simple shepherds' village with a notable 11th-century church, near the entrance to the remarkable Gorges de Kakouetta. 20km south of Tardets-Sorholus.

The valley of the Uhaitxa river drains limestone hills that have been scoured into deep gorges, their pastures and wooded slopes dotted with hay-barns and small farms. Deep within

this pastoral landscape lies Ste-Engrâce, once a place of pilgrimage and now sought out by walkers, for whom there is a *gîte d'étape* near the church. The imposing church is one of the few Romanesque buildings in the Basque country to have survived the centuries virtually unscathed. Inside, the triple nave leads to three semicircular apses supported by massive pillars.

The village itself consists of scattered farmhouses, thick-walled, whitewashed and with steeply sloping slate roofs.

St-Etienne-de-Baigorry

A picturesque humpback bridge spans the Nive des Aldudes to link the two parts of this typical Basque village, 11km west of St-Jean-Pied-de-Port.

With the delightful Vallée des Aldudes spreading to the south, St-Etienne is a long, straggling village divided by meadows. It has a number of fine, typically Basque and well-

The two parts of St-Etienne-de-Baigorry are linked by an ancient humpback bridge across the River Nive des Aldudes

restored 18th-century houses, some with lintel carvings or handsome doors, and a lovely tree-lined central square. Below the château (a rarity in these parts), across the cobbled 17th-century bridge with its Roman foundations, the Etchaux forge was built in the 18th century to manufacture cannon. The church of St-Etienne, rebuilt in the 18th century on

Romanesque foundations, has three typical Basque wooden galleries, as well as three fine retables.

Up the valley, the high pastureland of the Pays Quint is a Pyrenean anomaly, where French farmers graze their animals on Spanish soil. Down the valley, the vineyards of Irouléguy produce a well-known Basque wine.

St-Lizier

On a hilltop overlooking the Salat river two cathedrals, a 17th-century bishop's palace and the walls that encircle it proclaim the former stature of this little town, 2km north of St-Girons.

On this lovely site overlooking the River Salat and facing the Pyrenees, the Romans built the ramparts of St-Lizier some 1,700 years ago. Sections of wall remain, and within them atmospheric cobbled alleys wind uphill among stout stone or half-timbered houses, from the cathedral to the turreted 14th-century bishop's palace. Neither it, nor the upper church of Notre-Dame de la Sède in its shadow (also once a cathedral), is open to visitors.

The lower cathedral was originally constructed in the 10th century, partly using Roman masonry, and substantially rebuilt 200 years later. The beautiful cloister is of two storeys, the lower one built in the 12th century and the upper one added in the 16th century. The lower storey is supported by slender marble columns with richly carved capitals. The eye-catching octagonal tower was added in the 14th century in the style of St-Sernin in Toulouse.

APHAT-D'OSPITALE

Chapel of St-Blaise

The little hamlet of Aphat-d'Ospitale lies east of St-Jean-Pied-de-Port.

Three of the main pilgrim routes to the shrine of Santiago de Compostela came together at Ostabat-Asme, to the north-east of St-Jean-Pied-de-Port, and from there great processions of travellers converged on St-

Jean before tackling the Roncevaux pass into Spain. The tiny hamlet of Aphat-d'Ospitale offered a rest-house for the pilgrims, and beside the main road, in the grounds of a farm, there stands a low, insignificant-looking building that is, in fact, the almost derelict 12th-century Chapelle St-Blaise.

This tiny place of worship is just one of many such chapels strung along the pilgrims' route.

A tiny chapel to be discovered on the ancient Way of St James

The fine and imposing abbey church of St-Savin contains many interesting treasures

ST-SAVIN

Ecclesiastical grandeur, a chequered history and a scenic position on a hillside above the basin of Argelès-Gazost make this little village unusually interesting. 17km south of Lourdes.

The Benedictine monks of the abbey here grew powerful through exploitation of the curative waters of Cauterets, and for centuries governed the surrounding areas virtually as an independent pastoral state. Their authority was somewhat reduced in 1317, however, when discontented local communes forced upon them a power-sharing agreement. The abbey church and its imposing bell-tower still dominate the village. Built of honey-coloured stone in the 11th and 12th centuries and fortified in the 14th, it stands at the end of a street lined with attractive houses, some of them half-timbered. It retains a Romanesque portal, a 12th-century stoup for *cagots* (the outcast descendants of lepers), the tomb of St-Savin, and a Renaissance organ cabinet decorated with grotesque faces whose eyes and mouths move in hideous grimaces whenever it is played. The treasury, in the chapterhouse, contains one of the finest collections of religious artefacts in the Pyrenees.

BASQUE TOMBSTONES

Explore churchyards and cemeteries in the Pays Basque and you will soon notice the tombstones with a wedge-shaped base topped by a disc. Most date from the 16th century on, but they obviously continue a much older tradition, and antiquarians have been quick to point out their resemblance to Celtic wheel-headed crosses. The decorations on the discs vary widely. Some show trade tools or heraldic devices, others overtly Christian motifs such as the monograms IHS and INRI. A few depict the sun, or a design of interlaced triangles, or, most interesting of all, the so-called 'Basque cross'. This is a floriate version of the broken cross or swastika, looking rather like four commas with their tails meeting at the centre. The swastika is an ancient Hindu emblem and its appearance here has helped to fuel speculation about the mysterious origins of the Basque people.

VILLEFRANCHE-DE-CONFLENT

Massive ramparts surrounding medieval streets bear witness to the strategic importance of this ancient outpost of the kingdom of Aragon. 6km south-west of Prades.

Ringed by sturdy man-made defences, Villefranche is also hemmed in by the natural fortifications of the narrow walls of the Têt gorge. From the 11th century it was an outpost of Aragon, but was annexed in 1659.

The houses, with lovely Romanesque or Gothic doors and windows, are simple but very fine, arranged on a number of side alleys off two main streets.

Vauban's *pièce de résistance* here was the massive Fort-Liberia, above the village, designed to render it unassailable from the surrounding heights.

PLANES

CHURCH OR MOSQUE?

Planès is in the Cerdagne, south-east of Mont-Louis.

The most remarkable church in the Cerdagne serves the village of Planès, with a fine view of the Carlit mountains from its position below the Col de la Perche.

The church itself is ancient, and very unusual in shape and construction. It has no nave as such, but makes up for this omission with three half-domed, semi-circular apses, giving it the shape of a clover-leaf. The cupola roofing each apse in turn supports a larger, central cupola, from which emerges the bell-tower.

It is thought that the whole building was once covered by a timber dome with surrounding balcony, and there has been much speculation locally that it was formerly used as a mosque.

SECRET FRANCE
PROVENCE

For most visitors to France the names Provence and Côte d'Azur conjure up the Mediterranean coast, hot, sunny days spent on beaches or drinking coffee in beach cafés, or lazy days exploring the expensive delights of Nice and Monaco, or the more cosmopolitan pleasures of Marseille. But there is another side to the area. Provence – here taken to cover the whole of the area from Nîmes to the Italian border, from the sea to Mont Ventoux and eastward through the high hills of the Mercantour National Park – is a region of magical light, bleached landscapes, olive groves, herb-scented *garrigue*, vineyards and Roman and medieval antiquities.

Because of its coastline, Provence has always been susceptible to attack from the sea; pirates came this way, and so did more determined invaders, particularly the Saracens, who settled parts of Provence and maintained a presence for many years, until they were eventually driven out by the Franks. Then, following the peace of Charlemagne's reign, Provence found itself once more a frontier land. First came the conflicts between France and Savoy, followed by those associated with the Popes of Avignon; these were followed in turn by the Wars of Religion of the 16th century, and finally came the border disputes between France and Italy.

Not surprisingly, village people and their feudal lords felt the need to fortify their homes. The easiest way to do this was to place the village at the top of a hill, adding a castle and walls to nature's defences to produce an impregnable fortress. These are

the hill villages of old Provence, one of the great joys of the area, and often missed by the visitor who seeks sea and sun alone.

There are lavender fields that provide the raw material for the perfume industry, and the stupendous Verdon Gorge, one of the natural wonders of Europe. The hills of Haute Provence lie within the borders of the Mercantour National Park, home to most of Europe's mountain animal species, while the Camargue, famous for its white horses and black bulls, also offers sanctuary to some of Europe's most exotic birds.

It might seem an impossibility to find anything in the region that has escaped the notice of legions of tourists, yet among the upland areas, and even closer to the coast, there are hidden places that are a real delight: isolated chapels, unexplored landscapes, haunted castles and spectacular rock formations.

lavende de Provence

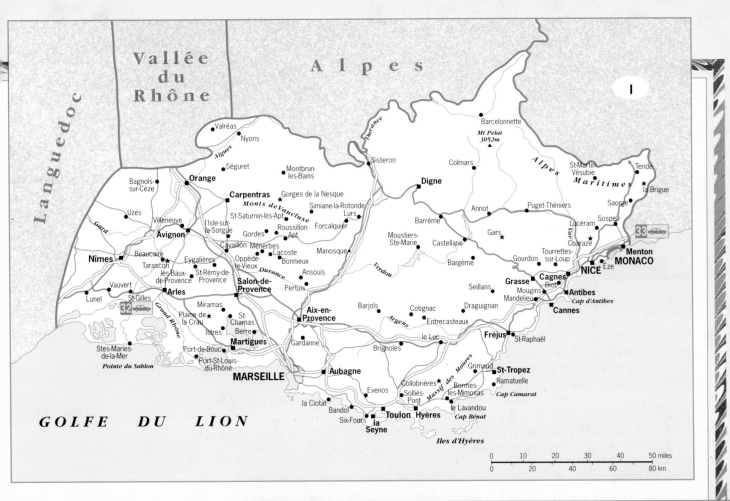

Languedoc

Vallée
du
Rhône

Alpes

Maritimes

Valréas
Nyons
Aigues
Séguret
Montbrun-
les-Bains
Bagnols-
sur-Cèze
Orange
Uzès
Villeneuve
Carpentras
Gorges de la Nesque
Monts de Vaucluse
Simiane-la-Rotonde
St-Saturnin-lès-Apt
Lurs
l'Isle-sur-
la-Sorgue
Roussillon
Gordes
Apt
Forcalquier
Gard
Avignon
Cavaillon
Ménerbes
Lacoste
Nîmes
Beaucaire
Eygalières
Oppède-
le-Vieux
Bonnieux
Ansouis
Durance
Tarascon
les-Baux-
de-Provence
St-Rémy-de-
Provence
Salon-de-
Provence
Pertuis
Vauvert
Lunel
Vauvert
St-Gilles
Arles
Miramas
Plaine de
la Crau
St-
Chamas
Berre
Aix-en-
Provence
Martigues
Gardanne
Port-de-Bouc
Stes-Maries-
de-la-Mer
Pointe du Sablon
Port-St-Louis-
du-Rhône
Grand Rhône
MARSEILLE
Aubagne
Evenos
la Ciotat
Bandol
Six-Fours
la
Seyne
Toulon
Hyères

Durance
Sisteron
Colmars
Barrême
Moustiers-
Ste-Marie
Castellane
Bargème
Verdon
Barjols
Cotignac
Entrecasteaux
Argens
le Luc
Brignoles
Collobrières
Solliès-
Pont
Bormes-
les-Mimosas
le Lavandou
Cap Bénat
Iles d'Hyères

Digne

Barcelonnette
Mt Pelat
3052m
Annot
Puget-Théniers
St-Martin-
Vésubie
Tende
la Brigue
Saorge
Gars
Lucéram
Sospel
Var
Coaraze
Gourdon
Tourrettes-
sur-Loup
Grasse
Mougins
Seillans
Draguignan
Cagnes
Biot
NICE
Eze
MONACO
Menton
Antibes
Cap d'Antibes
Mandelieu
Cannes
Fréjus
St-Raphaël
Massif des Maures
Grimaud
St-Tropez
Ramatuelle
Cap Camarat

GOLFE DU LION

0   10   20   30   40   50 miles
0   20   40   60   80 km

The region of Provence has a particularly wide range of attractions, and while it attracts many visitors, there are still tranquil corners to be discovered, including historic, sun-baked old towns and villages, right, and the wildlife reserve of the Camargue delta, below centre
Below, the architecture has a flair of its own
Below, far right, famous for its heady perfumes, the area also produces delicately flavoured cakes and sweets such as these calissons

ROMAN INFUENCES

The Pont du Gard, the three-tiered aqueduct spanning the Gardon valley, is probably the most abiding image surviving from the Roman occupation of Provence. They first gained a foothold here at Marseilles, endowing it with a rich architectural heritage. The theatre, amphitheatre and avenue of marble tombs at Arles; the temple and amphitheatre at Nîmes; and the theatre at Orange: these are among the best-known Roman remains outside Italy, and among the most popular tourist destinations in the region. Lesser-known places include Vaison-la-Romaine, which gives an excellent idea of the layout of a Roman town; and the extensive ruins of Glanum near St-Rémy-de-Provence.

ANNOT

A substantial and ancient settlement, at once Alpine and Provençal in character, overlooking the River Vaire and surrounded by strange rock formations. 75km north-west of Nice.

The most ancient settlement in the valley, having been inhabited since the Roman road from Cimiez (on the northern edge of Nice) was constructed through the valley on its way to Digne. Annot as we see it today dates from the 11th century, when it was resited so that it was less susceptible to flooding.

Set around a large Provençal square and shaded by huge plane trees, the old quarter is the loveliest part of the village. From the medieval fortified town gate the main street, Grande Rue, lined with Renaissance houses, leads to the church of St-Pons, part Romanesque and part Gothic, with part of the apse raised to serve as a watchtower. Next to it is the 17th-century Chapelle des Pénitents Blancs. Leading off the main square are fascinating narrow alleyways, with fine carved lintels to either side.

ANSOUIS

Beautifully sited on the southern edge of the Lubéron, this historic village spreads picturesquely down a south-facing slope dominated by its medieval castle. 8km north-west of Pertuis.

Ansouis is dominated by its castle, built originally in the 11th century. The northern façade, built into the rock, still looks like a fortress, but the fine Louis XIII façade has the friendlier air of a country mansion.

Beneath the 13th-century curtain wall lies the Place des Hôtes, from which lead off narrow streets of pretty medieval and Renaissance houses. The village clock tower, topped by an iron-work bell cage, rises from the old ramparts. The only surviving gateway in the ramparts is the Petit Portail, from which the rue du Château rises steeply to the castle, passing close to the severe, 13th-century presbytery, behind its 18th-century façade. The Romanesque village church, dedicated to St Martin, is of about the same age and was originally the *salle de justice* of the castle.

BARGEME

A tiny, spectacularly sited hilltop village – the highest in the Var – which time seems to have passed by, still dominated by its medieval castle and Romanesque church. 40km north-east of Draguignan.

At over 1,000m of altitude, and crowned by the lofty towers of its castle, Bargème dominates the beautiful hilly landscape for miles around. The castle is first mentioned in the 13th century and the church dates back to the 11th.

SECRET PLACES

LA BRIGUE

THE PAINTINGS OF NOTRE-DAME DES FONTAINES

La Brigue lies east of St-Dalmas-de-Tende. Just east of the village is the chapel of Notre-Dame des Fontaines. A path leads to the house-like, white-painted chapel.

Close to this spot rise seven springs that water the valley. In the 14th century they were sealed by an earthquake, but the valley dwellers prayed to the Virgin, and the springs miraculously re-opened. In gratitude they built a chapel, which became a place of pilgrimage.

In the mid-15th century the chapel walls were painted with scenes from the life of Christ, and the frescos are extraordinary both for their number, and for their composition and execution. They offer an uncompromising view of the fate awaiting those who stray from the Christian path, and an equally direct assessment of the trial and crucifixion of Christ.

Look out for the gruesome figure of the hanged Judas

The castle ruins are still extremely imposing, dominating the skyline with the bell-tower of the Romanesque church, beautifully constructed from the local white stone. Its superb altarpiece was the work of local craftsmen in the 16th century.

But the real joy in Bargème is to wander the streets, admiring the stone-built houses and the fine flowers and trees, and enjoying a special tranquillity in such a high and remote location.

BARJOLS

Standing in a lush valley at the confluence of three streams, this old village possesses nearly 30 fountains. 22km north of Brignoles.

The old part of Barjols, arranged round a huge square, has an array of fine houses, perhaps the best being the ancient Hotel de Pontevès with its beautiful Renaissance façade. Vaulted passageways link the houses, and everywhere there are little squares with fountains, as well as a dozen wash houses. The most remarkable fountain – huge, mushroom-shaped and encrusted with moss – can be found near the Mairie.

Water was essential for the tanning industry on which Barjols' prosperity was once based. The Romanesque church, partly rebuilt in Gothic style in the 16th century, contains some exquisite woodcarving.

LES BAUX-DE-PROVENCE

A beautiful, half-ruined fortified village in a spectacular site that is among the loveliest in the whole of France. 20km north-east of Arles.

Hollowed out partly from the solid rock, les Baux stands on a natural rock island, an outlier of the Alpilles, surrounded by an 80m, virtually sheer drop to the surrounding valleys.

Les Baux consists of the lower, 'living' village and an upper, deserted village, which together with towers, walls, stairs and windows carved from the living rock, make an unforgettable sight, both to view from a distance and to visit.

Entrance to the lower part is through the Porte Mage, beyond which the village consists of little more than a pair of streets in which virtually every house is remarkable. The old

Les Baux-de-Provence's spectacular position on top of a rock island provides extensive views across the plains

Mairie, a 17th-century vaulted building, is now a museum devoted to *santons*, the Provençal terracotta figurines. Not far beyond the Porte Eyguières, once the only gate into the village, is the Hôtel des Porcelets, a 16th-century house that is now a museum of contemporary art. Close by are the Chapelle des Pénitents Blancs, decorated with murals by Yves Brayer, and the village church, a 12th-century building with an elegant campanile. In Grande Rue is the Hôtel de Manville, perhaps the most impressive of all the village houses, a 16th-century building with fine Renaissance windows. On Rue des Fours are the old communal bread ovens, and beyond is Rue de Trencat, carved straight out of the rock.

The atmospheric ruins of the deserted upper village lie further beyond this. It is estimated that in the heyday of les Baux there were as many as 100 buildings on the rock. Here are the impressive remnants of the 13th-century castle keep and two towers, two chapels, a few houses and some enigmatic foundations and walls.

TOUR 32 – 130KM
ARLES AND THE CAMARGUE

To the west of Marseille lies the Camargue, one of the most remarkable areas in Europe, a land of salt-marshes, that supports some of the most exotic birdlife in Europe. On the northern edge of the Camargue is Arles, the capital of Roman Provence, with some of the finest Roman remains in Europe, and famous as the home of Vincent Van Gogh. The route starts from Arles and visits the Camargue, where it may be possible to spot some of the spectacular wildlife of the region. On the return to Arles the tour takes in one of the most complete medieval cities in France.

ROUTE DIRECTIONS

Leave Arles on the **D570** and follow it all the way to Stes-Maries-de-la-Mer, the road going between rice fields and giving tantalising glimpses of the Camargue.

Return from Stes-Marie along the same road for about 13km, then turn left along the **D38c**, later the **D58**, towards Aigues-Mortes. Stay on this road, crossing the Petit Rhône and a canal just before reaching Aigues, and follow signs into the town.

Leave Aigues-Mortes on the **D979**, signed for Nîmes, and follow this past St-Laurent-d'Aigouze. About 6km beyond St-Laurent, and 1.5km after a level crossing, turn right towards Vauvert. Continue for 3km, then just after a double bend turn left on to the **D135** towards Nîmes. Continue on the **D135** until it meets the **D42** south of Nîmes and here turn south on the **D42**, following signs to St-Gilles and Garons (airport).

Continue to St-Gilles, entering the town under a big white bridge that takes the Philippe-Lamour canal over the road. Continue straight ahead into the centre of St-Gilles, and go down the main street. Cross another canal (the Rhône Canal), a level crossing and the bridge over the Petit Rhône to reach the **N572**, and follow this back into Arles.

PLACES OF INTEREST

MAS DU PONT DE ROUSTY

This old sheepfold houses a museum with displays explaining the area's unique geography, its natural history, and the way of life of the people of the Camargue over the centuries. From the Rousty bridge a path leads out into the saltmarshes providing a close-up view of this extraordinary place. Close to the Pont de Rousty is a bird sanctuary and information centre. They cannot guarantee you

Top, storks are one of the many rare bird species found in the Camargue Above, carvings on the main doorway of the cathedral of St-Tromphime in Arles

a sight of the numerous species that live in or migrate through the Camargue, but they can tell you more about them.

STES MARIES-DE-LA-MER
See page 245.

AIGUES-MORTES

Louis IX built the port here in the mid-13th century in order to embark on the Seventh Crusade. Later the port was fortified with the addition of the ramparts, and the medieval fortress town remains virtually intact.

There is an excellent view of the layout of the town and its defences from the top of the great Constance Tower. The Wick Tower is so-called because here a lamp burned perpetually, ready to light the powder of cannons. The Gothic

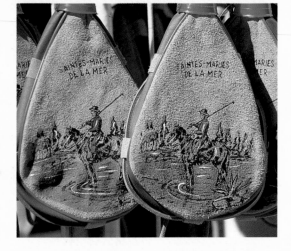

Notre-Dame-des-Sablons in Place St-Louis, contains a 14th-century Christ. The Chapelle des Pénitants Gris dates from the 17th century, and includes and altarpiece carved by Sabatier.

ST-GILLES

It would seem that the Camargue was a favourite destination for early Christian missionaries. St-Gilles came here from Greece in the 8th century to live a hermit's life and spread word of the new

Traditional-style wine-holders make good souvenirs of the Camargue

religion. When he died a church was raised over his remains, which in time became a Benedictine monastery.

The abbey was badly damaged during the Albigensian Crusade, but was restored in the 17th century. It is a beautiful building, its west front, with three doors, being a masterpiece of early medieval carving.

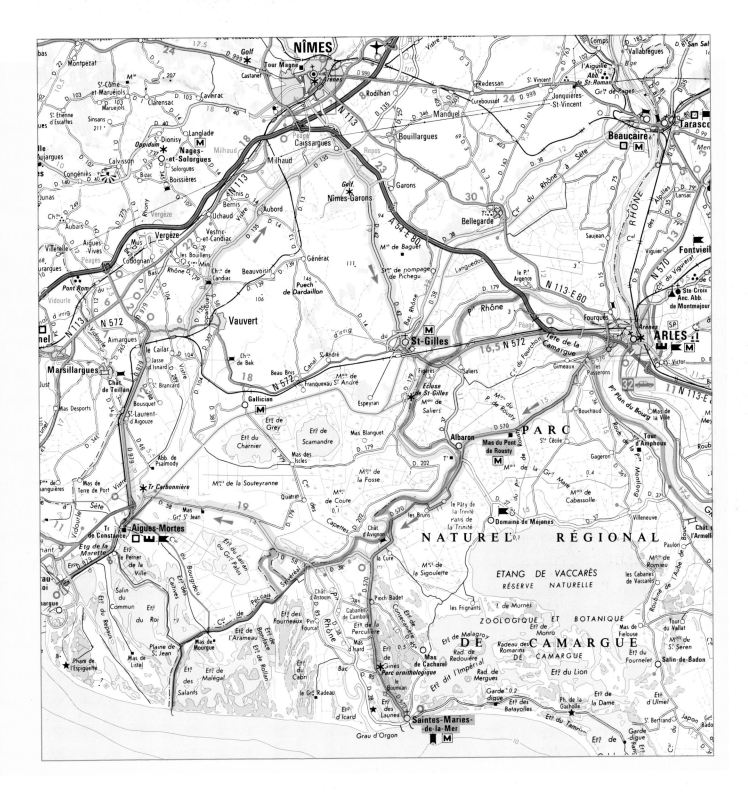

BIOT

A picturesque village just inland from the Côte d'Azur, famous for its flowers and its links with the artist Léger. 5km north of Antibes.

First settled by the Greeks over 2,000 years ago, Biot was famed for its pottery until the 18th century, and the craft tradition persists, with a thriving glassworks and ceramic trade. It was this trade that attracted the artist Fernand Léger to the village in the late 1950s, and his house is now a museum.

The heart of the village is the Place des Arcades, a beautiful square with arcading dating from the 13th and 14th centuries. In the old part of the village, the Musée d'Histoire Locale presents the history of the village.

BONNIEUX

This ancient hilltop village with its many beautiful houses is one of the most picturesque spots in the Lubéron. 26km east of Cavaillon.

Steep, stepped pathways in the village lead up through the terraces and past beautiful old houses to reach the old church, built in the 12th century. From a cedar-shaded terrace by the church the view out across the Lubéron is breathtaking. Sadly the church is no longer open, but the key can be obtained from the Syndicat d'Initiative. Until recently it housed four superb 15th-century paintings, brightly coloured, vibrant works on wood, which have now been transferred to the new village church.

BORMES-LES-MIMOSAS

In a picturesque setting at the western end of the Massif des Maures and close to the coast, this beautiful hill village is alive with the scent of mimosa, chamomile and eucalyptus. 6km west of le Lavandou.

Bormes has a *circuit touristique*, a waymarked trail through its sometimes steep and narrow streets, and there is no better way to see the village. Starting from the Mairie, it passes the remains of a windmill. Beyond is a fine 16th-century chapel dedicated to St-François de Paule, who is said to have saved Bormes from plague in 1481.

Beyond the 18th-century church of St-Trophyme, signs marked '*parcours fleuri*' lead to a flower-filled walk round the castle, built by the Comtes de Marseille in the 13th century. A stepped alley leads down into the heart of the village, continuing on to Roumpi Cuou, the longest of the village's slippery alleys.

COLMARS

One of the finest and most complete fortified villages in Haute Provence, in a magnificent mountain setting. 45km south of Barcelonnette.

In the 14th century the village became a frontier stronghold of the Duc de Savoie, and was put to the torch by the infamous Raymond de Turenne, and in 1690, when war between France and Savoy seemed imminent, Louis XIV instructed Vauban to reinforce the fortifications. Colmars was therefore surrounded by a

The flower-lined tourist walk through Bormes

SECRET PLACES

GORGES DE LA NESQUE

THE ROCK OF WAX

The road into the Gorges de la Nesque is off the D942 between Sault and Mormoiron. Follow it into the gorge, stopping at a sharp bend to the right, where there is a viewpoint (*belvédère*) to the left.

From the *belvédère* is a splendid view of the gorge and the Rocher du Cire that towers above it. The 870m cliffs of the Rocher are honeycombed with caves, and generations of bees have used these natural hives, the outpourings of their wax having given the rock its occasional odd lustre, and earned it its name – the Rock of Wax.

The rock has been known about for many years. The 19th-century poet and Nobel prizewinner, Frédéric Mistral, famous for his preservation of the Provençal language, mentioned the in his epic poem *Calendal*. Mistral's words may be read, etched on a tablet at high wall, topped with loopholes for archers and finished with defensive towers. Close to each fort was a gateway through the walls, which still lead inside to the stone walkways and wooden placements of the internal defences. The village itself contains some fine Renaissance houses. The church which stands very close to the wall and whose slender tower can easily be seen above it, was built in the 16th and 17th centuries and is a delicate mixture of Romanesque and Gothic.

COTIGNAC

The ruined towers of its medieval castle and fantastically sculpted, high tufa cliffs riddled with caves dominate this picturesque old village, 25km north of Brignoles.

The early inhabitants of Cotignac lived in the many caves and tunnels in the 80m-high cliff, though in medieval times they decided to reinforce the natural defences of the site with a castle, of which two ruined towers remain. The village beneath, built mostly in the 17th and 18th centuries, is open and airy, with a sense of space enhanced by shady plane trees and the occasional fountain. The most ornate of these, in the Cours Gambetta, is the Fontaine des Quatre Saisons, with each season represented by a mask. At the centre of the village is the Place de la Mairie, and close by are a bell-tower, and the 16th-century Romanesque village church, with an 18th-century façade. A couple of caves in the tufa cliff, one of which has some very fine dripstone formations, are open to visitors.

ENTRECASTEAUX

A typically Provençal village with a notable château and fine gardens, 25km west of Draguignan.

Entrecasteaux is justifiably proud of its public gardens, said to have been laid out as a small park for the château by the great Le Nôtre. One of the attractive streets round the fortified Gothic church has to negotiate a huge flying buttress. Of the same age as the church is the superb humpbacked bridge over the Bresque.

The whole village is dominated by the château, a long and narrow 17th-century building, very plain in design. Built by the Count of Grignan, it eventually passed to the village, but the council was unable to maintain it and it fell into disrepair. When it seemed possible that it might have to be dismantled, it was rescued by Ian McGarvie-Munn. The château is now open to the public, and contains interesting collections of Provençal and Chinese furniture and porcelain.

Cotignac is dominated by the ruins of its medieval castle

EVENOS

The ruins of a castle perched on the edge of an extinct volcano loom over this half-ruined hilltop village. 17km north-west of Toulon.

Set on a peak dominating the gorges of the Ollioules, a strategically important valley for the control of the approaches to Toulon, Evenos has always been an obvious candidate for fortification. Above the village looms the imposing mass of the 16th-century castle, built of sombre volcanic basalt except for one limestone tower, known as the Tour Blanche. The church, a tiny but dignified 13th-century building, has a statue of the Virgin whose face is said to have a likeness of the Empress Eugénie, and several candelabra, all the gift of Napoleon III, Bonaparte's nephew.

The village beyond the castle's triple wall is a picturesque and semi-ruined jumble of little houses, all built of a mixture of basalt and limestone and clinging to the steep, narrow streets, and all enjoying the magnificent view.

the viewpoint, which is off the main beaten track. The viewpoint and tablet are reached via a path that is, at times, somewhat precarious.

A natural home for bees over the centuries, the stone appears lustrous with wax in a certain light

EYGALIERES

In the foothills of the Chaîne des Alpilles lies this pretty, ancient village. 15km south-west of Cavaillon.

The site of Eygalières was occupied in Neolithic times and there was certainly a Roman presence, and in each case the attraction was the water that has its spring here.

The present village rises in a series of picturesque tiers up the hillside, linked by narrow, winding streets. At the top are the square Tour de l'Horloge and the ruins of the medieval castle, reached through the Porte de Laure, from which there is a wide view of the Alpilles and the Durance valley. The village church is 12th-century, though the older Chapelle des Pénitents Blancs is the more interesting building. Exhibitions of the work of local artists are held here in the summer months.

During World War II the Resistance was very active in this area: in the part of the village known as la Lègue is a cabin that sheltered their leader, Jean Moulin, in January 1942.

EZE

Perched high above the sea and the fashionable beaches of the Côte d'Azur, this is one of the best and most picturesque of Provençal *villages perchés*. 10km north-east of Nice.

Records of a settlement here go as far back as the 11th century and the village was fortified in the 14th. In the 17th century, during the hostilities between the kingdoms of France and

Savoy, it was fortified again, and the fortifications were well tested in several sieges and battles over the following two centuries. Only after the plebiscite of 1860, when the village became French, did peace finally come. Today the village is still entered through the

Gordes offers inviting, shady cafes as well as many interesting buildings

only gate in the ancient ramparts, formerly approached via a drawbridge. Inside, the old streets are the most picturesque on the coast: steep, cobbled and narrow, and occasionally arcaded as they pass beneath the tall, narrow houses. They lead eventually to the Place du Planet, where, beside a fountain stands the Chapelle des Pénitents Blancs, an elegant 14th-century building decorated with enamelled tiles telling the story of the life of Christ. Inside is a fine 13th-century Catalan Crucifix. A few

metres away stands the village church, rebuilt in the 18th century and containing an 18th-century statue of the Assumption. Close by, around the ruins of the castle, is a remarkable tropical garden planted with a large collection of cacti and succulents, some of them very rare. From the castle there is a superb view of the Côte d'Azur and, on a clear day, of Corsica.

GORDES

The archetypal Provençal hill village, its lovely golden sandstone houses dominated by the ancient château and church. 18km north-east of Cavaillon.

Steep, narrow alleys climb up the sandstone hill, passing some delightful old houses such as the 17th-century Palais St-Firmin, a portalled mansion on rue du Four which is perhaps the most picturesque house in Gordes. At the top of the hill are the 18th-century church and the Renaissance château, first built in the 12th century, and remodelled early in the 16th century to become one of the very few in Renaissance style in Provence. It contains a museum of the work of the Hungarian-born artist Victor Vasarely, who restored the château and was largely responsible for the influx of artists who helped to reconstruct the village in the post-war years. The village was severely damaged in 1944 when it was bombarded by the Germans for being the centre of the local Resistance. It was awarded the Croix de Guerre in 1948, an extraordinary achievement.

THE PLAINE DE LA CRAU

West of the Carmague lies a little-known and infrequently visited area that is rich in wildlife. The Crau plain, the ancient flood plain of the River Durance, is traversed by the N568.

The Crau is a rocky plain, with low, bleached scrub cover, and, with its occasional pools, it is an ideal spot for reptiles, amphibians and insects. It is one of the last strongholds of the Montpellier snake, a harmless creature which can grow up to 2.5m long. There are four other species of snake, none of them poisonous, including a water snake.

The birds of prey are similar to those of the Camargue – look out for Bonelli's eagle, the short-toed eagle, marsh, hen and Montagu's harriers, goshawk and lesser kestrel. The Calendra lark, black-eared wheatear, pin-tailed sandgrouse and the cream-bibbed pratincole are also seen here.

GOURDON

This little fortified village, perched precariously on a rocky spur above the gorges of the River Loup, offers a superb panorama of the surrounding countryside. 14km north-east of Grasse.

Gourdon's position, high above the valley, means it has been inhabited and fortified for many centuries, there being evidence of both Ligurian and Roman occupations. Later the Saracens held the site, and it is on the foundations of their fortress that the present imposing 13th-century castle was built. Inside is a historical museum housing fine collections of armour, furniture and religious art. A gallery of naive painting includes work by Douanier Rousseau. The terraced gardens, laid out by Le Nôtre, have now been given over to the native flora of the pre-Alps. From the gardens there is a superb view of the coast around Cap d'Antibes.

In the village there is an even more magnificent panorama of the Loup gorges and the Massif d'Esterel from the square by the church. The church is 12th-century, though largely remodelled in the 16th, and some of the village houses are of similar vintage, with beautiful façades.

GRIMAUD

A beautiful medieval village with lovely views of the Massif des Maures and the bay of St-Tropez, now a thriving craft centre. 10km west of St-Tropez.

Grimaud derives its name from Monaco's Grimaldi family, who controlled the local area in the 11th century. It was around this time that

the castle, of which the ruins still dominate the village, was built. Having survived at least two wars, it eventually fell victim to the anger of Louis XIV, who feared its potential as a base for Provence to defy the crown and control the local coast. Today it offers a wonderful view of the tight streets of medieval Grimaud, a village to wander

Perched high in the hills just inland, Ezé commands fine views out to sea

about at leisure. Below the castle is the 13th-century chapel of St-Roch, traditionally used to bless the local harvest. The village church, on older foundations, is a superb 11th-century Romanesque building.

COARAZE

CURSED CHATEAU DE ROCCA-SPARVIERA

On top of the peak close to the village of Coaraze, north of Nice stand the ruins of the Château de Rocca-Sparviera, the Castle of the Sparrow-hawk. Built at the point where ridges meet, overlooking the valleys of the Duranus and Coaraze, the castle once dominated both those valleys, controlling the Vésubie valley.

A story is told that in medieval times Jeanne, Queen of Provence, fled from Avignon to this remote area to seek sanctuary from the men who had killed her husband. With her were her young twin sons, a few men and an old monk known for his love of wine. They settled in the castle, which even then was partly in ruins and said to be cursed.

At Christmas the Queen went down into the village to hear Midnight Mass, but when she returned she found to her horror that the monk had killed her sons in a drunken stupor. In despair she left the castle, cursing it by saying that never again would a bird sing near it. Some say that the curse lives on, and that although the castle offers fine views, the silence makes it an uncomfortable place to stay for long.

LACOSTE

A pretty hilltop village at the north-western end of the Lubéron hills, dominated by the remains of its huge château, once home to the Marquis de Sade. 21km east of Cavaillon.

The partially ruined château that looms above this tiny village has been the source of both its fame and its notoriety. In the 18th century it came into the de Sade family. The Marquis de Sade, Lord of Lacoste for some 30 years, escaped to the château to avoid prison; but in the end spent more time in prison than he did at Lacoste. The Revolution released him from the Bastille, but it also destroyed the château. It has been painstakingly restored, along with many of the village houses, by the present owner.

The village is entered through one of the old gates in the well-preserved medieval town walls, and is typical of the region, with vaulted passages between and sometimes beneath the houses. Above the Hôtel de Ville is an elegant bell-tower with a delicate wrought-iron bell cage, from which there are fine views.

LUCERAM

A historic village, rich in works of art, set on a rocky hilltop surrounded by a cirque of peaks in a wildly beautiful setting. 27km north-east of Nice.

Lucéram managed to avoid the major conflicts of medieval France, though it acquired ramparts and a

watchtower which still stands. Instead, the grandiose beauty of its setting attracted religious settlements and commanderies of the Knights Templar and Hospitaller, reflected in the village church. A 15th-century building remodelled in the 18th century in fine Italian rococo style, it contains some superb works of art, notably five altar-pieces by artists of the school of Louis Bréa, dating from the late 15th and early 16th centuries, and another by

Jean Canavesio. The church treasure also includes some beautiful work, including a 15th-century silver statue of Ste-Marguerite, a 14th-century statue-reliquary and a 16th-century alabaster Virgin.

The village is as Italianate in style as the church it surrounds, with a picturesque jumble of medieval and Renaissance houses linked by steep, occasionally stepped, streets and vaulted alleys. Crowds come to Lucéram every

TARASCON

THE TARASQUE

Tarascon is north of Arles on the River Rhône.

The Tarasque, a fearful monster, said to be half-lion, half-crocodile, once lived in the river here, favouring a diet of washer-women, plucked from the river's edge, and young women whom it sneaked through the town at night to catch. Knightly combat was in vain, and in desperation the townsfolk sent to Stes-Maries-de-la-Mer for help. St Martha came, and subdued the monster by sprinkling it with holy water and showing it a cross. She then led it to a deeper part of the river, where it dived down, never to be seen again.

The legend is celebrated in Tarascon with a lively annual festival.

A local monster of legend, cause for celebration

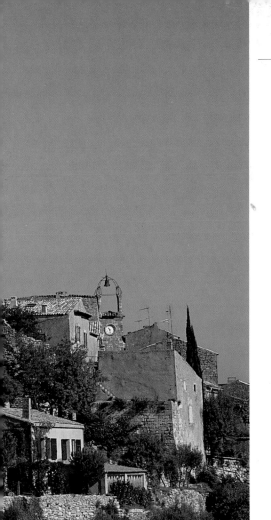

The remains of the château at Lecost, once the home of the de Sade family, dominate this typical Provencal village

Christmas to watch an ancient ceremony in which local shepherds bring in their sheep to be blessed.

LURS

Hidden away in the Montagne de Lure, above the valley of the Durance, this sleepy village in its beautiful setting can be seen from miles around. 11km east of Forcalquier.

In the 9th century Charlemagne gave land here to the Bishop of Sisteron, who built a summer residence and then a seminary. As the bishops' favoured residence, the village grew prosperous, and by medieval times it had 3,000 inhabitants and an impressive castle to defend them. When the seminary fell into disuse the village declined, until it was finally abandoned early this century. However, in 1945 a group of artists settled in the village and began the gradual and painstaking

process of restoration. In the centre of the village is the quaintly named Place des Feignants or the idlers' square. Beyond lie the church and a series of delightful, narrow and winding streets of medieval houses. Leading from the remains of the old castle is the Promenade des Evêques, a favourite walk of the Sisteron bishops.

MENERBES

Scene of a heroic five-year siege during the Wars of Religion, this lovely old village sprawls along a promontory on a northern spur of the Lubéron. 18km east of Cavaillon.

Ménerbes is a strangely elusive village, its oldest parts semi-ruined, the more interesting buildings – the castle and church – not easy of access. Yet among the higher alleyways the visitor can gain an insight into village life in the late 16th century. Here, the Calvinists resisted a Catholic force for over five years during the Wars of Religion. The Catholics, amazed by the fortitude of the Ménerbeans, never found the secret passage, running north from the Mairie, that allowed the villagers to creep out at night for provisions. The passage has collapsed in

places and is unsafe. The same is also true of the 13th-century castle, which still manages to look formidable.

MONTBRUN-LES-BAINS

Set on a sunny, south-facing hillside, its tall houses built on a series of terraces overlooked by the remains of its medieval château, Montbrun-les-Bains is now known for its thermal spa. 12km north of Sault.

Although Montbrun's picturesque medieval quarter is preserved, the château, originally built in the 14th century is mostly in ruins. The 12th-century church has a rather plain exterior, which belies the richness of its interior. There are many ornate and luxurious decorations, paintings and wood panelling, and the elaborate altar was created by one of the celebrated Bernus family. A 14th-century crenellated bell tower that contained one of the four fortified entrances to the village gives its name to the Place du Beffroi.

The spa waters here were probably discovered by the Romans, though it was the end of the 19th century before it became an established centre. The sulphurous water is said to be excellent for bronchial infections and rheumatism.

A SWEETER TASTE

Provençal cooking has given *bouillabaisse* to the world and gained a reputation for its rich use of tomatoes, olive oil and garlic. Less known but also worth trying are the local sweets and desserts. Look out for *beignets de fleurs d'acacia*, pancakes flavoured with acacia, and *torta bléa*, a cake with raisins and pine seed. In Apt, a little town in the Calavon valley, crystallised fruits are made by extracting the water from the fruit and replacing it with a sugar solution. Honey and almonds go into the nougat at Montélimar and Sault. Almonds flavour *calissons* from Aix and the biscuits, or *croquants*, which in Nîmes are still baked by the same family, the Villarets, in the ovens which they have used since the 18th century. (Their shop is on the Rue Nationale.)

MOUGINS

This picturesque old village on its dramatic hilltop site was once a great stronghold. 6km north of Cannes.

It is astonishing to think that this tiny village was once more important than Cannes, when the latter was a fishing village vulnerable to attacks by pirates, and the measure of a village's worth was its fortification. Mougins' rocky spire was an impressive natural defence, reinforced in medieval times by an encircling rampart to create a formidable fortress. The gateway through which the visitor walks – no cars are allowed in Mougins – is called the Porte Sarrasine, or saracen gate, and though it dates from the 15th century, clearly recalls an early siege of occupation. The Place de la Mairie is full of cafés, restaurants and craft shops. Picasso spent his last years here, and photographs of him, along with work by many famous photographers, can be seen in the museum.

MOUSTIERS-STE-MARIE

At the western end of the spectacular Verdon gorges, this ancient village lies on an immensely tall natural rocky amphitheatre, west of Castellane.

A medieval lord of the village, called Blacas, installed the great chain and star that hang dizzily across the high gorge behind the village, supposedly to celebrate his release from captivity during one of the Crusades. In the 17th century

---

TOUR 33 – 100KM

THE RIVIERA AND THE MERCANTOUR NATIONAL PARK

There could hardly be a greater contrast than that between the Riviera coast and the Mercantour National Park. The one is glitter and noise, the other peace and unspoilt beauty. The tour combines these elements, starting in the pleasant Riviera town of Menton, and travelling, sometimes along narrow, winding roads, into the hills of Haute-Provence. The return is down the Vésubie valley, through vineyards and olive groves.

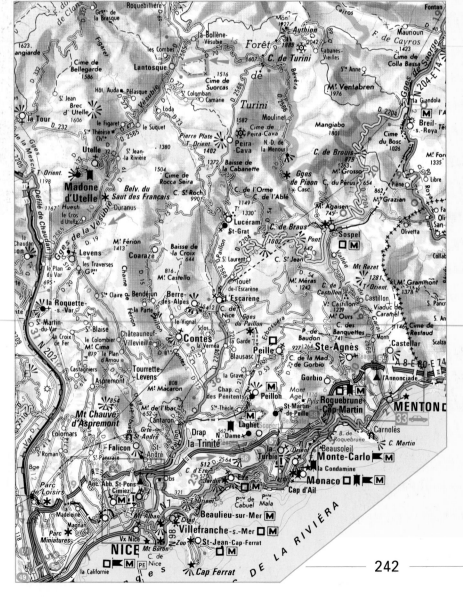

ROUTE DIRECTIONS

From the centre of Menton take the road signed for the autoroute (A8) and Sospel. At the junction with the autoroute take the D2566 through Castillon. Drive through Sospel, following signs for the Col de Turini, still on the D2566.

At the col, follow the main road (D70) towards la-Bollène-Vésubie. Continue through la Bollène until you reach a T-junction. Follow signs to Nice and St-Martin-Vésubie to reach a valley bottom. Follow signs for Lantosque and Nice, turning left on to the main road. After 1km you can turn right through Lantosque, or take the bypass. The road through the village rejoins the main road: if you go that way, turn right towards Nice.

Continue into St-Jean-la-Rivière. Where the road to Nice bears left at a junction go straight on if you wish to visit Madone d'Utelle.

About 1km beyond St-Jean, bear left at a road fork following signs to Nice 'par Levens' (be sure to follow 'par Levens' as both directions are signed for Nice). Continue along the road into Levens, leaving on the road signed for Nice.

Just after St-André you will go under the A8. Turn left at the traffic lights here, following signs to Sospel, cross a river, and go straight over at the next set of traffic lights to pass back under the A8 again. Take the next turn right, crossing the river and a level crossing. Go left at traffic lights towards la Trinité and Drap. Go right off a roundabout towards la Turbie and Laghet, and follow the road to the sanctuary at Laghet.

Pass under the A8 again, and turn left at the next junction (an autoroute slip road) towards Menton. Go left again at the next junction towards la Turbie and Monaco.

Go through la Turbie, following signs for Roquebrune and Menton. Turn right at the traffic lights towards Nice and Beausoleil. Go left at the next set of traffic lights towards Cap-Martin.

Where the road goes sharp left, go straight ahead on to a smaller road, heading towards Mayerling and Cap-Martin to reach the sea. Follow this road back into Menton.

PLACES OF INTEREST

SOSPEL

The old bridge in this pretty village was built in the 11th century, although the central tower is of 20th-century vintage, the original having been destroyed in World War II. The 15th-century fountain and nearby arcaded houses in the cathedral square are a delight. The church of St-Michel has a Romanesque bell-tower, and contains a retable said to be by François Bréa.

the village became prosperous, and famous for its pottery, finished with a blue and beautiful, almost luminously clear glaze. The industry had died out by the late 19th century but has now been revived. Some of the original Moustiers-ware can be seen in the Musée de la Faïence.

The church has a superb multi-storey bell-tower with a distinctly Italian air. A fine view of the village can be had from the chapel of Notre-Dame de Beauvoir, an interesting

12th-century building on the site of the original 5th-century chapel.

OPPEDE-LE-VIEUX

Beautifully positioned on a rocky spur on the southern face of the Petit Lubéron, this sleepy, half-ruined village is full of atmosphere and charm. 12km east of Cavaillon.

During the Wars of Religion, the villagers were Protestant, while their

feudal lord, Baron Oppède, was an active Catholic. He sent as many as 800 of the villagers to Marseille to be sold as slaves. Subsequently depopulated, the village was abandoned at the end of the last century, but has recently been 'rediscovered' and some of the houses renovated. The picturesque houses are at first almost indistinguishable from the rocky outcrops among the olive groves. Crowning the site are the 13th-century church and the imposing ruins of the castle.

Above, la-Bollene-Vesubie is hidden away in the hills of Haute-Provence
Left, the sea front at Menton

MADONE D'UTELLE
Reached by a signed road that winds up the hill from St Jean-la-Rivière is the tiny mid-9th-century pilgrimage chapel of the Madonna of Utelle, restored at some time during the 19th century.

Close to the chapel is a panoramic dial which indicates and identifies all the visible peaks of the Maritime Alps.

LA TURBIE
This ancient village sits astride the Via Julia, a Roman road built by Julius Caesar to link Genoa with Cimiez, on the northern outskirts of Nice. The church of Michael the Archangel was built as lately as the 18th century and has a fine baroque interior decorated with frescos and paintings and an onyx altar. The spectacular triumphal arch the Alpine Trophy was built in about 6BC to celebrate the victories of Augustus the Emperor over 44 local tribes. From the 14th century onwards, it was used as a fortress, and in 1705 Louis XIV attempted to blow it up when he feared it would fall into Spanish hands. Now restored, it stands beside a museum that houses a model of the Trophy in its prime.

ROQUEBRUNE-CAP-MARTIN
Close to Menton lies Roquebrune, a tightly packed village of steep, narrow, vaulted alleys dominated by a medieval castle keep bristling with defensive features. About 200 metres beyond the village, on the road to Menton, is an olive tree claimed to be over 1,000 years old. Cap-Martin provides fine views of Menton and the Italian coast.

RAMATUELLE

This marvellous old Provençal village just south of the Golfe de St-Tropez is surrounded by the luxuriant plant life so typical of the Maures area of the Riviera. 9km south of St-Tropez.

The position of Ramatuelle, on the eastern flank of the Moulins de Paillas gives a clue to its history – this is a market and viticultural village rather than a defensive one. The Romans founded a settlement here, followed by the Saracens, who in turn were succeeded by the monks of the abbey of St-Victor. Defensive walls were never built, but the houses on the outside of the village were arranged to form a defensive ring. Within this ring are narrow, winding alleys with vaulted passages and fine archways, many of the houses being hung with honeysuckle and jasmine. The Romanesque church has a fine doorway carved from the dark rock known as serpentine and dated 1620, and houses some very fine carved woodwork, particularly two baroque altarpieces.

ROUSSILLON

Lying at the heart of great ochre deposits, this hilltop village used to be known throughout the world for its dyes. At sunset, village and cliff erupt in a symphony of red-browns, presenting one of the most dramatic colour shows in Provence. 24km north-east of Cavaillon.

The pretty, narrow Rue de l'Arcade leads past simple old houses in a spectacular range of shades of ochre to reach the rather austere 12th-century church, greatly altered in the 18th century. To the west of the village, past the Tour de l'Horloge, one of the village's old defence towers, is the Porte Aurouse, from where there is a superb view of the ochre rock formations known as the Aiguilles du Val des Fées, or needles of the valley of fairies. A short walk away to the east of the village, is the Chaussée des Géants, a giants' causeway – a spectacular range of jagged ochre-red cliffs set against deep green forest.

The ochre rock formations at Roussillon, which range in colour from yellow-orange to red-brown, glow in the sun

---

SECRET PLACES

GARS

A CURIOUS DISAPPEARING STREAM

Gars lies between Collongues and St-Auban, west of Roquesteron.

A spring in the main street, the village's chief water supply, is known to mysteriously dry up, suddenly and without warning, every 25 years. It remains dry for perhaps a few days or a week, and then flows again. The last time this occurred, just a few years ago, it was the middle of the night, and the villagers were awoken by the sudden silence.

COLLOBRIERES

CHARTREUSE DE LA VERNE

One of the most beautiful monastic sites in all France

About 6km east of Collobrières a rough, narrow road heads south to Chartreuse de la Verne

Verne was a very early Carthusian house, founded in 1170, and has a number of small cells for the monks, each of whom had his own garden. There were also communal rooms, a bakery and refectory, and cloisters.

Verne has a troubled history, having been rebuilt several times, and was finally abandoned at the time of the Revolution, although it has been partially restored since.

Entry is through an ornate serpentine porch. Inside, the *hôtellerie* (guest's quarters) has been magnificently restored. A rebuilt monk's cell is a model of simple dignity.

A walk through the gallery of the cloister leads to the rear entrance, which was fortified. Outside the gate are the remains of the monks' windmill, and a magnificent mountain view.

Narrow streets in the hilltop village of Roussillon wind between old, ochre-coloured houses

ST MARTIN-VESUBIE

A mountain village in a spectacular setting, surrounded by the highest peaks of the southern Alps. 65km north of Nice.

Perched on its rocky spur above the confluence of the Vésubie, the Boréon and the Madone-de-Fenestre streams, St-Martin-Vésubie has a fine old quarter recalling its medieval origins.

The architecture of the village has a distinctly alpine air, with tall houses reaching for the sun, their façades hung with as many as three wooden balconies on different levels. These are interspersed with fine arcaded Gothic buildings, the best of which are on Rue du Docteur-Cagnoli, a narrow street with a central rainwater gutter.

Standing in the middle of the street is the Chapelle des Pénitents Blancs, an 18th-century building with a carved façade and distinctive bulb-shaped bell-tower. Rue de l'Eglise leads to the church, a delightful 17th-century building in regional baroque style.

ST-SATURNIN-LES-APT

A fortified village dominated by its castle ruins and Romanesque chapel and set on one of the foothills. 30km south-east of Carpentras.

The former importance of this ancient walled village can still be seen in the remains of its impressive fortifications: the Porte Ayguier, erected in 1420, the Tour de l'Horloge and Tour du Portalet, several hundred years older, and the ruined castle, which dates from the 11th century. Close by is the Chapelle de St-Saturnin, a beautiful Romanesque building that served the castle. From both castle and chapel there is a fine view across the plateau and the Lubéron. The best of the village lies close to the church, rebuilt in the 19th-century in neo-Romanesque style. Inside there is a beautiful 15th-century wooden *pietà*.

Eleven kilometres to the south-west is the Colorado de Rustrel, a huge and spectacular ochre quarry.

COLONISING THE COTE D'AZUR

The novelist Tobias Smollett was in the vanguard of tourist fashion when he came to Nice in 1763 and found it a town of only 12,000 people. The British – and Americans and Russians – who followed him put the Riviera on the map, and followed him, too, in combining enthusiasm for the landscape with near-contempt for the locals. Tempted by the odd mixture of the promise of a health-giving climate and gambling at nearby Monte Carlo, visitors and expatriates were determined to enjoy these delights amid the atmosphere of their own culture: golf clubs, tennis clubs, cricket clubs, Anglican churches, English reading rooms and English-language newspapers. The list of the famous and sometimes notorious who came would easily fill a directory of its own, and includes: among royalty, Queen Victoria and the Duke of Windsor; among politicians, Gladstone and Churchill; and, among writers, Robert Louis Stevenson, Katherine Mansfield, D H Lawrence, Yeats and Somerset Maugham (the last three also died here). Inevitably, the heyday of the English colony ended with World War II, and today the French have been allowed to rediscover the coast.

STES-MARIES-DE-LA-MER

The magical village that seems to emerge from the sea at the heart of the Camargue, where gypsies from all over the world gather every May. 40km south-west of Arles.

According to legend, a few years after Christ's death the Virgin Mary's two half-sisters, Mary and Mary Salome, together with their servant Sarah, were set adrift in a boat from Jerusalem and came to land here. When they died they were reputedly buried in the chapel they had raised here, and in the 12th century their remains were discovered and a church was built around them. The church, with its massive crenellated walls, dominates the village.

The Musée Baroncelli contains fascinating displays on the flora, fauna and traditional life of the Camargue, with a wonderful view from the terrace.

SAORGE

A medieval stronghold clinging to a high ledge in the wild and rocky setting of the Roya gorges, 47km north of Menton.

It would be hard to imagine a setting more dramatic than the rocky gorges to which the ancient houses of Saorge cling. By medieval times it had become an important stronghold, and in the 17th century it was a large and prosperous community.

The village houses, dating mainly from the 15th to the 17th centuries, are laid out along twisting, cobbled streets, sometimes so steep that they turn into flights of steps. Rebuilt in the 16th century after fire had ravaged the village, and with substantial 17th- and 18th-century baroque additions, the church contains an unusual Genoese organ, dating from the 19th-century, and transported here by sea and mule.

Set among olive trees at the southern end of the village are the restored remains of a Franciscan monastery, originally built in the 17th century. From the terrace by the monastery church there is a wonderful view of the village and the Roya gorges.

Access to the village of Saorge is only on foot, and cars should be left at the perimeter.

The houses of Saorge climb in tiers up the cliff face, and the winding streets can only be explored on foot

SEGURET

A beautiful and typically Provençal wine village set against the craggy foothills of the Dentelles de Montmirail, now popular with artists and tourists alike. 9km south-west of Vaison-la-Romaine.

Three medieval gateways guard Séguret: the Porte de la Bise to the north, the Port Neuf to the south, and the picturesque 12th-century Porte Reynier. All are reminders of the medieval ramparts, whose course can be traced by the old streets of the village.

Within, the steep, cobbled streets are lined with lovely stone houses, often hung with vines and virginia creeper and with sundials on their façades, interspersed with cyprus trees, vaulted passageways and little squares. One of the prettiest of these contains a 15th-century fountain with water trickling from the mouths of four masks.

At the top of the village are the

SECRET PLACES

MENTON

MENTON LEMONS

According to local legend, when God expelled Adam and Eve from the Garden of Eden, Eve hid a lemon about her person before leaving. After a time Adam and Eve reached Menton, quickly deciding it was an earthly paradise. Eve planted the seeds from her lemon, and all the local lemon trees are said to stem from them.

For centuries Menton's prosperity was based on the lemon crop, and Menton lemons were highly regarded by connoisseurs. Even today the annual Lemon festival, which takes place on Shrove Tuesday, is the town's major event.

During the 19th century, when Menton, along with Roquebrune, was part of the Principality of Monaco, the locals agitated long and hard to become part of France, knowing that France offered a much better market for their lemons than Italy.

A local delicacy fêted in a colourful annual festival

ruins of the old castle, and beneath is the fine 12th-century church of St-Denis with its small square bell-tower.

SIMIANE-LA-ROTONDE

One of the most picturesque of all Provençal hilltop villages, crowned by a unique rotunda, and overlooking lavender fields which stretch far into the distance. 32km west of Forcalquier.

Set between the Plateau de Vaucluse and the Durance valley, Simiane combines the typical characteristics of a hilltop village with a sylvan setting of great beauty and shimmering views of the surrounding lavender fields.

Narrow winding streets flanked by tall stone houses, many with finely carved doorways from the 17th or 18th century, lead steeply up to the celebrated rotunda which has given the village its name. This unique building was in fact the keep of the 12th-century castle which once stood here, and is all that remains. Its austere exterior is in extreme contrast to the richly decorated interior, with finely carved capitals and graceful rib-vaulting.

The old streets of the village are a delight, focusing on the covered market hall and the 16th-century church of Ste-Victoire. From the top of the village, there is a superb view of the surrounding countryside, enhanced by the sight of a number of old windmills.

TENDE

A remote mountain village set on the banks of the Roya, close to the Parc National du Mercantour, which remained under Italian jurisdiction until 1947. 60km north of Menton.

The ancient alleys of Tende, with their ironwork, elaborate doorways and stairways, are distinctly Italian, while the atmosphere of the village with its cafés and restaurants, is unquestionably French.

In this remarkable site its tall, mostly 15th-century houses seem to be piled on top of one another towards the valley rim. At the top is the enormous 20m-high wall that once protected the Château de Lascaris, which was dismantled in 1692. Near by is the unusual terraced village cemetery. It is dominated by the church, a huge, late 15th-century edifice built as a cathedral by the Italian architect Lazzarino, and widely held to be the finest example of the Gothic style in the Alpes Maritimes.

TOURRETTES-SUR-LOUP

A virtually untouched medieval village standing on a sheer-sided rock plateau, now popular with artists and crafts people and a centre for the growing of violets. 7km west of Vence.

Together with lavender and jasmine, violets form the basis of the Provence perfume industry, and Tourrettes is one of the chief growing centres. From the village the view of the surrounding terraced land, with its olive groves, stands of pine trees and the violet fields, is unforgettable.

The old village, which seems hardly to have changed since medieval times, is entered through a bell-tower gateway. Within, the Grand-Rue which carves an elegant arc through the village, offers tempting views down fine narrow alleys.

PERFUME

The mimosa that turns the hills behind Cannes and Mandelieu golden in January and February is the most picturesque sign of the perfume industry, which also feeds, at appropriate times of the year, on violets, jonquils, orange blossom, lavender, roses, mignonettes and tuberoses. The industry's centre is Grasse, where it was introduced in the 1580s by an Italian glovemaker brought to France by Catherine de' Medici on her marriage to Henri II – perfume then being fashionable for masking the smell of leather in gloves. Today the town has more than 30 factories, which make an essence from the local blooms by distilling them, or by extracting the odour from individual petals with grease (a labour-intensive process known as *enfleurage*), or by using chemical solvents. By no means all the

factory names will be familiar to visitors, since the essence they produce is often shipped to Paris houses for blending into the brands such as Chanel and Givenchy, for which France is famous.

SECRET FRANCE
CORSICA

Corsica is the jewel of the Mediterranean islands. Located 180km off the French coast, it is the fourth largest after Sicily, Sardinia and Cyprus, being 184km long and 83km wide. Often referred to as the 'Isle of Beauty' or the 'Scented Isle', few phrases can capture the contrasting wealth of natural beauty and the individual character of this glorious island.

Corsica is a continent in miniature, its diverse landscape encompassing a mountainous interior of dramatic gorges, glacial lakes, gushing mountain torrents, magnificent pine and chestnut forests and jagged peaks soaring to over 2,000m. Ringing this rugged central massif is a 1,000km halo of superb sandy beaches, creeks, bays and an impressive cliffed coastline. Contrasts also extend to the weather; hot and dry in the summer, with snow-covered mountains and mild coasts in winter. Across the island the celebrated perfume of the Corsican *maquis*, a tangled undergrowth of fragrant herbs, flowers and bushes, fills the warm spring and summer air.

Five hundred years of Italian rule under the Pisans and Genoese had a profound influence across the island, especially in the pattern and style of the towns and villages. Italian-style hilltop hamlets and villages developed by mountain springs, safe from all-too-frequent attacks from the sea. Few settlements existed on the coast, except for well-fortified ports, a few small fishing harbours and a ring of headland watchtowers. Since World War II, with the eradication of the anopheles mosquito and the development of tourism, the east coast lowlands has seen the development of small resorts along the coast. In the villages, the Pisans built many of the rustic, unadorned churches, and the Genoese added a few grand Romanesque churches, but it was during a rare period of peace and prosperity during the baroque era that many of the richly adorned church interiors and tall bell-towers seen today were built.

Traditional village life revolved around shepherding, fishing and harvesting olives and chestnuts. Improved communications and the importation of goods saw a decline in these established ways and with it a rapid depopulation of the hill villages. In the past 20 years, however, this trend has been somewhat stemmed with the development of jobs in forestry and tourism, and more recently there has been a revival in the old traditions, such as olive pressing, fruit growing and honey production, this time by the younger generation.

hélianthème de Corse

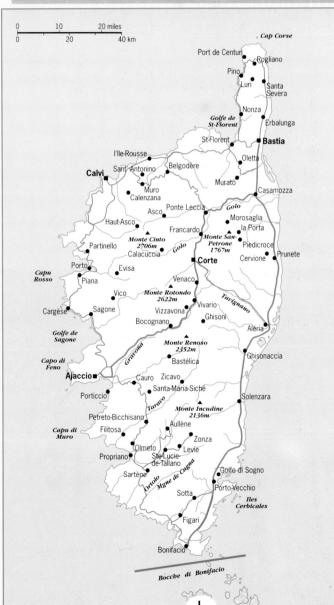

Above, the rugged mountains of Corsica form a dramatic backdrop to villages such as Vivario
Below, rough terracing on the steep hillside betrays the hand of man

Above, one of the island's specialities is its fragrant, low-growing herbage, the maquis
Left, a typical alley winds through the houses of Piana, with their outside stairways and shallow, red-tiled roofs

Map labels:

Cap Corse
Port de Centuri
Rogliano
Pino
Luri
Santa Severa
Nonza
Erbalunga
Golfe de St-Florent
St-Florent
Bastia
I'lle-Rousse
Oletta
Sant-Antonino
Belgodère
Calvi
Murato
Muro
Casamozza
Calenzana
Golo
Asco
Ponte Leccia
Morosaglia
Haut-Asco
Francardo
la Porta
Monte Cinto 2706m
Monte San-Petrone 1767m
Golo
Piedicroce
Partinello
Calacuccia
Cervione
Prunete
Porto
Evisa
Corte
Capu Rosso
Piana
Venaco
Vico
Monte Rotondo 2622m
Tavignano
Cargèse
Sagone
Vizzavona
Vivario
Ghisoni
Bocognano
Aléria
Golfe de Sagone
Gravona
Monte Renoso 2352m
Bastélica
Ghisonaccia
Capo di Feno
Cauro
Zicavo
Ajaccio
Santa-Mária-Siché
Solenzara
Porticcio
Taravo
Monte Incudine 2136m
Petreto-Bicchisano
Capu di Muro
Filitosa
Aullène
Zonza
Olmeto
Levie
Propriano
Ste-Lucie-de-Tallano
Golfo di Sogno
Sartène
Ortolo
Mgne de Cagna
Porto-Vecchio
Sotta
Iles Cerbicales
Figari
Bonifacio
Bocche di Bonifacio

0   10   20 miles
0   20   40 km

LA PORTA

Set in the heart of the Castagniccia, among rolling hills and sweet chestnut groves, la Porta contains one of the finest examples of Corsican baroque religious architecture. 38km north-east of Corte.

In the past la Porta has witnessed many battles against Romans, Vandals, Arabs, Genoese and the French. Today, a peaceful atmosphere pervades the narrow streets and alleyways, lined with tall, shuttered buildings painted in warm pastel shades of beige and terracotta. Locals sit on benches in the Piazza di u Piano passing time, chatting and watching the visitors, who seek out the village to view the richly-adorned ochre and white-painted church of St John the Baptist, built in the 17th century, its façade ornately decorated with pinnacles and scrolls, and the adjacent five-storey 18th-century campanile, which is considered to be the finest baroque bell-tower on the island. The church is generally open – unlike many on the island – and displays a fine painted ceiling, a 17th-century figure of Christ painted on wood and a magnificent Italian organ, built by a monk in 1780.

Nonza's 16th-century church, surrounded by a maze of narrow old streets

NONZA

Clinging to the cliffs 150m above its distinctive black beach on the rugged west coast of Cap Corse, and topped by the remains of a Genoese watchtower, is the ancient settlement of Nonza. 32km north-west of Bastia.

Surrounded by chestnut and plane trees, Nonza was the birthplace of Ste-Julie, a martyr crucified by the Romans for her Christian beliefs in AD303. The fine 16th-century church is dedicated to her and contains an impressive marble altar, dating from 1694, and a 16th-century painting of the Crucifixion. Reached via the steep path to the beach is the fountain of Ste-Julie, supposedly the place where she was killed and the destination of a pilgrimage each May.

Narrow, steeply stepped alleyways wind through the jumble of traditional stone houses that perch on the cliffside, their miniature terraces and balconies bedecked with flower pots, and bright bougainvillaea adds a splash of colour to the grey walls. Ascend to the tower for a magnificent bird's-eye view across the cluster of slated roof-tops to the church and down the coast across the Gulf of St Florent to the Désert des Agriates and the Monte Cinto massif, dominating the horizon on a clear day.

STE-LUCIE-DE-TALLANO

Set against a backdrop of beautiful mountain and valley scenery high above the Rizzanèse valley, and endowed with many fine treasures, lies the traditional village of Ste-Lucie-de-Tallano. 20km east of **Propriano.**

Ste-Lucie was the home of the great Corsican chief, Rinuccio della Rocca, who not only fought the Genoese, but was an admirer and collector of Renaissance art, and in 1492 bestowed many of his treasures and paintings to the Franciscan monastery, which stands above the village. He also donated a 15th-century marble font in the shape of a hand to the parish church, which, along with the large fountain and plane-shaded square forms the central core of the village. Clustered around the church are a delightful collection of tall, rustic buildings, narrow streets and alleyways.

Despite it being on a relatively busy, if narrow, route into the mountains, a relaxed atmosphere extends throughout the village. The splendour of the location of this community can best be appreciated from the terrace of the old monastery, or from the road as it winds its way up the hillside above the village.

CORSICA

Interesting details decorate many buildings in Ste-Lucie-de-Tallano

archways and between dwellings gradually prepares one for the anticipated magnificent panorama that greets the eye from the top; from the sandy beaches at Algajola to the high peaks inland.

VICO

Nestling among the *maquis* on the wooded slopes of the Liamone valley, well off the beaten track, with picturesque old streets and splendid views, is the peaceful settlement of Vico. 50km north of Ajaccio.

Historically important, in the 16th century, Vico was a bishopric, the capital of Cinarca and the birthplace of Auguste-Françoise Vico, Governor of Sardinia, and Casanelli d'Istria, who became the bishop of Ajaccio.

Rustic, well-weathered, five-storey buildings with balconied and shuttered façades line ancient streets, stepped passageways and the single main street, which boasts two squares. Standing proud in one is the fountain and statue of Casanelli d'Istria; the other is a boules pitch with benches, a splendid view and two conveniently placed, homely bars with terraces.

Just to the east of the village, and affording fine views of Vico and the high mountains, is the monastery of St-Francis. The 15th-century church contains a wood carving of Christ, reputed to be the oldest in Corsica.

ST-ANTONINO

The oldest village in Corsica, timeless and unspoilt, St-Antonino perches high on a rocky outcrop with stunning views out to sea. 18km east of Calvi.

Nicknamed the 'eyrie', and giving the appearance of being walled, St-Antonino dates back to the 9th century and originally grew up around a castle. It remains totally unspoiled and typically Corsican. A maze of narrow, cobbled streets, vaulted passageways and flights of steps zigzag up between granite-grey shuttered houses built into the rock, with pots of red geraniums on the tiny balconies and courtyards providing the only colour.

Breathtaking cameo views through

EMPEROR'S CRADLE

Napoleon Bonaparte is generally regarded as the greatest Corsican of all time. Born in 1769 into a partisan family, Napoleon dreamed of Corsican independence and of himself as the island's saviour. His dramatic rise in the army quelled such desires, however, and resulted in his doing little to help his native island in its quest for liberation. Instead, he forged links between Corsica and France, and made Ajaccio the island's capital. Known as the 'Emperor's cradle', Ajaccio delights in Napoleon's fame – statues, plaques and monuments dedicated to the Bonaparte family can be seen at every turn, and the life of Corsica's most famous son is retold in displays at both his birthplace and the museum.

SECRET PLACES

CORSICA'S MAQUIS

A very special island with its own unique, fragrant flora.

Corsica is often called the 'fragrant isle', and the origin of this is in the special vegetation of the island.

The word 'maquis' derives from the Corsican word *mucchio* or rock-rose and is the name given to the vast area of luxuriant scrubland that covers much of the island. Many species of shrub, heather, aromatic herbs and scented flowers make up

this dense undergrowth, the thickness and height of which depends on such factors as altitude, rainfall and soil conditions. The beauty of the *maquis* is best experienced from mid-April to mid-June, when the slopes are a glorious sea of colour and the air is filled with a lingering, heady perfume.

During World War II the *maquis* hid French

partisans escaping the Italian and German troops, and was the name adopted by the resistance organisations.

The lush undergrowth provides the islands with excellent quality honey, fruits and liqueurs and serves Corsicans as a hunting ground where they can pursue wild boar.

INDEX

ACKNOWLEDGEMENTS

The Automobile Association wishes to thank the following photographers and libraries
for their assistance in the preparation of this book.

J. ALLAN CASH PHOTOLIBRARY 62b, 124a, 125, 175, 206

THE BRIDGEMAN ART LIBRARY 141 (Musee Conde Chantilly/Giraudon)

MICHAEL BUSSELLE 129, 157b, 169, 170a, 176, 180/1, 203c, 205

JAMES DAVIS TRAVEL PHOTOGRAPHY front cover

MARY EVANS PICTURE LIBRARY 251b

INTERNATIONAL PHOTOBANK 38a

JOHN LLOYD 98b, 102b, 108/9, 160a, 160b, 161, 162, 163b, 164/5a, 164/5b, 165, 204b

JOHN MILLAR 43a, 43b, 44/5, 47, 48/9, 48, 51, 52b, 53, 55a, 68a, 69, 71a, 167b, 207a, 217, 218, 227, 228, 229a

ROGER MOSS 89a

NATURE PHOTOGRAPHERS LTD 59 (B.Burbidge), 128a (P.Sterry), 142b (P.Sterry), 181b (P.Sterry),
249c (B.Burbidge), 251c (S.C.Bisserot)

PICTURES COLOUR LIBRARY 73, 84b, 88a, 239

IAN POWYS 61, 63

RETROPGRAPH ARCHIVE 55b (Martin Breese)

SCOPE 127a (Guillard), 132b (Sierpinski)

BARRIE SMITH 71c, 149b, 149c, 151a, 178/9, 182b, 215b, 225a

SPECTRUM COLOUR LIBRARY 15, 18, 19a, 57b, 153a, 170b, 177a, 178b, 184b, 192, 200a, 200b

ZEFA PICTURE LIBRARY (UK) LTD 171, 178a

JOHN WHITE 168b

The remaining photographs are held in the Association's own picture library
(AA PHOTO LIBRARY) with contributions from:

A BAKER 13c, 14a, 238a

P BENNETT 215a, 216a, 219a, 220b, 222/3, 223, 224, 226b

I BURGUM 121b

J EDMANSON back cover;a, c, 10/1, 24b, 71b, 72a, 74a, 74b, 75, 76, 77a, 77b, 78/9, 78, 79a, 79c,
80a, 80b, 80/1, 81a, 82a, 82b, 83, 84c

P KENWOOD 46, 123a, 123b, 123c, 126, 127b, 128b, 128/9, 130b, 131, 132a, 133,
134a, 134b, 135, 137a, 137b, 137c, 137d, 138a, 138b, 139, 140a, 140b, 142a, 144a, 144b, 145, 146, 147a, 147b, 157a, 182a,
185a, 185b, 186b, 191a, 191b, 194/5, 194b, 196a, 198, 199a, 199b

J MILLAR 180

R MOORE 29b, 30b, 33, 34/5, 35, 37a, 40a

R NEILLANDS 26/7

D NOBLE 84d, 87b, 89b, 90, 91

T OLIVER 46/7, 49a, 50b, 57a, 57c, 58/9, 60a, 62a, 64a, 65, 66a, 149a, 150, 151b, 152, 153b, 154a, 154b, 154c,
155, 203a, 203b, 203d, 204a, 207b, 208/9a, 208/9b, 209, 210, 210/1, 212b, 213a, 213b, 243a

K
D ROBER   , 68b
C SAW   41
M SHORT 97a, 97b, 97c, 98a,   a, 110b, 110c, 110d, 112a,
112b,   a
B SMITH 60b, 86, 12   201a, 201b, 232a

R STRANGE 2/3, 157c, 158   c, 231d, 232b, 233, 234a,
234b, 2   47

R VICTO   6, 27